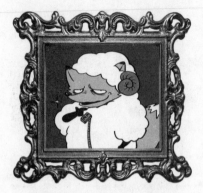

Hitsuji Gondaira

Thank you very much for picking up this book.
They may be a weird family, but I hope you will come to love them.

Hitsuji Gondaira's first series, *Demon Prince Poro's*
Diaries, was published in *Weekly Shonen Jump* in 2017.
He started work on *Mission: Yozakura Family* in 2019.

MISSION: YOZAKURA FAMILY

VOL. 1
SHONEN JUMP Edition

STORY AND ART BY
HITSUJI GONDAIRA

TRANSLATION AND LETTERING
PINKIE-CHAN

DESIGN
JIMMY PRESLER

RETOUCH LETTERER
JOHN HUNT

EDITOR
RAE FIRST

YOZAKURA-SANCHI NO DAISAKUSEN © 2019 by Hitsuji Gondaira
All rights reserved. First published in Japan in 2019 by SHUEISHA Inc., Tokyo.
English translation rights arranged by SHUEISHA Inc.

The stories, characters, and incidents mentioned
in this publication are entirely fictional.

Printed in Canada

Published by VIZ Media, LLC
P.O. Box 77010
San Francisco, CA 94107

10 9 8 7 6 5 4 3 2 1
First printing, October 2022

PARENTAL ADVISORY
MISSION YOZAKURA FAMILY is rated T for Teen
and is recommended for ages 13 and up for
realistic and fantasy violence.

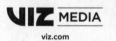 MEDIA

viz.com

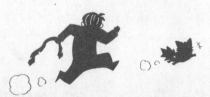

MISSION: Yozakura family

1

The Cherry Blossom Ring

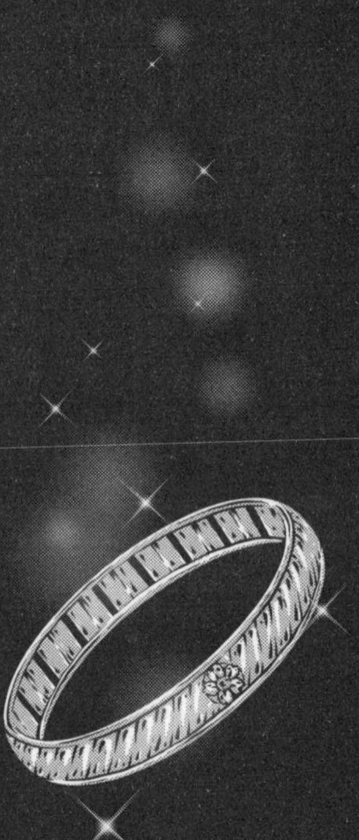

Story and Art by
Hitsuji Gondaira

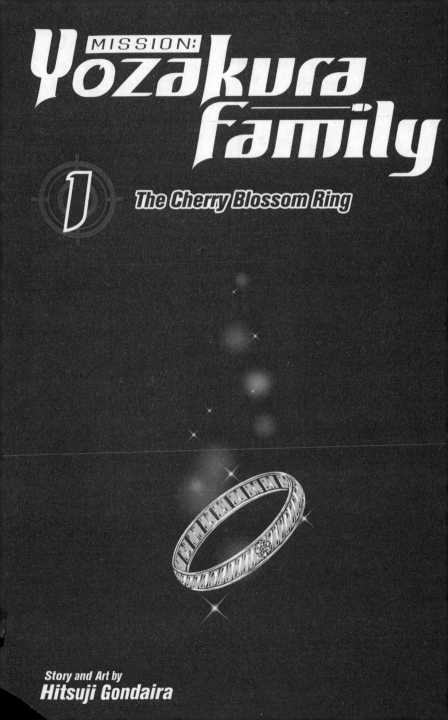

Mission: Yozakura Family Vol. 1

The Cherry Blossom Ring

Mission Objectives

Number	Mission titles
005	☑ Mission 1: The Cherry Blossom Ring
061	☑ Mission 2: The Yozakura Family's Lifeline
087	☑ Mission 3: Feelings
111	☑ Mission 4: Recovering the Ring
131	☑ Mission 5: Hostage
151	☑ Mission 6: Flower Bin Delivery Headquarters
171	☑ Mission 7: Surprise Attack
	☐
	☐
	☐
	☐

Mission:
Yozakura Family

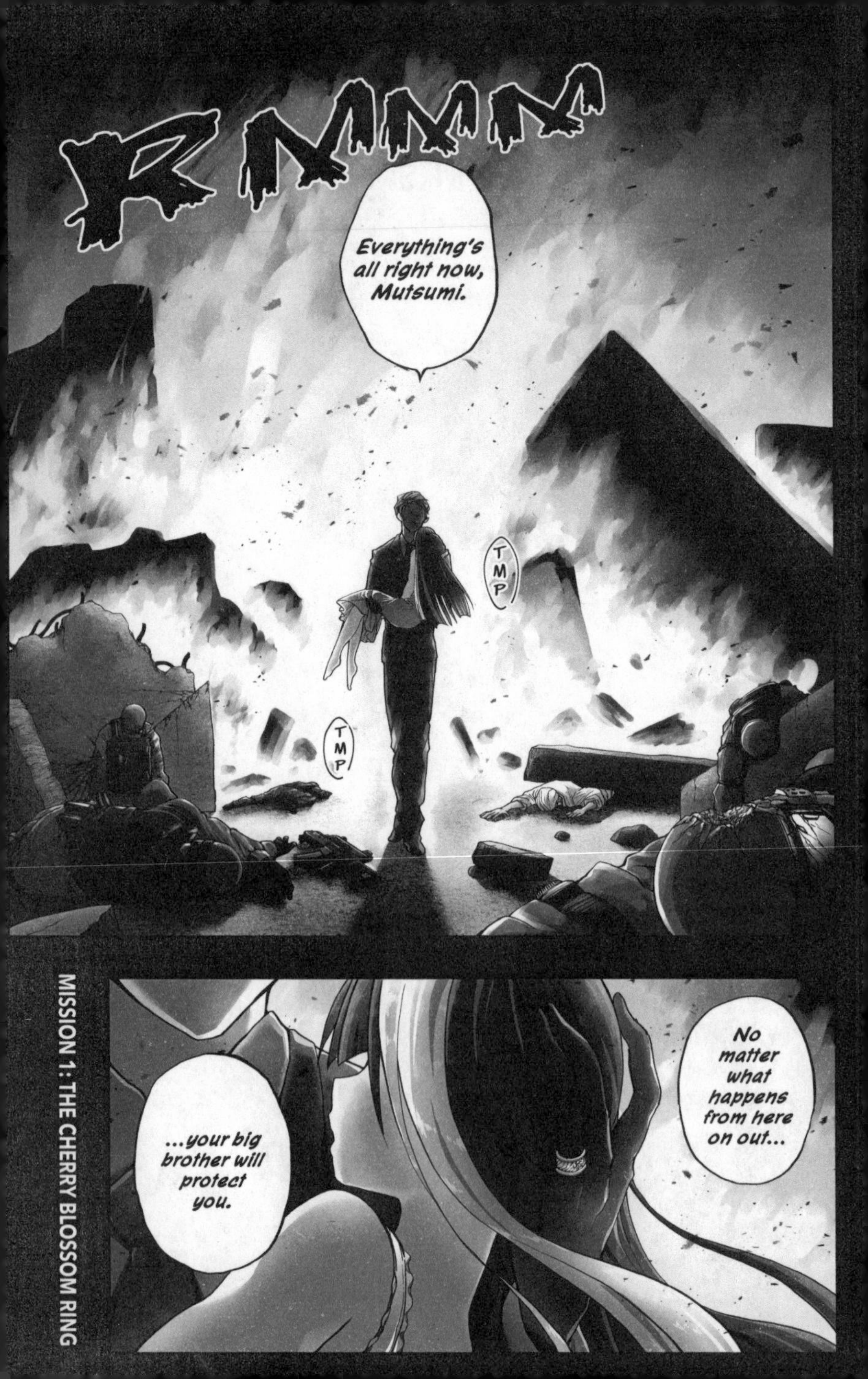
RMMM
Everything's all right now, Mutsumi.
TMP
TMP
MISSION 1: THE CHERRY BLOSSOM RING
No matter what happens from here on out...
...your big brother will protect you.

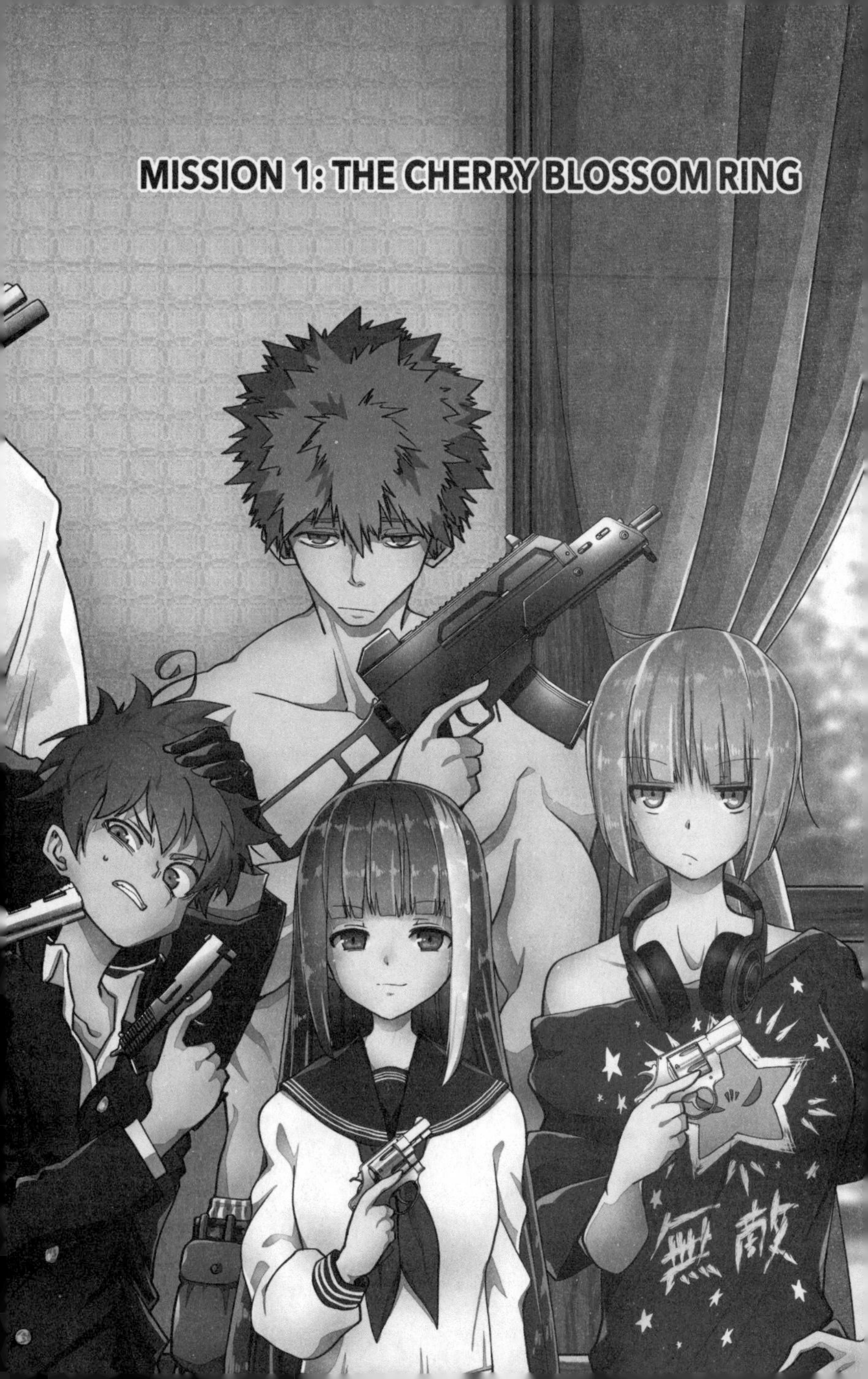
MISSION 1: THE CHERRY BLOSSOM RING
無敵

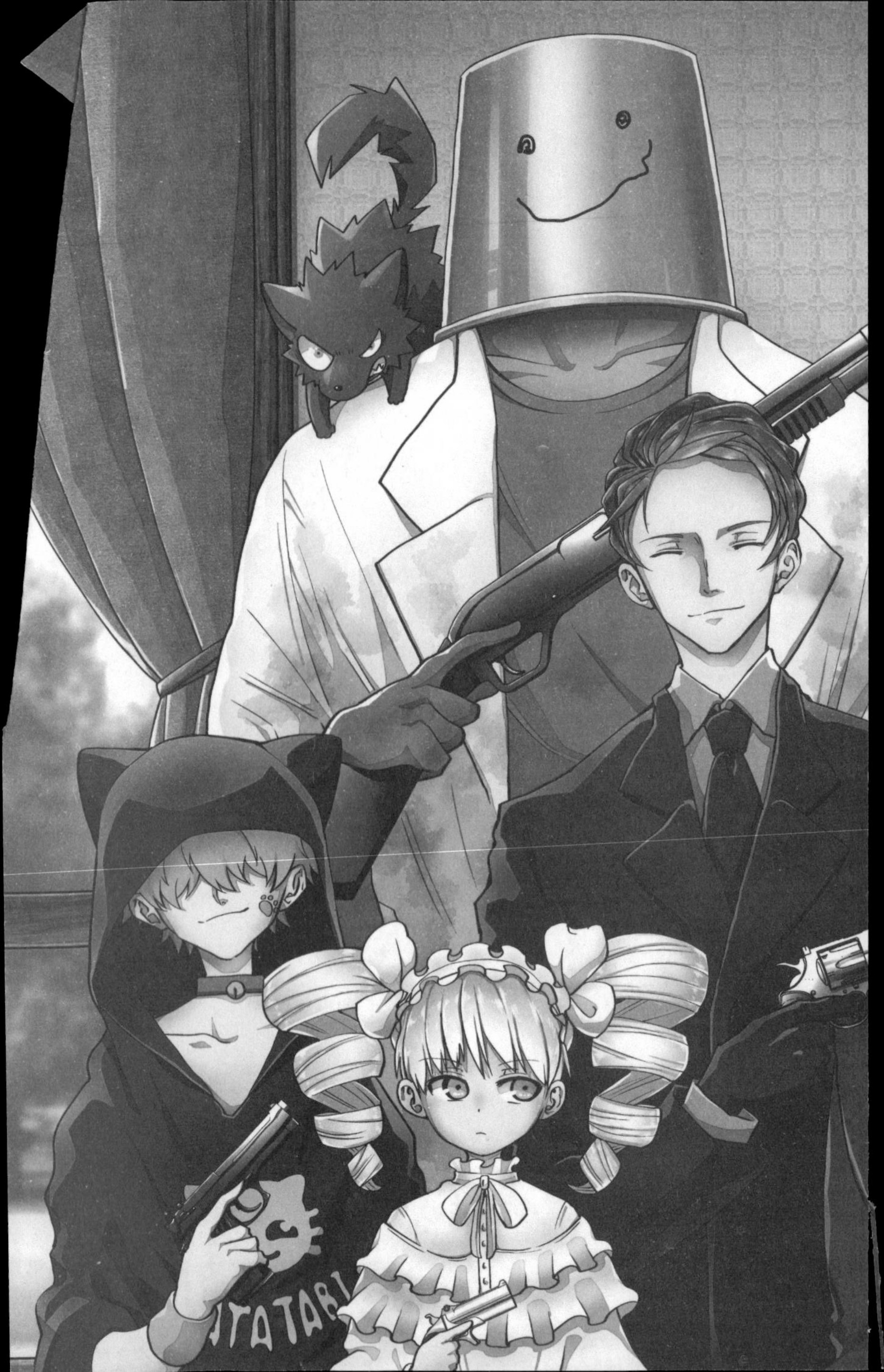
TATABI

MISSION: Yozakura family

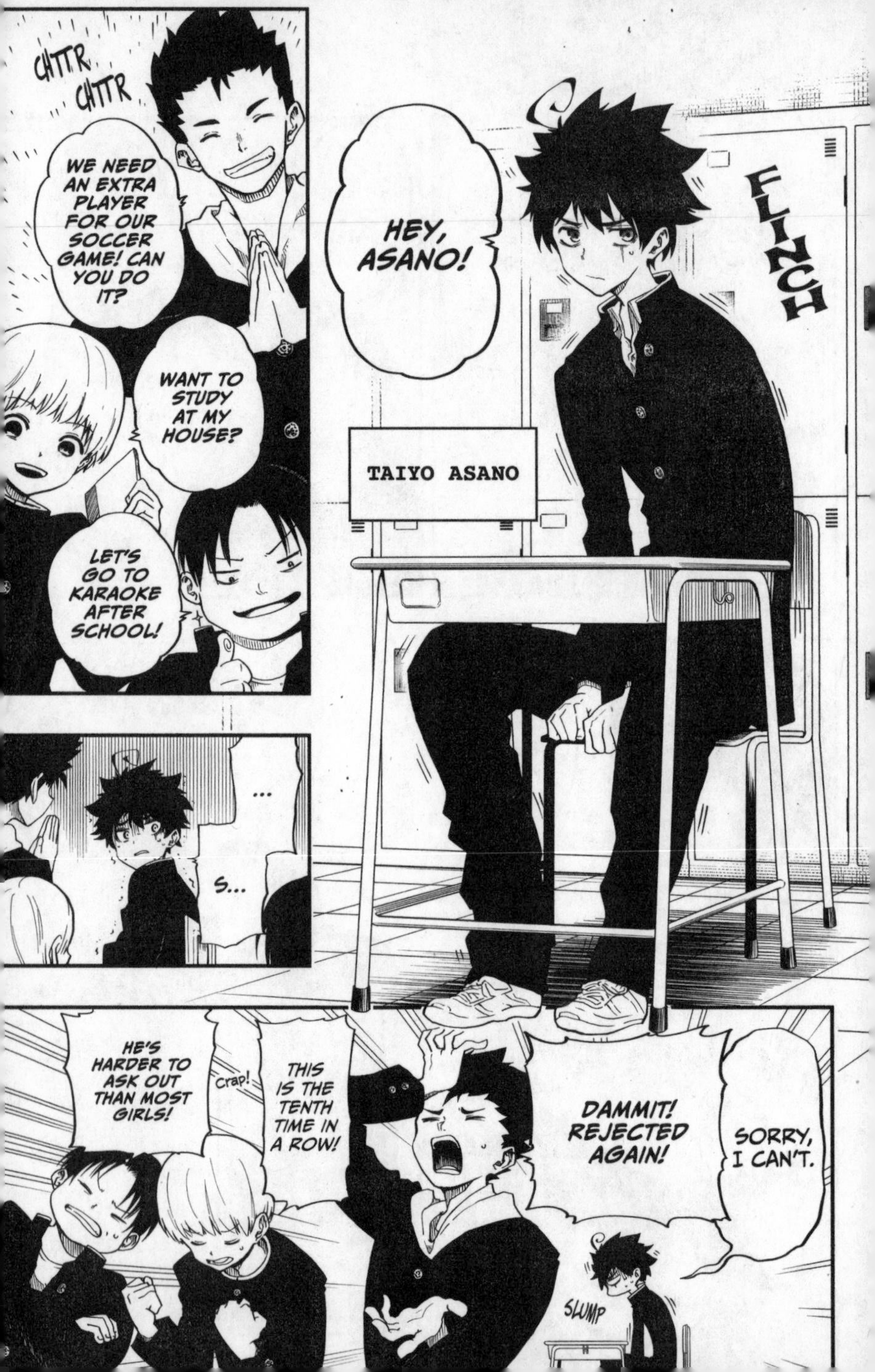
FLINCH
HEY, ASANO!
TAIYO ASANO
CHTTR CHTTR
WE NEED AN EXTRA PLAYER FOR OUR SOCCER GAME! CAN YOU DO IT?
WANT TO STUDY AT MY HOUSE?
LET'S GO TO KARAOKE AFTER SCHOOL!
...
S...
SORRY, I CAN'T.
SLUMP
DAMMIT! REJECTED AGAIN!
THIS IS THE TENTH TIME IN A ROW!
Crap!
HE'S HARDER TO ASK OUT THAN MOST GIRLS!

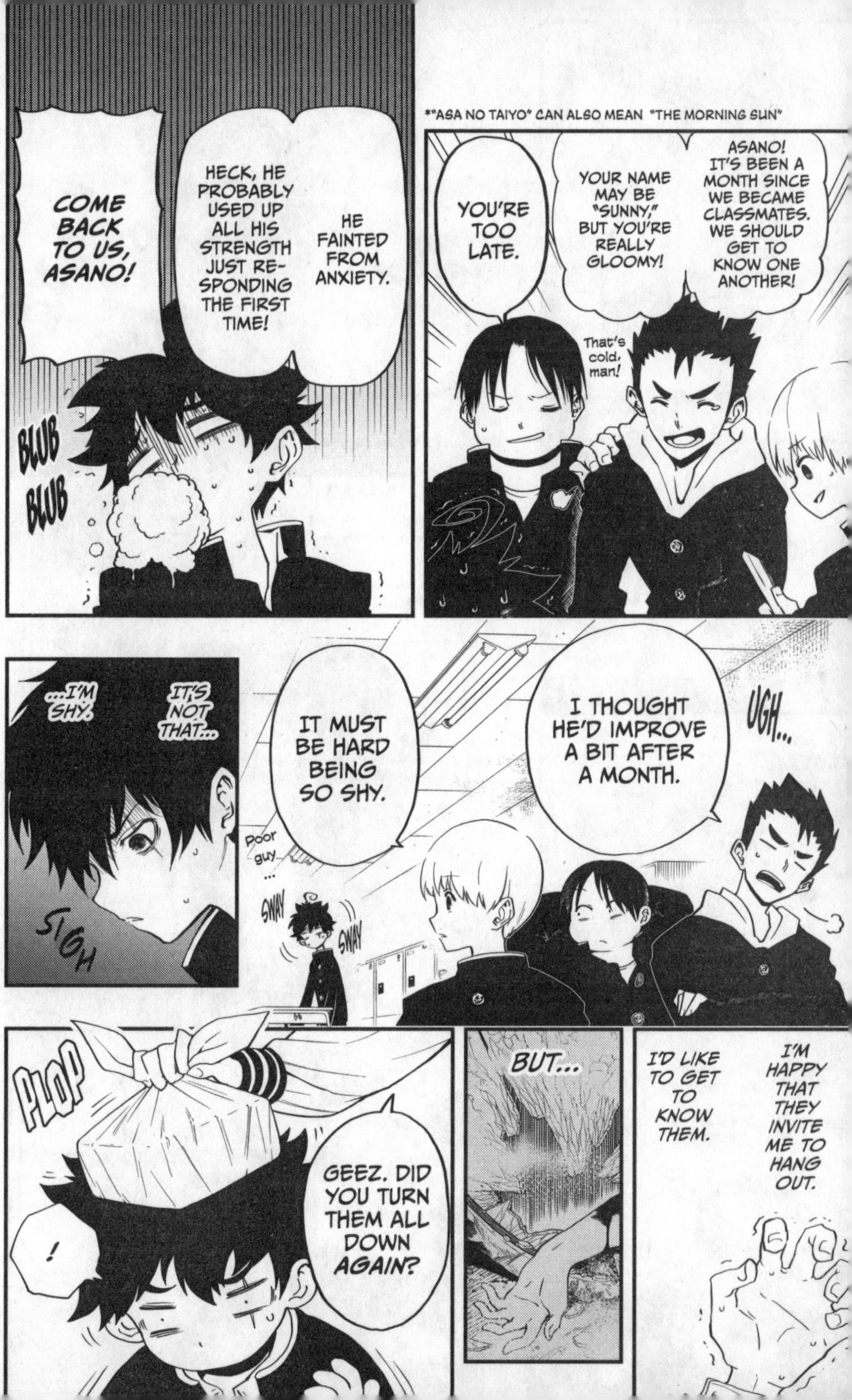
*"ASA NO TAIYO" CAN ALSO MEAN "THE MORNING SUN"
ASANO! IT'S BEEN A MONTH SINCE WE BECAME CLASSMATES. WE SHOULD GET TO KNOW ONE ANOTHER!
YOUR NAME MAY BE "SUNNY," BUT YOU'RE REALLY GLOOMY!
YOU'RE TOO LATE.
That's cold, man!
HE FAINTED FROM ANXIETY.
HECK, HE PROBABLY USED UP ALL HIS STRENGTH JUST RE-SPONDING THE FIRST TIME!
COME BACK TO US, ASANO!
BLUB BLUB
UGH...
I THOUGHT HE'D IMPROVE A BIT AFTER A MONTH.
IT MUST BE HARD BEING SO SHY.
Poor guy...
SWAY SWAY
IT'S NOT THAT...
...I'M SHY.
SIGH
I'M HAPPY THAT THEY INVITE ME TO HANG OUT.
I'D LIKE TO GET TO KNOW THEM.
BUT...
PLOP
GEEZ. DID YOU TURN THEM ALL DOWN AGAIN?
!

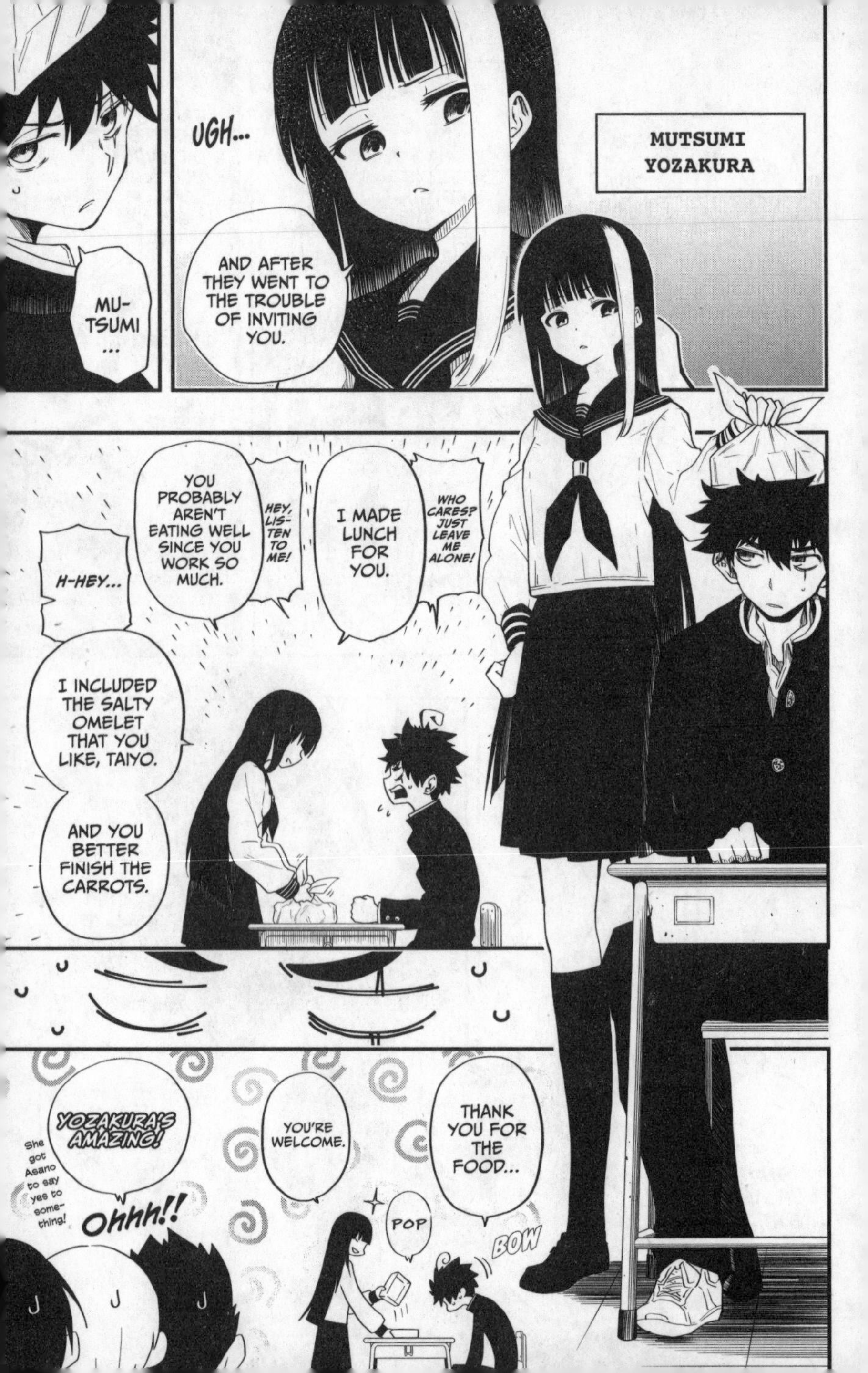
MUTSUMI YOZAKURA
UGH...
AND AFTER THEY WENT TO THE TROUBLE OF INVITING YOU.
MU-TSUMI...
I MADE LUNCH FOR YOU.
WHO CARES? JUST LEAVE ME ALONE!
HEY, LIS-TEN TO ME!
YOU PROBABLY AREN'T EATING WELL SINCE YOU WORK SO MUCH.
H-HEY...
I INCLUDED THE SALTY OMELET THAT YOU LIKE, TAIYO.
AND YOU BETTER FINISH THE CARROTS.
THANK YOU FOR THE FOOD...
BOW
YOU'RE WELCOME.
POP
YOZAKURA'S AMAZING!
Ohhh!!
She got Asano to say yes to some-thing!

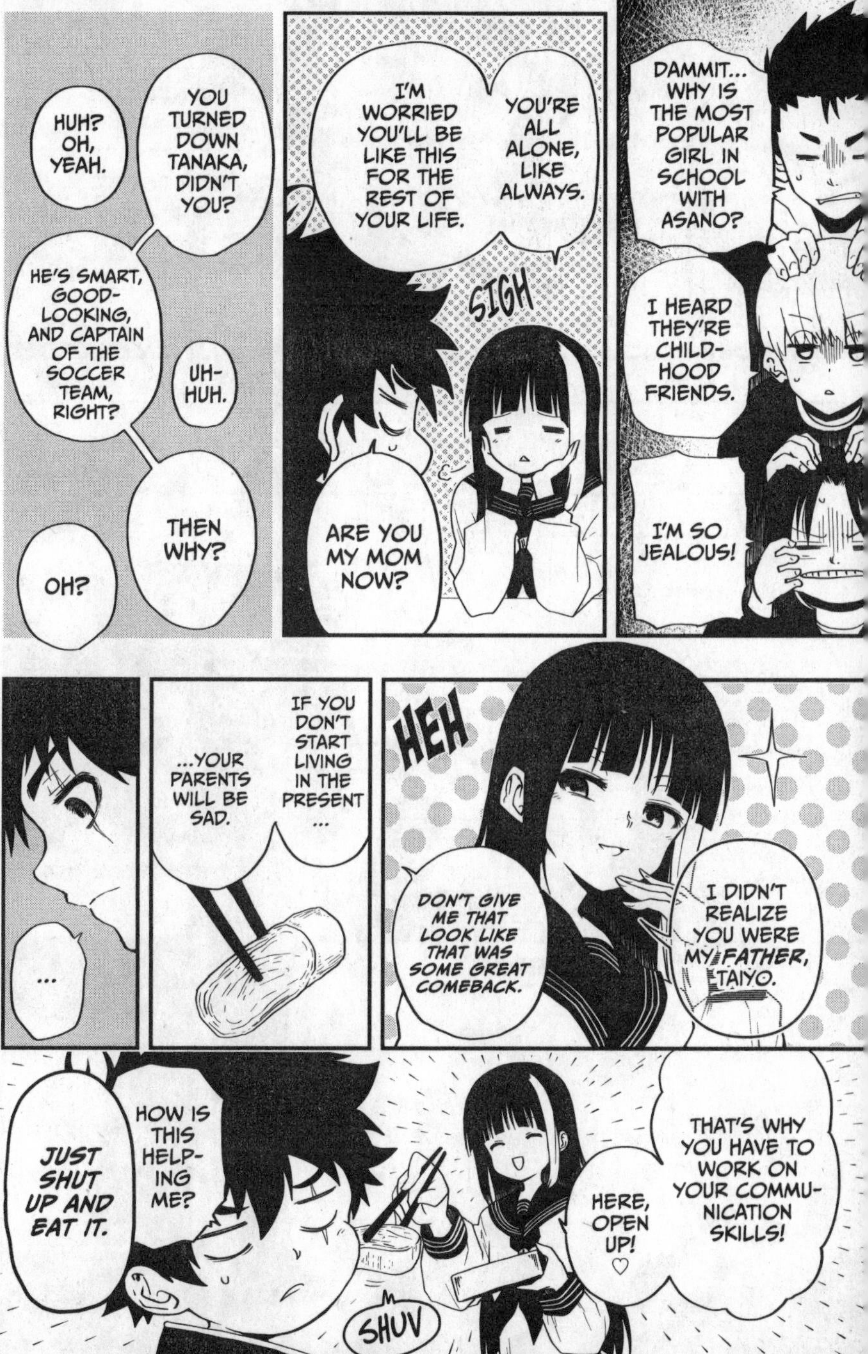
DAMMIT... WHY IS THE MOST POPULAR GIRL IN SCHOOL WITH ASANO?
I HEARD THEY'RE CHILD-HOOD FRIENDS.
I'M SO JEALOUS!
YOU'RE ALL ALONE, LIKE ALWAYS.
I'M WORRIED YOU'LL BE LIKE THIS FOR THE REST OF YOUR LIFE.
SIGH
ARE YOU MY MOM NOW?
YOU TURNED DOWN TANAKA, DIDN'T YOU?
HUH? OH, YEAH.
HE'S SMART, GOOD-LOOKING, AND CAPTAIN OF THE SOCCER TEAM, RIGHT?
UH-HUH.
THEN WHY?
OH?
HEH
I DIDN'T REALIZE YOU WERE MY FATHER, TAIYO.
DON'T GIVE ME THAT LOOK LIKE THAT WAS SOME GREAT COMEBACK.
IF YOU DON'T START LIVING IN THE PRESENT...
...YOUR PARENTS WILL BE SAD.
...
THAT'S WHY YOU HAVE TO WORK ON YOUR COMMU-NICATION SKILLS!
HERE, OPEN UP! ♡
HOW IS THIS HELP-ING ME?
JUST SHUT UP AND EAT IT.
SHUV

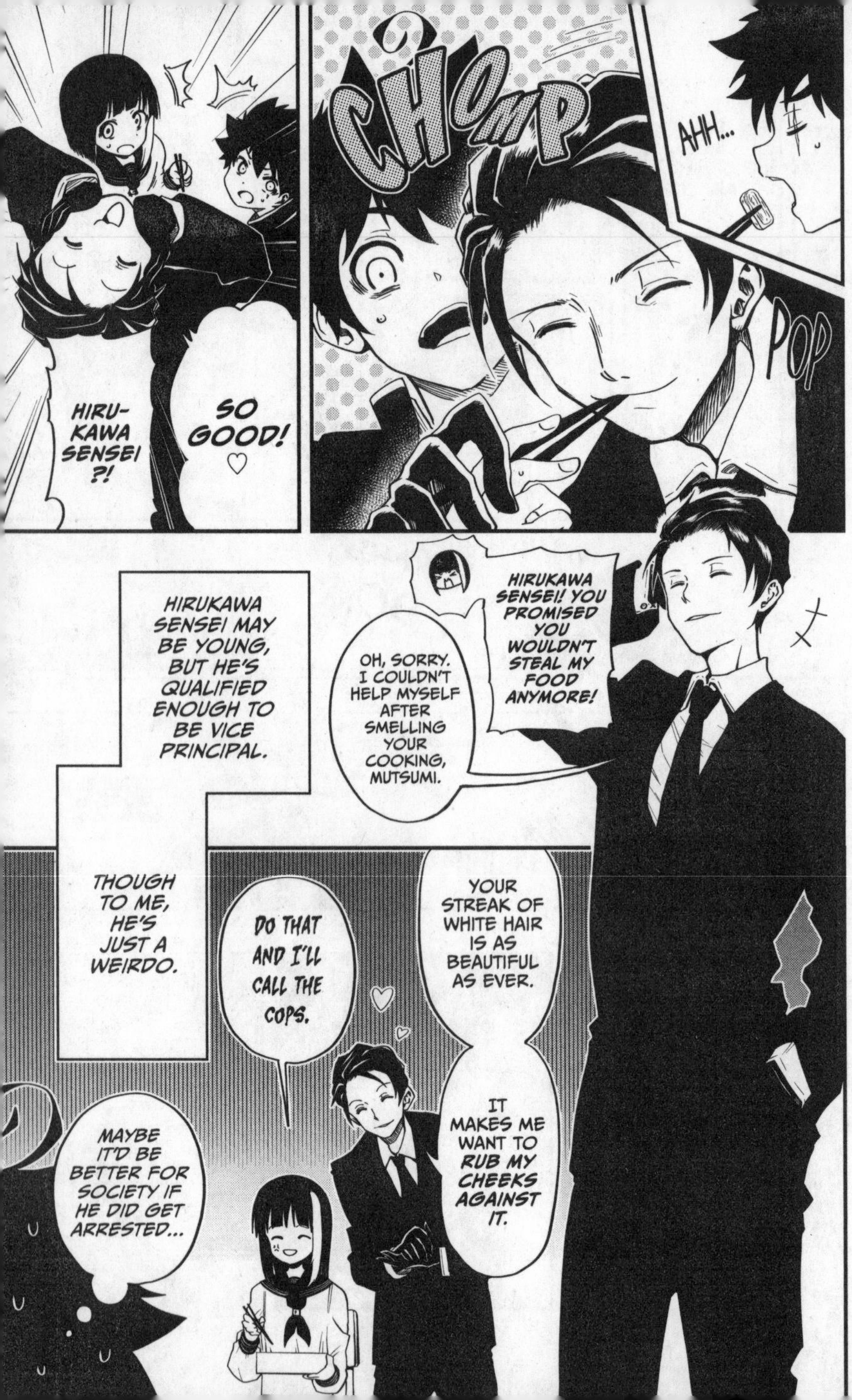
AHH...
POP
CHOMP
SO GOOD! ♡
HIRUKAWA SENSEI?!
HIRUKAWA SENSEI! YOU PROMISED YOU WOULDN'T STEAL MY FOOD ANYMORE!
OH, SORRY. I COULDN'T HELP MYSELF AFTER SMELLING YOUR COOKING, MUTSUMI.
HIRUKAWA SENSEI MAY BE YOUNG, BUT HE'S QUALIFIED ENOUGH TO BE VICE PRINCIPAL.
THOUGH TO ME, HE'S JUST A WEIRDO.
YOUR STREAK OF WHITE HAIR IS AS BEAUTIFUL AS EVER.
IT MAKES ME WANT TO RUB MY CHEEKS AGAINST IT.
DO THAT AND I'LL CALL THE COPS.
MAYBE IT'D BE BETTER FOR SOCIETY IF HE DID GET ARRESTED...

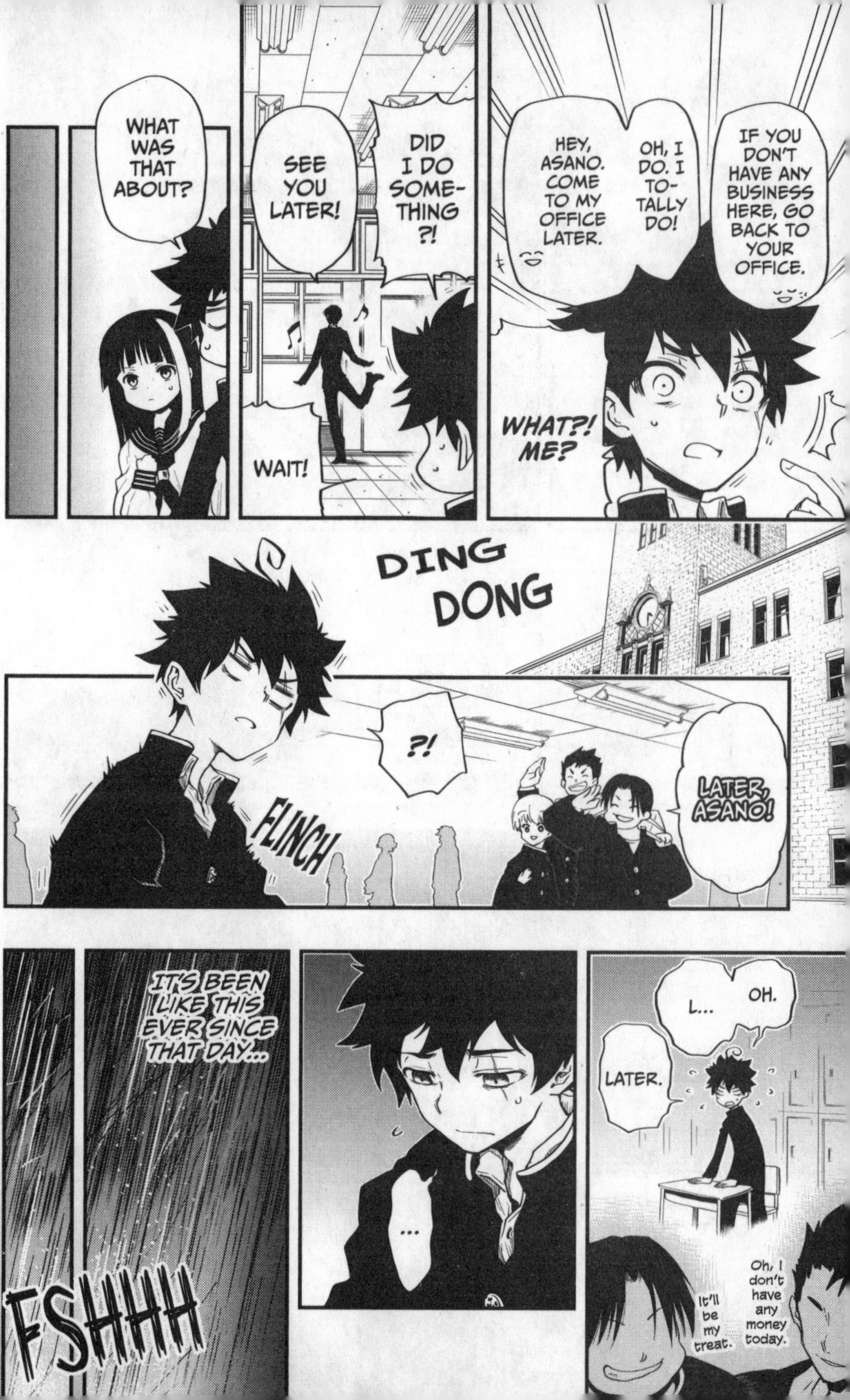
IF YOU DON'T HAVE ANY BUSINESS HERE, GO BACK TO YOUR OFFICE.
OH, I DO. I TOTALLY DO!
HEY, ASANO. COME TO MY OFFICE LATER.
WHAT?! ME?
DID I DO SOMETHING?!
SEE YOU LATER!
WAIT!
WHAT WAS THAT ABOUT?
DING DONG
LATER, ASANO!
?!
FLINCH
OH.
L...
LATER.
Oh, I don't have any money today.
It'll be my treat.
...
IT'S BEEN LIKE THIS EVER SINCE THAT DAY...
FSHHH

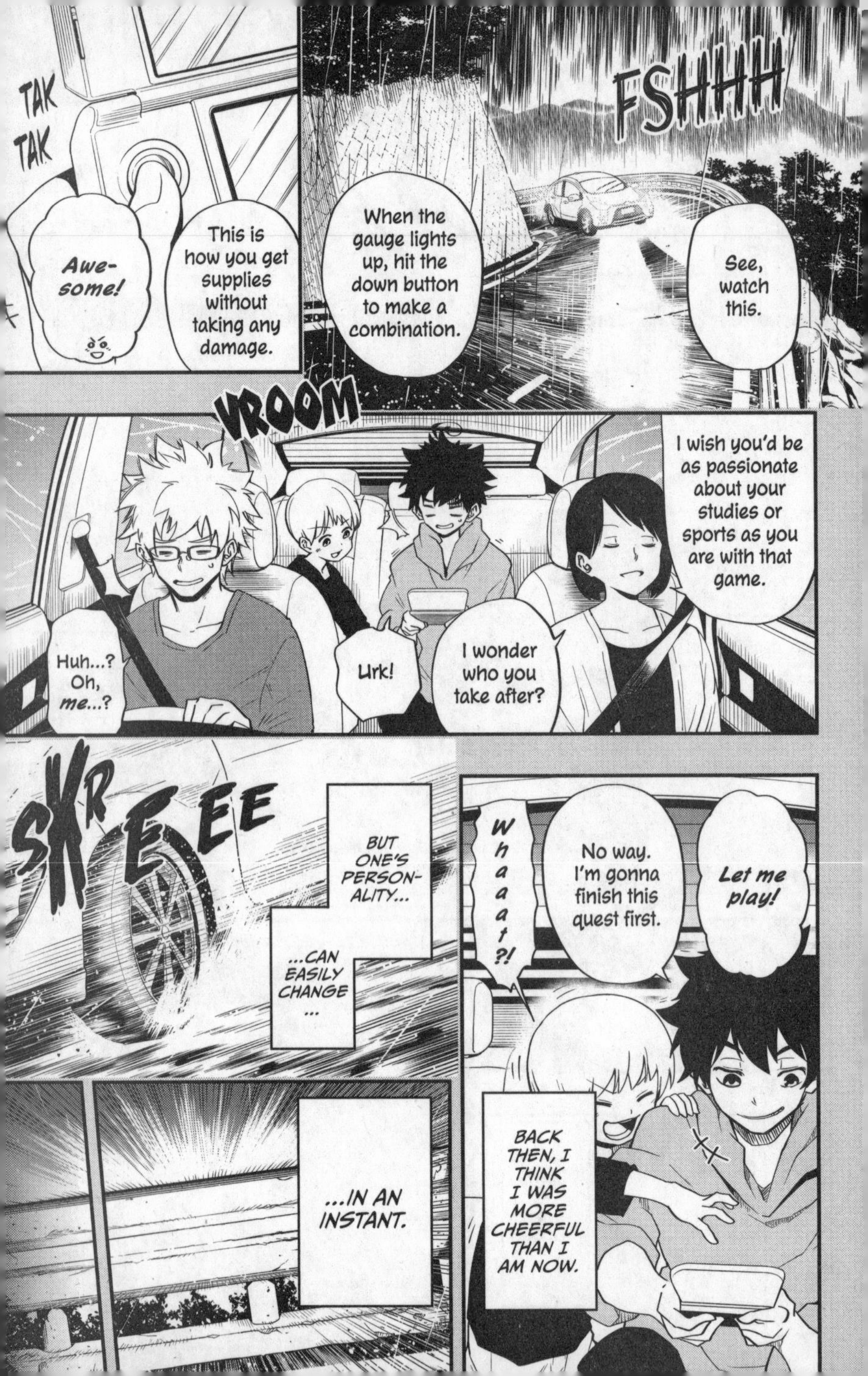
FSHHH
See, watch this.
When the gauge lights up, hit the down button to make a combination.
This is how you get supplies without taking any damage.
Awe-some!
TAK TAK
VROOM
I wish you'd be as passionate about your studies or sports as you are with that game.
I wonder who you take after?
Urk!
Huh...? Oh, me...?
Let me play!
No way. I'm gonna finish this quest first.
Whaaaat?!
BACK THEN, I THINK I WAS MORE CHEERFUL THAN I AM NOW.
SKREEE
BUT ONE'S PERSONALITY...
...CAN EASILY CHANGE...
...IN AN INSTANT.

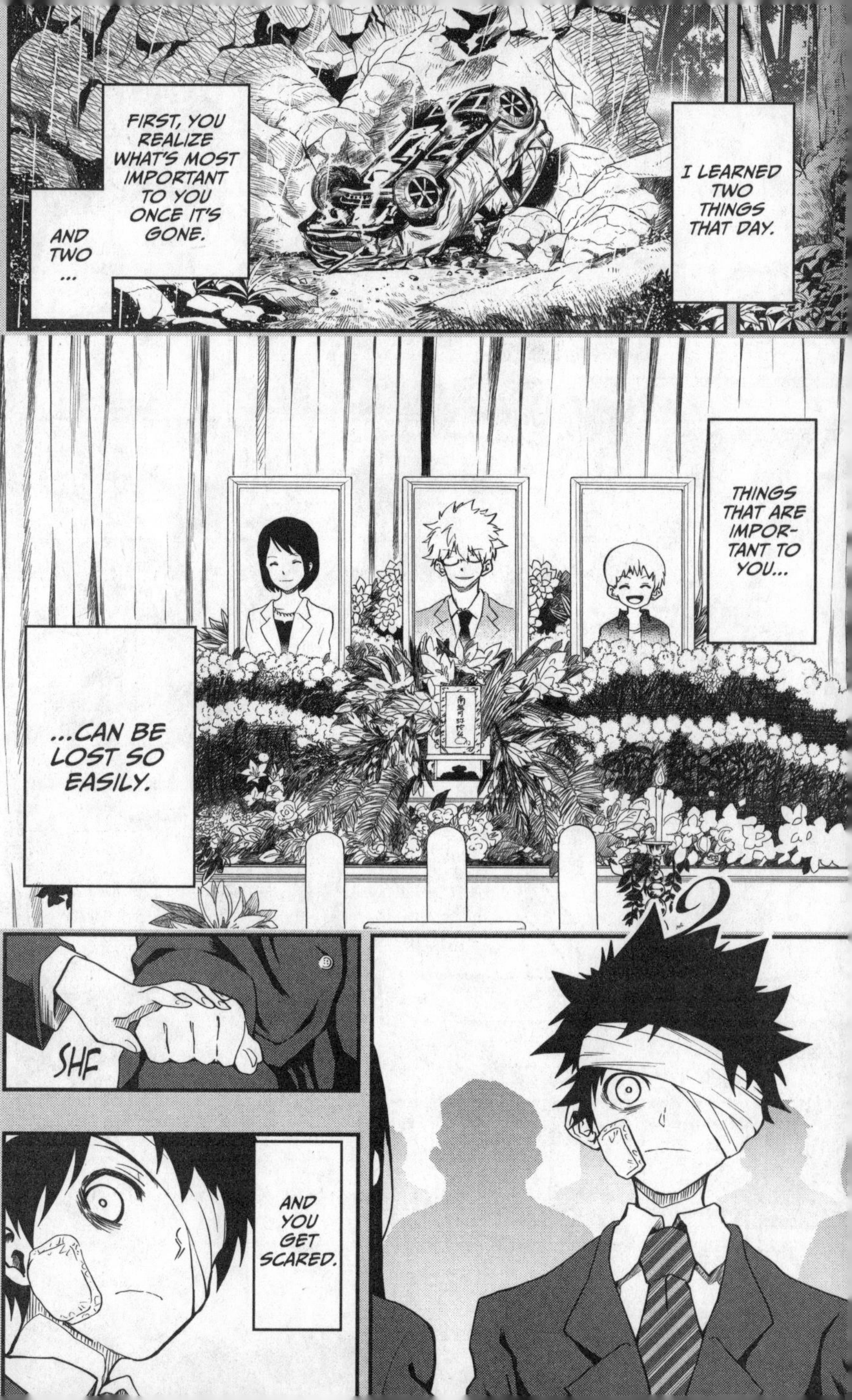
I LEARNED TWO THINGS THAT DAY.
FIRST, YOU REALIZE WHAT'S MOST IMPORTANT TO YOU ONCE IT'S GONE.
AND TWO ...
THINGS THAT ARE IMPOR-TANT TO YOU...
...CAN BE LOST SO EASILY.
SHF
AND YOU GET SCARED.

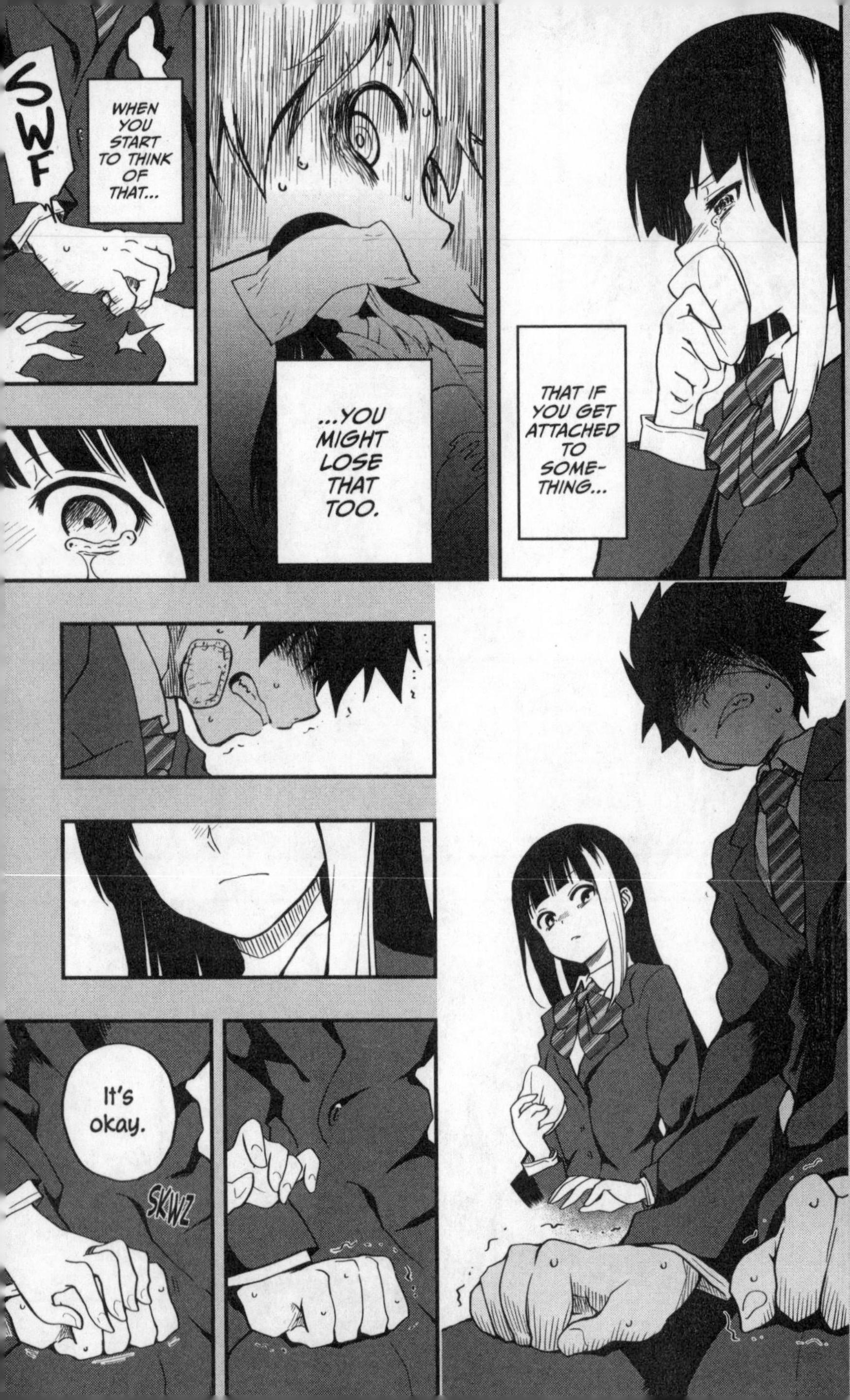
THAT IF YOU GET ATTACHED TO SOME-THING...
...YOU MIGHT LOSE THAT TOO.
WHEN YOU START TO THINK OF THAT...
SWF
It's okay.
SKWZ

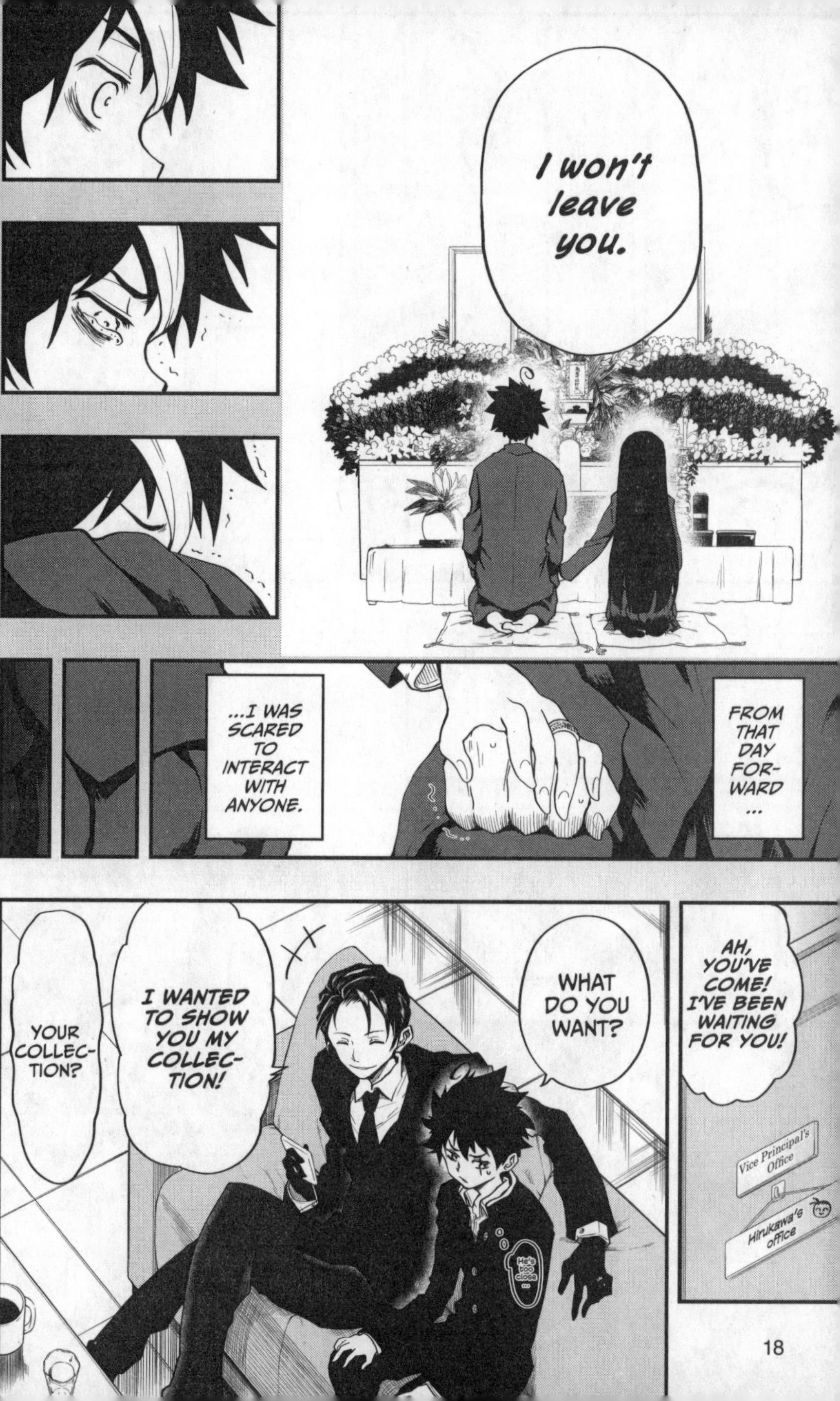
I won't leave you.
FROM THAT DAY FORWARD...
...I WAS SCARED TO INTERACT WITH ANYONE.
AH, YOU'VE COME! I'VE BEEN WAITING FOR YOU!
Vice Principal's Office
Hirukawa's office
WHAT DO YOU WANT?
I WANTED TO SHOW YOU MY COLLECTION!
YOUR COLLECTION?
He's too close...

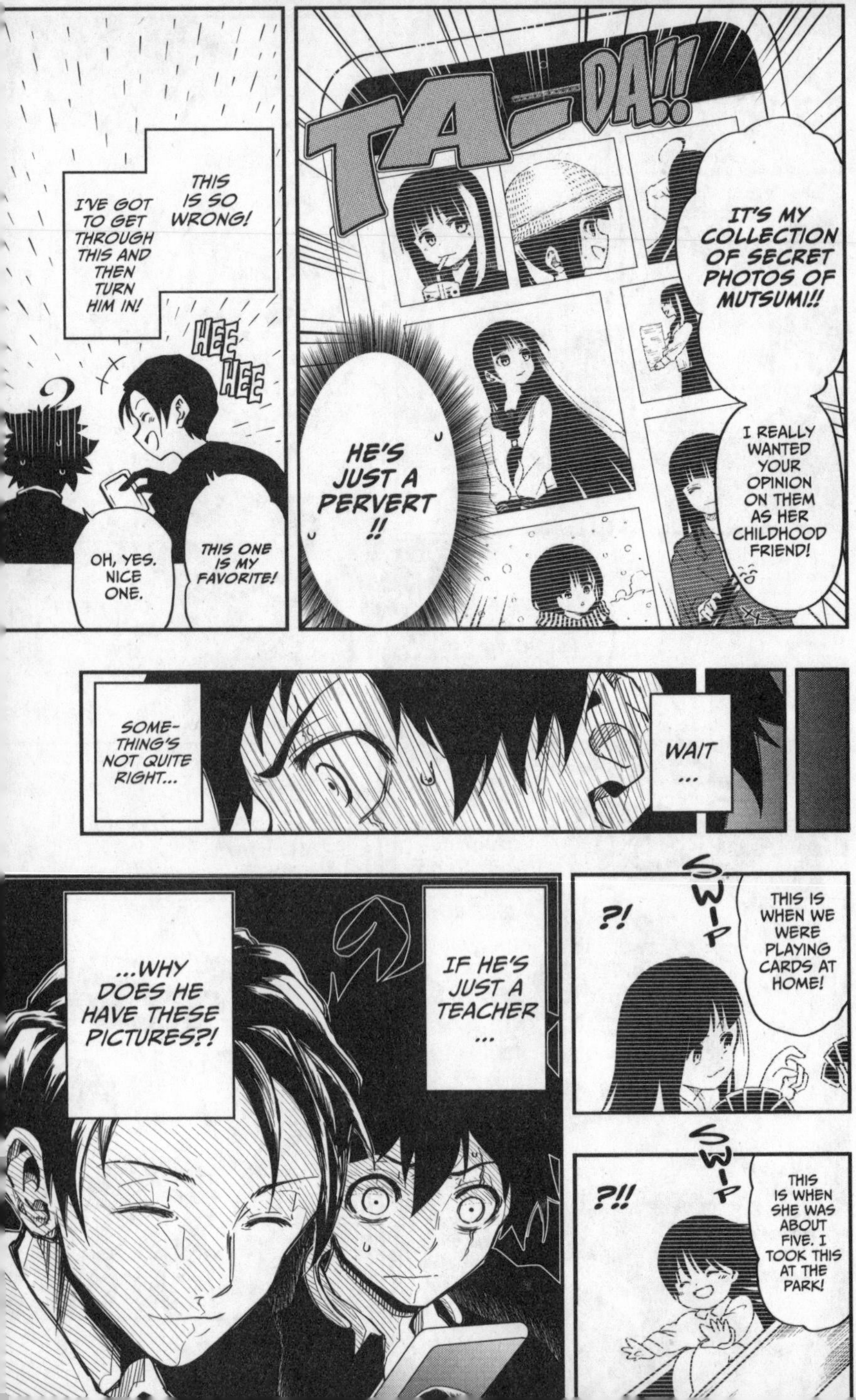
TA-DA!!
IT'S MY COLLECTION OF SECRET PHOTOS OF MUTSUMI!!
I REALLY WANTED YOUR OPINION ON THEM AS HER CHILDHOOD FRIEND!
HE'S JUST A PERVERT!!
THIS IS SO WRONG!
I'VE GOT TO GET THROUGH THIS AND THEN TURN HIM IN!
HEE HEE
THIS ONE IS MY FAVORITE!
OH, YES. NICE ONE.
WAIT ...
SOME-THING'S NOT QUITE RIGHT...
SWIP
THIS IS WHEN WE WERE PLAYING CARDS AT HOME!
?!
SWIP
THIS IS WHEN SHE WAS ABOUT FIVE. I TOOK THIS AT THE PARK!
?!!
IF HE'S JUST A TEACHER ...
...WHY DOES HE HAVE THESE PICTURES?!

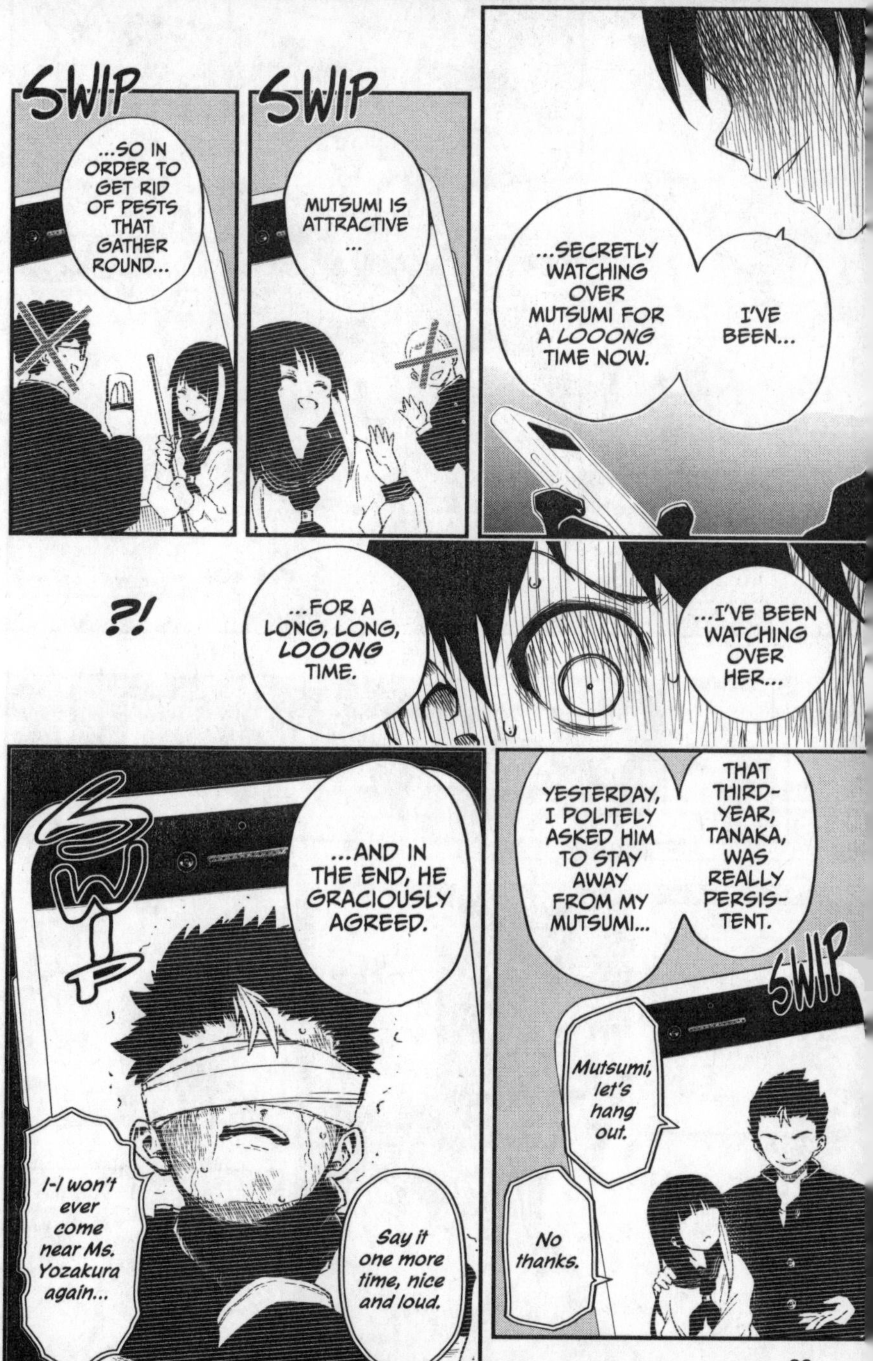
I'VE BEEN...
...SECRETLY WATCHING OVER MUTSUMI FOR A LOOOONG TIME NOW.
SWIP
MUTSUMI IS ATTRACTIVE ...
SWIP
...SO IN ORDER TO GET RID OF PESTS THAT GATHER ROUND...
...I'VE BEEN WATCHING OVER HER...
...FOR A LONG, LONG, LOOOONG TIME.
?!
THAT THIRD-YEAR, TANAKA, WAS REALLY PERSIS-TENT.
YESTERDAY, I POLITELY ASKED HIM TO STAY AWAY FROM MY MUTSUMI...
SWIP
Mutsumi, let's hang out.
No thanks.
SWIP
...AND IN THE END, HE GRACIOUSLY AGREED.
Say it one more time, nice and loud.
I-I won't ever come near Ms. Yozakura again...

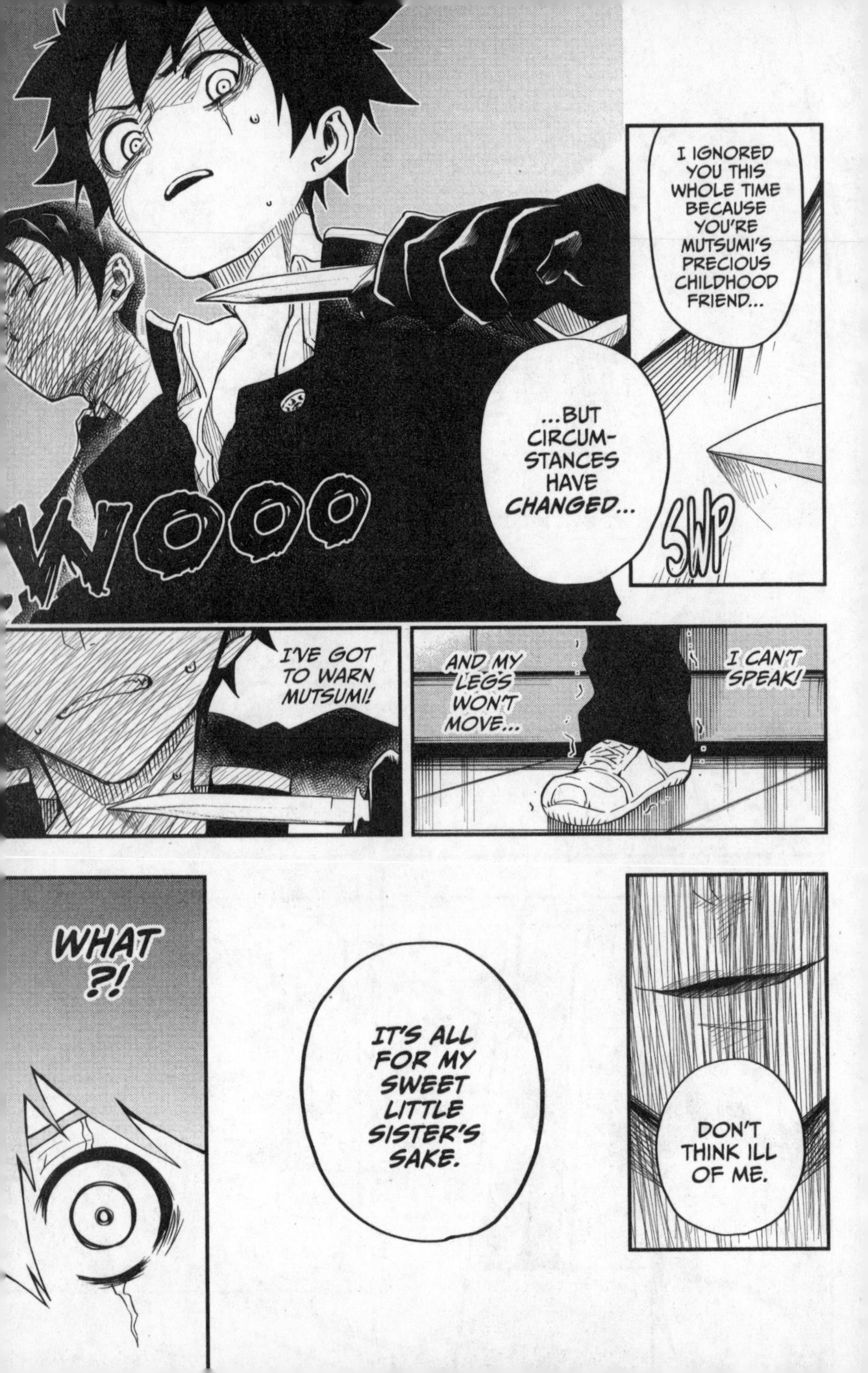
I IGNORED YOU THIS WHOLE TIME BECAUSE YOU'RE MUTSUMI'S PRECIOUS CHILDHOOD FRIEND...
...BUT CIRCUM-STANCES HAVE CHANGED...
SWP
WOOO
I CAN'T SPEAK!
AND MY LEGS WON'T MOVE...
I'VE GOT TO WARN MUTSUMI!
DON'T THINK ILL OF ME.
IT'S ALL FOR MY SWEET LITTLE SISTER'S SAKE.
WHAT?!

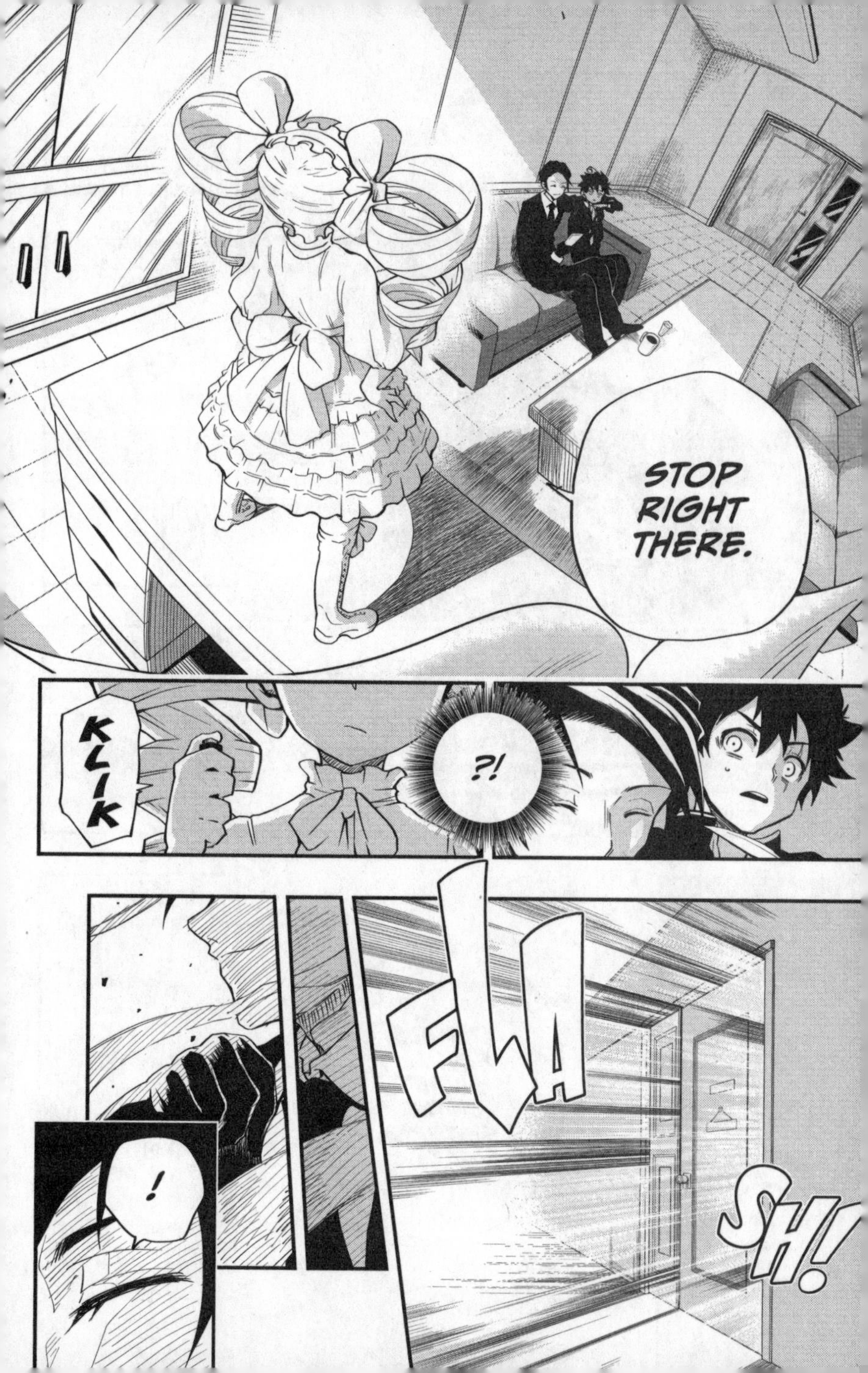
STOP RIGHT THERE.
?!
KLIK
FLASH!
!

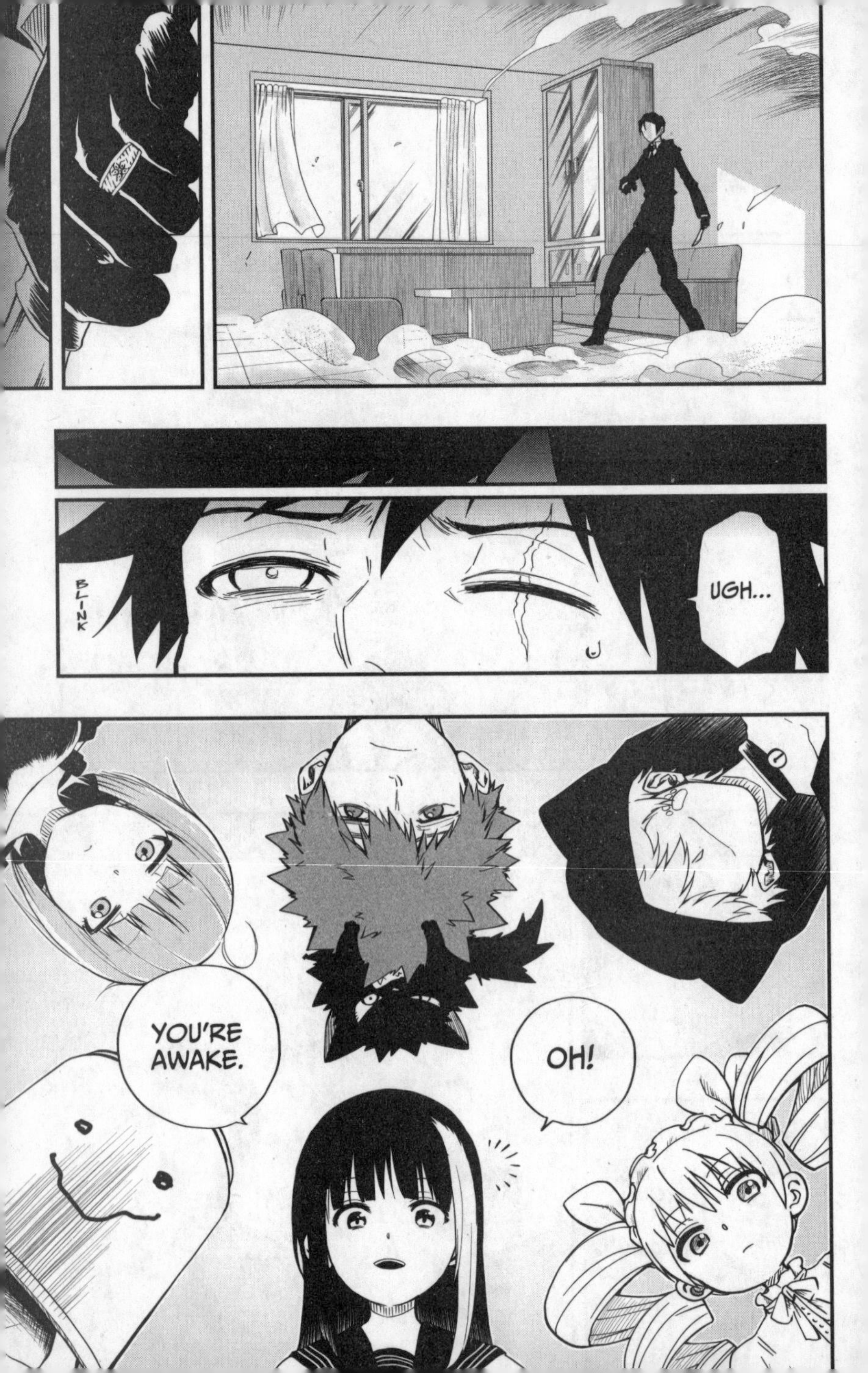
UGH...
BLINK
OH!
YOU'RE AWAKE.

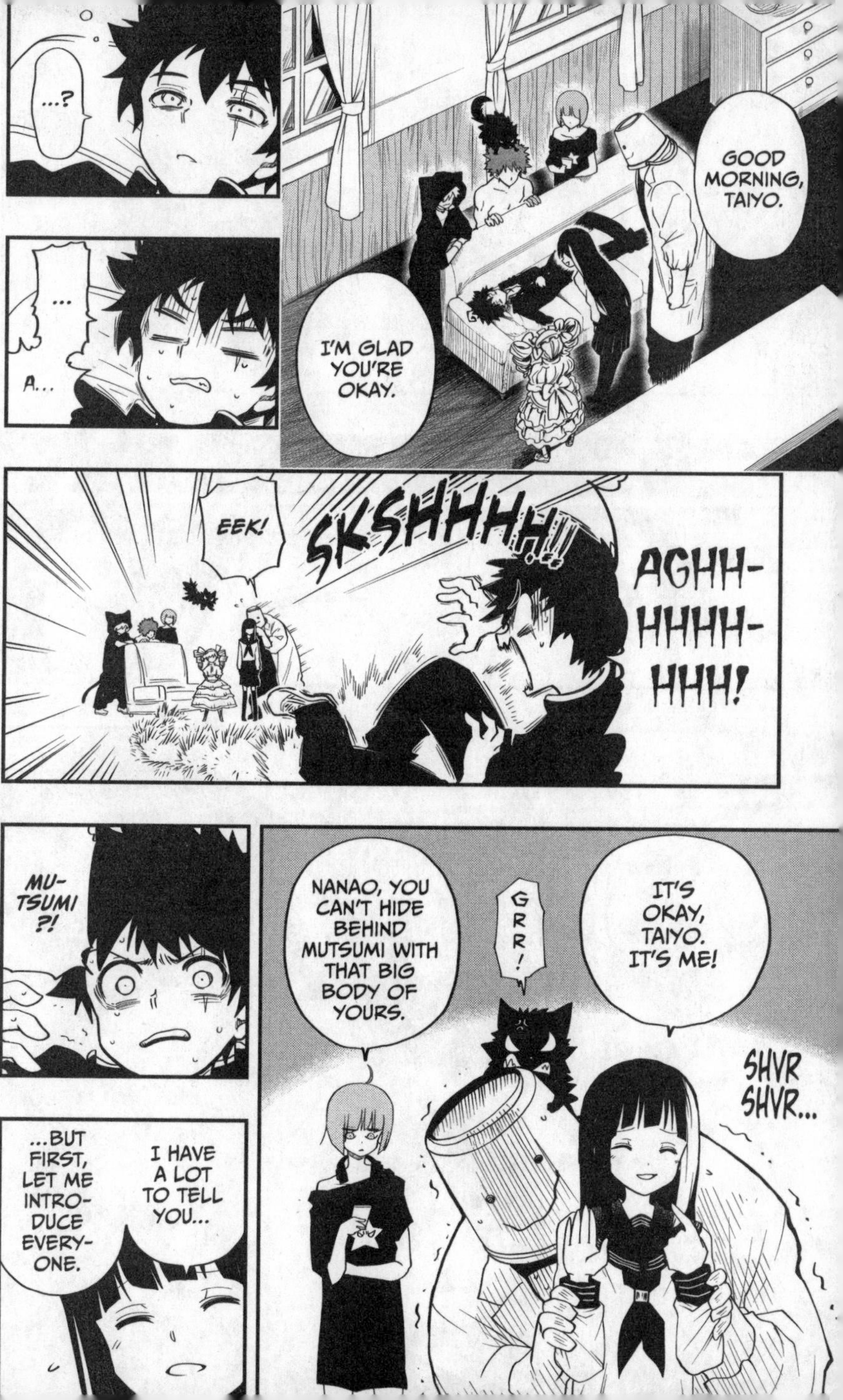
GOOD MORNING, TAIYO.
I'M GLAD YOU'RE OKAY.
...?
...
A...
AGHH-HHHH-HHH!
SKSHHHH!!
EEK!
IT'S OKAY, TAIYO. IT'S ME!
GRR!
NANAO, YOU CAN'T HIDE BEHIND MUTSUMI WITH THAT BIG BODY OF YOURS.
SHVR SHVR...
MUTSUMI?!
I HAVE A LOT TO TELL YOU...
...BUT FIRST, LET ME INTRODUCE EVERYONE.

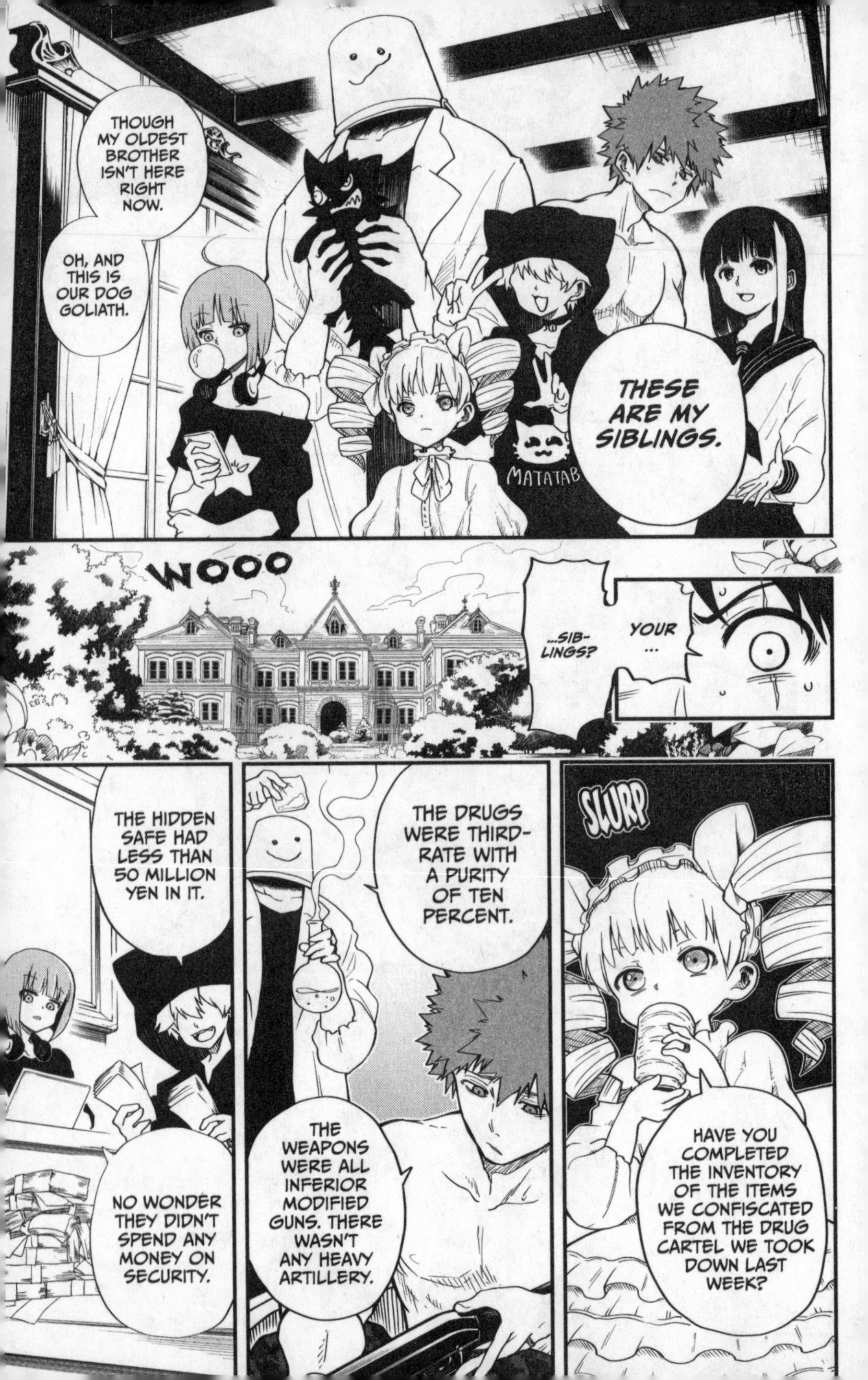
THESE ARE MY SIBLINGS.
MATATAB
THOUGH MY OLDEST BROTHER ISN'T HERE RIGHT NOW.
OH, AND THIS IS OUR DOG GOLIATH.
YOUR ...
...SIB-LINGS?
WOOO
SLURP
HAVE YOU COMPLETED THE INVENTORY OF THE ITEMS WE CONFISCATED FROM THE DRUG CARTEL WE TOOK DOWN LAST WEEK?
THE DRUGS WERE THIRD-RATE WITH A PURITY OF TEN PERCENT.
THE WEAPONS WERE ALL INFERIOR MODIFIED GUNS. THERE WASN'T ANY HEAVY ARTILLERY.
THE HIDDEN SAFE HAD LESS THAN 50 MILLION YEN IN IT.
NO WONDER THEY DIDN'T SPEND ANY MONEY ON SECURITY.

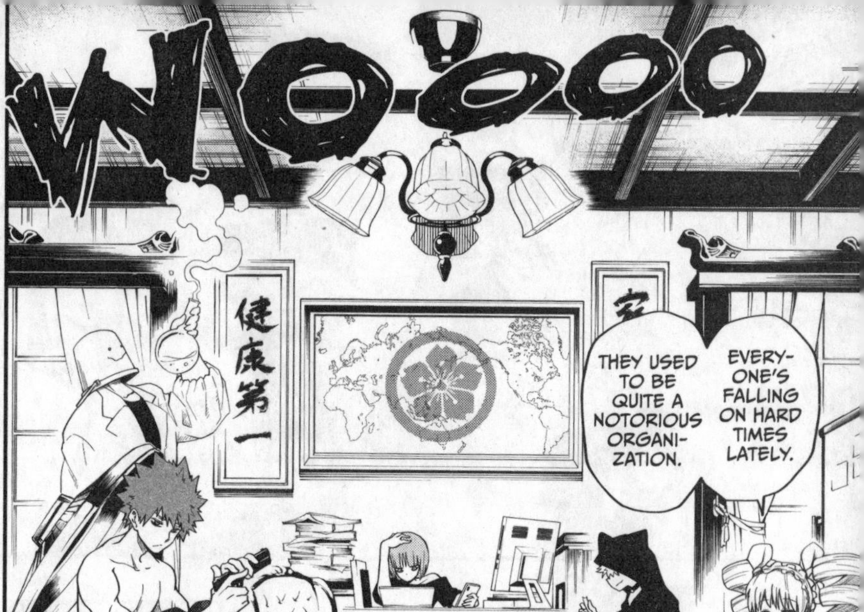
WHOOOO
健康第一
EVERY-ONE'S FALLING ON HARD TIMES LATELY.
THEY USED TO BE QUITE A NOTORIOUS ORGANI-ZATION.
MY FAMILY ARE ALL SPIES.
RIP
RIP
GRR!
THAT'S WHY I KEPT EVERYTHING ABOUT MY FAMILY A SECRET.

*SIGN: HEALTH COMES FIRST

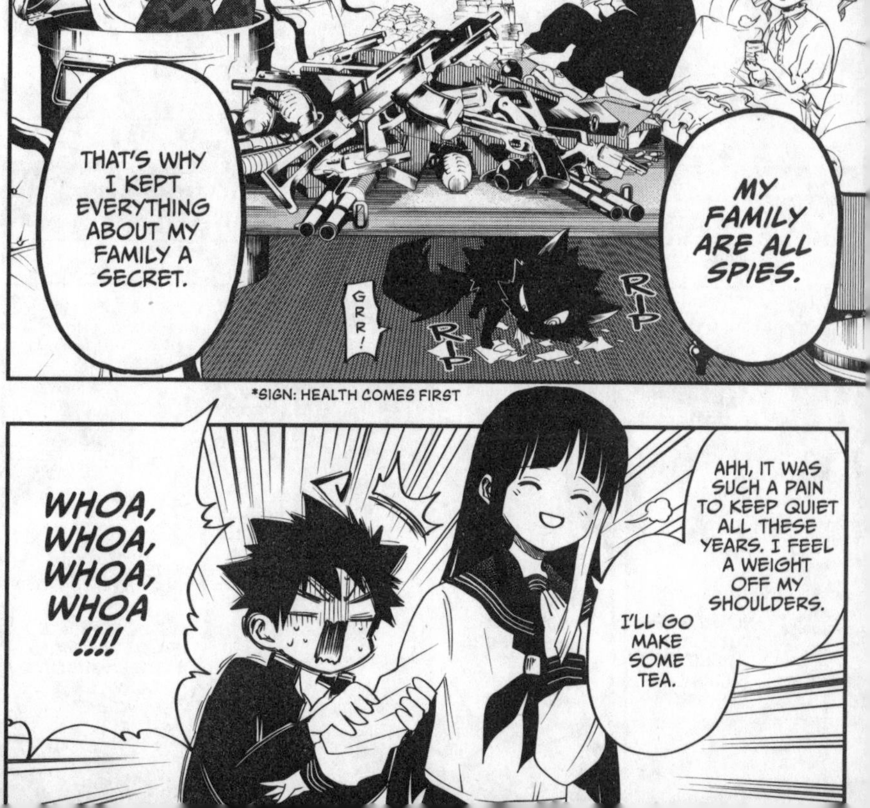
AHH, IT WAS SUCH A PAIN TO KEEP QUIET ALL THESE YEARS. I FEEL A WEIGHT OFF MY SHOULDERS.
I'LL GO MAKE SOME TEA.
WHOA, WHOA, WHOA, WHOA!!!!

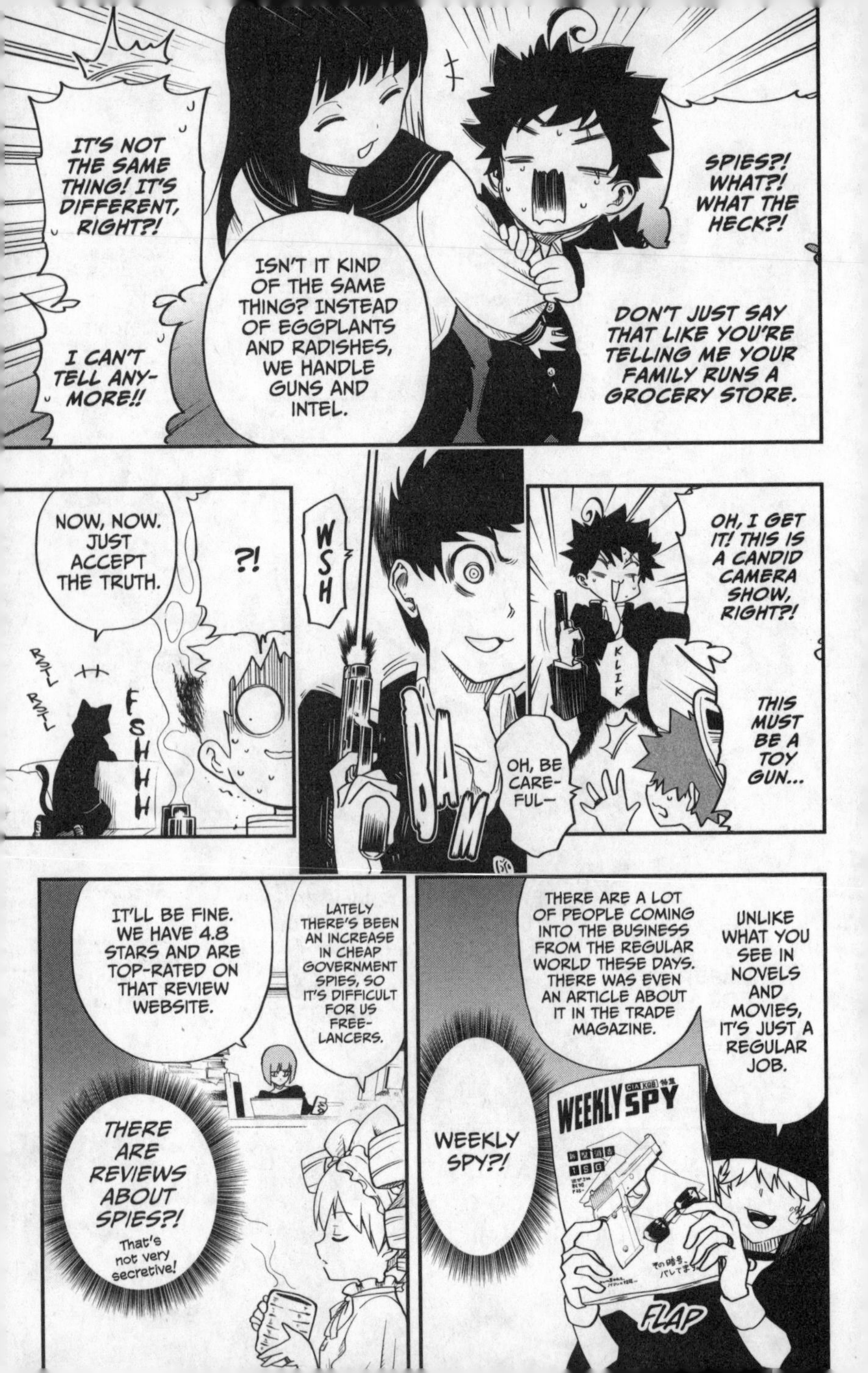
SPIES?! WHAT?! WHAT THE HECK?!
DON'T JUST SAY THAT LIKE YOU'RE TELLING ME YOUR FAMILY RUNS A GROCERY STORE.
ISN'T IT KIND OF THE SAME THING? INSTEAD OF EGGPLANTS AND RADISHES, WE HANDLE GUNS AND INTEL.
IT'S NOT THE SAME THING! IT'S DIFFERENT, RIGHT?!
I CAN'T TELL ANY-MORE!!
OH, I GET IT! THIS IS A CANDID CAMERA SHOW, RIGHT?!
KLIK
THIS MUST BE A TOY GUN...
OH, BE CARE-FUL—
WSH
BAM
NOW, NOW. JUST ACCEPT THE TRUTH.
?!
FSHHH
RSTL RSTL
UNLIKE WHAT YOU SEE IN NOVELS AND MOVIES, IT'S JUST A REGULAR JOB.
THERE ARE A LOT OF PEOPLE COMING INTO THE BUSINESS FROM THE REGULAR WORLD THESE DAYS. THERE WAS EVEN AN ARTICLE ABOUT IT IN THE TRADE MAGAZINE.
WEEKLY CIA KGB SPY
WEEKLY SPY?!
FLAP
LATELY THERE'S BEEN AN INCREASE IN CHEAP GOVERNMENT SPIES, SO IT'S DIFFICULT FOR US FREE-LANCERS.
IT'LL BE FINE. WE HAVE 4.8 STARS AND ARE TOP-RATED ON THAT REVIEW WEBSITE.
THERE ARE REVIEWS ABOUT SPIES?!
That's not very secretive!

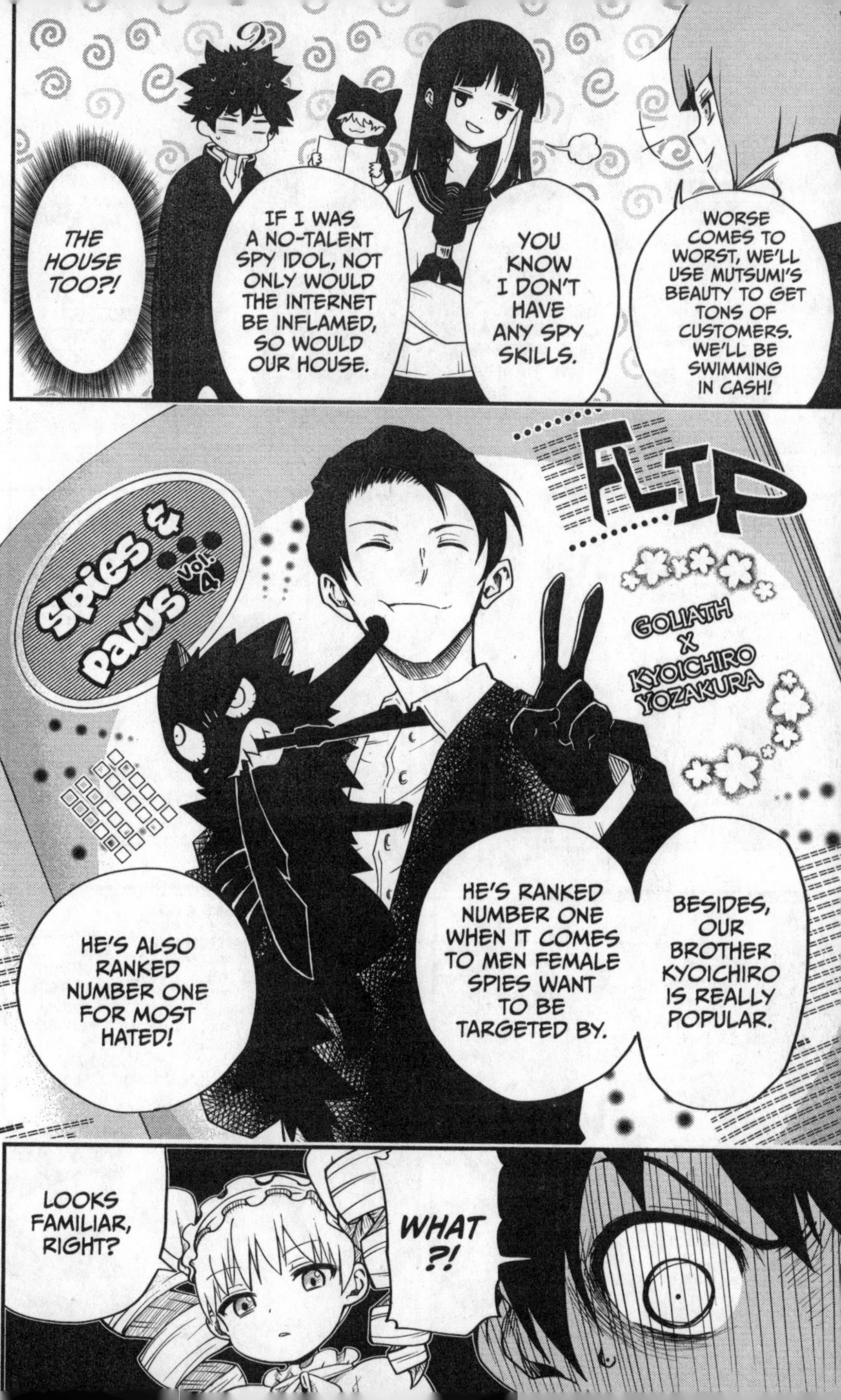
WORSE COMES TO WORST, WE'LL USE MUTSUMI'S BEAUTY TO GET TONS OF CUSTOMERS. WE'LL BE SWIMMING IN CASH!
YOU KNOW I DON'T HAVE ANY SPY SKILLS.
IF I WAS A NO-TALENT SPY IDOL, NOT ONLY WOULD THE INTERNET BE INFLAMED, SO WOULD OUR HOUSE.
THE HOUSE TOO?!
FLIP
GOLIATH X KYOICHIRO YOZAKURA
Spies & Paws Vol. 4
BESIDES, OUR BROTHER KYOICHIRO IS REALLY POPULAR.
HE'S RANKED NUMBER ONE WHEN IT COMES TO MEN FEMALE SPIES WANT TO BE TARGETED BY.
HE'S ALSO RANKED NUMBER ONE FOR MOST HATED!
WHAT?!
LOOKS FAMILIAR, RIGHT?

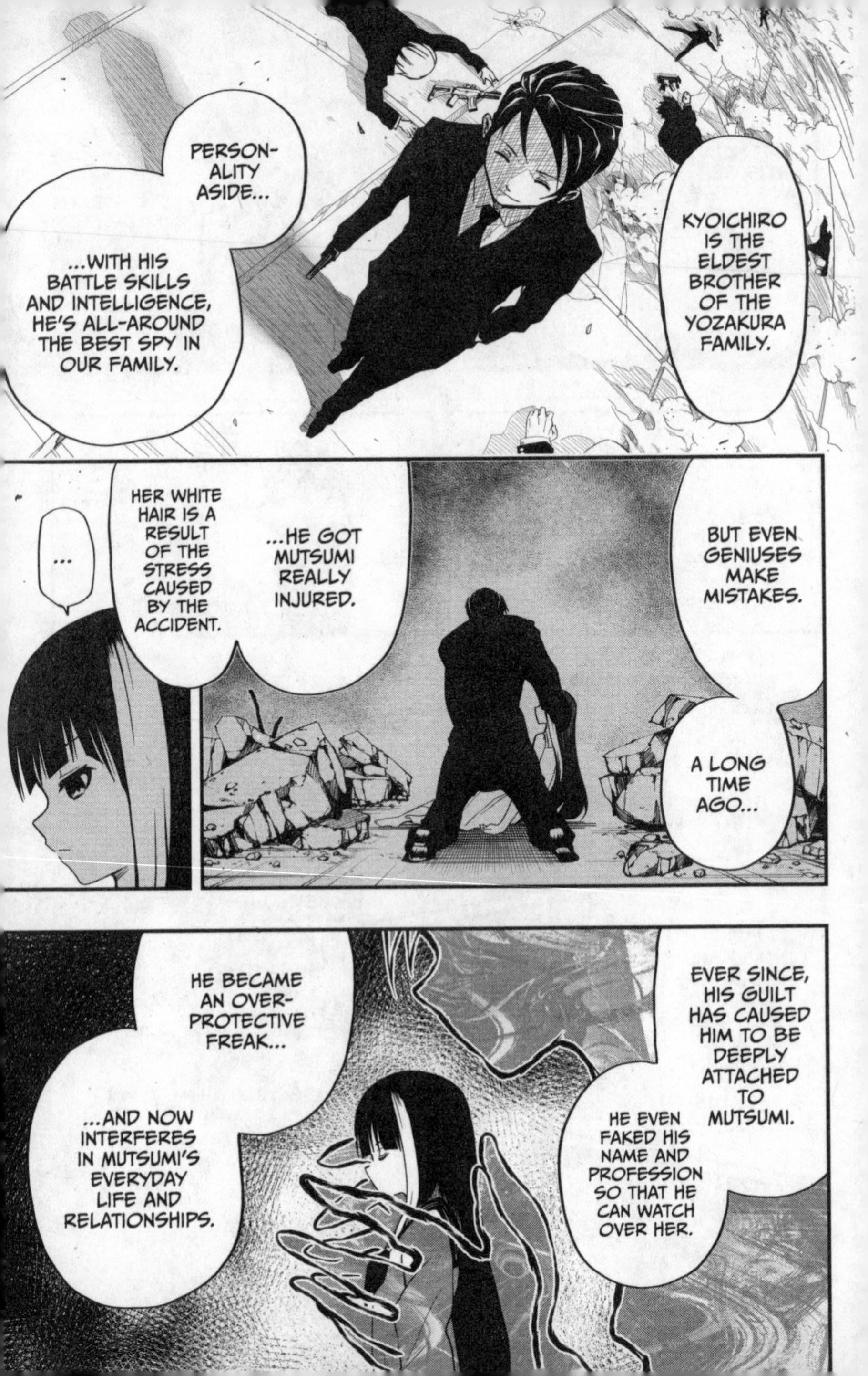
KYOICHIRO IS THE ELDEST BROTHER OF THE YOZAKURA FAMILY.
PERSON-ALITY ASIDE...
...WITH HIS BATTLE SKILLS AND INTELLIGENCE, HE'S ALL-AROUND THE BEST SPY IN OUR FAMILY.
BUT EVEN GENIUSES MAKE MISTAKES.
A LONG TIME AGO...
...HE GOT MUTSUMI REALLY INJURED.
HER WHITE HAIR IS A RESULT OF THE STRESS CAUSED BY THE ACCIDENT.
...
EVER SINCE, HIS GUILT HAS CAUSED HIM TO BE DEEPLY ATTACHED TO MUTSUMI.
HE EVEN FAKED HIS NAME AND PROFESSION SO THAT HE CAN WATCH OVER HER.
HE BECAME AN OVER-PROTECTIVE FREAK...
...AND NOW INTERFERES IN MUTSUMI'S EVERYDAY LIFE AND RELATIONSHIPS.

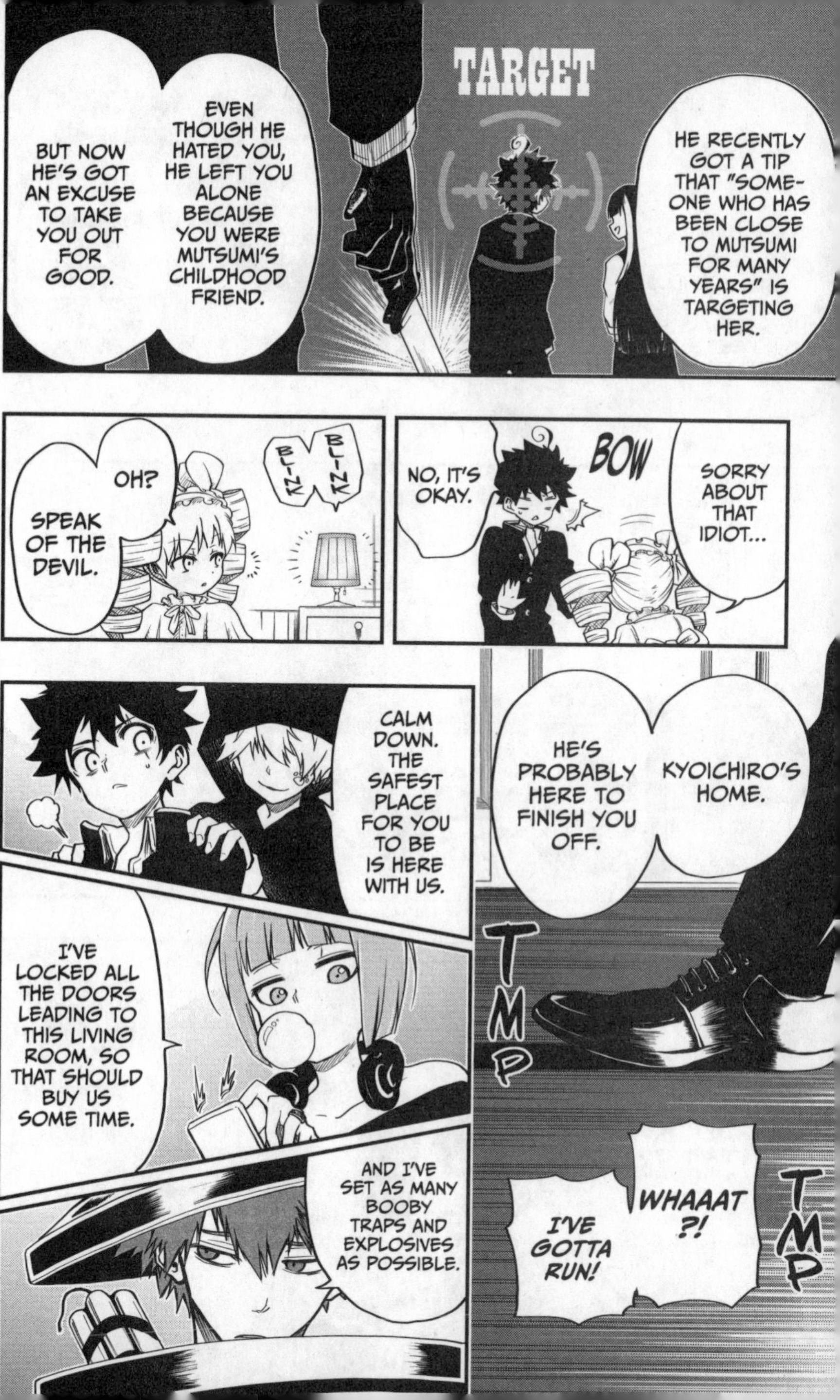
TARGET
HE RECENTLY GOT A TIP THAT "SOME-ONE WHO HAS BEEN CLOSE TO MUTSUMI FOR MANY YEARS" IS TARGETING HER.
EVEN THOUGH HE HATED YOU, HE LEFT YOU ALONE BECAUSE YOU WERE MUTSUMI'S CHILDHOOD FRIEND.
BUT NOW HE'S GOT AN EXCUSE TO TAKE YOU OUT FOR GOOD.
SORRY ABOUT THAT IDIOT...
BOW
NO, IT'S OKAY.
BLINK
BLINK
OH?
SPEAK OF THE DEVIL.
KYOICHIRO'S HOME.
HE'S PROBABLY HERE TO FINISH YOU OFF.
TMP
WHAAAT?!
I'VE GOTTA RUN!
TMP
CALM DOWN. THE SAFEST PLACE FOR YOU TO BE IS HERE WITH US.
I'VE LOCKED ALL THE DOORS LEADING TO THIS LIVING ROOM, SO THAT SHOULD BUY US SOME TIME.
AND I'VE SET AS MANY BOOBY TRAPS AND EXPLOSIVES AS POSSIBLE.

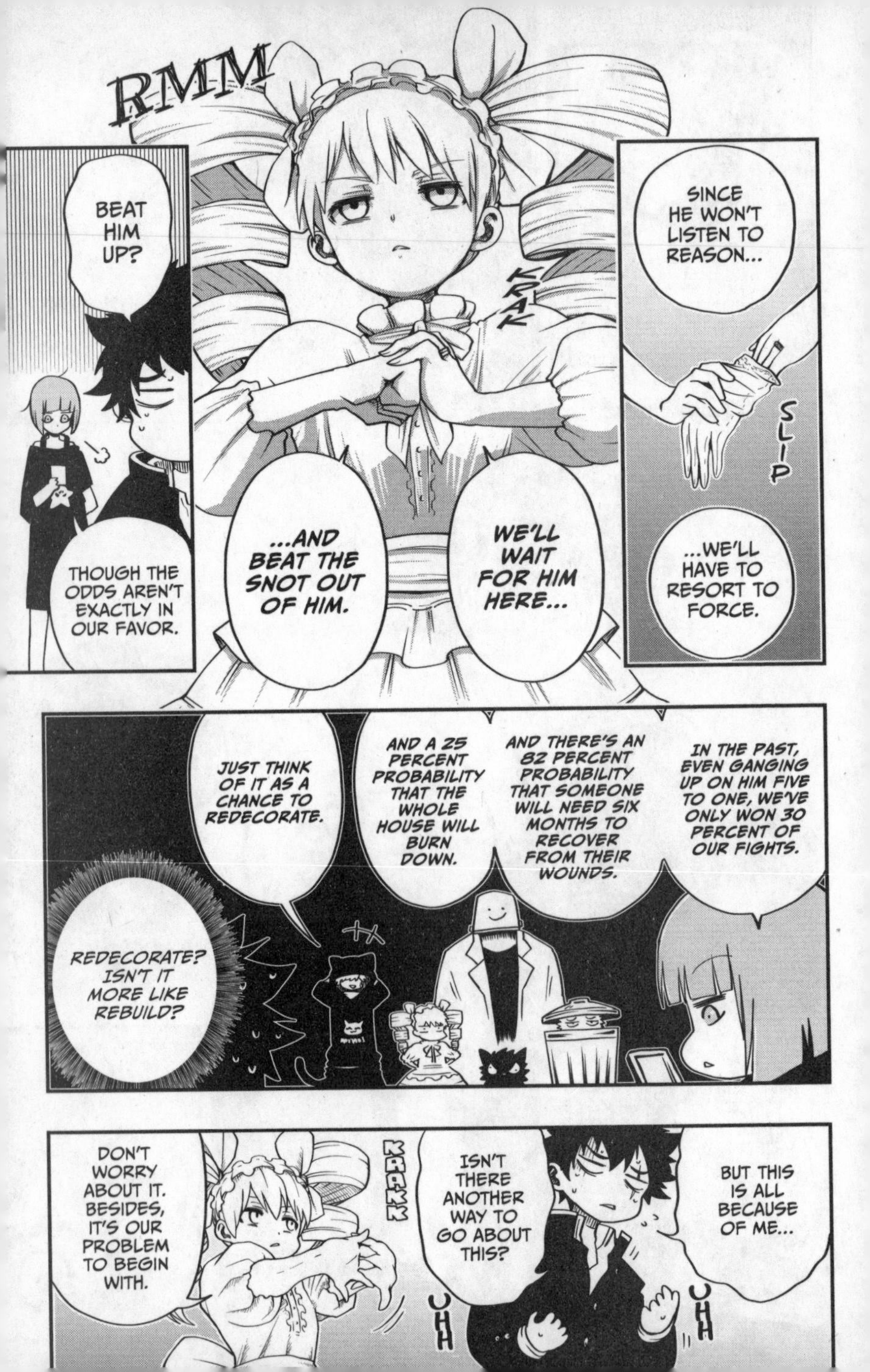
SINCE HE WON'T LISTEN TO REASON...
SLIP
...WE'LL HAVE TO RESORT TO FORCE.
RMM
KRAK
WE'LL WAIT FOR HIM HERE...
...AND BEAT THE SNOT OUT OF HIM.
BEAT HIM UP?
THOUGH THE ODDS AREN'T EXACTLY IN OUR FAVOR.
IN THE PAST, EVEN GANGING UP ON HIM FIVE TO ONE, WE'VE ONLY WON 30 PERCENT OF OUR FIGHTS.
AND THERE'S AN 82 PERCENT PROBABILITY THAT SOMEONE WILL NEED SIX MONTHS TO RECOVER FROM THEIR WOUNDS.
AND A 25 PERCENT PROBABILITY THAT THE WHOLE HOUSE WILL BURN DOWN.
JUST THINK OF IT AS A CHANCE TO REDECORATE.
REDECORATE? ISN'T IT MORE LIKE REBUILD?
BUT THIS IS ALL BECAUSE OF ME...
UHH
ISN'T THERE ANOTHER WAY TO GO ABOUT THIS?
UHH
KRAKK
DON'T WORRY ABOUT IT. BESIDES, IT'S OUR PROBLEM TO BEGIN WITH.

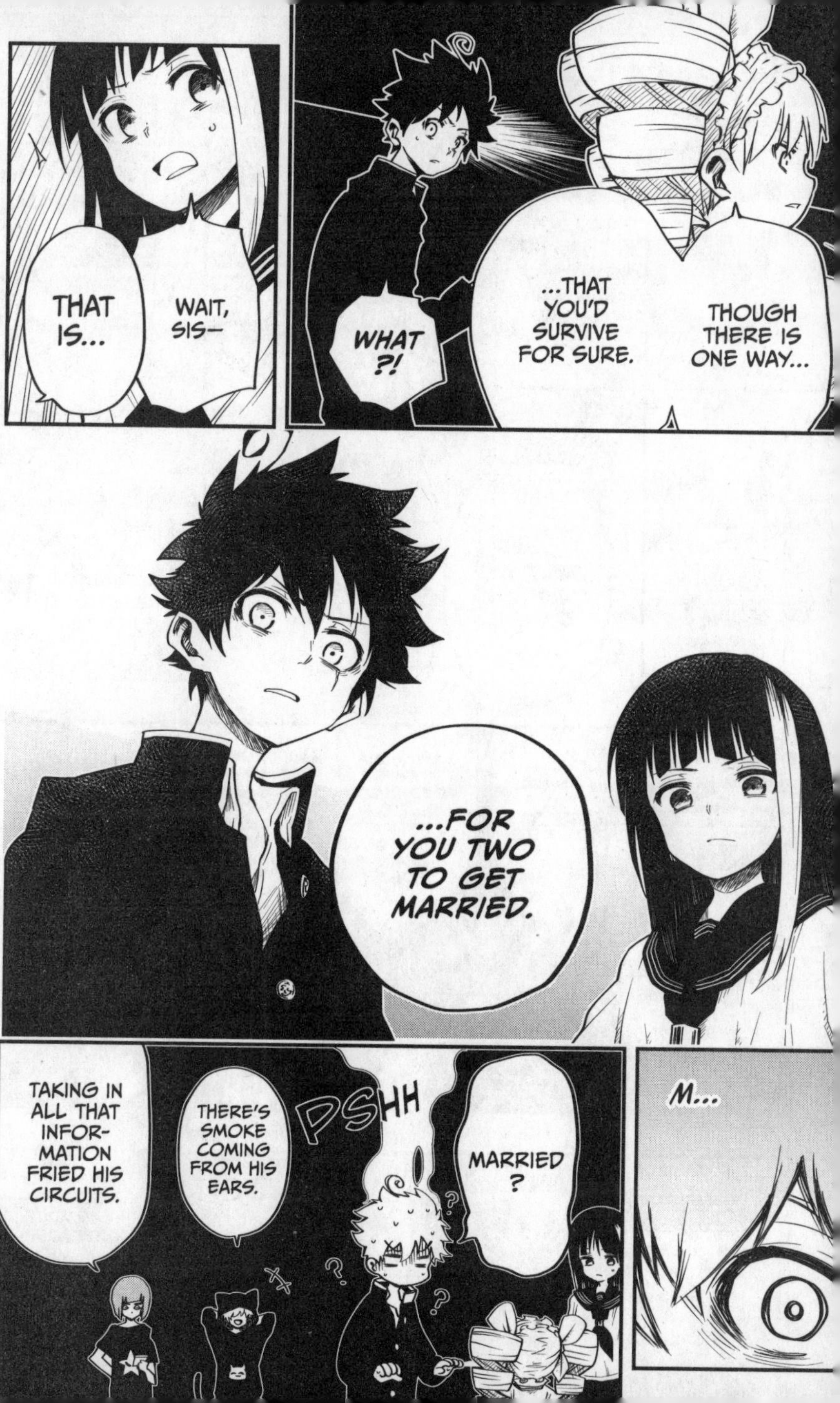
THOUGH THERE IS ONE WAY...
...THAT YOU'D SURVIVE FOR SURE.
WHAT?!
WAIT, SIS—
THAT IS...
...FOR YOU TWO TO GET MARRIED.
M...
MARRIED?
PSHH
THERE'S SMOKE COMING FROM HIS EARS.
TAKING IN ALL THAT INFOR-MATION FRIED HIS CIRCUITS.

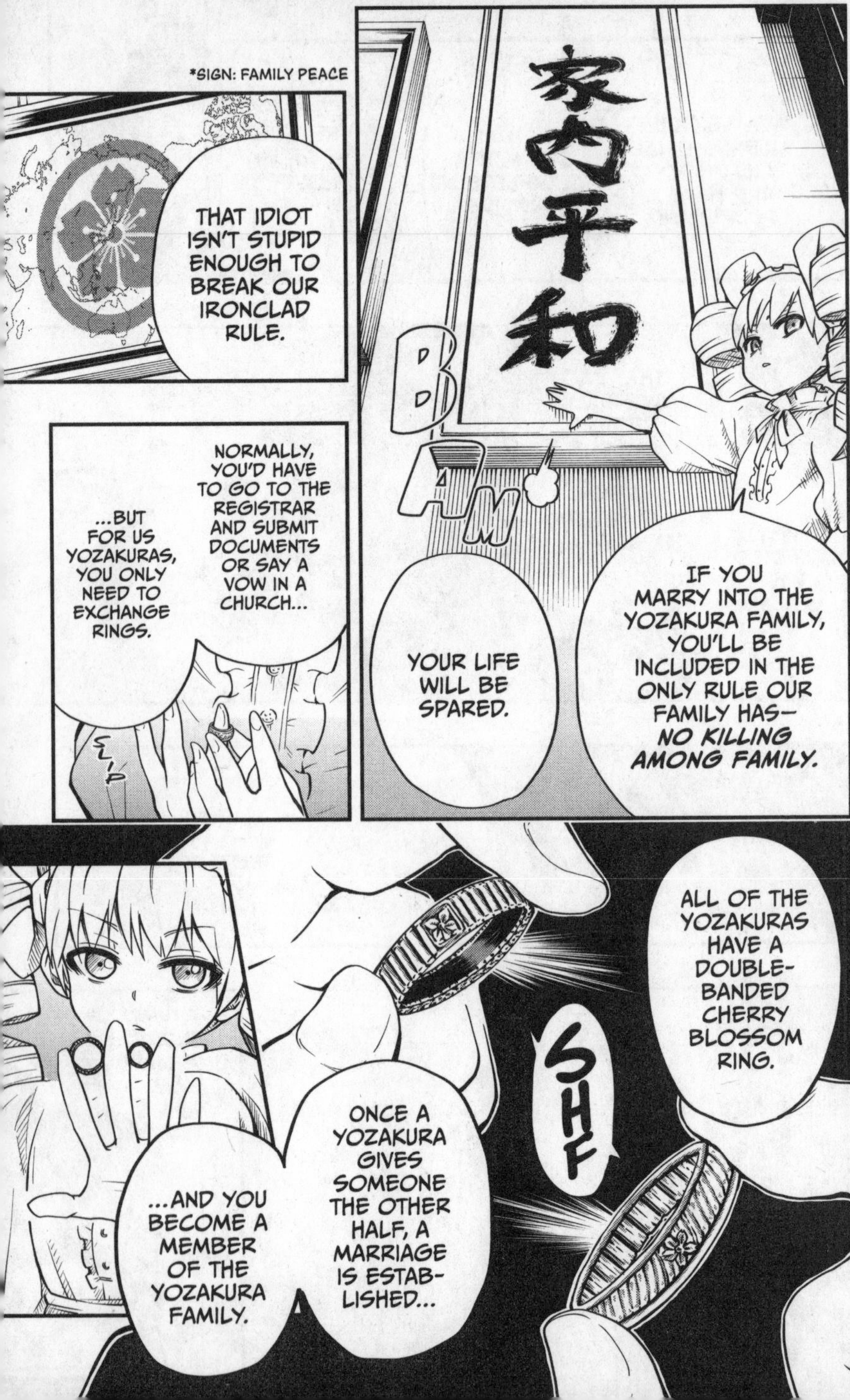
*SIGN: FAMILY PEACE
家内平和
BAM
IF YOU MARRY INTO THE YOZAKURA FAMILY, YOU'LL BE INCLUDED IN THE ONLY RULE OUR FAMILY HAS— *NO KILLING AMONG FAMILY.*
YOUR LIFE WILL BE SPARED.
THAT IDIOT ISN'T STUPID ENOUGH TO BREAK OUR IRONCLAD RULE.
NORMALLY, YOU'D HAVE TO GO TO THE REGISTRAR AND SUBMIT DOCUMENTS OR SAY A VOW IN A CHURCH...
...BUT FOR US YOZAKURAS, YOU ONLY NEED TO EXCHANGE RINGS.
SLIP
ALL OF THE YOZAKURAS HAVE A DOUBLE-BANDED CHERRY BLOSSOM RING.
SHF
ONCE A YOZAKURA GIVES SOMEONE THE OTHER HALF, A MARRIAGE IS ESTAB-LISHED...
...AND YOU BECOME A MEMBER OF THE YOZAKURA FAMILY.

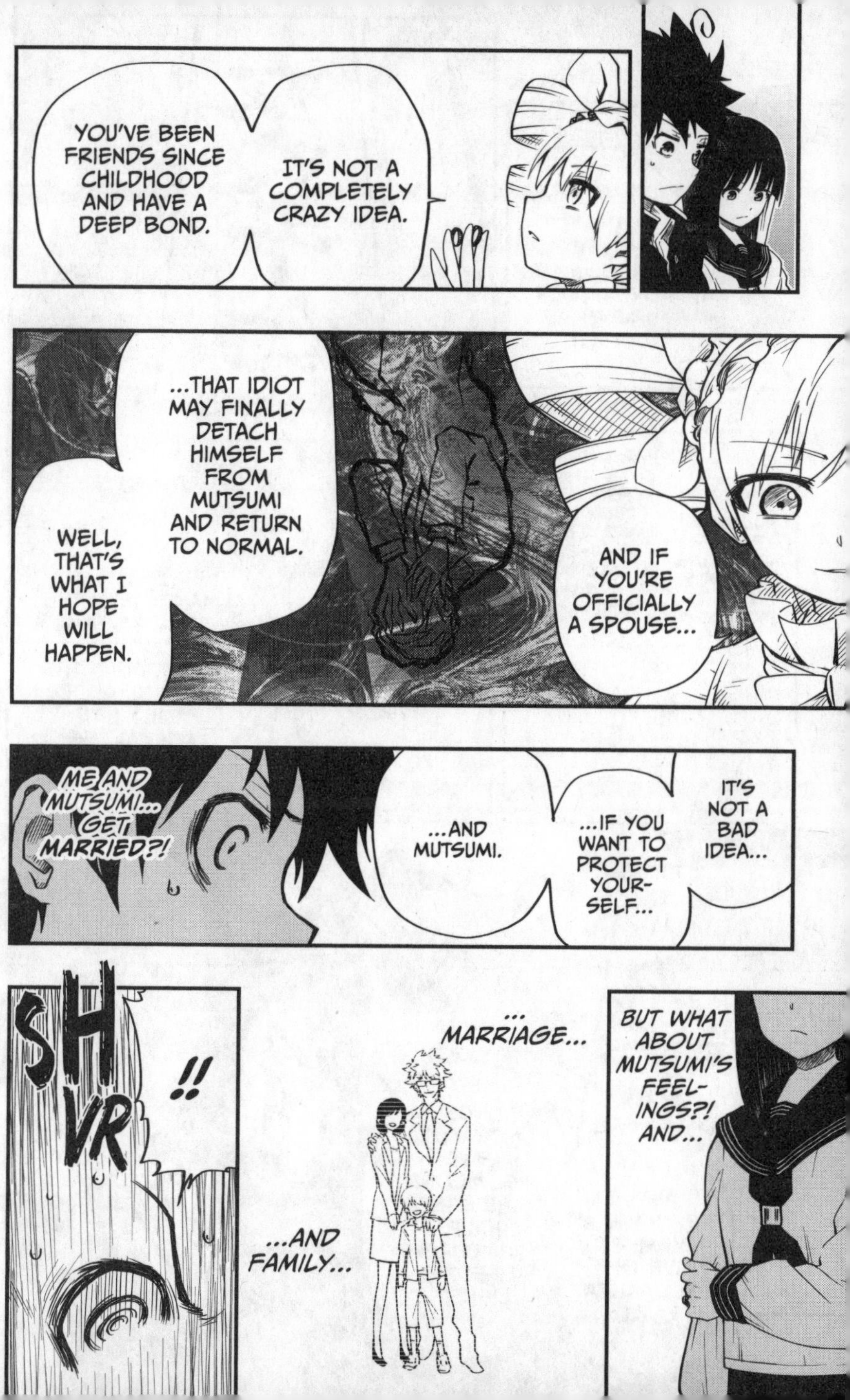
IT'S NOT A COMPLETELY CRAZY IDEA.
YOU'VE BEEN FRIENDS SINCE CHILDHOOD AND HAVE A DEEP BOND.
AND IF YOU'RE OFFICIALLY A SPOUSE...
...THAT IDIOT MAY FINALLY DETACH HIMSELF FROM MUTSUMI AND RETURN TO NORMAL.
WELL, THAT'S WHAT I HOPE WILL HAPPEN.
IT'S NOT A BAD IDEA...
...IF YOU WANT TO PROTECT YOURSELF...
...AND MUTSUMI.
ME AND MUTSUMI... GET MARRIED?!
BUT WHAT ABOUT MUTSUMI'S FEELINGS?! AND...
... MARRIAGE...
...AND FAMILY...
SHVR
!!

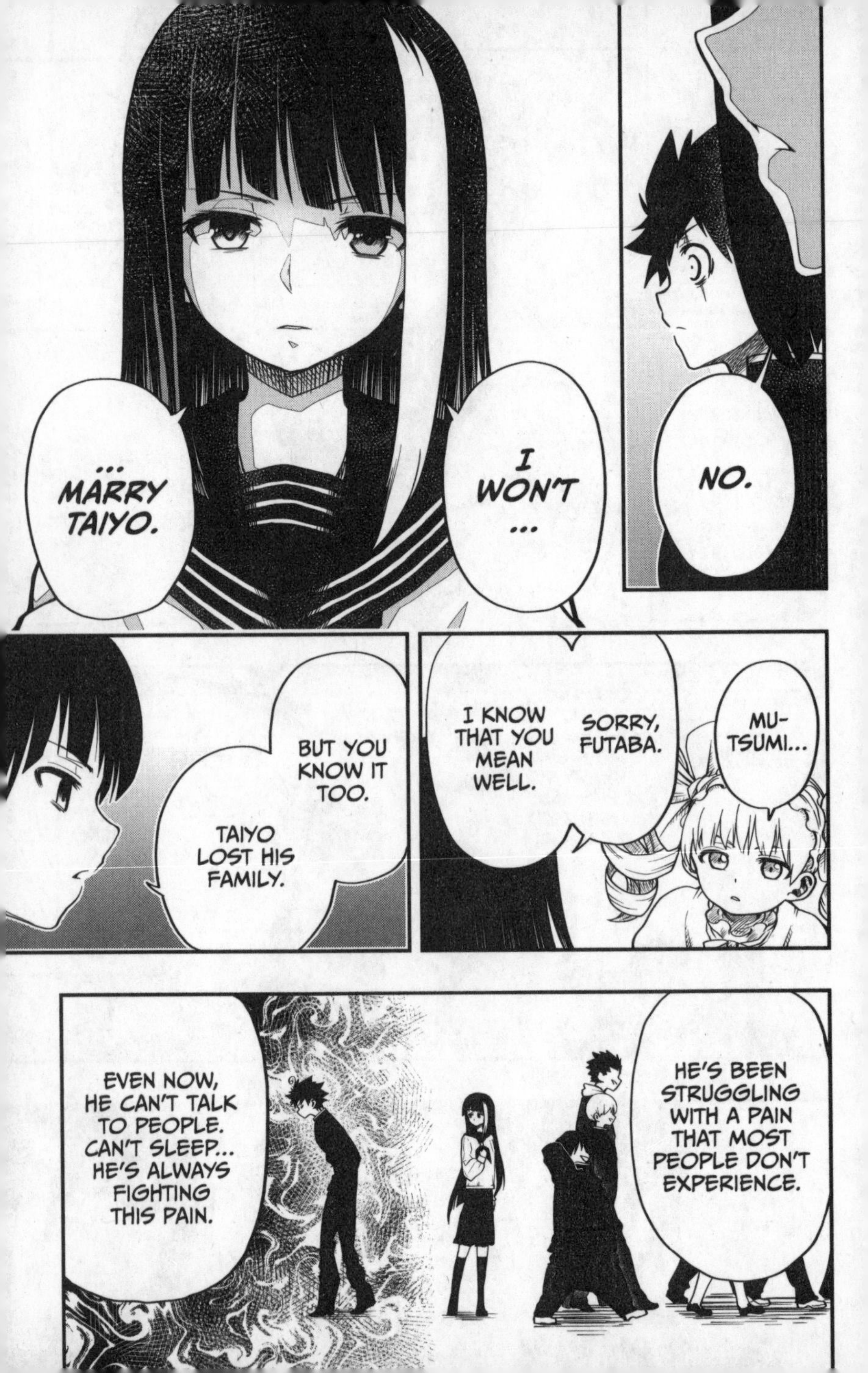
NO.
I WON'T ...
... MARRY TAIYO.
MU-TSUMI...
SORRY, FUTABA.
I KNOW THAT YOU MEAN WELL.
BUT YOU KNOW IT TOO.
TAIYO LOST HIS FAMILY.
HE'S BEEN STRUGGLING WITH A PAIN THAT MOST PEOPLE DON'T EXPERIENCE.
EVEN NOW, HE CAN'T TALK TO PEOPLE. CAN'T SLEEP... HE'S ALWAYS FIGHTING THIS PAIN.

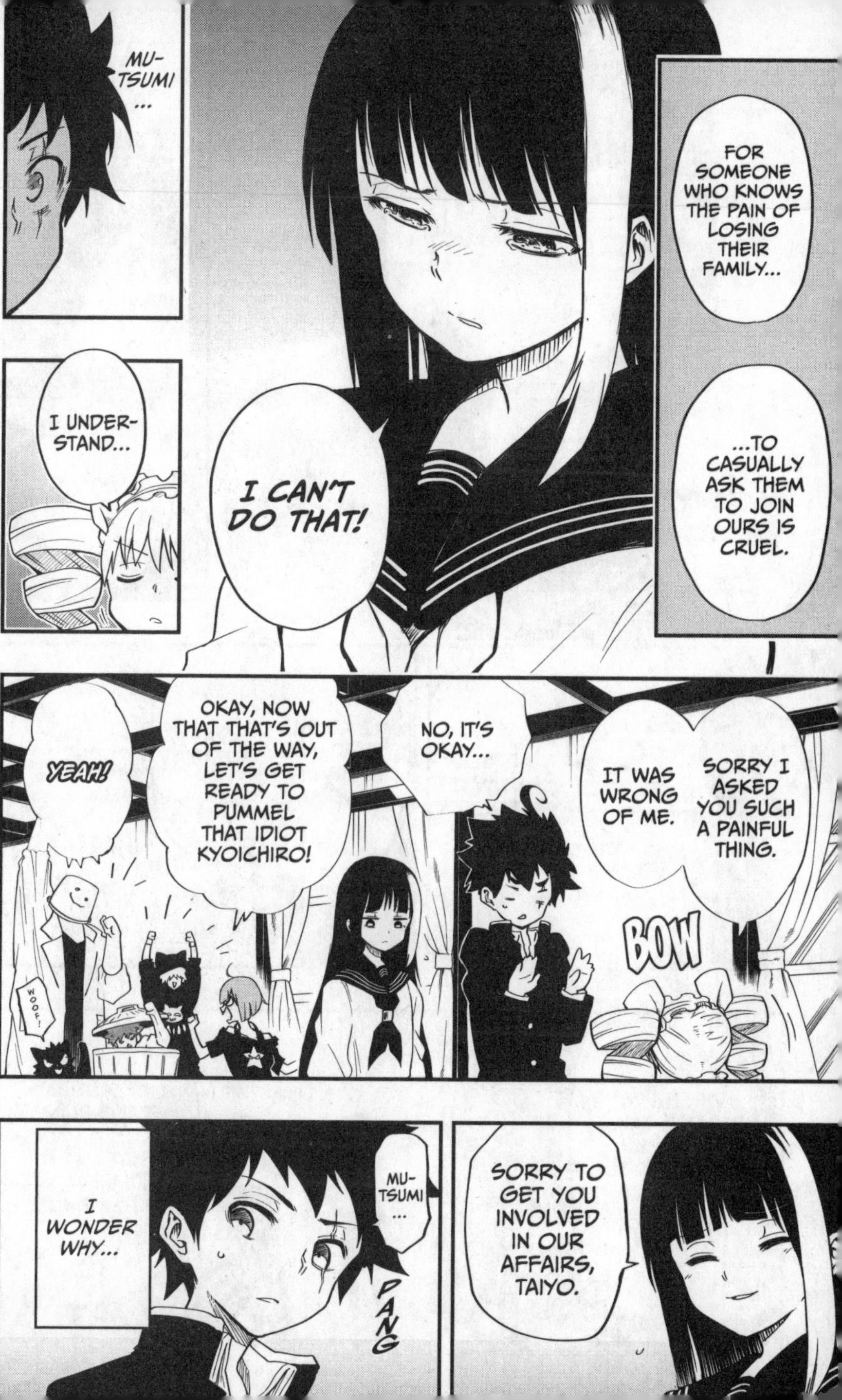
FOR SOMEONE WHO KNOWS THE PAIN OF LOSING THEIR FAMILY...
...TO CASUALLY ASK THEM TO JOIN OURS IS CRUEL.
I CAN'T DO THAT!
MU-TSUMI...
I UNDER-STAND...
SORRY I ASKED YOU SUCH A PAINFUL THING.
IT WAS WRONG OF ME.
BOW
NO, IT'S OKAY...
OKAY, NOW THAT THAT'S OUT OF THE WAY, LET'S GET READY TO PUMMEL THAT IDIOT KYOICHIRO!
YEAH!
WOOF!
SORRY TO GET YOU INVOLVED IN OUR AFFAIRS, TAIYO.
MU-TSUMI...
PANG
I WONDER WHY...

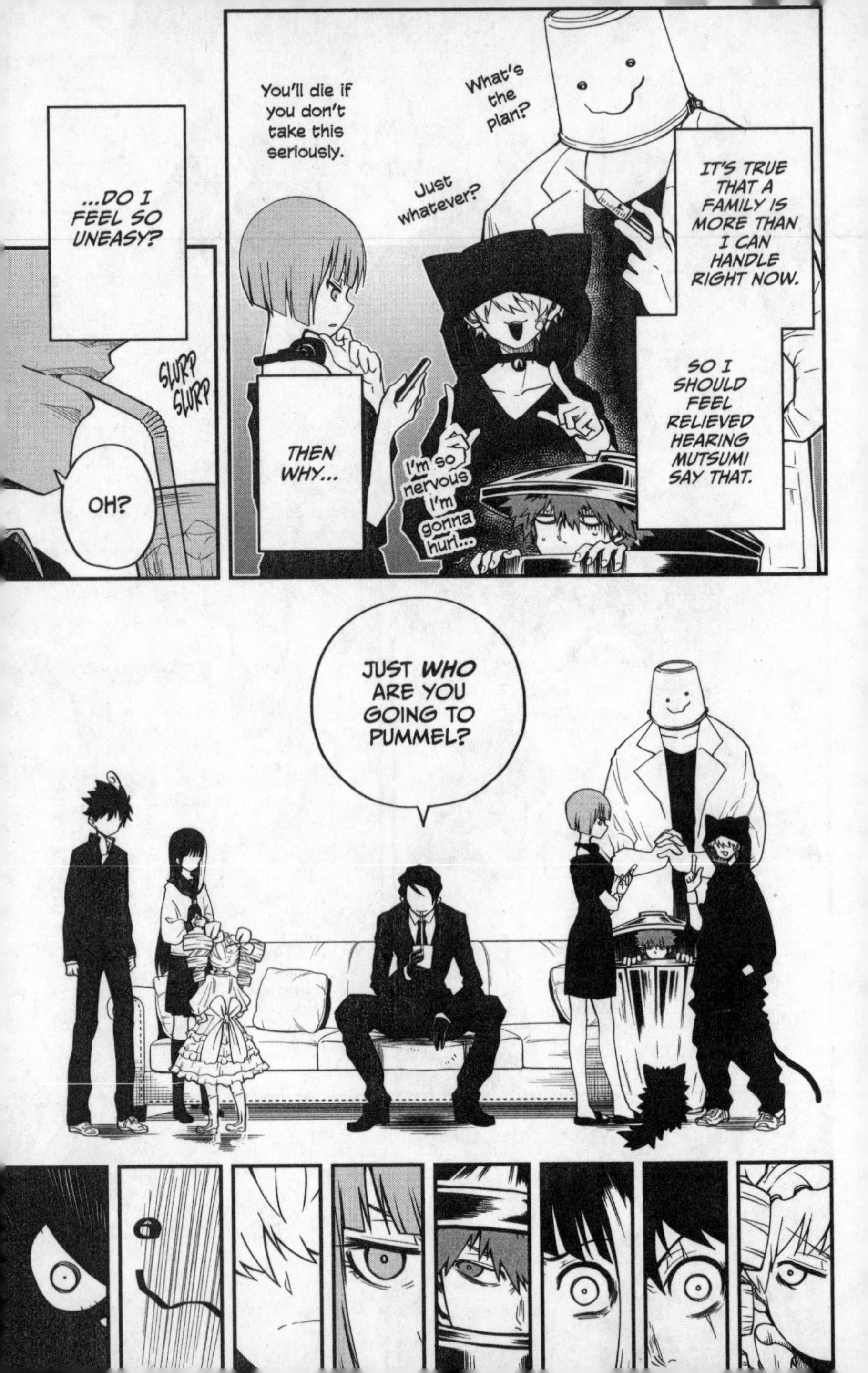
What's the plan?
You'll die if you don't take this seriously.
IT'S TRUE THAT A FAMILY IS MORE THAN I CAN HANDLE RIGHT NOW.
Just whatever?
SO I SHOULD FEEL RELIEVED HEARING MUTSUMI SAY THAT.
I'm so nervous I'm gonna hurl...
THEN WHY...
...DO I FEEL SO UNEASY?
SLURP SLURP
OH?
JUST WHO ARE YOU GOING TO PUMMEL?

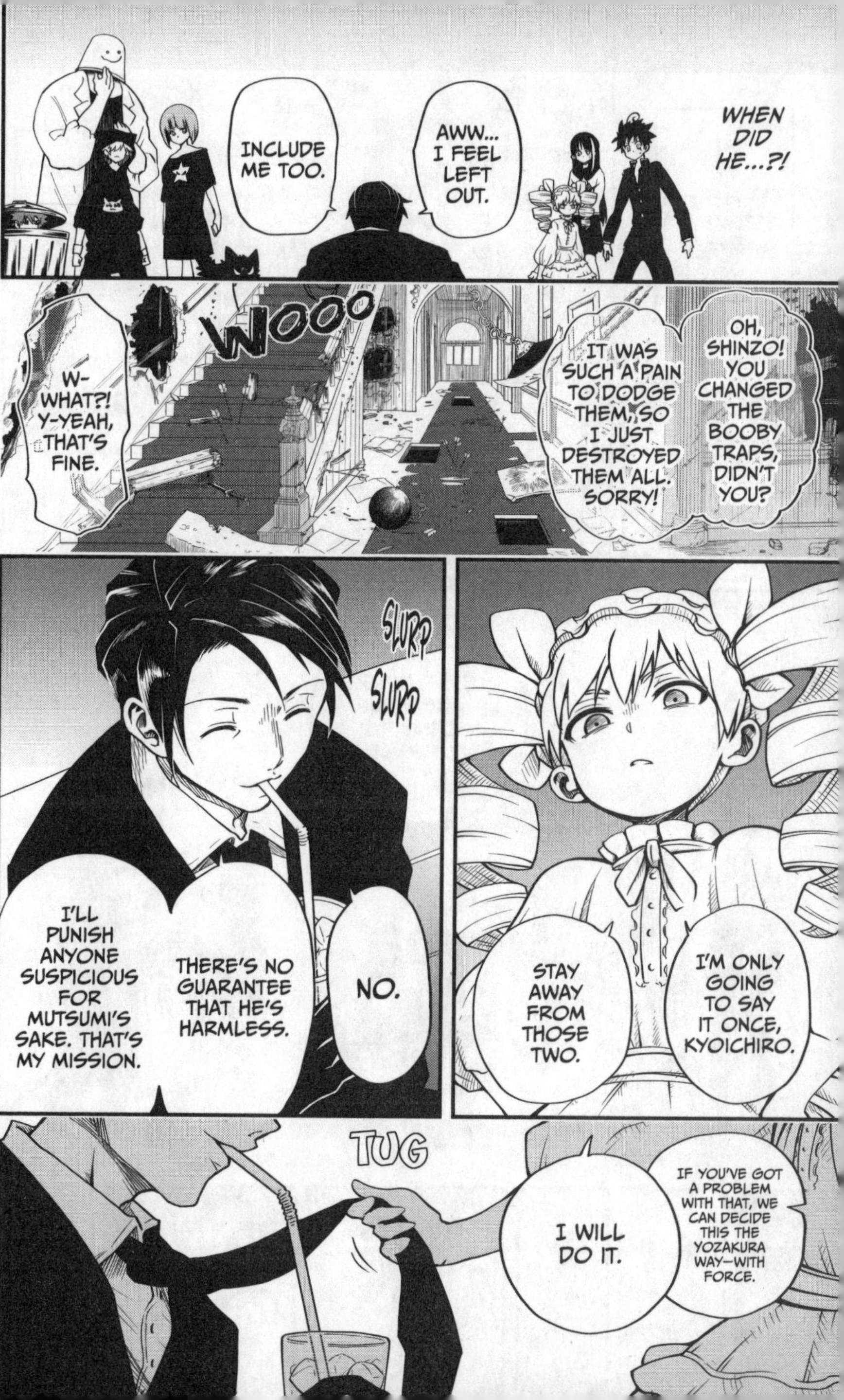
WHEN DID HE...?!
AWW... I FEEL LEFT OUT.
INCLUDE ME TOO.
OH, SHINZO! YOU CHANGED THE BOOBY TRAPS, DIDN'T YOU?
IT WAS SUCH A PAIN TO DODGE THEM, SO I JUST DESTROYED THEM ALL. SORRY!
WOOO
W-WHAT?! Y-YEAH, THAT'S FINE.
I'M ONLY GOING TO SAY IT ONCE, KYOICHIRO.
STAY AWAY FROM THOSE TWO.
SLURP
SLURP
NO.
THERE'S NO GUARANTEE THAT HE'S HARMLESS.
I'LL PUNISH ANYONE SUSPICIOUS FOR MUTSUMI'S SAKE. THAT'S MY MISSION.
IF YOU'VE GOT A PROBLEM WITH THAT, WE CAN DECIDE THIS THE YOZAKURA WAY—WITH FORCE.
I WILL DO IT.
TUG

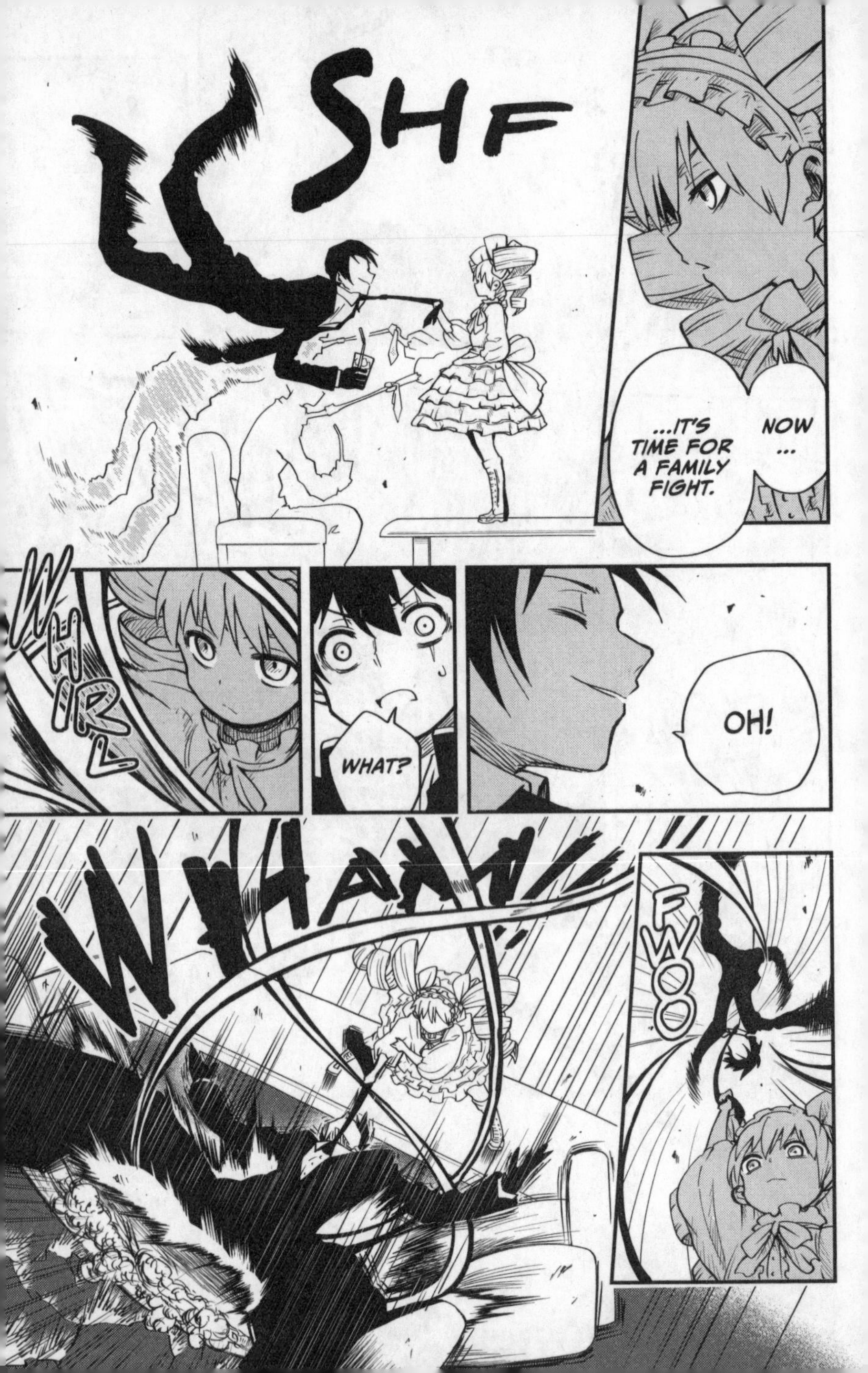
NOW ...
...IT'S TIME FOR A FAMILY FIGHT.
SHF
OH!
WHAT?
WHIRL
FWOO
WHAM!!

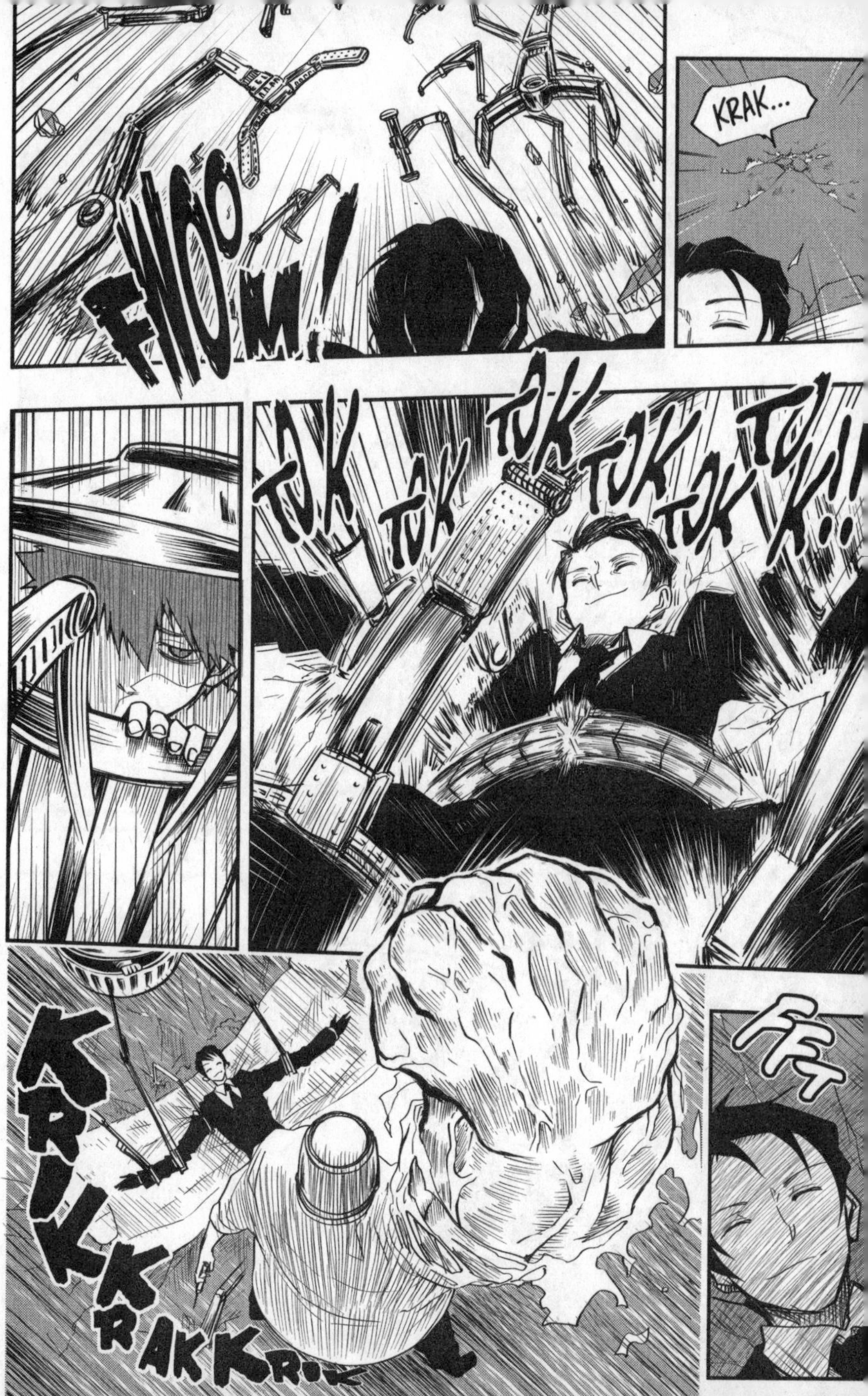
KRAK...
FWOOM!!
TOK TOK TOK TOK TOK TOK!!
FFT
KRIK KRAK KRIK

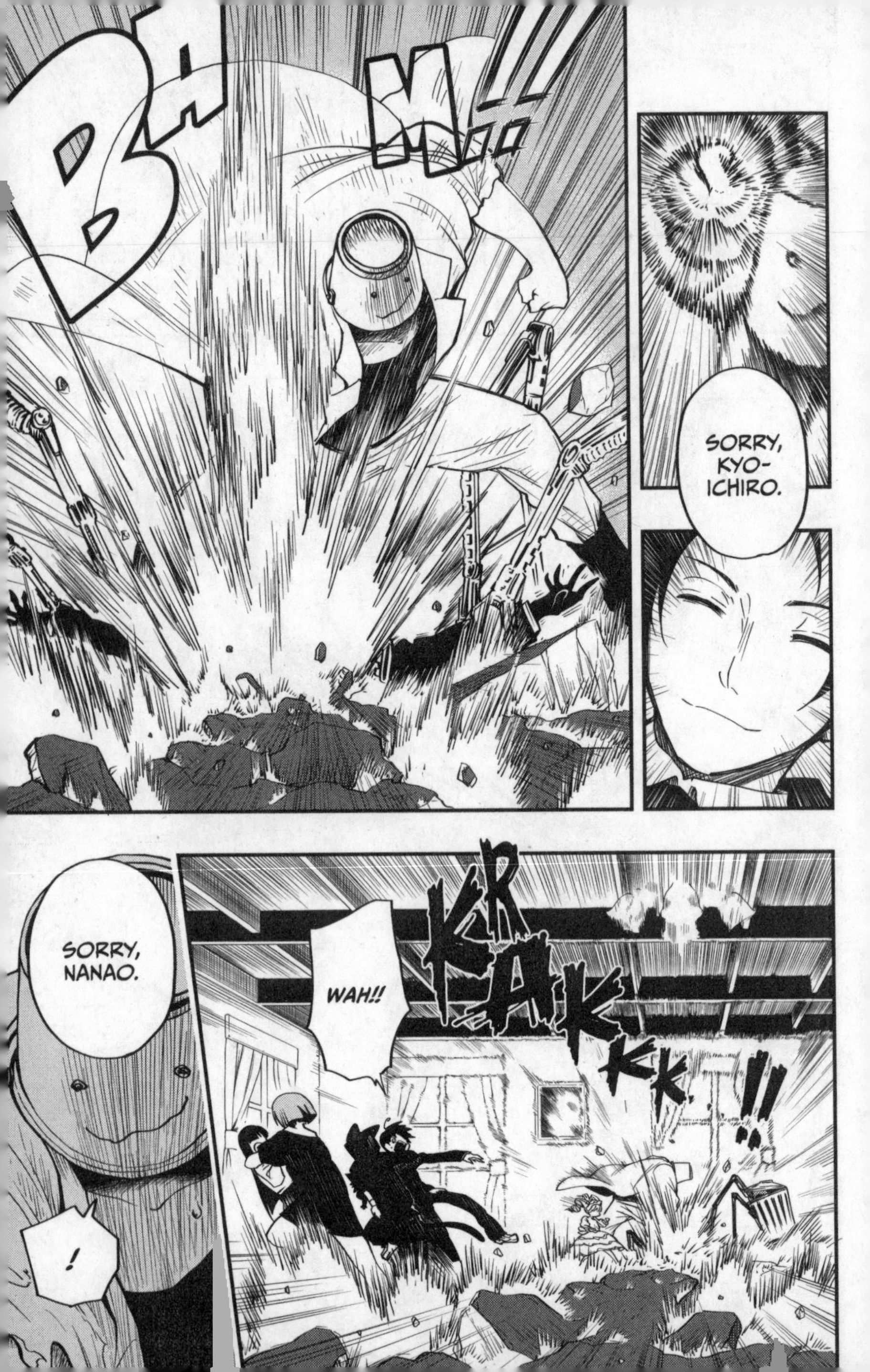
SORRY, KYO-ICHIRO.
BAM!!
WAH!!
KRAKKK!!
SORRY, NANAO.
!

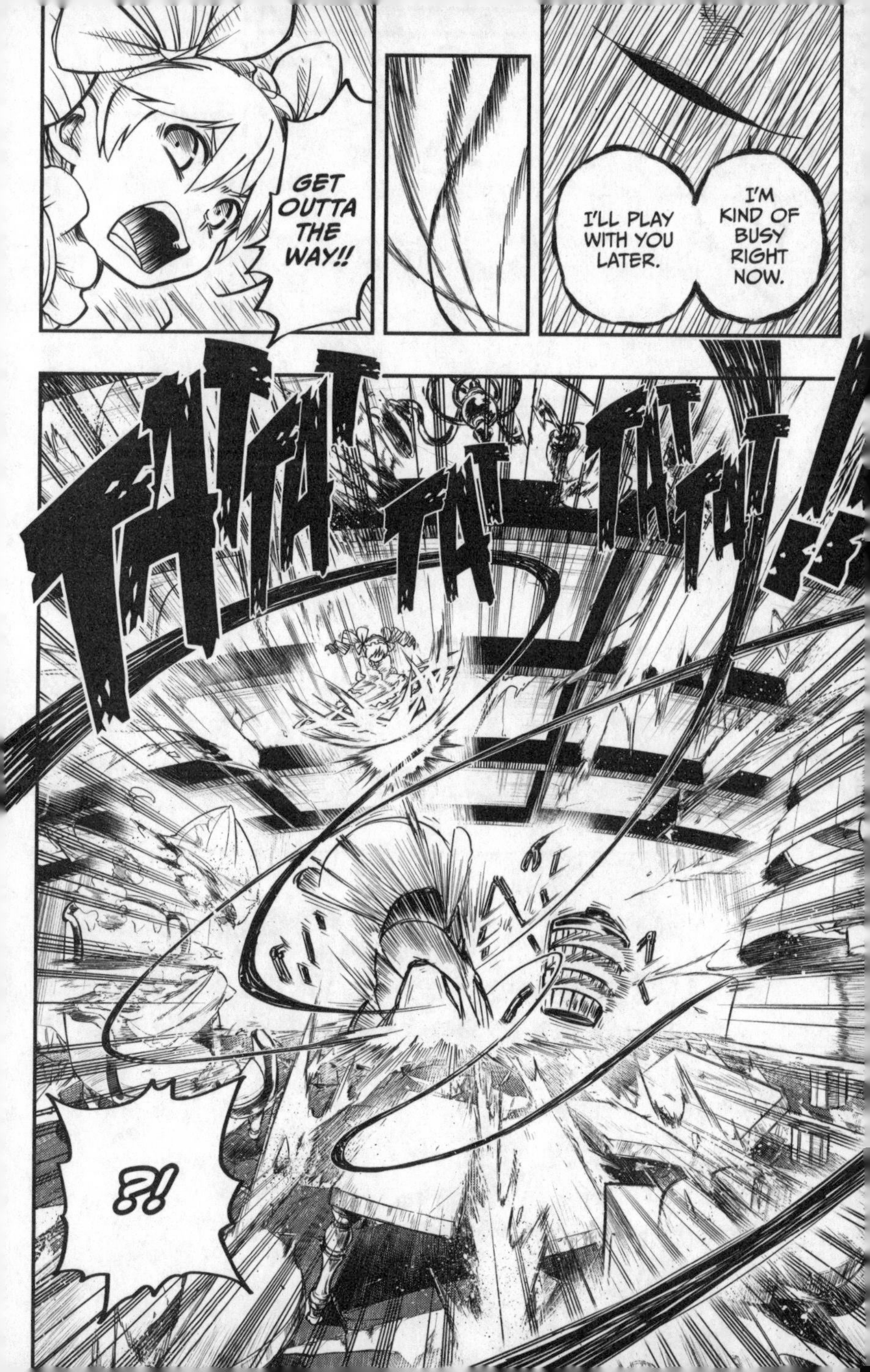
I'M KIND OF BUSY RIGHT NOW.
I'LL PLAY WITH YOU LATER.
GET OUTTA THE WAY!!
TATAT TAT TATAT!!
?!

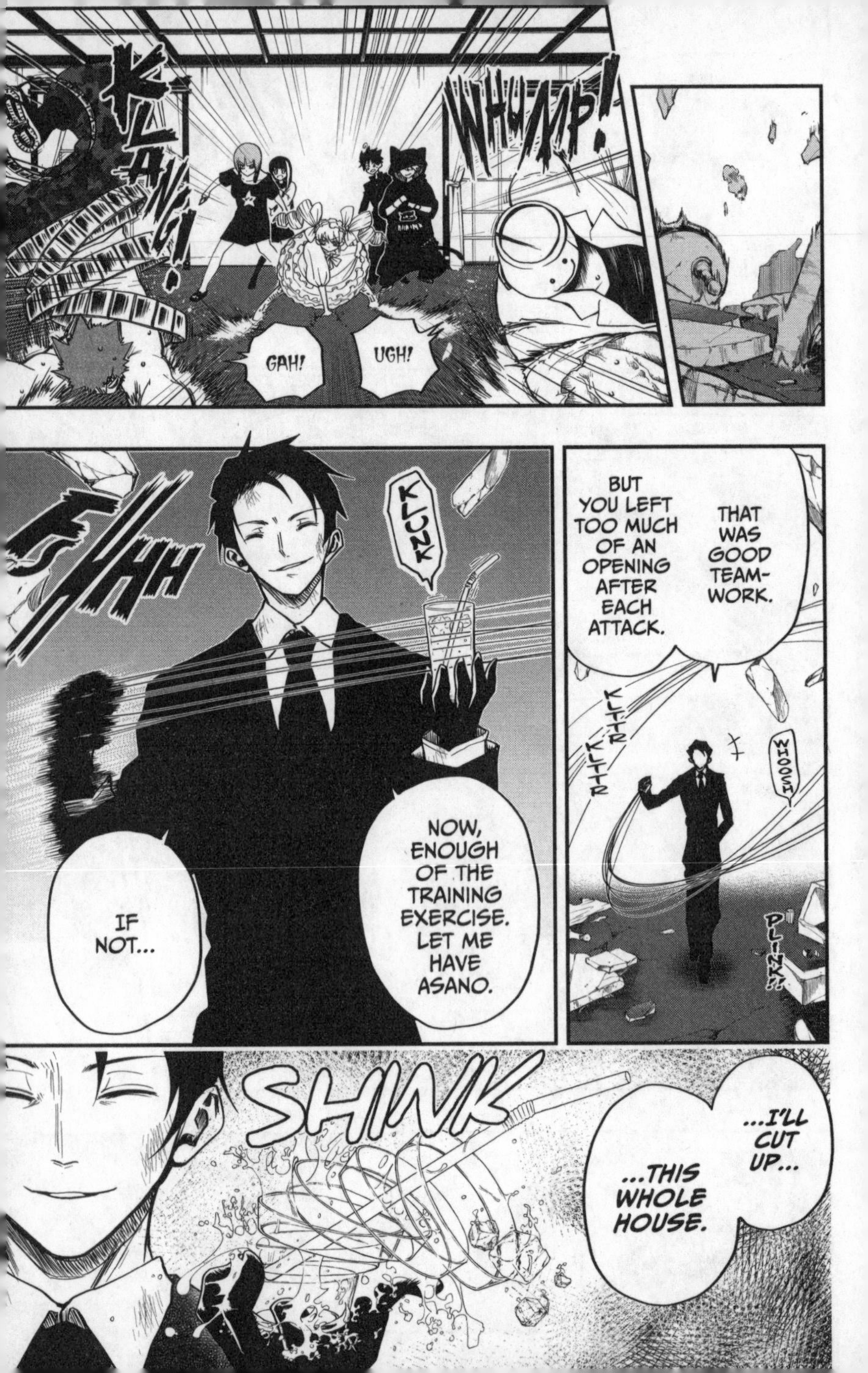
WHUMP!
KLANG!
UGH!
GAH!
THAT WAS GOOD TEAM-WORK.
BUT YOU LEFT TOO MUCH OF AN OPENING AFTER EACH ATTACK.
WHOOSH
KLTTR KLTTR
PLINK!
KLUNK
NOW, ENOUGH OF THE TRAINING EXERCISE. LET ME HAVE ASANO.
IF NOT...
SHINK
...I'LL CUT UP...
...THIS WHOLE HOUSE.

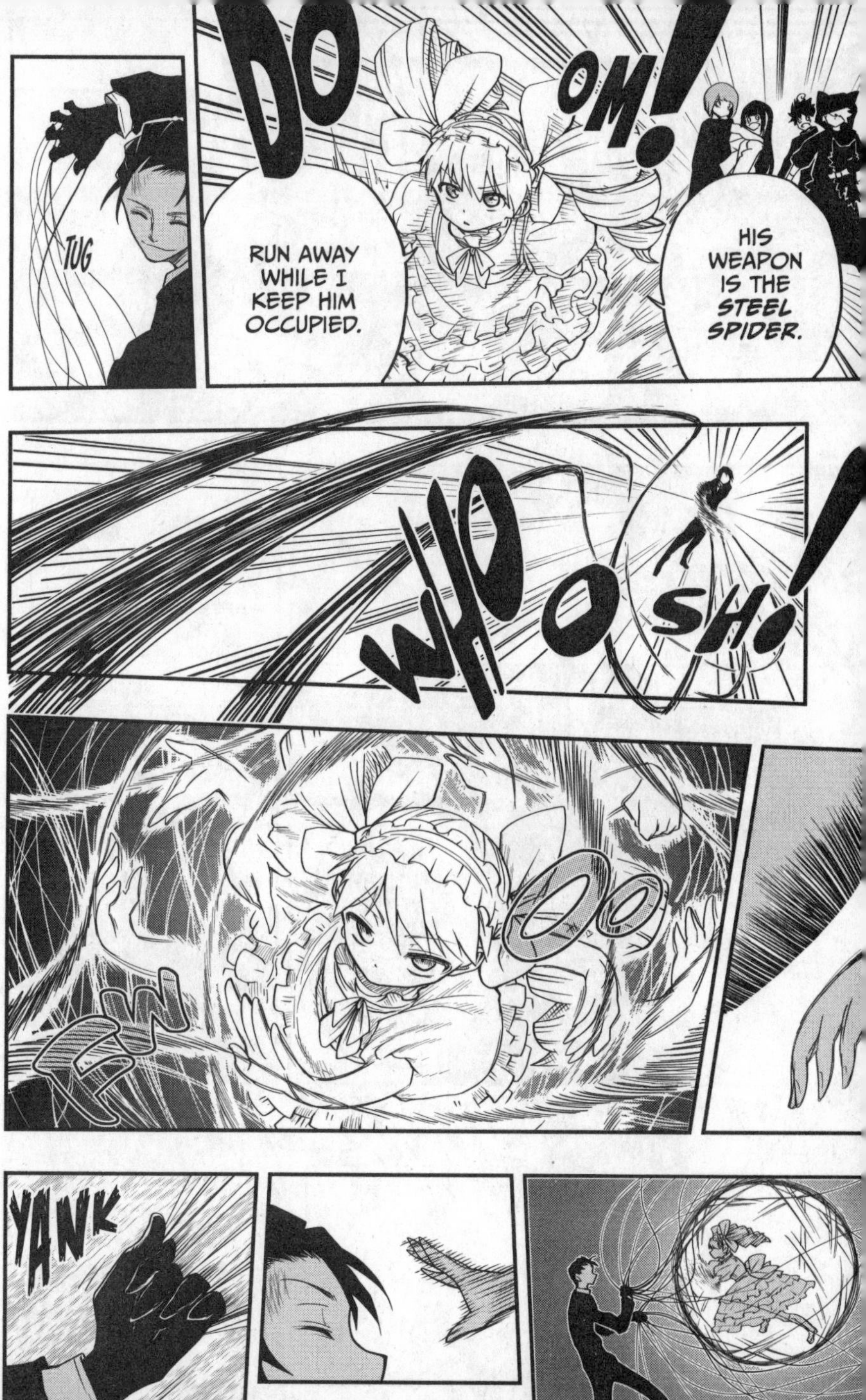
DOOM!
HIS WEAPON IS THE STEEL SPIDER.
RUN AWAY WHILE I KEEP HIM OCCUPIED.
TUG
WHOOSH!
FWOO
YANK

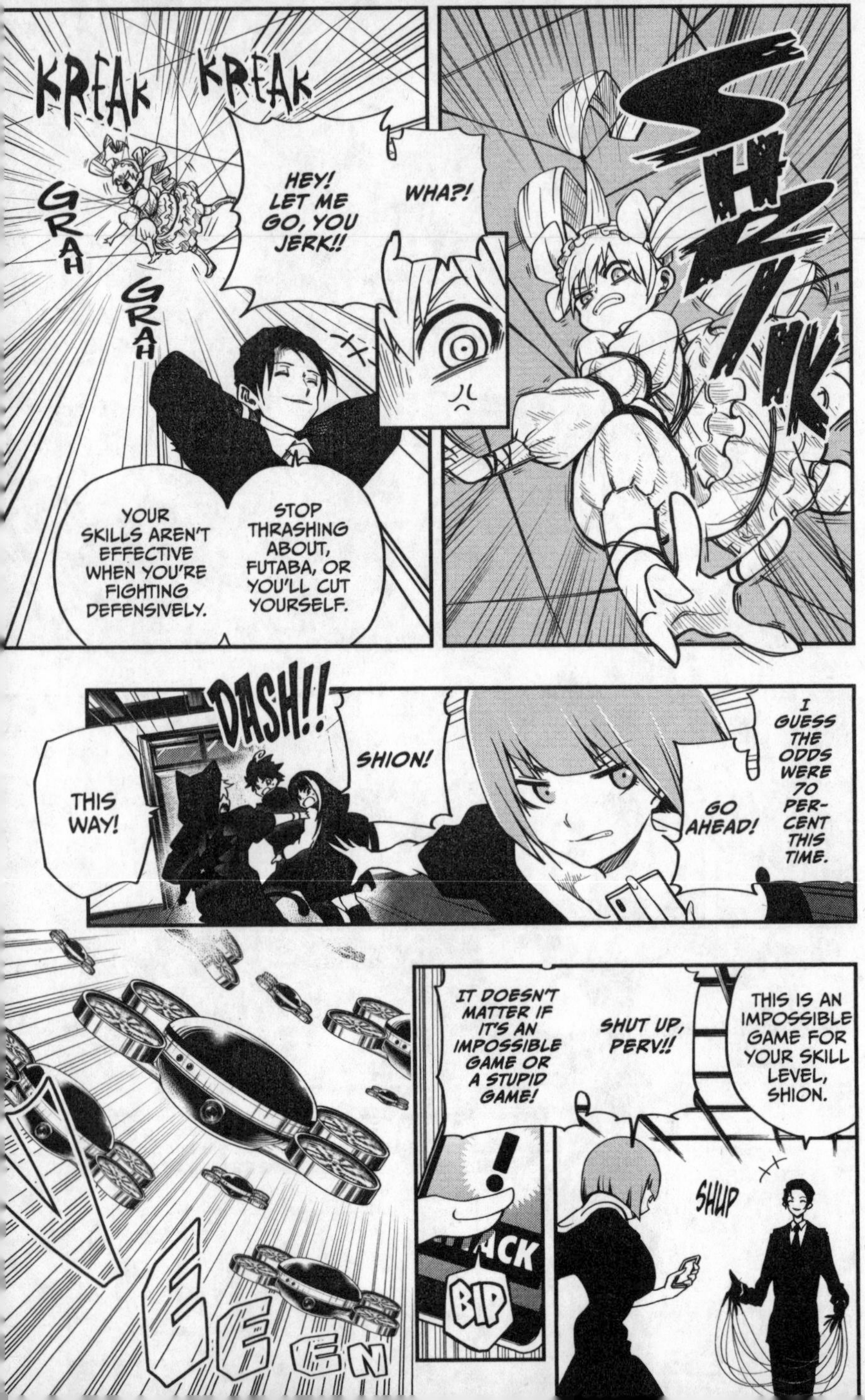
SHZIK
WHA?!
HEY! LET ME GO, YOU JERK!!
KREAK KREAK
GRAH
GRAH
STOP THRASHING ABOUT, FUTABA, OR YOU'LL CUT YOURSELF.
YOUR SKILLS AREN'T EFFECTIVE WHEN YOU'RE FIGHTING DEFENSIVELY.
I GUESS THE ODDS WERE 70 PER-CENT THIS TIME.
GO AHEAD!
SHION!
DASH!!
THIS WAY!
THIS IS AN IMPOSSIBLE GAME FOR YOUR SKILL LEVEL, SHION.
SHUT UP, PERV!!
IT DOESN'T MATTER IF IT'S AN IMPOSSIBLE GAME OR A STUPID GAME!
SHUP
!
BIP
EEEN

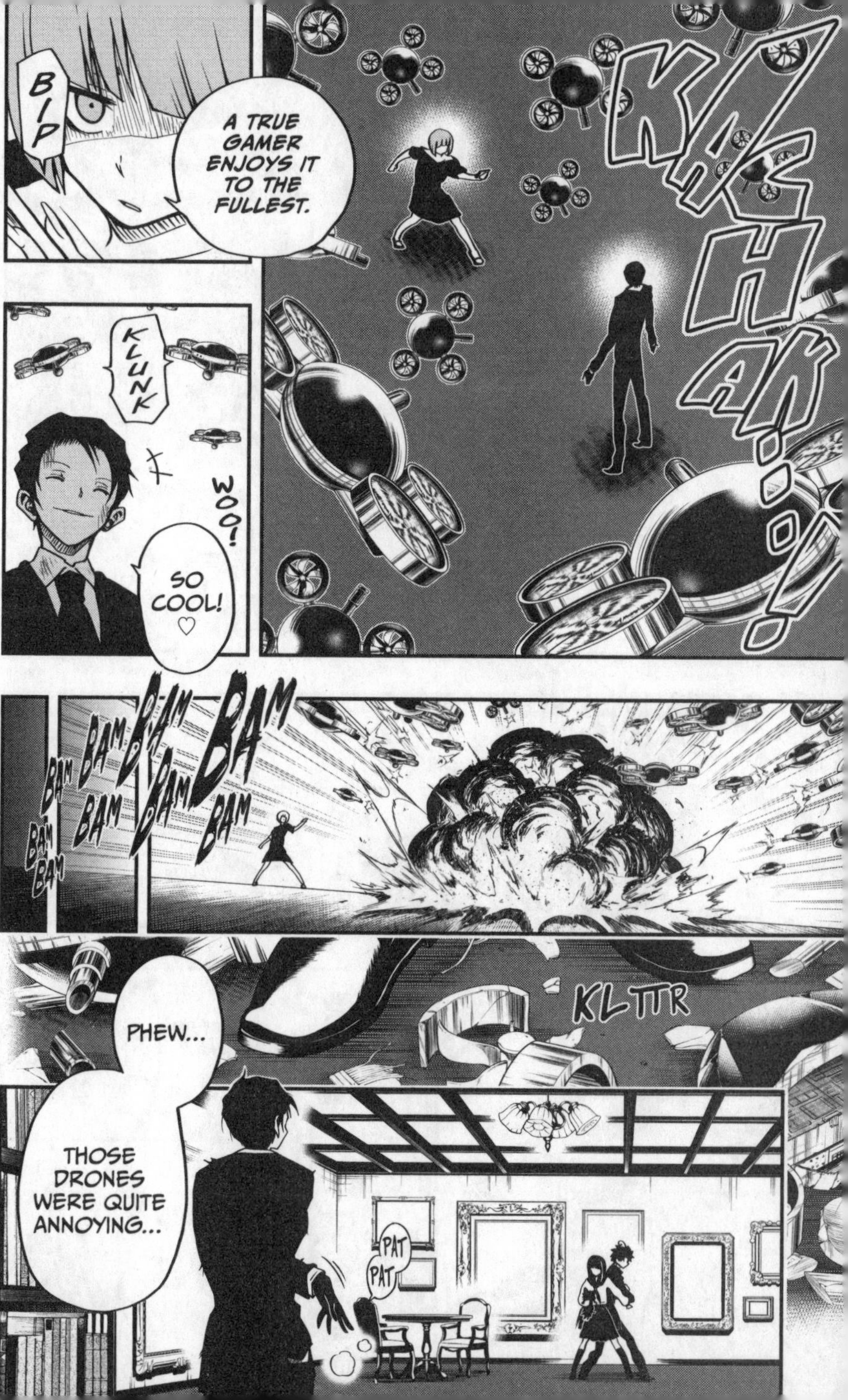
KAKHHAK!!
BIP
A TRUE GAMER ENJOYS IT TO THE FULLEST.
KLUNK
WOO!
SO COOL! ♡
BAM BAM BAM BAM BAM BAM BAM BAM BAM BAM BAM
KLTTR
PHEW...
THOSE DRONES WERE QUITE ANNOYING...
PAT PAT

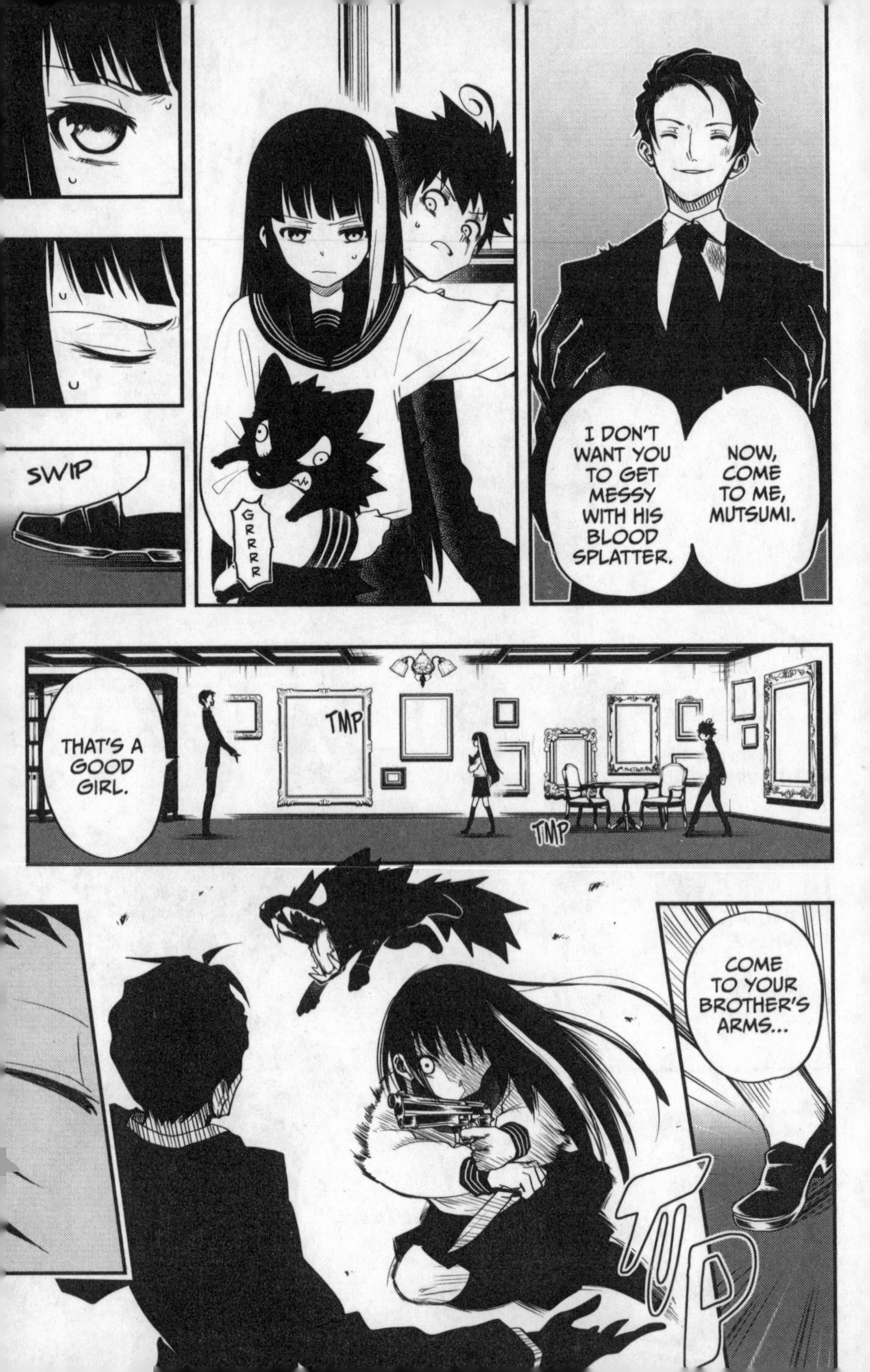
NOW, COME TO ME, MUTSUMI.
I DON'T WANT YOU TO GET MESSY WITH HIS BLOOD SPLATTER.
GRRRR
SWIP
TMP
TMP
THAT'S A GOOD GIRL.
COME TO YOUR BROTHER'S ARMS...

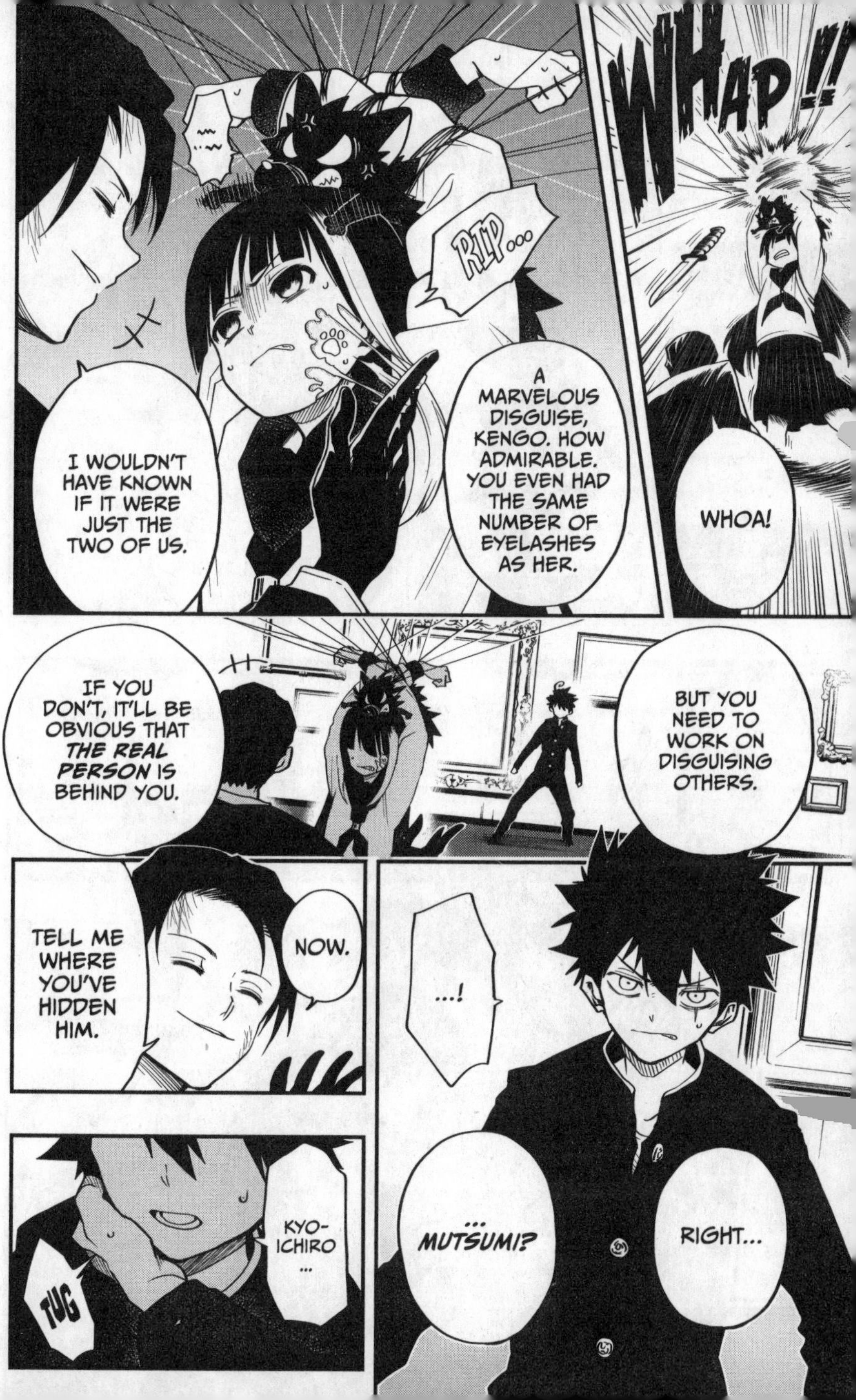
WHAP!!
WHOA!
RIP...
A MARVELOUS DISGUISE, KENGO. HOW ADMIRABLE. YOU EVEN HAD THE SAME NUMBER OF EYELASHES AS HER.
I WOULDN'T HAVE KNOWN IF IT WERE JUST THE TWO OF US.
BUT YOU NEED TO WORK ON DISGUISING OTHERS.
IF YOU DON'T, IT'LL BE OBVIOUS THAT *THE REAL PERSON* IS BEHIND YOU.
...!
RIGHT...
...MUTSUMI?
NOW.
TELL ME WHERE YOU'VE HIDDEN HIM.
KYO-ICHIRO...
TUG

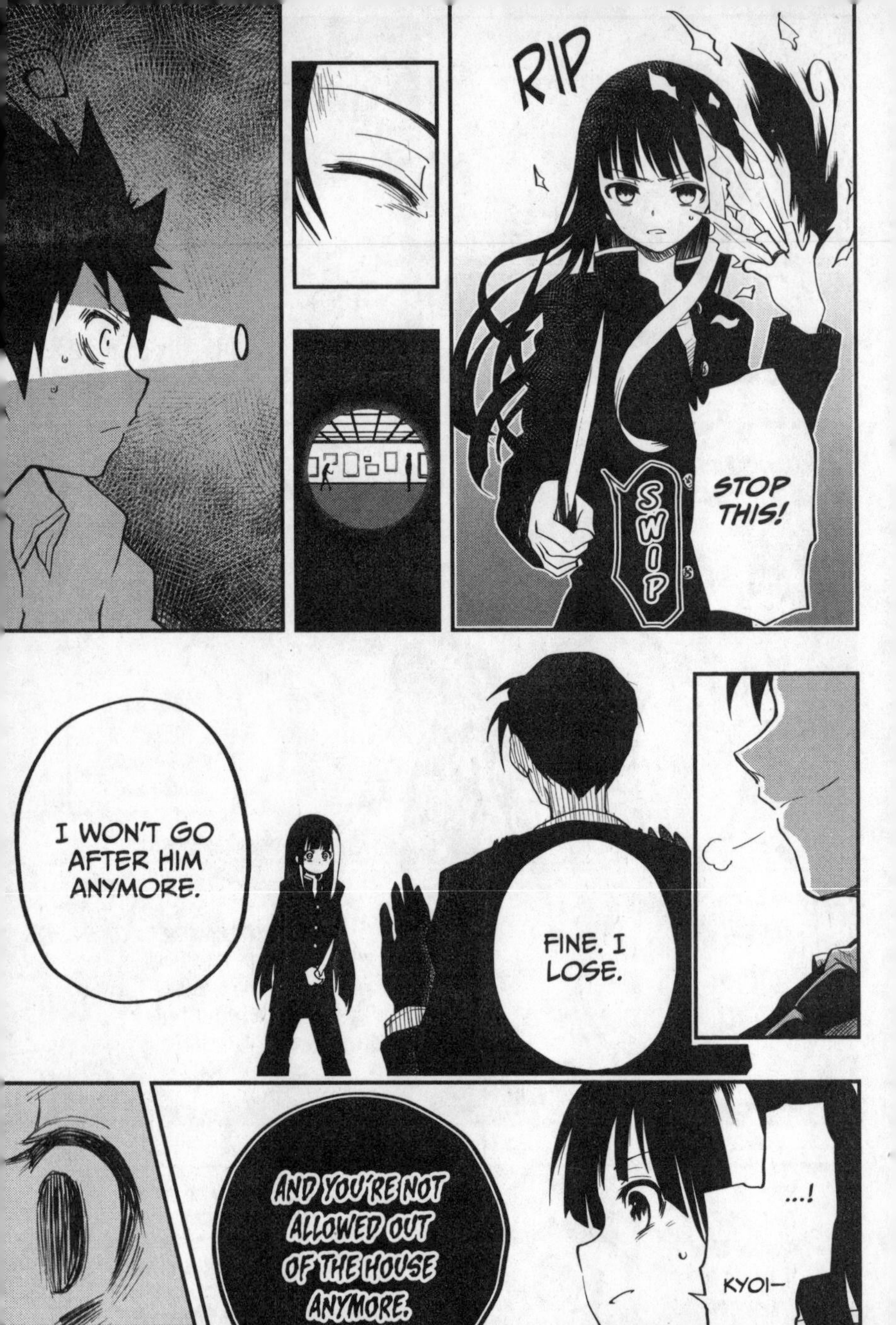
RIP
SWIP
STOP THIS!
FINE. I LOSE.
I WON'T GO AFTER HIM ANYMORE.
...!
KYOI—
AND YOU'RE NOT ALLOWED OUT OF THE HOUSE ANYMORE.

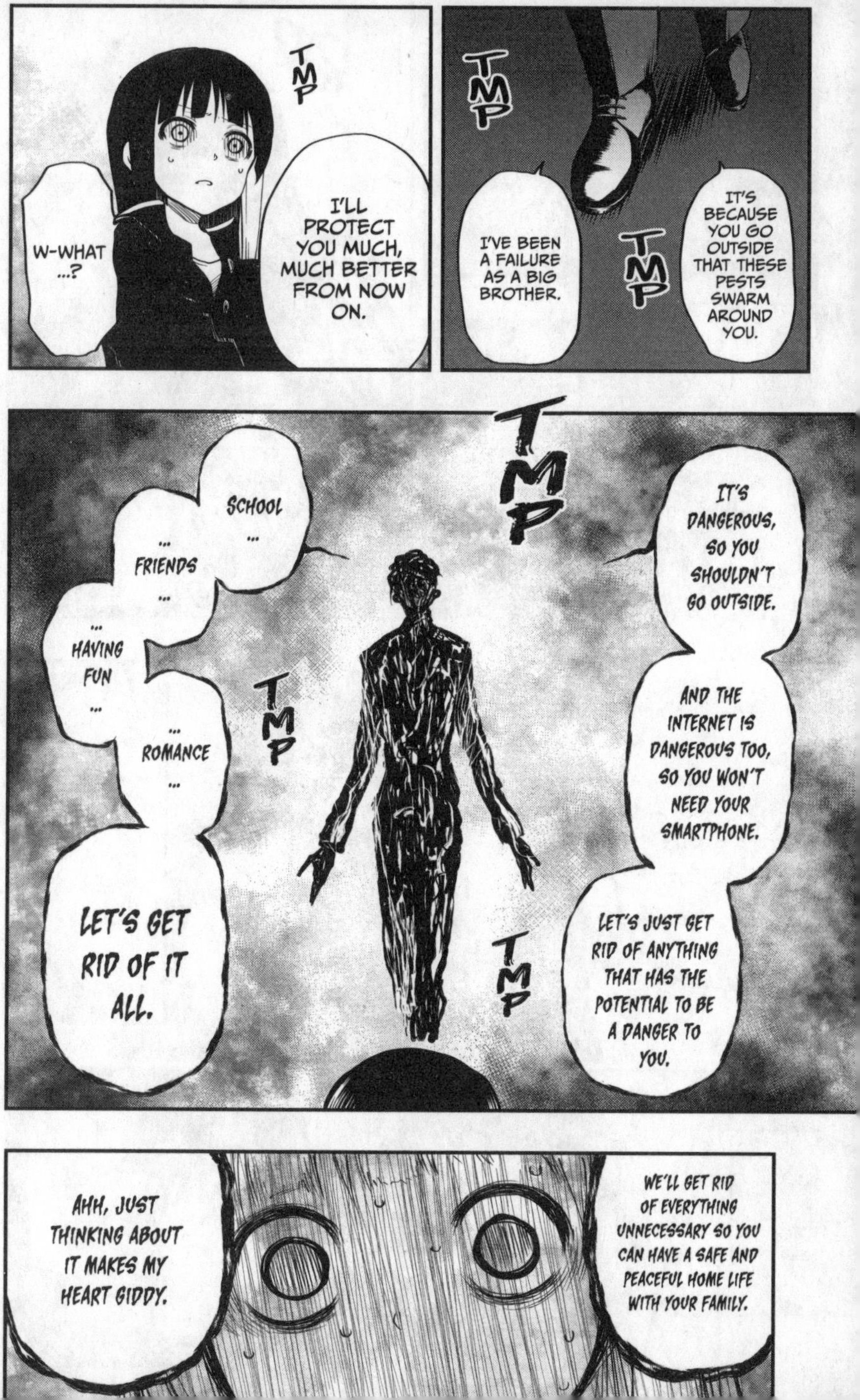
TMP
IT'S BECAUSE YOU GO OUTSIDE THAT THESE PESTS SWARM AROUND YOU.
TMP
I'VE BEEN A FAILURE AS A BIG BROTHER.
TMP
I'LL PROTECT YOU MUCH, MUCH BETTER FROM NOW ON.
W-WHAT ...?
TMP
IT'S DANGEROUS, SO YOU SHOULDN'T GO OUTSIDE.
AND THE INTERNET IS DANGEROUS TOO, SO YOU WON'T NEED YOUR SMARTPHONE.
LET'S JUST GET RID OF ANYTHING THAT HAS THE POTENTIAL TO BE A DANGER TO YOU.
TMP
TMP
SCHOOL ... ... FRIENDS ... ... HAVING FUN ... ... ROMANCE ...
LET'S GET RID OF IT ALL.
WE'LL GET RID OF EVERYTHING UNNECESSARY SO YOU CAN HAVE A SAFE AND PEACEFUL HOME LIFE WITH YOUR FAMILY.
AHH, JUST THINKING ABOUT IT MAKES MY HEART GIDDY.

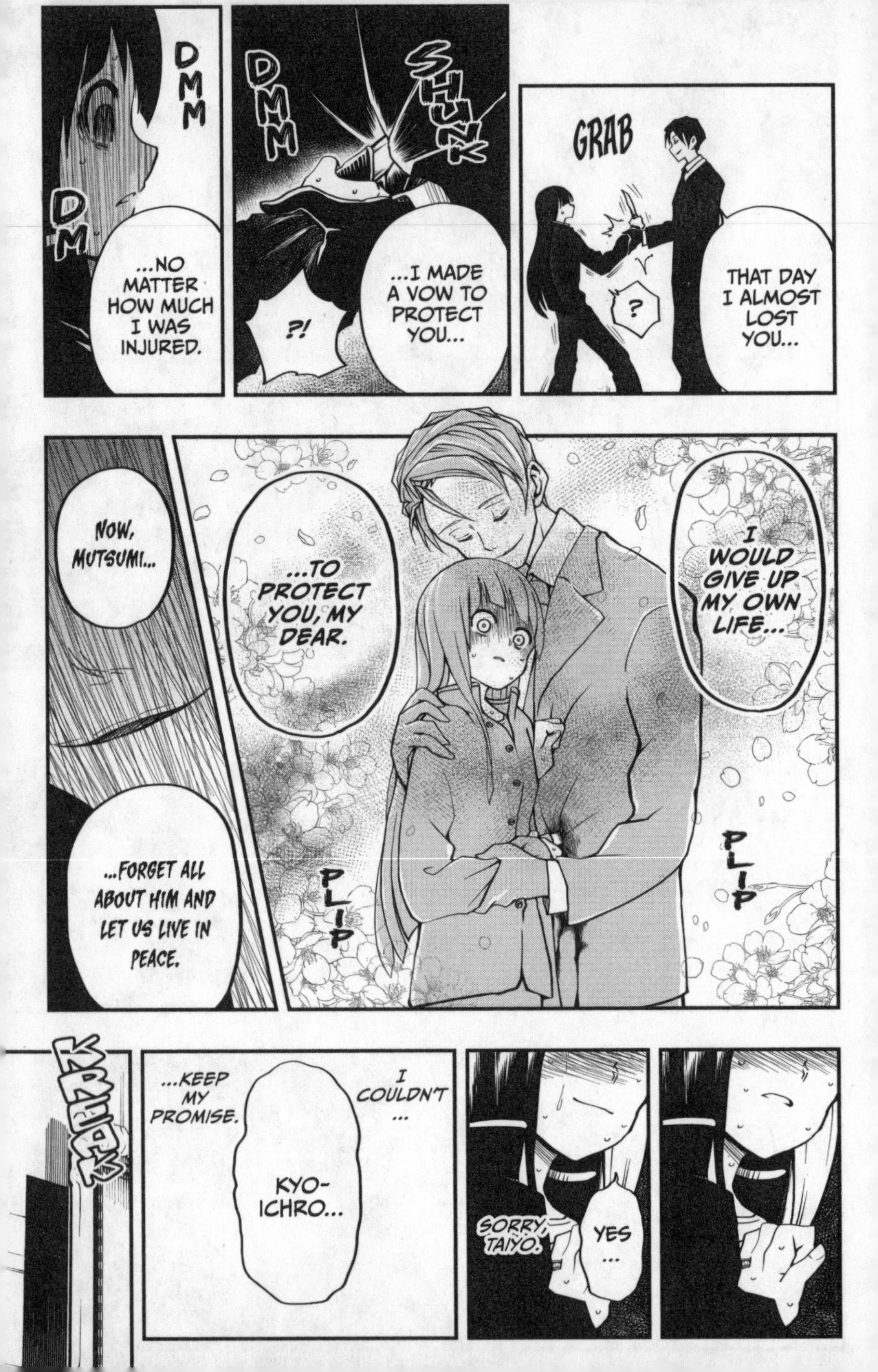
GRAB
THAT DAY I ALMOST LOST YOU...
?
SHUNK
DMM
...I MADE A VOW TO PROTECT YOU...
?!
DMM
DM
...NO MATTER HOW MUCH I WAS INJURED.
I WOULD GIVE UP MY OWN LIFE...
...TO PROTECT YOU, MY DEAR.
PLIP
PLIP
NOW, MUTSUMI...
...FORGET ALL ABOUT HIM AND LET US LIVE IN PEACE.
YES ...
SORRY, TAIYO.
I COULDN'T ...
KYO-ICHRO...
...KEEP MY PROMISE.
KREAK

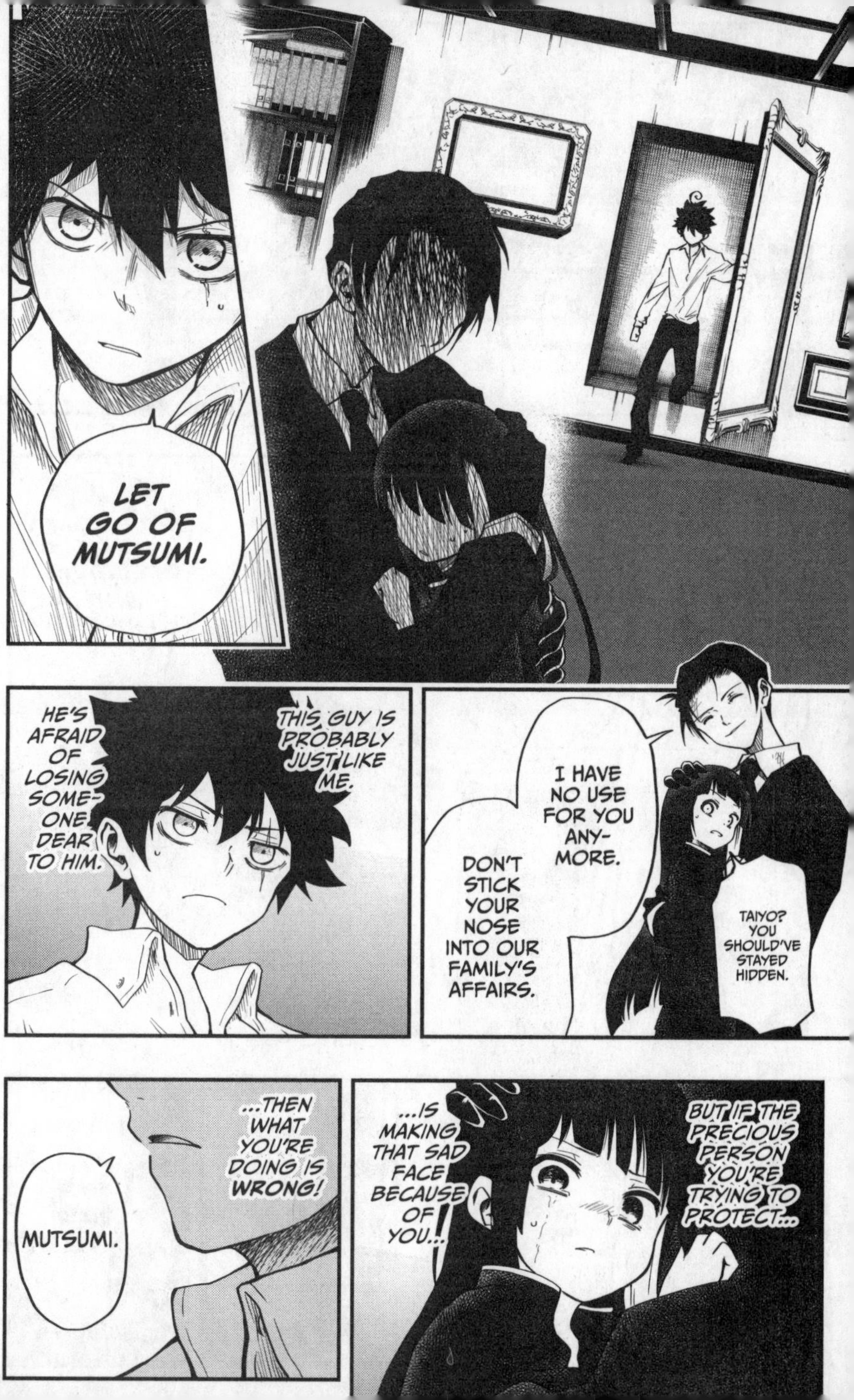
LET GO OF MUTSUMI.
I HAVE NO USE FOR YOU ANYMORE.
DON'T STICK YOUR NOSE INTO OUR FAMILY'S AFFAIRS.
TAIYO? YOU SHOULD'VE STAYED HIDDEN.
THIS GUY IS PROBABLY JUST LIKE ME.
HE'S AFRAID OF LOSING SOMEONE DEAR TO HIM.
BUT IF THE PRECIOUS PERSON YOU'RE TRYING TO PROTECT...
...IS MAKING THAT SAD FACE BECAUSE OF YOU...
...THEN WHAT YOU'RE DOING IS WRONG!
MUTSUMI.

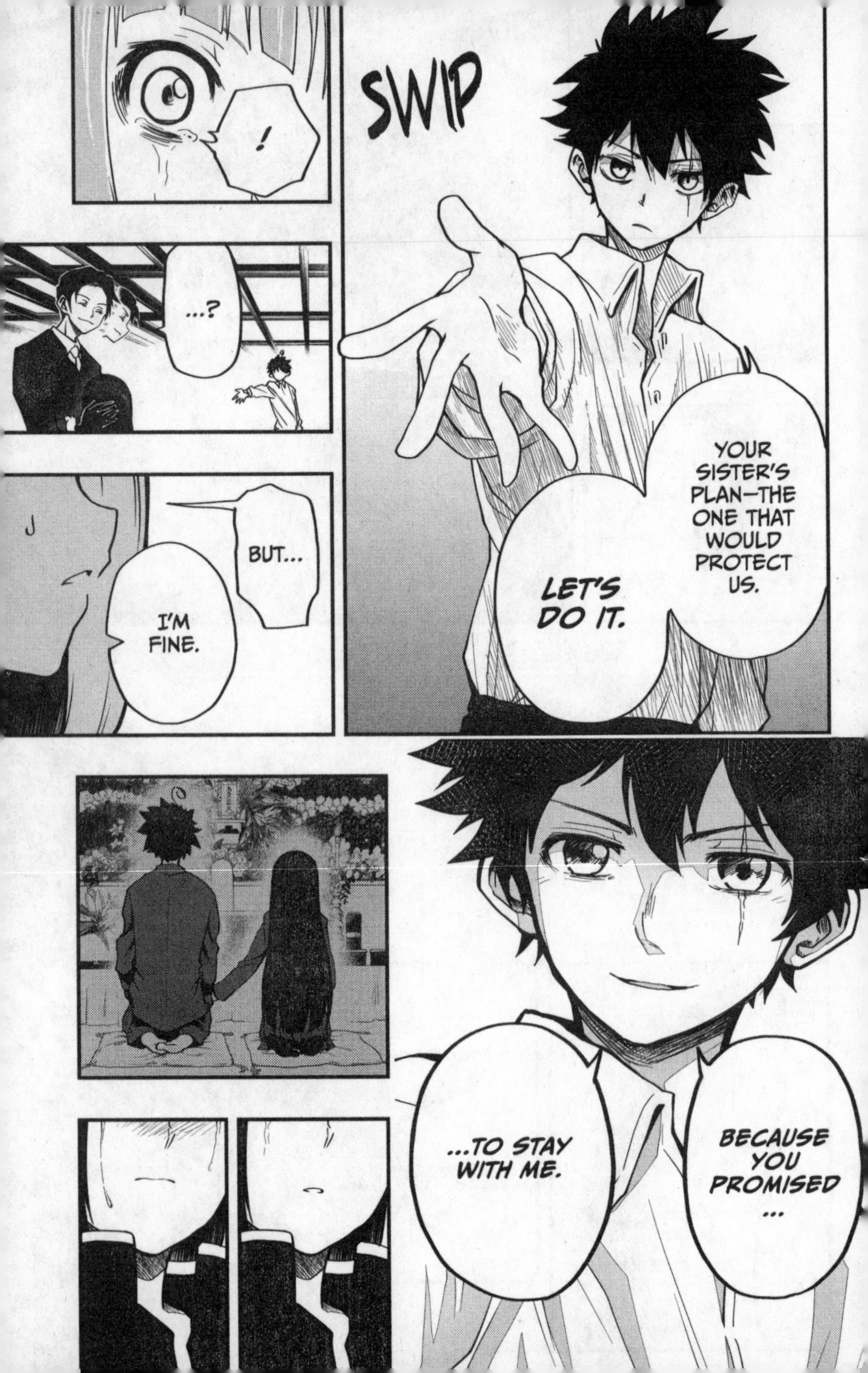
SWIP
YOUR SISTER'S PLAN—THE ONE THAT WOULD PROTECT US.
LET'S DO IT.
!
...?
BUT...
I'M FINE.
BECAUSE YOU PROMISED...
...TO STAY WITH ME.

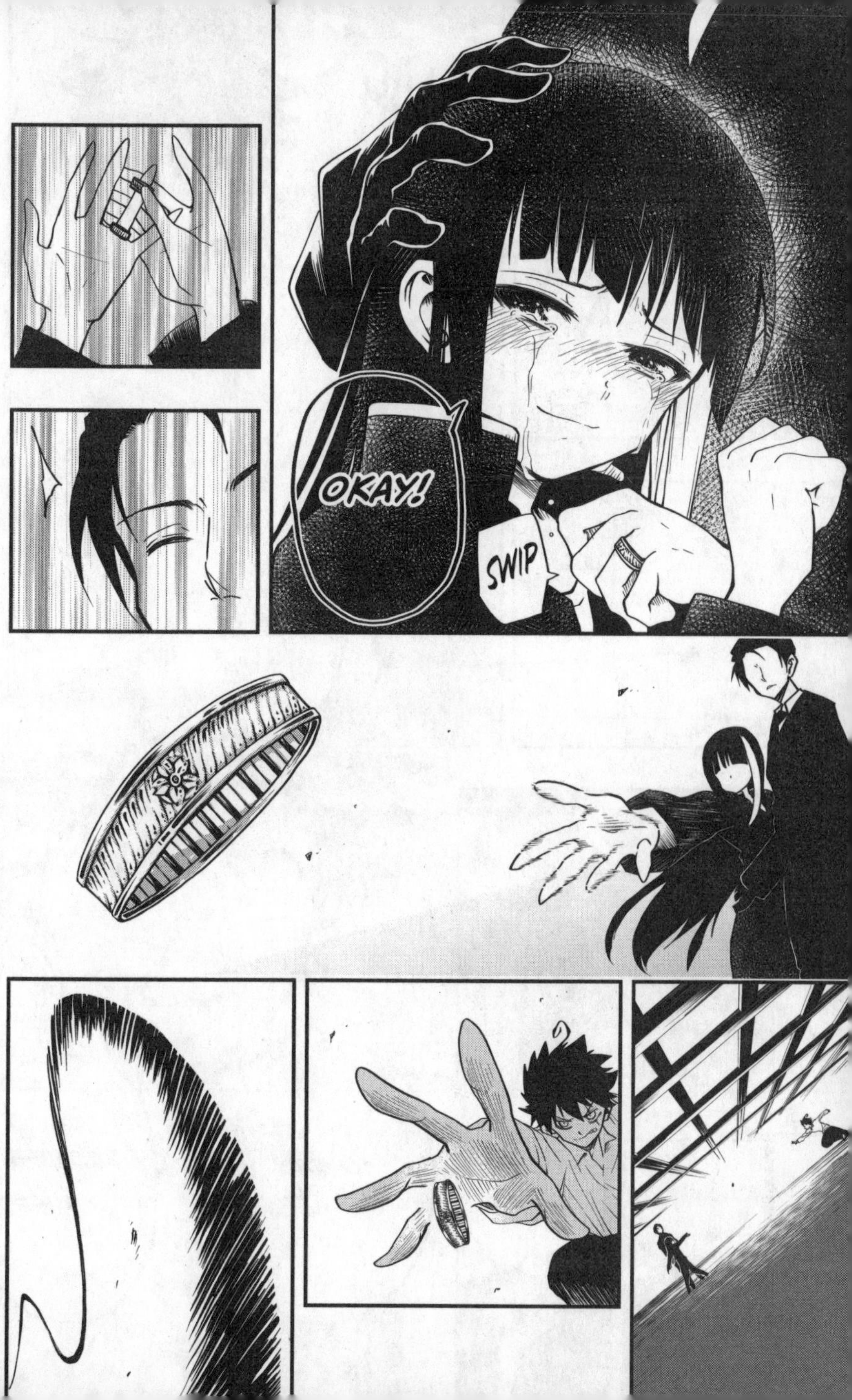
OKAY!
SWIP

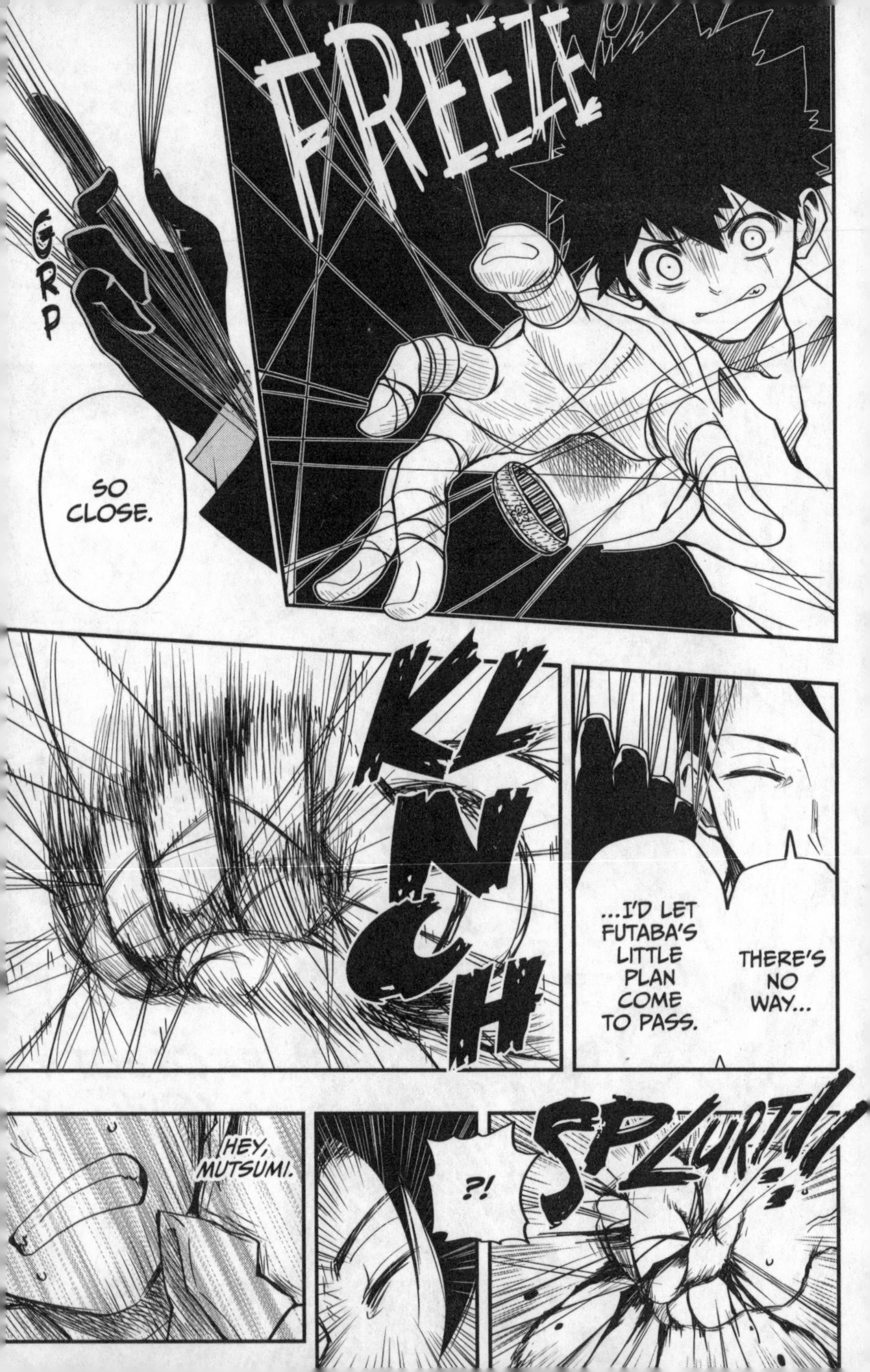
FREEZE
GRP
SO CLOSE.
THERE'S NO WAY...
...I'D LET FUTABA'S LITTLE PLAN COME TO PASS.
KLNCH
SPLURT!!
?!
HEY, MUTSUMI.

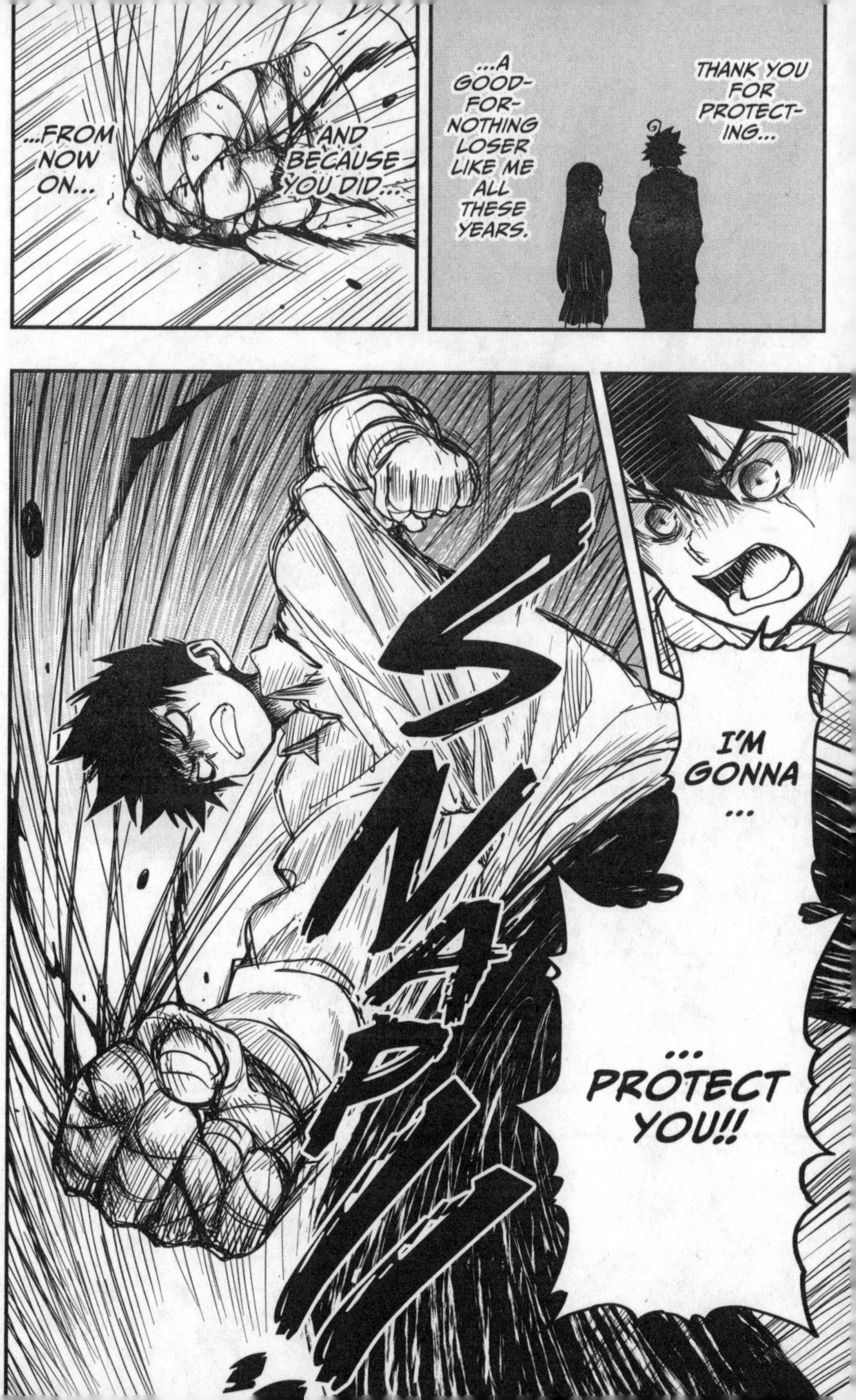
THANK YOU FOR PROTECTING...
...A GOOD-FOR-NOTHING LOSER LIKE ME ALL THESE YEARS.
AND BECAUSE YOU DID...
...FROM NOW ON...
I'M GONNA ...
... PROTECT YOU!!

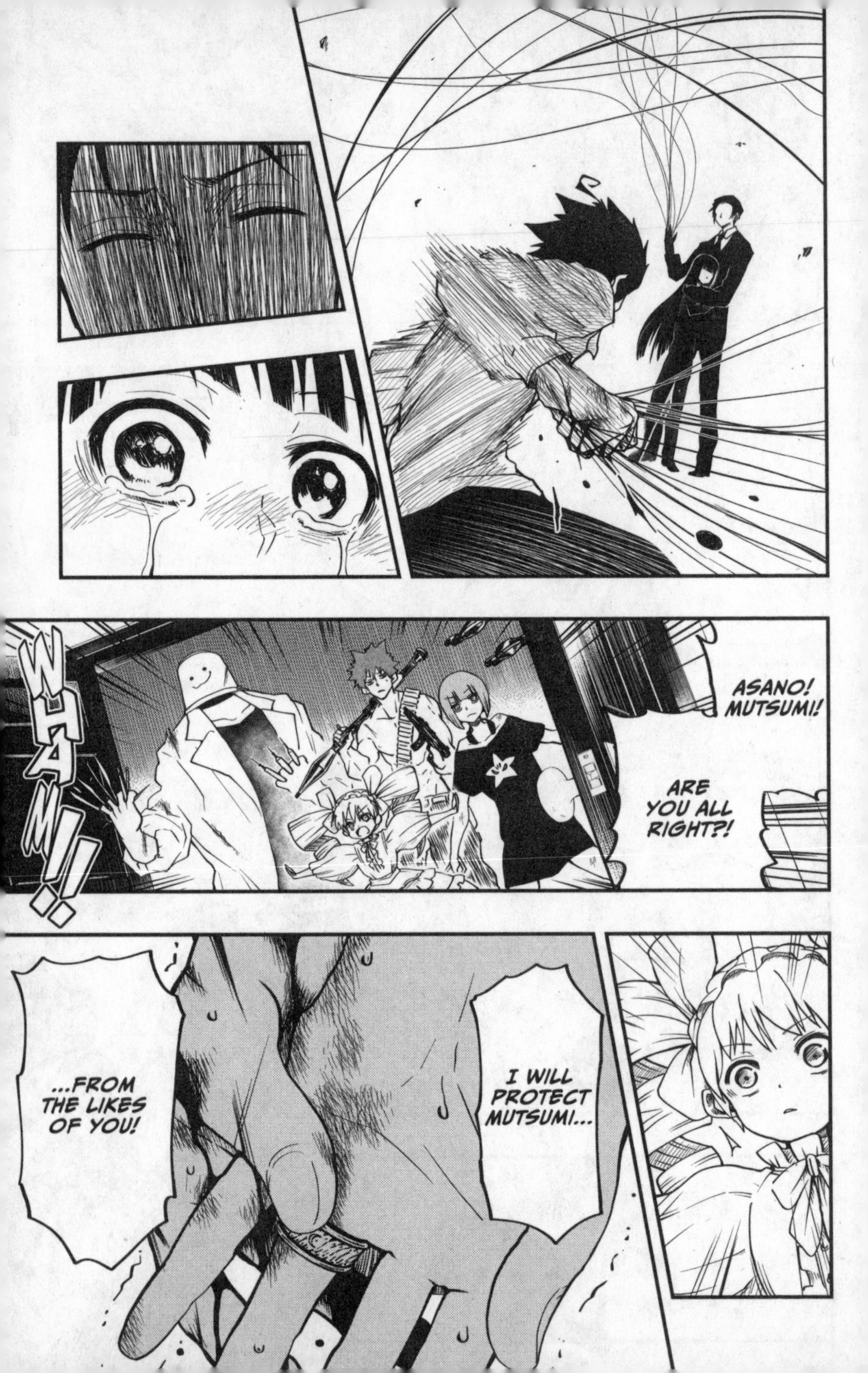
ASANO! MUTSUMI!
ARE YOU ALL RIGHT?!
WHAM!!
I WILL PROTECT MUTSUMI...
...FROM THE LIKES OF YOU!

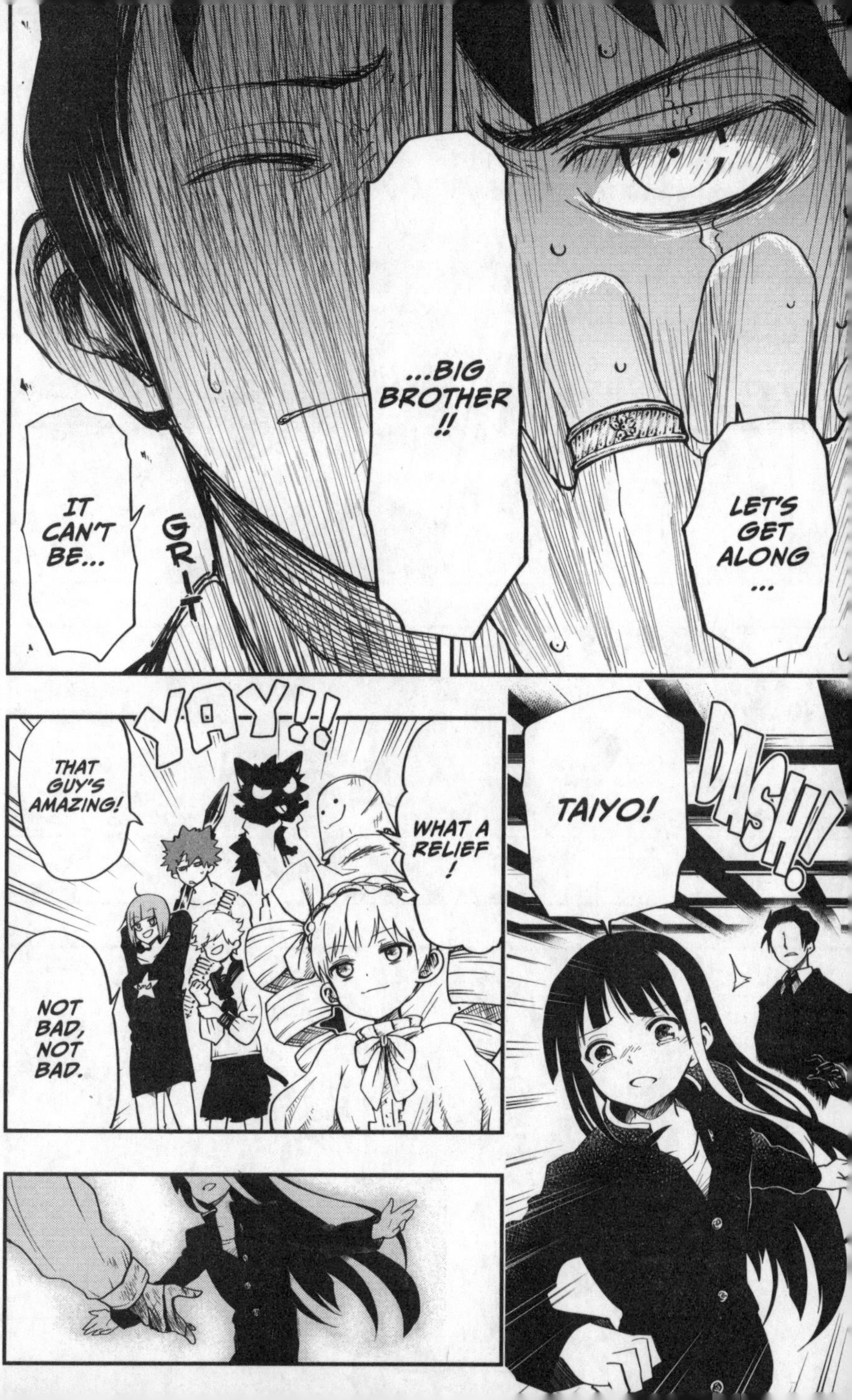
LET'S GET ALONG ...
...BIG BROTHER !!
IT CAN'T BE...
GRIT
DASH!
TAIYO!
YAY!!
WHAT A RELIEF!
THAT GUY'S AMAZING!
NOT BAD, NOT BAD.

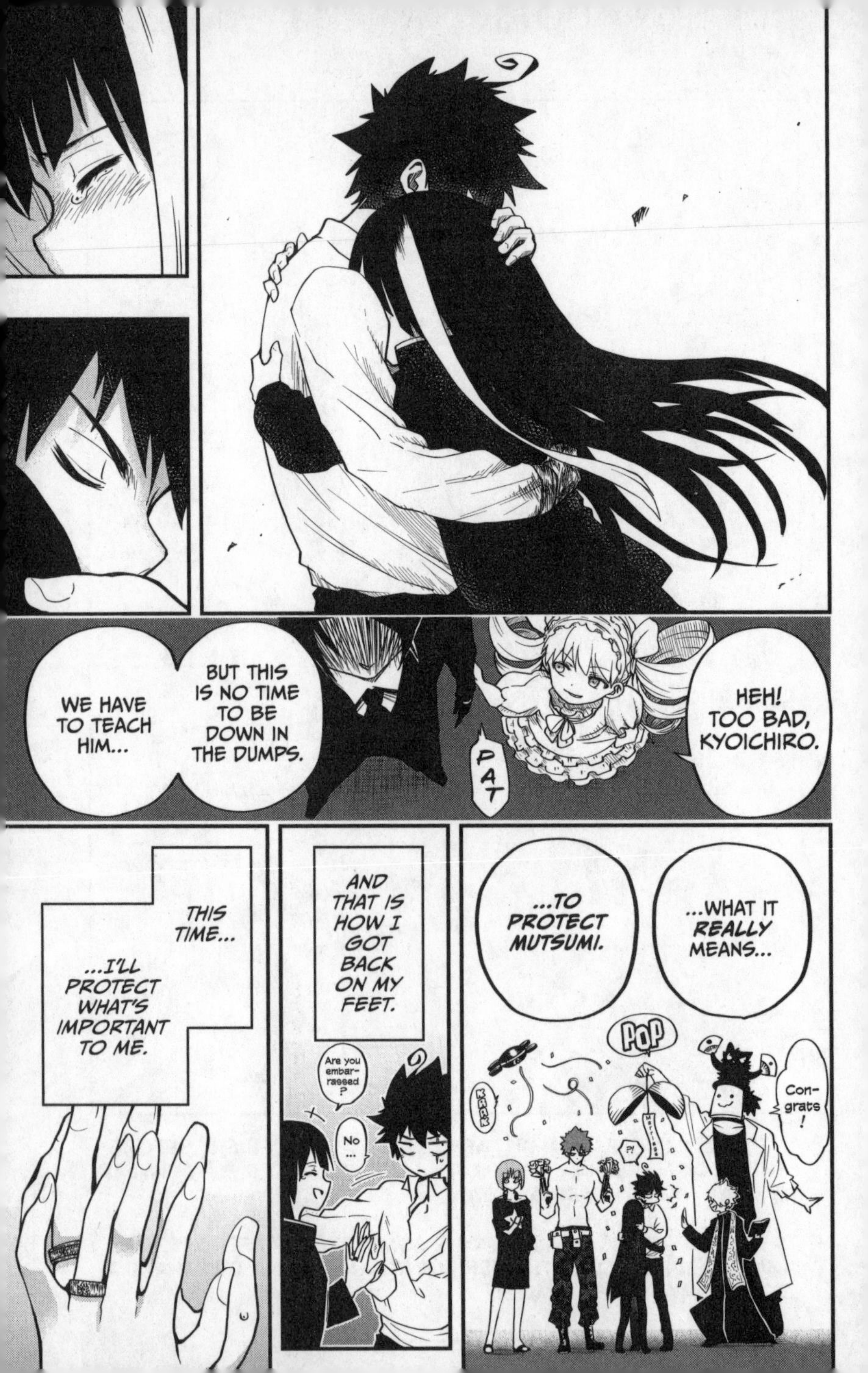
HEH! TOO BAD, KYOICHIRO.
PAT
BUT THIS IS NO TIME TO BE DOWN IN THE DUMPS.
WE HAVE TO TEACH HIM...
...WHAT IT REALLY MEANS...
...TO PROTECT MUTSUMI.
Congrats!
POP
?!
AND THAT IS HOW I GOT BACK ON MY FEET.
Are you embarrassed?
No...
THIS TIME...
...I'LL PROTECT WHAT'S IMPORTANT TO ME.

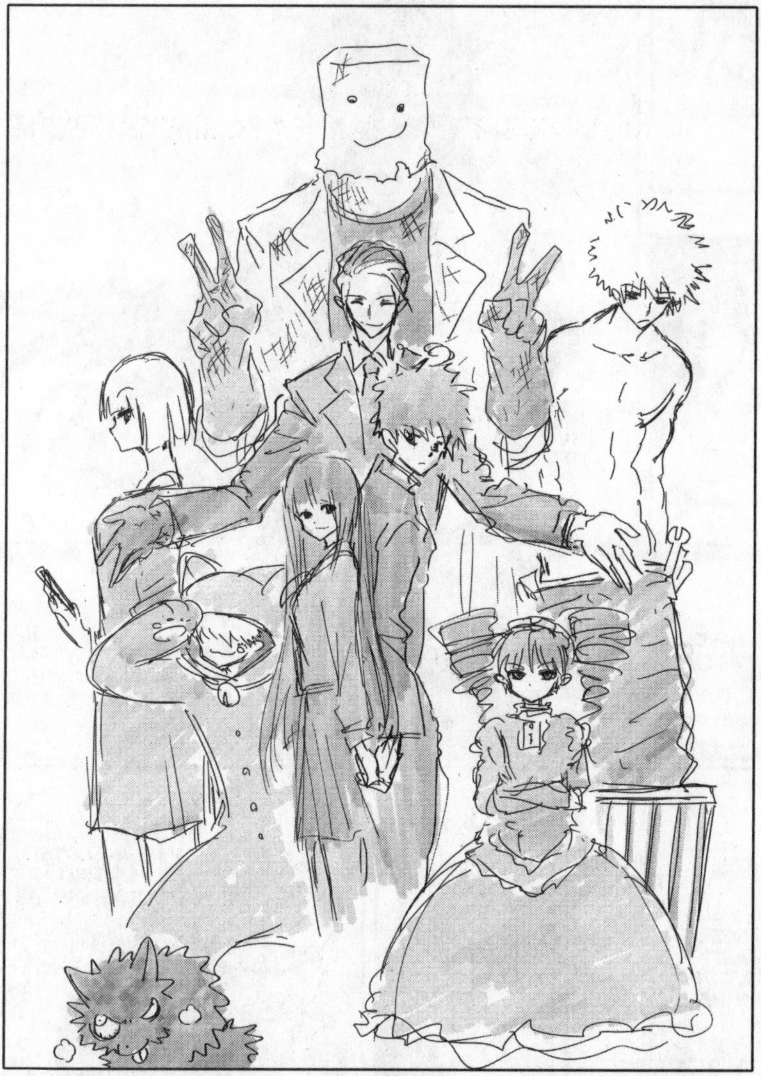

THIS IS AN ILLUSTRATION OF THE YOZAKURA FAMILY RIGHT BEFORE I SETTLED ON THE FINAL VERSION OF THE STORY. IT'S VERY SIMILAR TO WHAT YOU'RE READING NOW.

TO BE HONEST, THE FINAL STORY IS COMPLETELY DIFFERENT THAN WHAT WAS GREENLIT IN THE SERIALIZATION MEETING. BUT THAT'S A STORY FOR ANOTHER TIME...

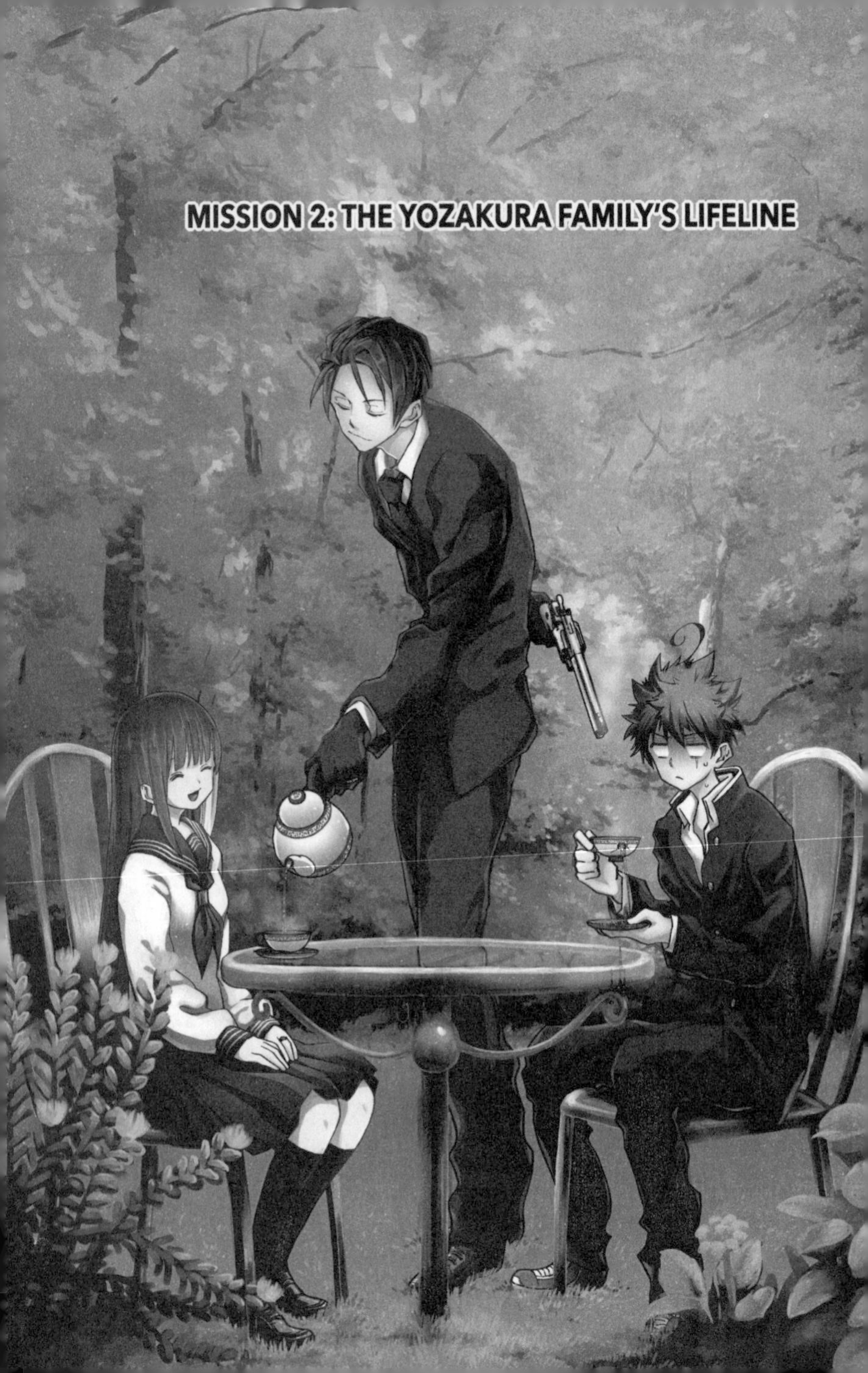
MISSION 2: THE YOZAKURA FAMILY'S LIFELINE

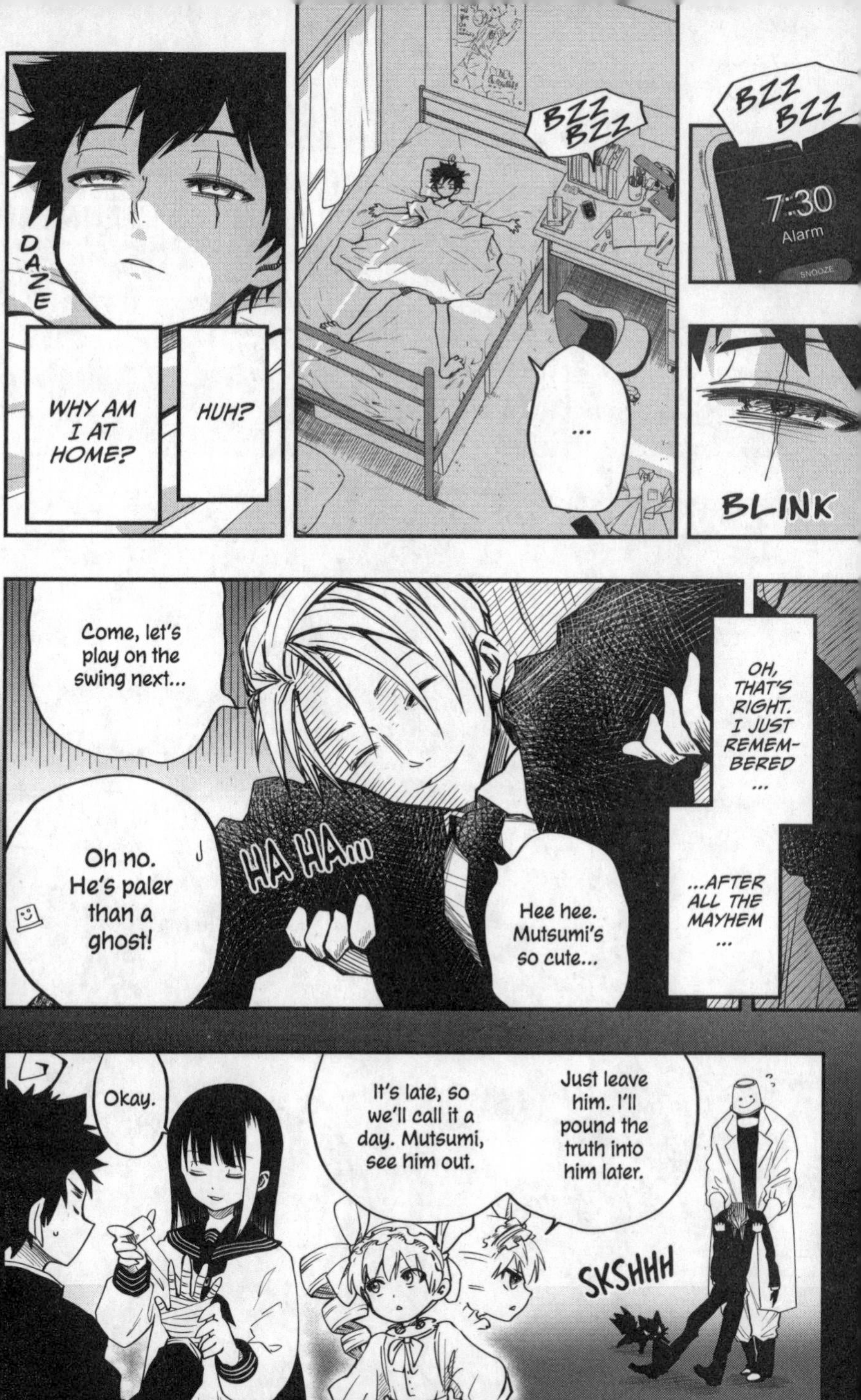
BZZ BZZ
7:30
Alarm
SNOOZE
BLINK
BZZ BZZ
...
HUH?
WHY AM I AT HOME?
DAZE
OH, THAT'S RIGHT. I JUST REMEMBERED ...
...AFTER ALL THE MAYHEM ...
Come, let's play on the swing next...
Hee hee. Mutsumi's so cute...
HA HA...
Oh no. He's paler than a ghost!
Just leave him. I'll pound the truth into him later.
SKSHHH
It's late, so we'll call it a day. Mutsumi, see him out.
Okay.

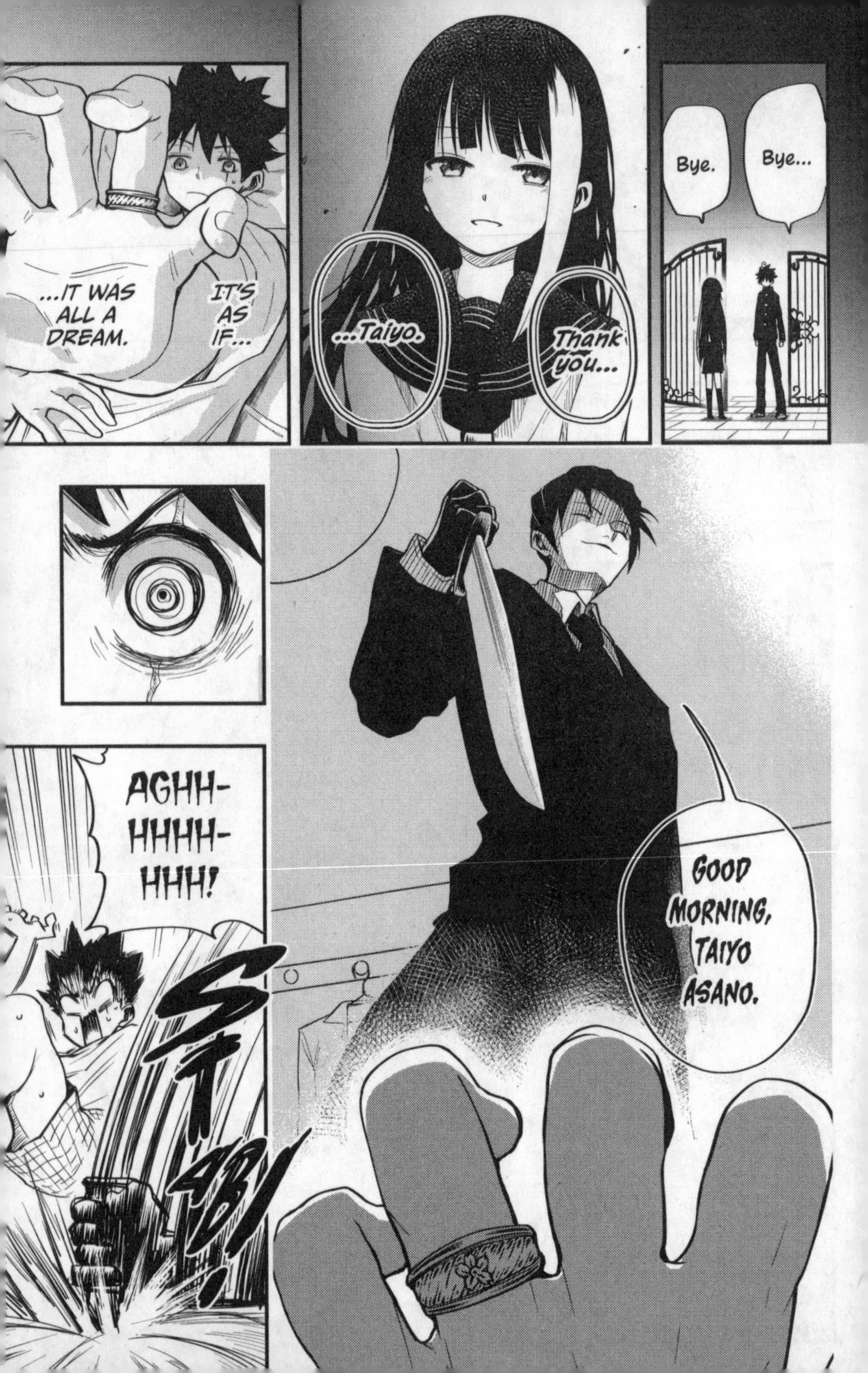
Bye...
Bye.
...Taiyo.
Thank you...
IT'S AS IF...
...IT WAS ALL A DREAM.
GOOD MORNING, TAIYO ASANO.
AGHH-HHHH-HHH!

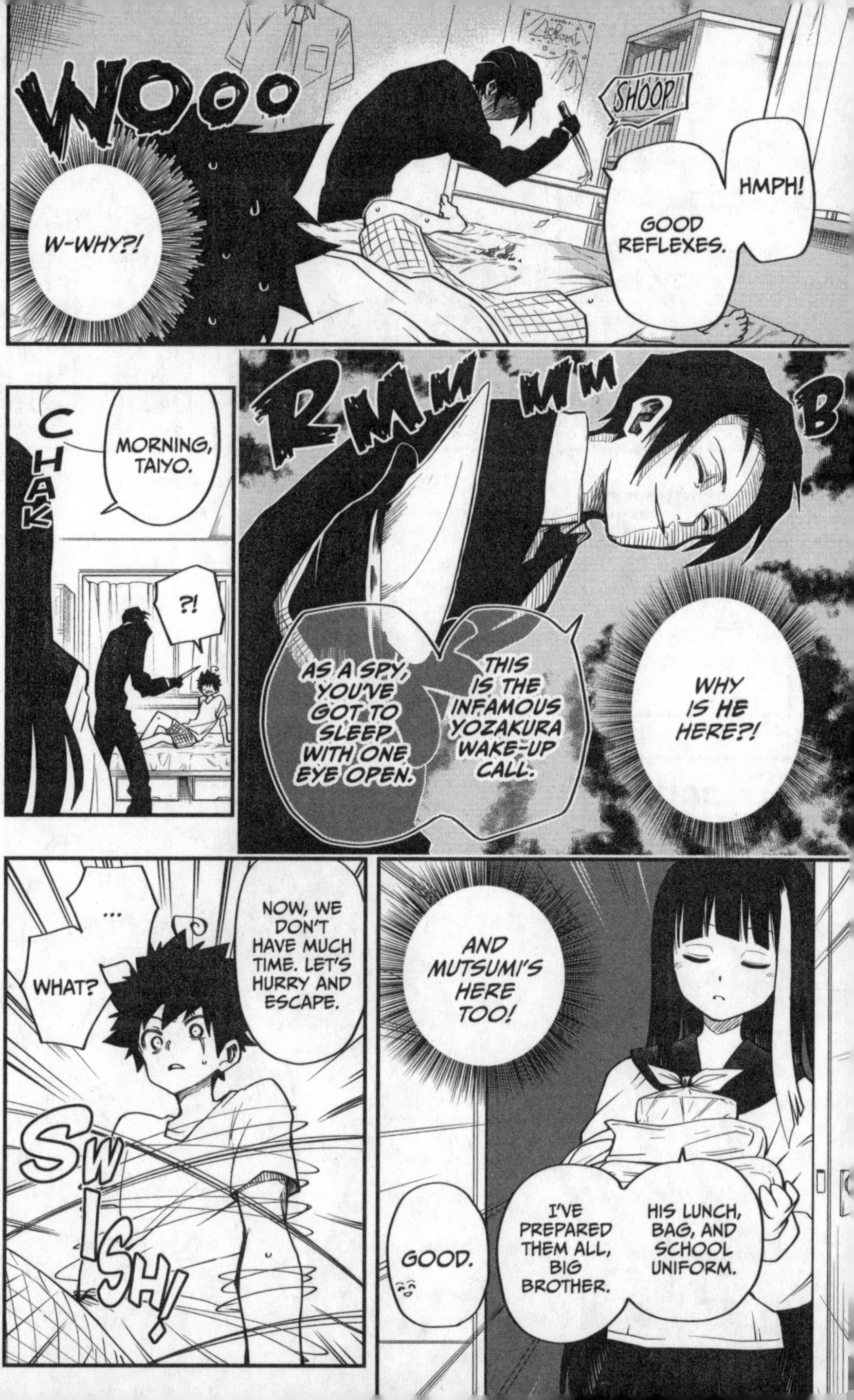
SHOOP
HMPH!
GOOD REFLEXES.
WOOO
W-WHY?!
RMMMMB
WHY IS HE HERE?!
THIS IS THE INFAMOUS YOZAKURA WAKE-UP CALL.
AS A SPY, YOU'VE GOT TO SLEEP WITH ONE EYE OPEN.
MORNING, TAIYO.
CHAK
?!
AND MUTSUMI'S HERE TOO!
HIS LUNCH, BAG, AND SCHOOL UNIFORM.
I'VE PREPARED THEM ALL, BIG BROTHER.
GOOD.
NOW, WE DON'T HAVE MUCH TIME. LET'S HURRY AND ESCAPE.
...
WHAT?
SWISH!

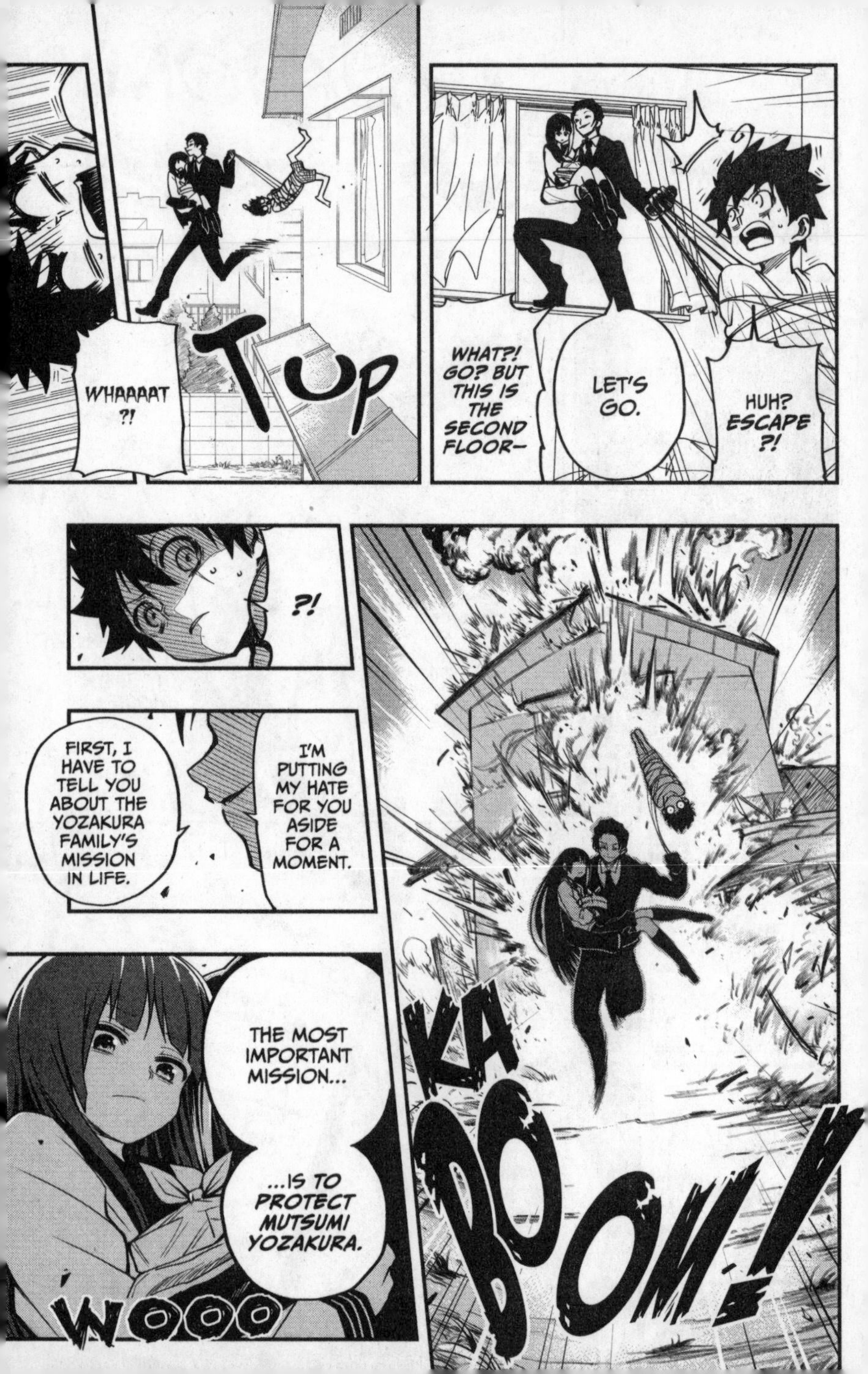
HUH? ESCAPE ?!
LET'S GO.
WHAT?! GO? BUT THIS IS THE SECOND FLOOR—
TUP
WHAAAAT ?!
KA BOOM!
?!
I'M PUTTING MY HATE FOR YOU ASIDE FOR A MOMENT.
FIRST, I HAVE TO TELL YOU ABOUT THE YOZAKURA FAMILY'S MISSION IN LIFE.
THE MOST IMPORTANT MISSION...
...IS TO PROTECT MUTSUMI YOZAKURA.
WOOO

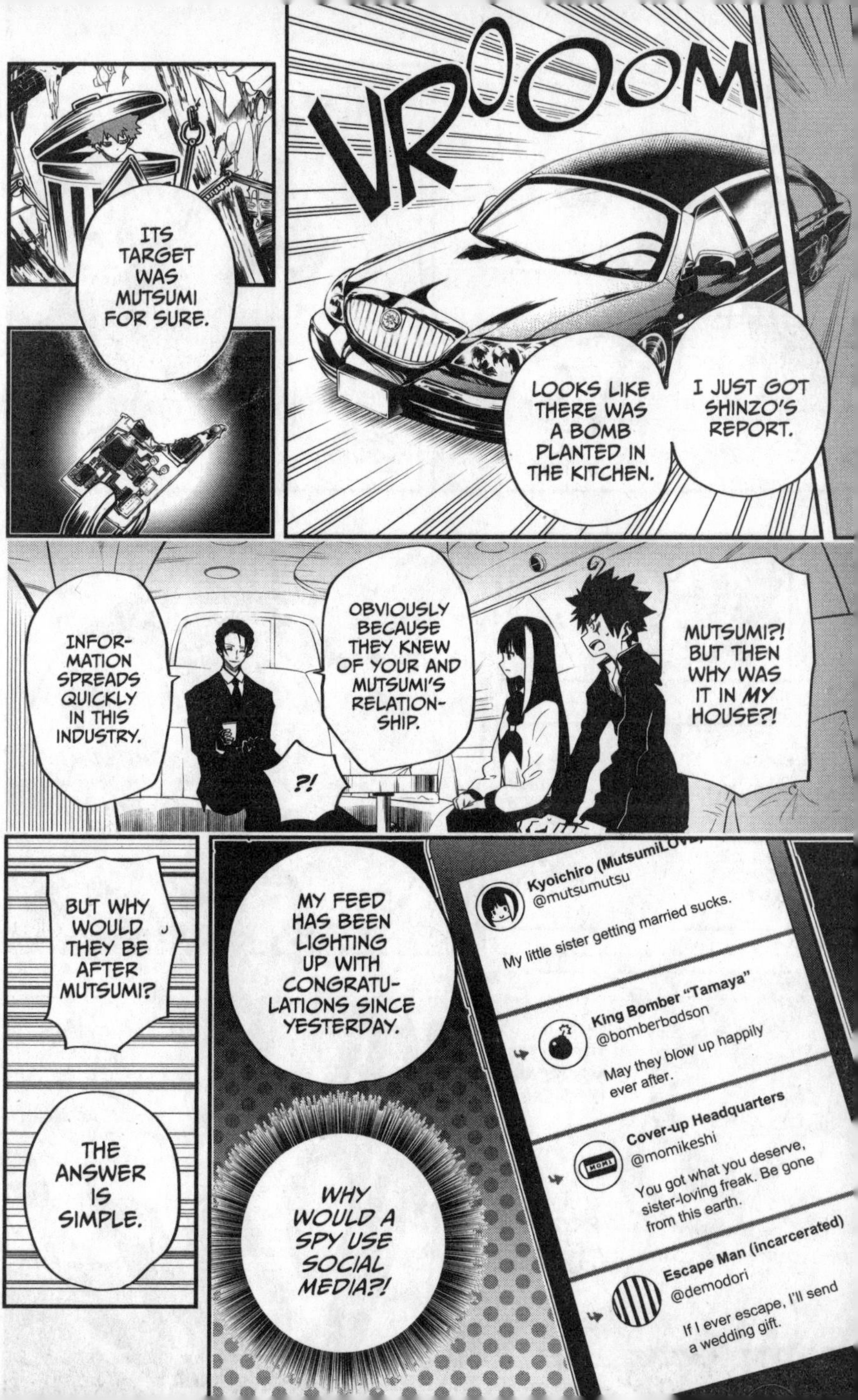
VROOOM
I JUST GOT SHINZO'S REPORT.
LOOKS LIKE THERE WAS A BOMB PLANTED IN THE KITCHEN.
ITS TARGET WAS MUTSUMI FOR SURE.
MUTSUMI?! BUT THEN WHY WAS IT IN *MY* HOUSE?!
OBVIOUSLY BECAUSE THEY KNEW OF YOUR AND MUTSUMI'S RELATION-SHIP.
INFOR-MATION SPREADS QUICKLY IN THIS INDUSTRY.
?!
Kyoichiro (MutsumiLOVE
@mutsumutsu
My little sister getting married sucks.
King Bomber "Tamaya"
@bomberbadson
May they blow up happily ever after.
Cover-up Headquarters
@momikeshi
You got what you deserve, sister-loving freak. Be gone from this earth.
Escape Man (incarcerated)
@demodori
If I ever escape, I'll send a wedding gift.
MY FEED HAS BEEN LIGHTING UP WITH CONGRATU-LATIONS SINCE YESTERDAY.
WHY WOULD A SPY USE SOCIAL MEDIA?!
BUT WHY WOULD THEY BE AFTER MUTSUMI?
THE ANSWER IS SIMPLE.

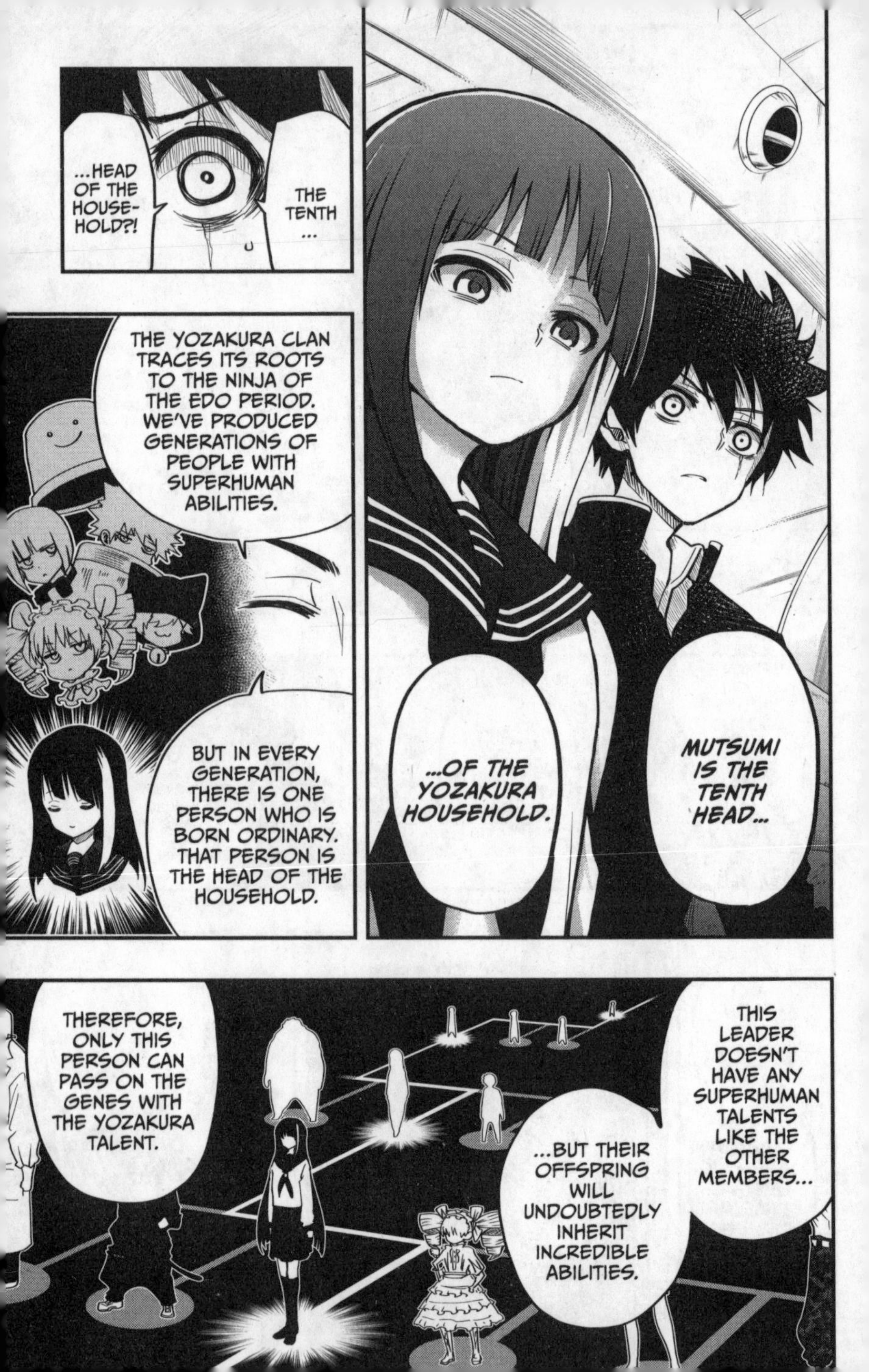
MUTSUMI IS THE TENTH HEAD...
...OF THE YOZAKURA HOUSEHOLD.
THE TENTH ...
...HEAD OF THE HOUSE-HOLD?!
THE YOZAKURA CLAN TRACES ITS ROOTS TO THE NINJA OF THE EDO PERIOD. WE'VE PRODUCED GENERATIONS OF PEOPLE WITH SUPERHUMAN ABILITIES.
BUT IN EVERY GENERATION, THERE IS ONE PERSON WHO IS BORN ORDINARY. THAT PERSON IS THE HEAD OF THE HOUSEHOLD.
THIS LEADER DOESN'T HAVE ANY SUPERHUMAN TALENTS LIKE THE OTHER MEMBERS...
...BUT THEIR OFFSPRING WILL UNDOUBTEDLY INHERIT INCREDIBLE ABILITIES.
THEREFORE, ONLY THIS PERSON CAN PASS ON THE GENES WITH THE YOZAKURA TALENT.

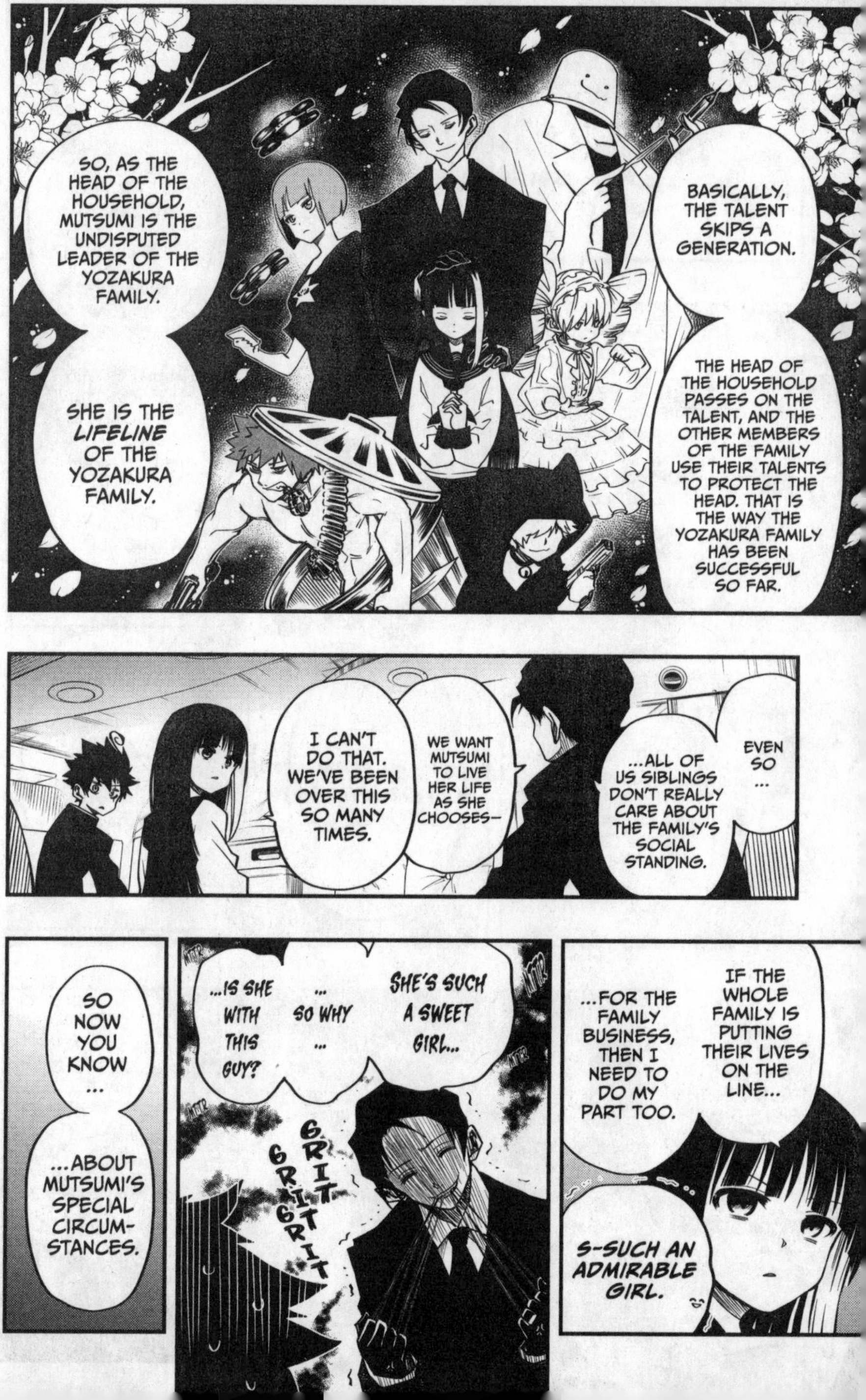
BASICALLY, THE TALENT SKIPS A GENERATION.
THE HEAD OF THE HOUSEHOLD PASSES ON THE TALENT, AND THE OTHER MEMBERS OF THE FAMILY USE THEIR TALENTS TO PROTECT THE HEAD. THAT IS THE WAY THE YOZAKURA FAMILY HAS BEEN SUCCESSFUL SO FAR.
SO, AS THE HEAD OF THE HOUSEHOLD, MUTSUMI IS THE UNDISPUTED LEADER OF THE YOZAKURA FAMILY.
SHE IS THE *LIFELINE* OF THE YOZAKURA FAMILY.
EVEN SO ...
...ALL OF US SIBLINGS DON'T REALLY CARE ABOUT THE FAMILY'S SOCIAL STANDING.
WE WANT MUTSUMI TO LIVE HER LIFE AS SHE CHOOSES—
I CAN'T DO THAT. WE'VE BEEN OVER THIS SO MANY TIMES.
IF THE WHOLE FAMILY IS PUTTING THEIR LIVES ON THE LINE...
...FOR THE FAMILY BUSINESS, THEN I NEED TO DO MY PART TOO.
S-SUCH AN ADMIRABLE GIRL.
SHE'S SUCH A SWEET GIRL...
... SO WHY ...
...IS SHE WITH THIS GUY?
GRIT GRIT GRIT GRIT
SO NOW YOU KNOW ...
...ABOUT MUTSUMI'S SPECIAL CIRCUMSTANCES.

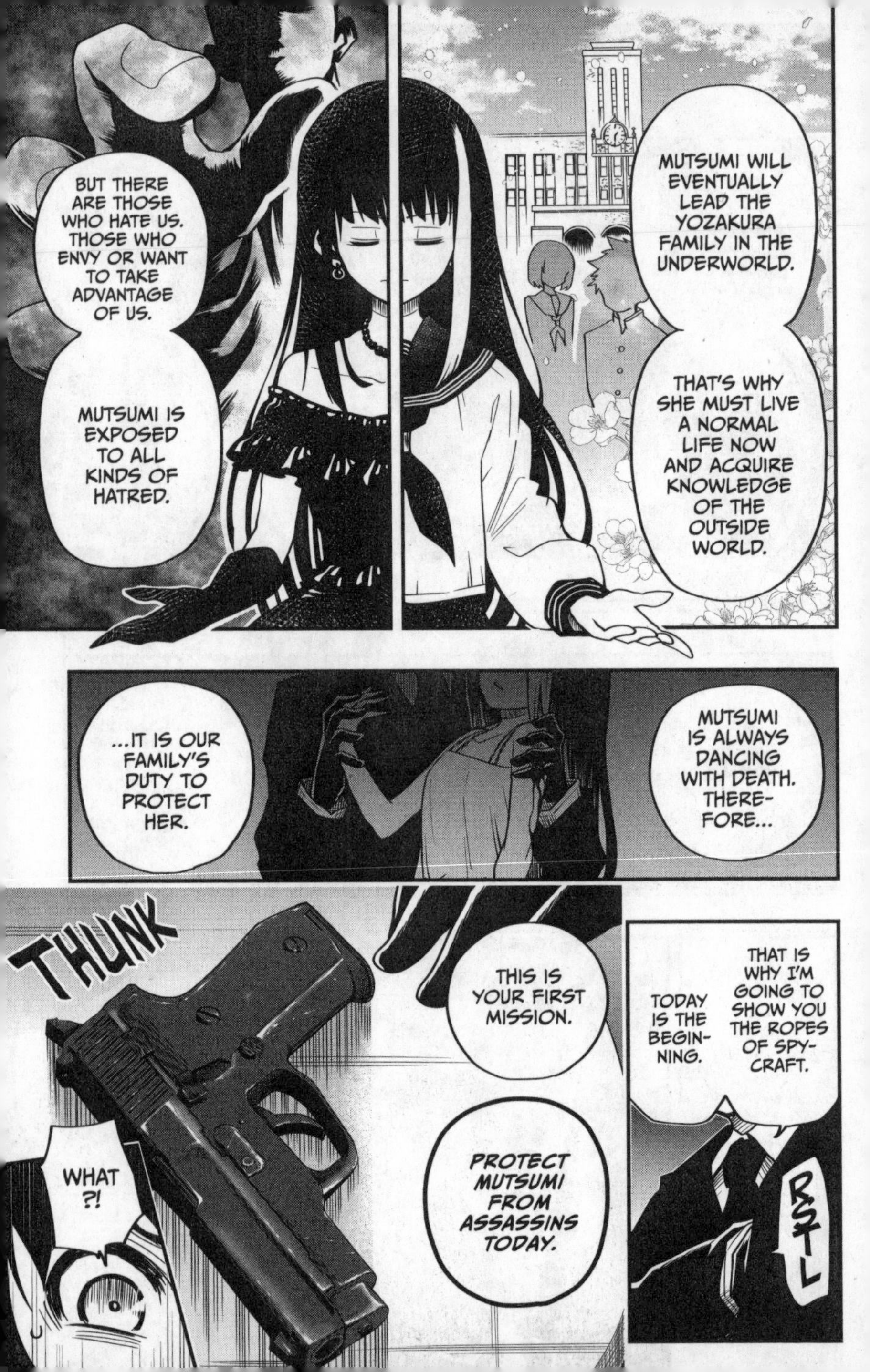
MUTSUMI WILL EVENTUALLY LEAD THE YOZAKURA FAMILY IN THE UNDERWORLD.
THAT'S WHY SHE MUST LIVE A NORMAL LIFE NOW AND ACQUIRE KNOWLEDGE OF THE OUTSIDE WORLD.
BUT THERE ARE THOSE WHO HATE US. THOSE WHO ENVY OR WANT TO TAKE ADVANTAGE OF US.
MUTSUMI IS EXPOSED TO ALL KINDS OF HATRED.
MUTSUMI IS ALWAYS DANCING WITH DEATH. THEREFORE...
...IT IS OUR FAMILY'S DUTY TO PROTECT HER.
THAT IS WHY I'M GOING TO SHOW YOU THE ROPES OF SPYCRAFT.
TODAY IS THE BEGINNING.
RSTL
THIS IS YOUR FIRST MISSION.
PROTECT MUTSUMI FROM ASSASSINS TODAY.
THUNK
WHAT?!

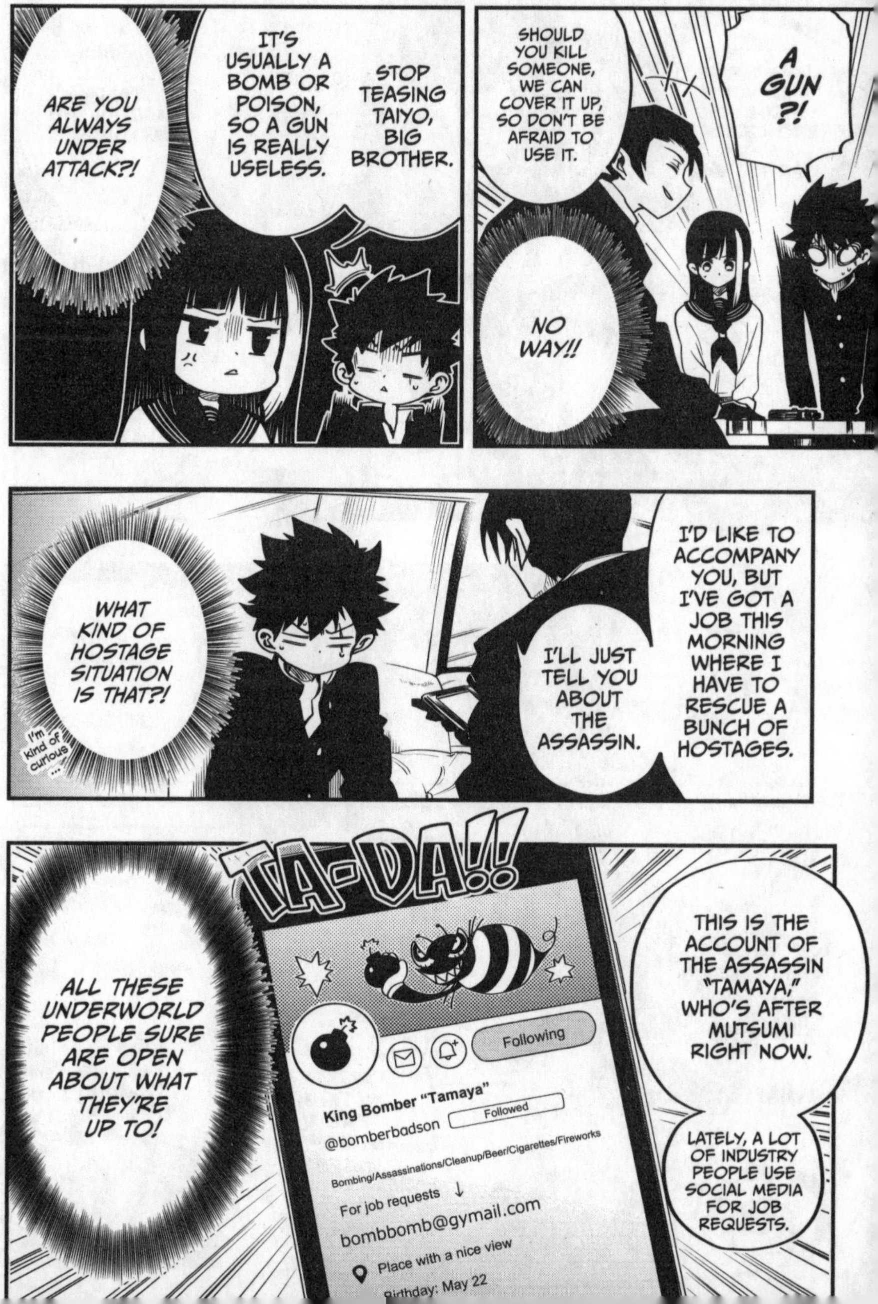
A GUN?!
SHOULD YOU KILL SOMEONE, WE CAN COVER IT UP, SO DON'T BE AFRAID TO USE IT.
NO WAY!!
STOP TEASING TAIYO, BIG BROTHER.
IT'S USUALLY A BOMB OR POISON, SO A GUN IS REALLY USELESS.
ARE YOU ALWAYS UNDER ATTACK?!
I'D LIKE TO ACCOMPANY YOU, BUT I'VE GOT A JOB THIS MORNING WHERE I HAVE TO RESCUE A BUNCH OF HOSTAGES.
I'LL JUST TELL YOU ABOUT THE ASSASSIN.
WHAT KIND OF HOSTAGE SITUATION IS THAT?!
I'm kind of curious...
THIS IS THE ACCOUNT OF THE ASSASSIN "TAMAYA," WHO'S AFTER MUTSUMI RIGHT NOW.
LATELY, A LOT OF INDUSTRY PEOPLE USE SOCIAL MEDIA FOR JOB REQUESTS.
TA-DA!!
Following
King Bomber "Tamaya"
Followed
@bomberbadson
Bombing/Assassinations/Cleanup/Beer/Cigarettes/Fireworks
For job requests ↓
bombbomb@gymail.com
Place with a nice view
Birthday: May 22
ALL THESE UNDERWORLD PEOPLE SURE ARE OPEN ABOUT WHAT THEY'RE UP TO!

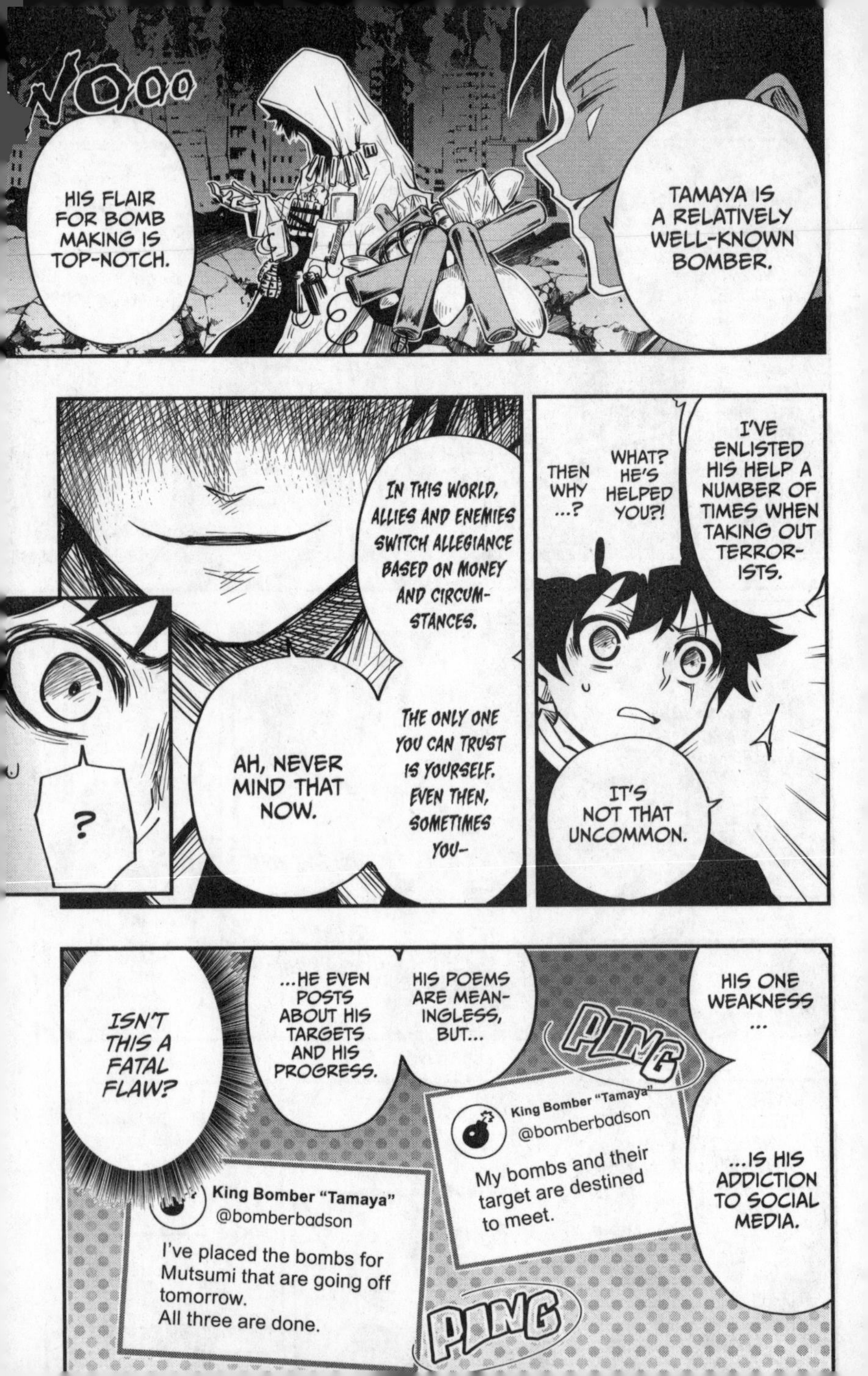
VOoo
TAMAYA IS A RELATIVELY WELL-KNOWN BOMBER.
HIS FLAIR FOR BOMB MAKING IS TOP-NOTCH.
I'VE ENLISTED HIS HELP A NUMBER OF TIMES WHEN TAKING OUT TERRORISTS.
WHAT? HE'S HELPED YOU?!
THEN WHY ...?
IT'S NOT THAT UNCOMMON.
IN THIS WORLD, ALLIES AND ENEMIES SWITCH ALLEGIANCE BASED ON MONEY AND CIRCUMSTANCES.
THE ONLY ONE YOU CAN TRUST IS YOURSELF. EVEN THEN, SOMETIMES YOU-
AH, NEVER MIND THAT NOW.
?
HIS ONE WEAKNESS ...
...IS HIS ADDICTION TO SOCIAL MEDIA.
PING
King Bomber "Tamaya"
@bomberbadson
My bombs and their target are destined to meet.
HIS POEMS ARE MEANINGLESS, BUT...
...HE EVEN POSTS ABOUT HIS TARGETS AND HIS PROGRESS.
PING
King Bomber "Tamaya"
@bomberbadson
I've placed the bombs for Mutsumi that are going off tomorrow.
All three are done.
ISN'T THIS A FATAL FLAW?

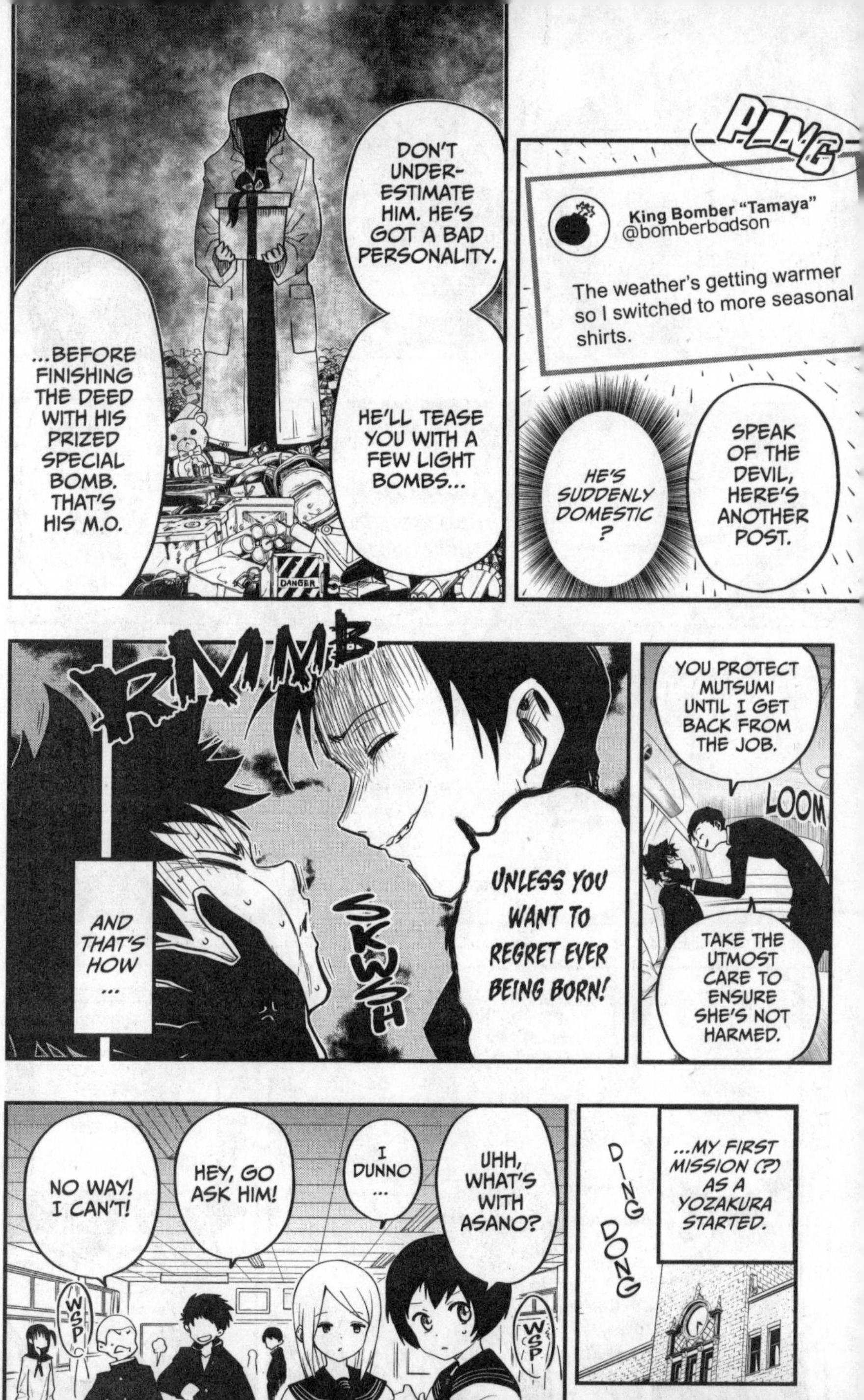
PING
King Bomber "Tamaya"
@bomberbadson
The weather's getting warmer so I switched to more seasonal shirts.
SPEAK OF THE DEVIL, HERE'S ANOTHER POST.
HE'S SUDDENLY DOMESTIC?
DON'T UNDER-ESTIMATE HIM. HE'S GOT A BAD PERSONALITY.
HE'LL TEASE YOU WITH A FEW LIGHT BOMBS...
...BEFORE FINISHING THE DEED WITH HIS PRIZED SPECIAL BOMB. THAT'S HIS M.O.
DANGER
YOU PROTECT MUTSUMI UNTIL I GET BACK FROM THE JOB.
LOOM
TAKE THE UTMOST CARE TO ENSURE SHE'S NOT HARMED.
RMMB
UNLESS YOU WANT TO REGRET EVER BEING BORN!
SKWSH
AND THAT'S HOW ...
DING DONG
...MY FIRST MISSION (?) AS A YOZAKURA STARTED.
UHH, WHAT'S WITH ASANO?
I DUNNO ...
WSP
HEY, GO ASK HIM!
NO WAY! I CAN'T!
WSP

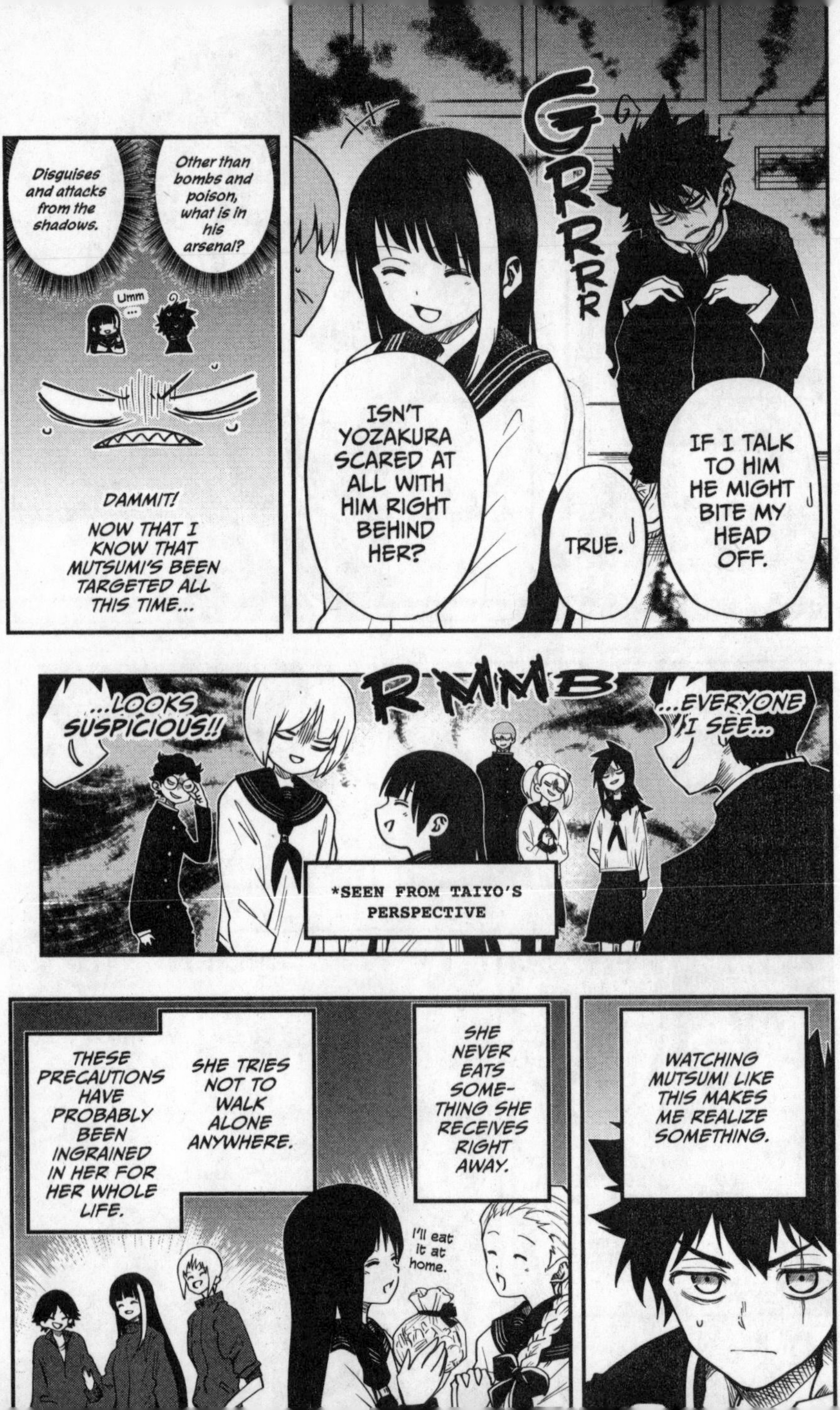
GRRRR
ISN'T YOZAKURA SCARED AT ALL WITH HIM RIGHT BEHIND HER?
IF I TALK TO HIM HE MIGHT BITE MY HEAD OFF.
TRUE.
Other than bombs and poison, what is in his arsenal?
Disguises and attacks from the shadows.
Umm ...
DAMMIT! NOW THAT I KNOW THAT MUTSUMI'S BEEN TARGETED ALL THIS TIME...
RMMB
...EVERYONE I SEE...
...LOOKS SUSPICIOUS!!
*SEEN FROM TAIYO'S PERSPECTIVE
WATCHING MUTSUMI LIKE THIS MAKES ME REALIZE SOMETHING.
SHE NEVER EATS SOME-THING SHE RECEIVES RIGHT AWAY.
I'll eat it at home.
SHE TRIES NOT TO WALK ALONE ANYWHERE.
THESE PRECAUTIONS HAVE PROBABLY BEEN INGRAINED IN HER FOR HER WHOLE LIFE.

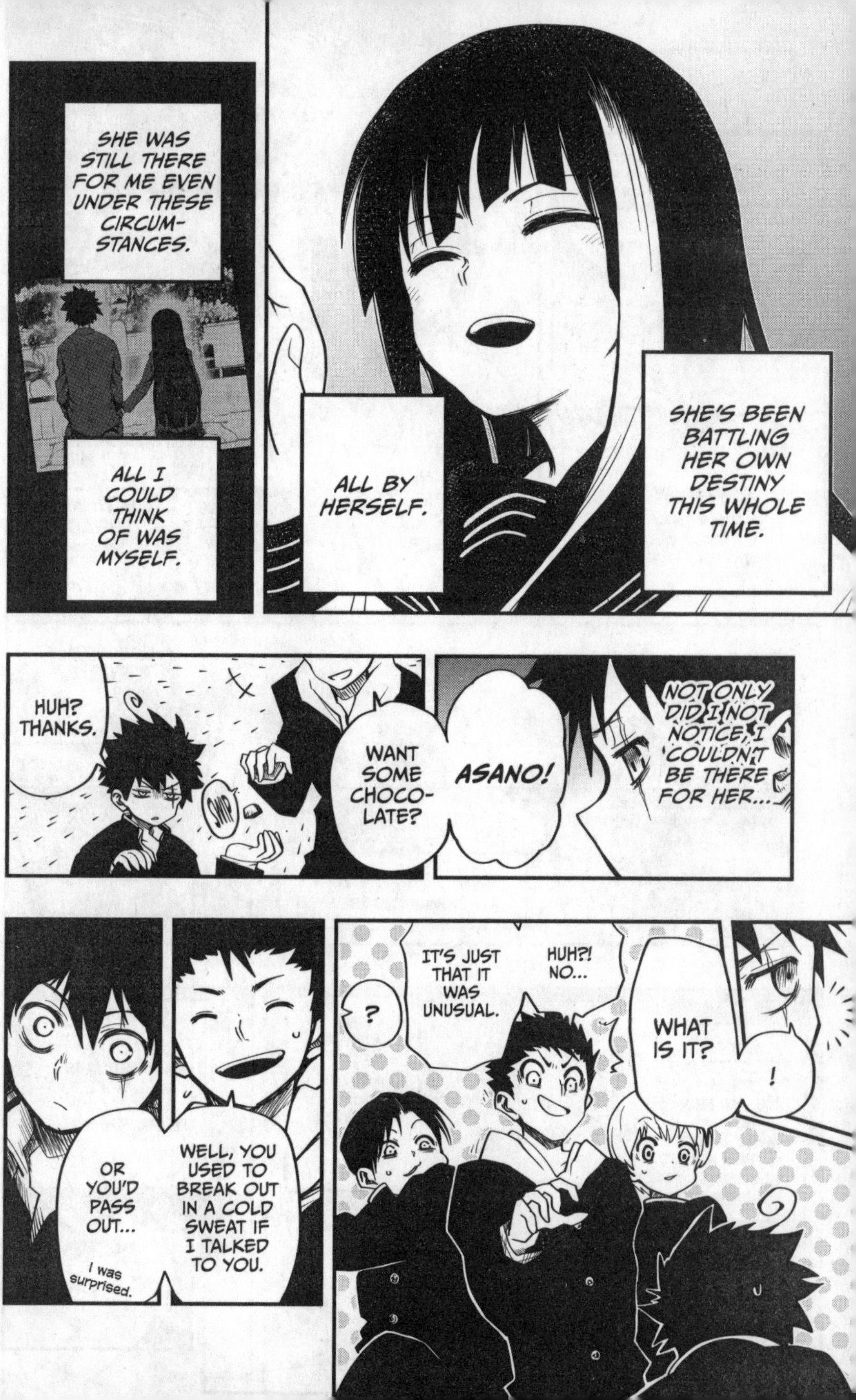
SHE'S BEEN BATTLING HER OWN DESTINY THIS WHOLE TIME.
ALL BY HERSELF.
SHE WAS STILL THERE FOR ME EVEN UNDER THESE CIRCUM-STANCES.
ALL I COULD THINK OF WAS MYSELF.
NOT ONLY DID I NOT NOTICE, I COULDN'T BE THERE FOR HER...
ASANO!
WANT SOME CHOCO-LATE?
HUH? THANKS.
!
WHAT IS IT?
HUH?! NO...
IT'S JUST THAT IT WAS UNUSUAL.
?
WELL, YOU USED TO BREAK OUT IN A COLD SWEAT IF I TALKED TO YOU.
OR YOU'D PASS OUT...
I was surprised.

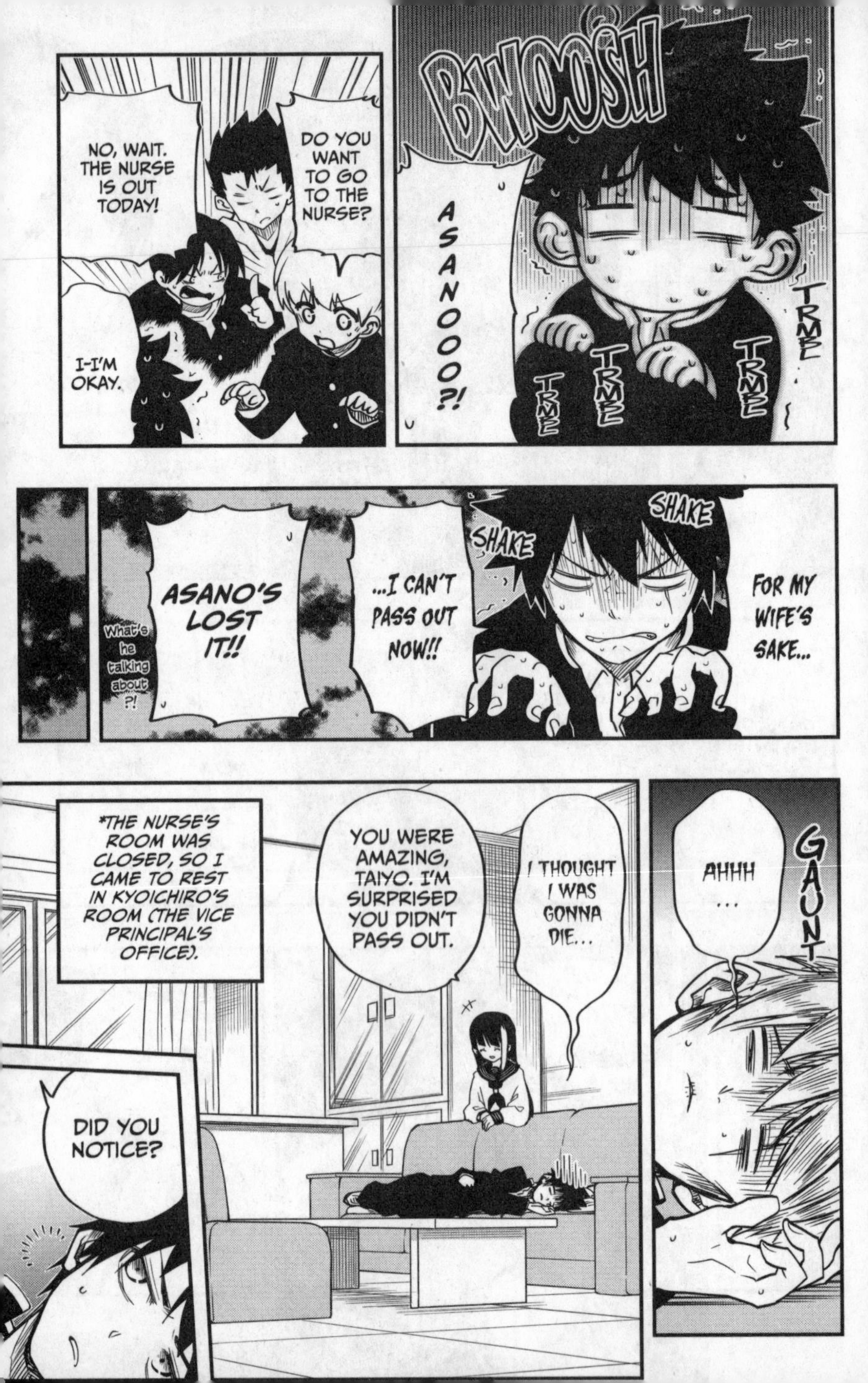
BWOOSH
ASANOOOO?!
TRMB
TRMB
TRMB
TRMB
DO YOU WANT TO GO TO THE NURSE?
NO, WAIT. THE NURSE IS OUT TODAY!
I-I'M OKAY.
FOR MY WIFE'S SAKE...
SHAKE
SHAKE
...I CAN'T PASS OUT NOW!!
ASANO'S LOST IT!!
What's he talking about?!
GAUNT
AHHH...
I THOUGHT I WAS GONNA DIE...
YOU WERE AMAZING, TAIYO. I'M SURPRISED YOU DIDN'T PASS OUT.
*THE NURSE'S ROOM WAS CLOSED, SO I CAME TO REST IN KYOICHIRO'S ROOM (THE VICE PRINCIPAL'S OFFICE).
DID YOU NOTICE?

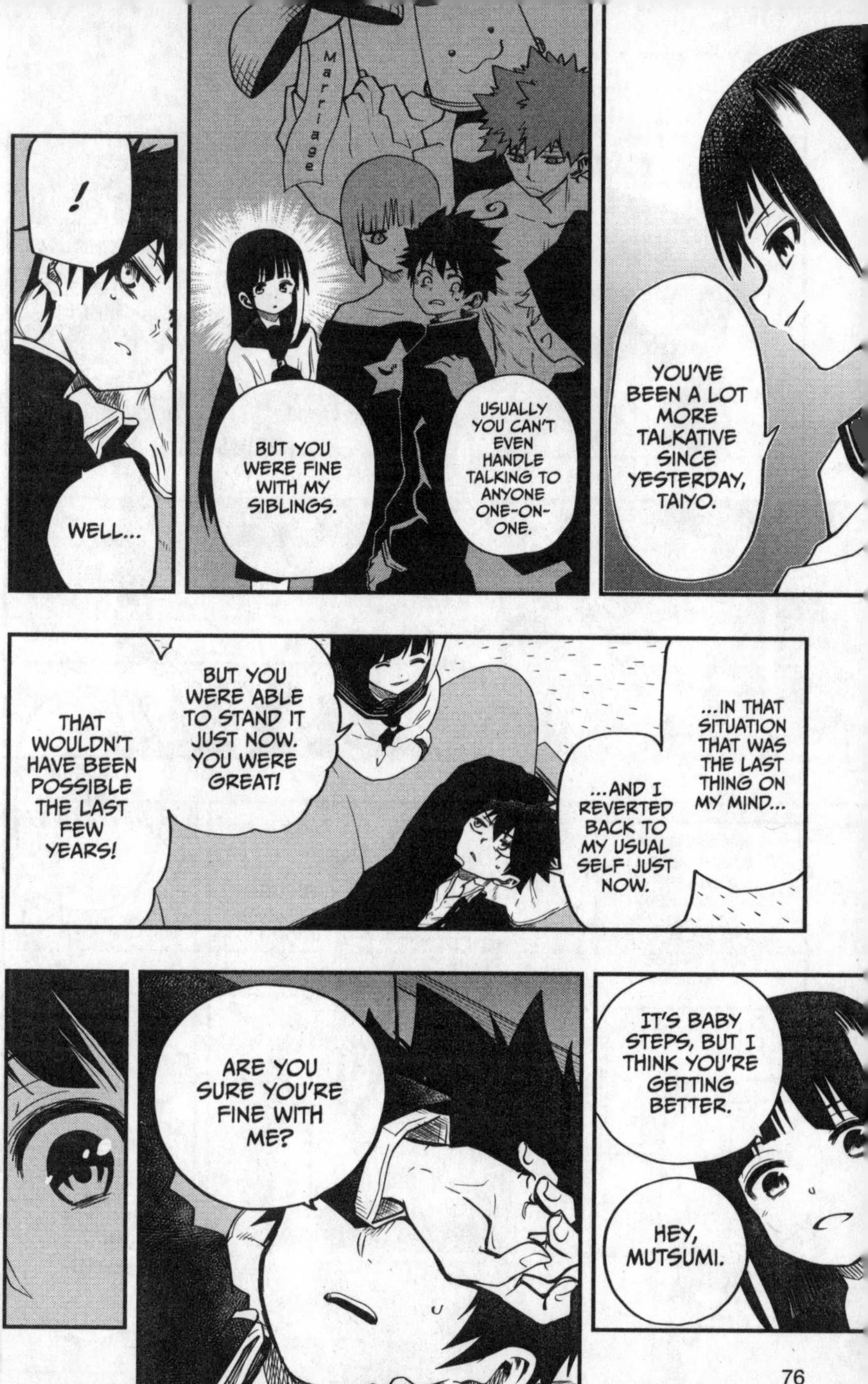
YOU'VE BEEN A LOT MORE TALKATIVE SINCE YESTERDAY, TAIYO.
Marriage
USUALLY YOU CAN'T EVEN HANDLE TALKING TO ANYONE ONE-ON-ONE.
BUT YOU WERE FINE WITH MY SIBLINGS.
!
WELL...
...IN THAT SITUATION THAT WAS THE LAST THING ON MY MIND...
...AND I REVERTED BACK TO MY USUAL SELF JUST NOW.
BUT YOU WERE ABLE TO STAND IT JUST NOW. YOU WERE GREAT!
THAT WOULDN'T HAVE BEEN POSSIBLE THE LAST FEW YEARS!
IT'S BABY STEPS, BUT I THINK YOU'RE GETTING BETTER.
HEY, MUTSUMI.
ARE YOU SURE YOU'RE FINE WITH ME?

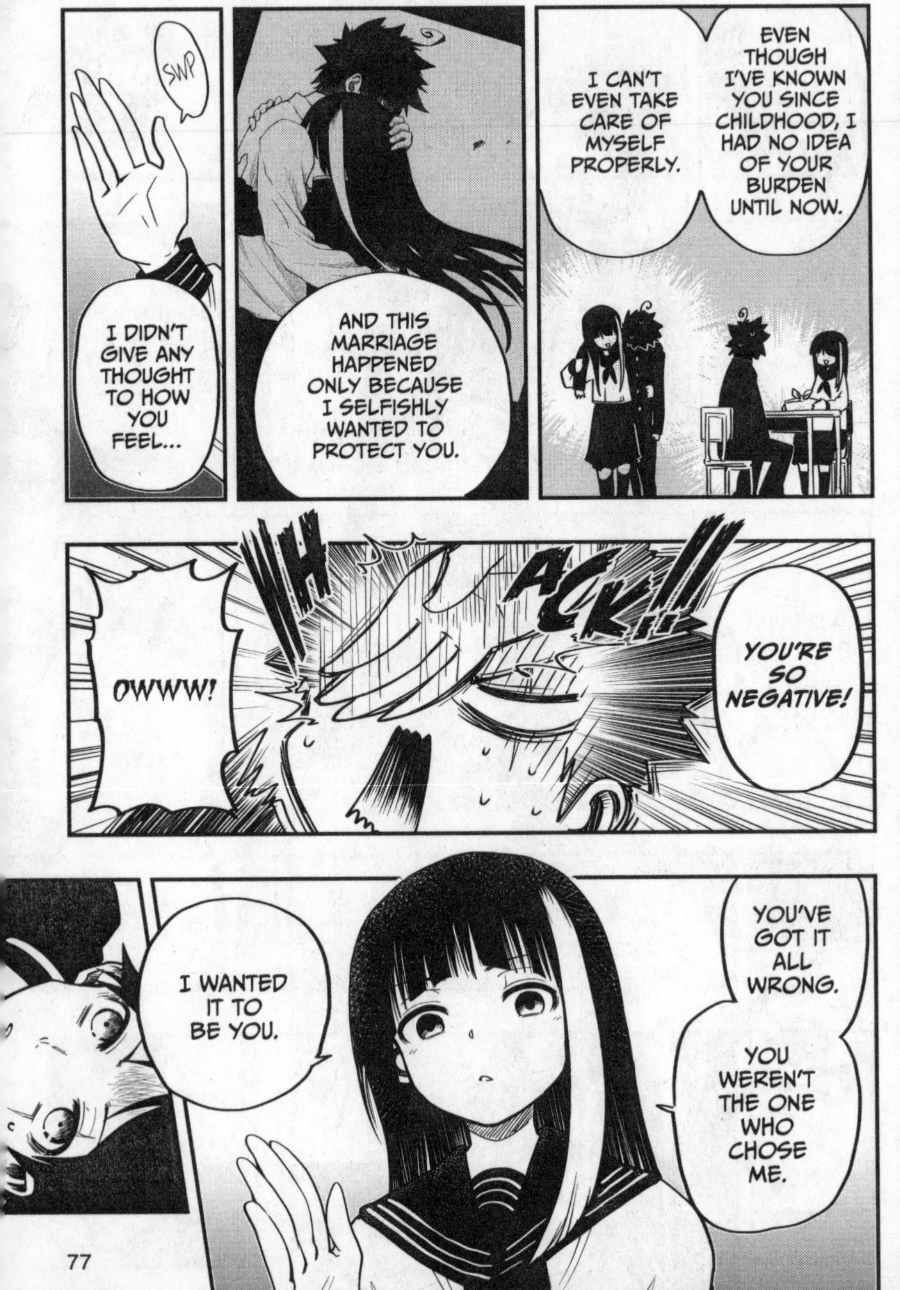
EVEN THOUGH I'VE KNOWN YOU SINCE CHILDHOOD, I HAD NO IDEA OF YOUR BURDEN UNTIL NOW.
I CAN'T EVEN TAKE CARE OF MYSELF PROPERLY.
AND THIS MARRIAGE HAPPENED ONLY BECAUSE I SELFISHLY WANTED TO PROTECT YOU.
SWP
I DIDN'T GIVE ANY THOUGHT TO HOW YOU FEEL...
YOU'RE SO NEGATIVE!
WHACK!!
OWWW!
YOU'VE GOT IT ALL WRONG.
YOU WEREN'T THE ONE WHO CHOSE ME.
I WANTED IT TO BE YOU.

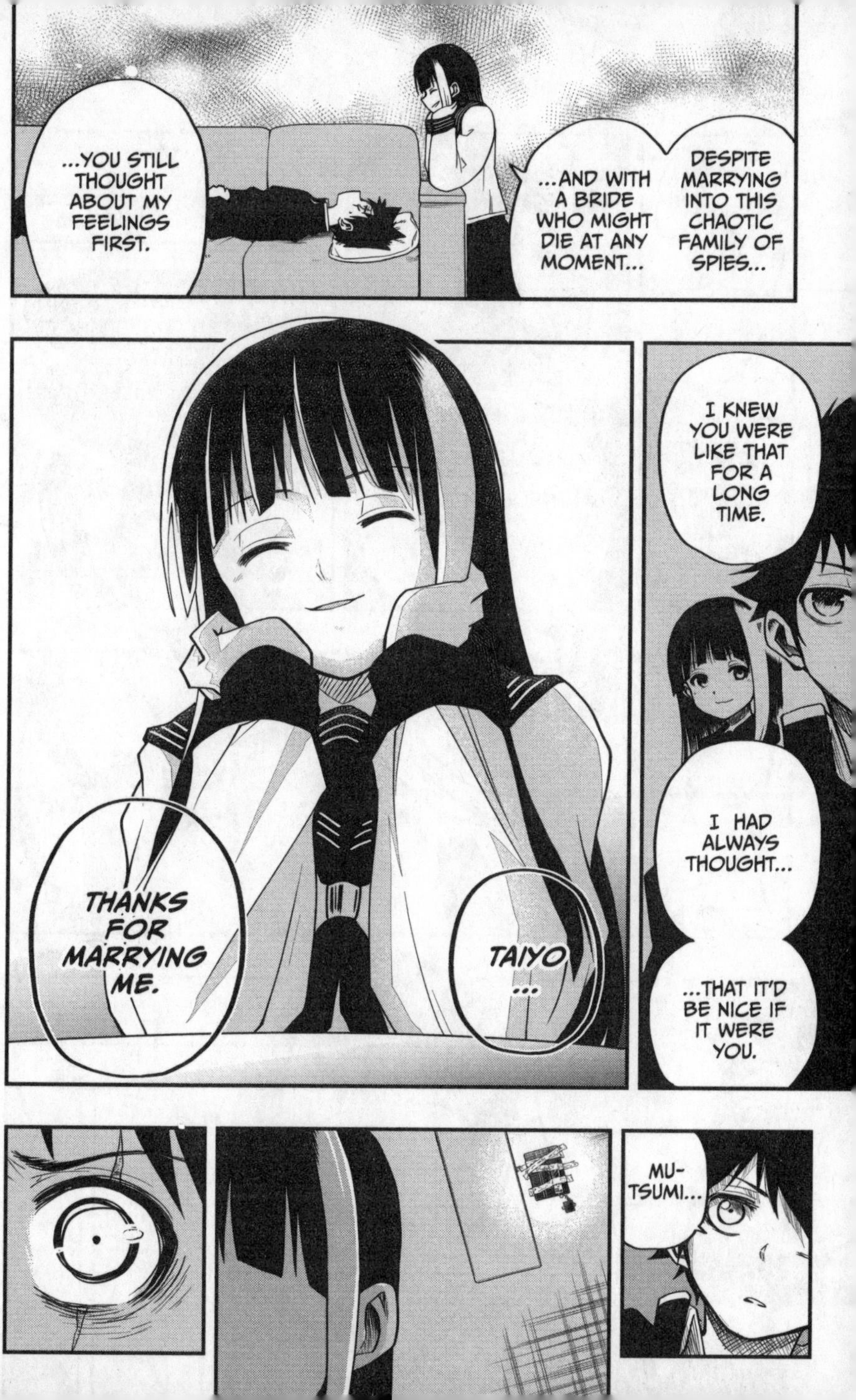
DESPITE MARRYING INTO THIS CHAOTIC FAMILY OF SPIES...
...AND WITH A BRIDE WHO MIGHT DIE AT ANY MOMENT...
...YOU STILL THOUGHT ABOUT MY FEELINGS FIRST.
I KNEW YOU WERE LIKE THAT FOR A LONG TIME.
I HAD ALWAYS THOUGHT...
...THAT IT'D BE NICE IF IT WERE YOU.
TAIYO...
THANKS FOR MARRYING ME.
MU-TSUMI...

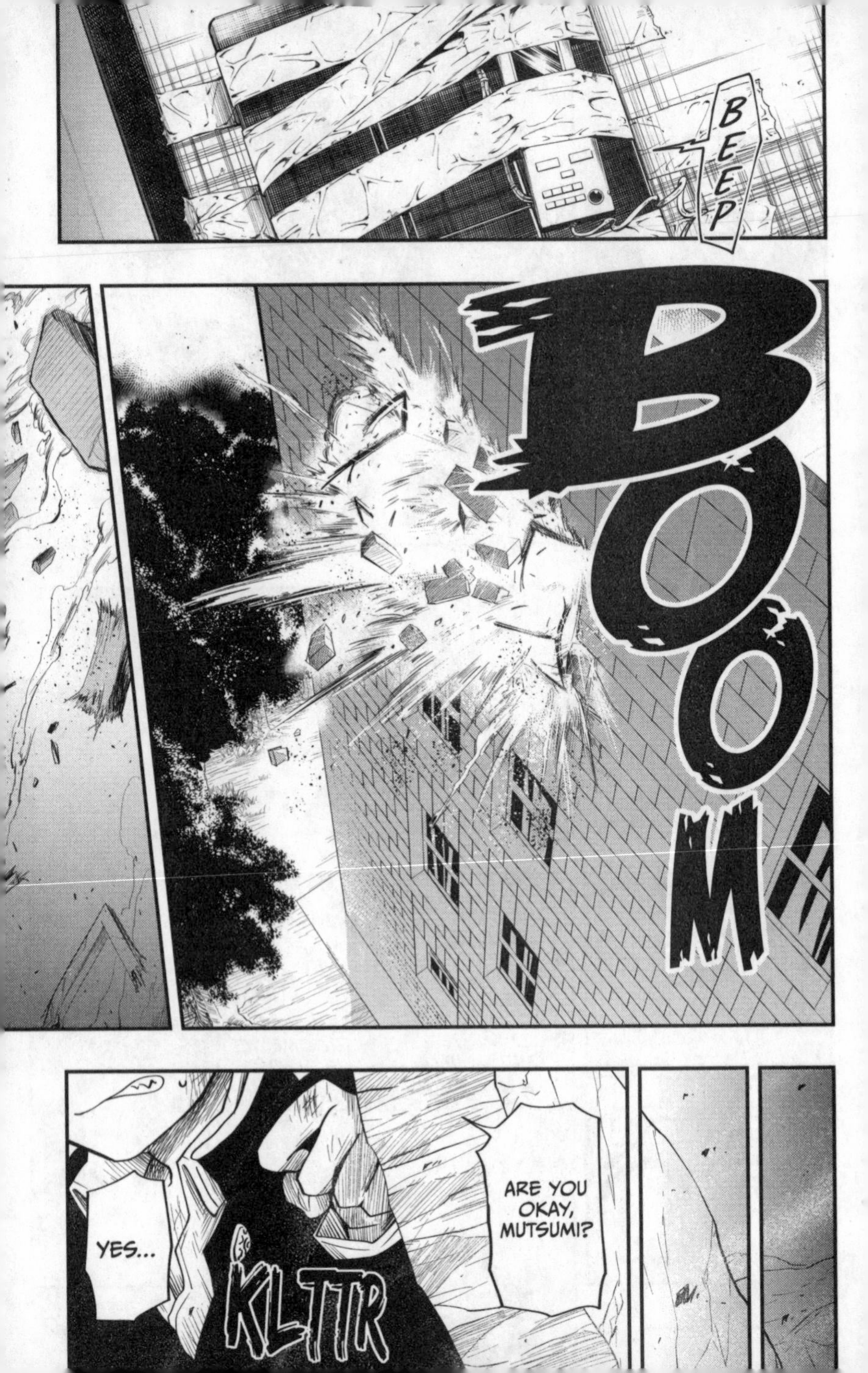
BEEP
BOOM
ARE YOU OKAY, MUTSUMI?
YES...
KLTR

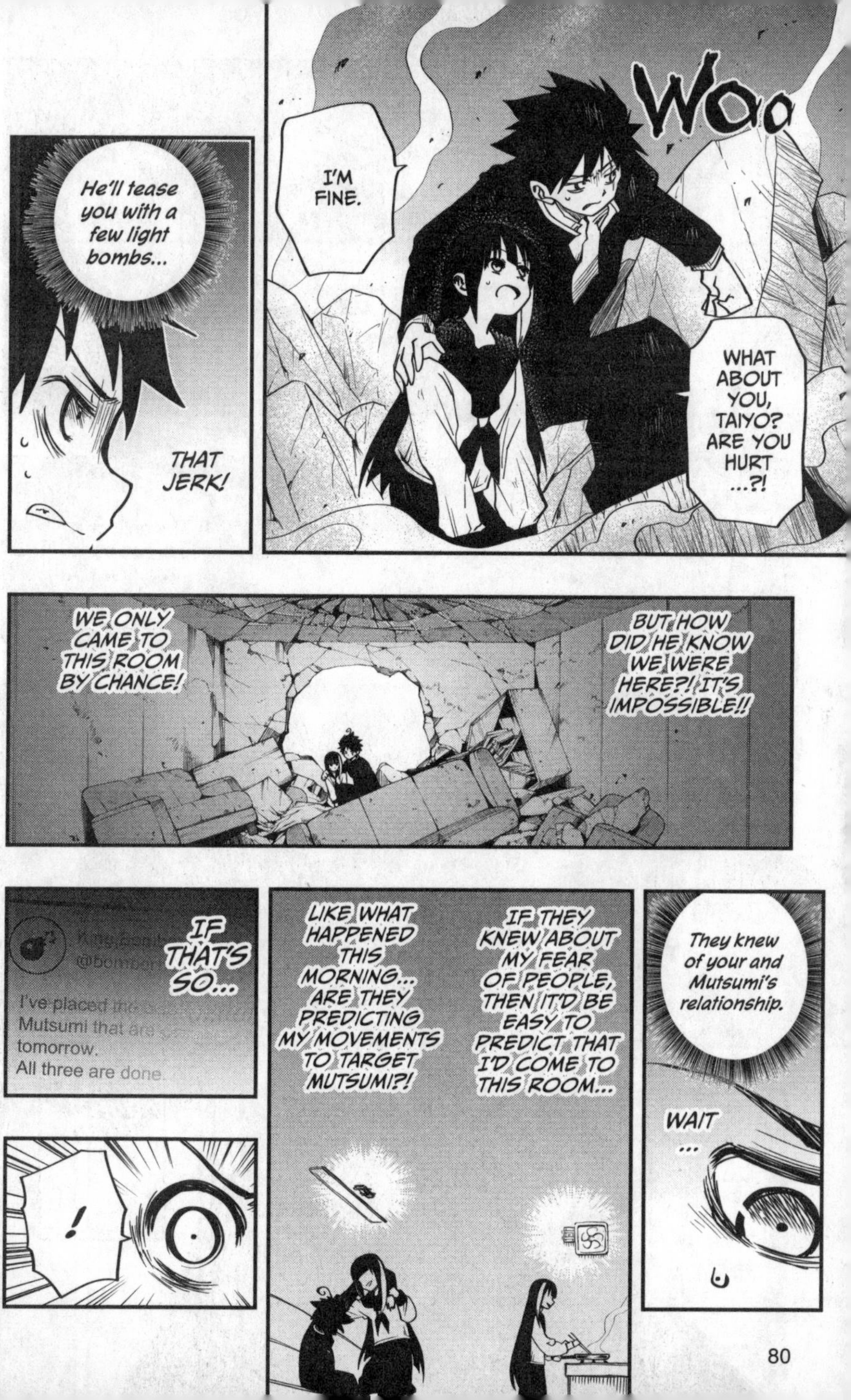
Waa
I'M FINE.
WHAT ABOUT YOU, TAIYO? ARE YOU HURT ...?!
He'll tease you with a few light bombs...
THAT JERK!
BUT HOW DID HE KNOW WE WERE HERE?! IT'S IMPOSSIBLE!!
WE ONLY CAME TO THIS ROOM BY CHANCE!
They knew of your and Mutsumi's relationship.
WAIT ...
IF THEY KNEW ABOUT MY FEAR OF PEOPLE, THEN IT'D BE EASY TO PREDICT THAT I'D COME TO THIS ROOM...
LIKE WHAT HAPPENED THIS MORNING... ARE THEY PREDICTING MY MOVEMENTS TO TARGET MUTSUMI?!
IF THAT'S SO...
I've placed
Mutsumi that
tomorrow.
All three are done.
!

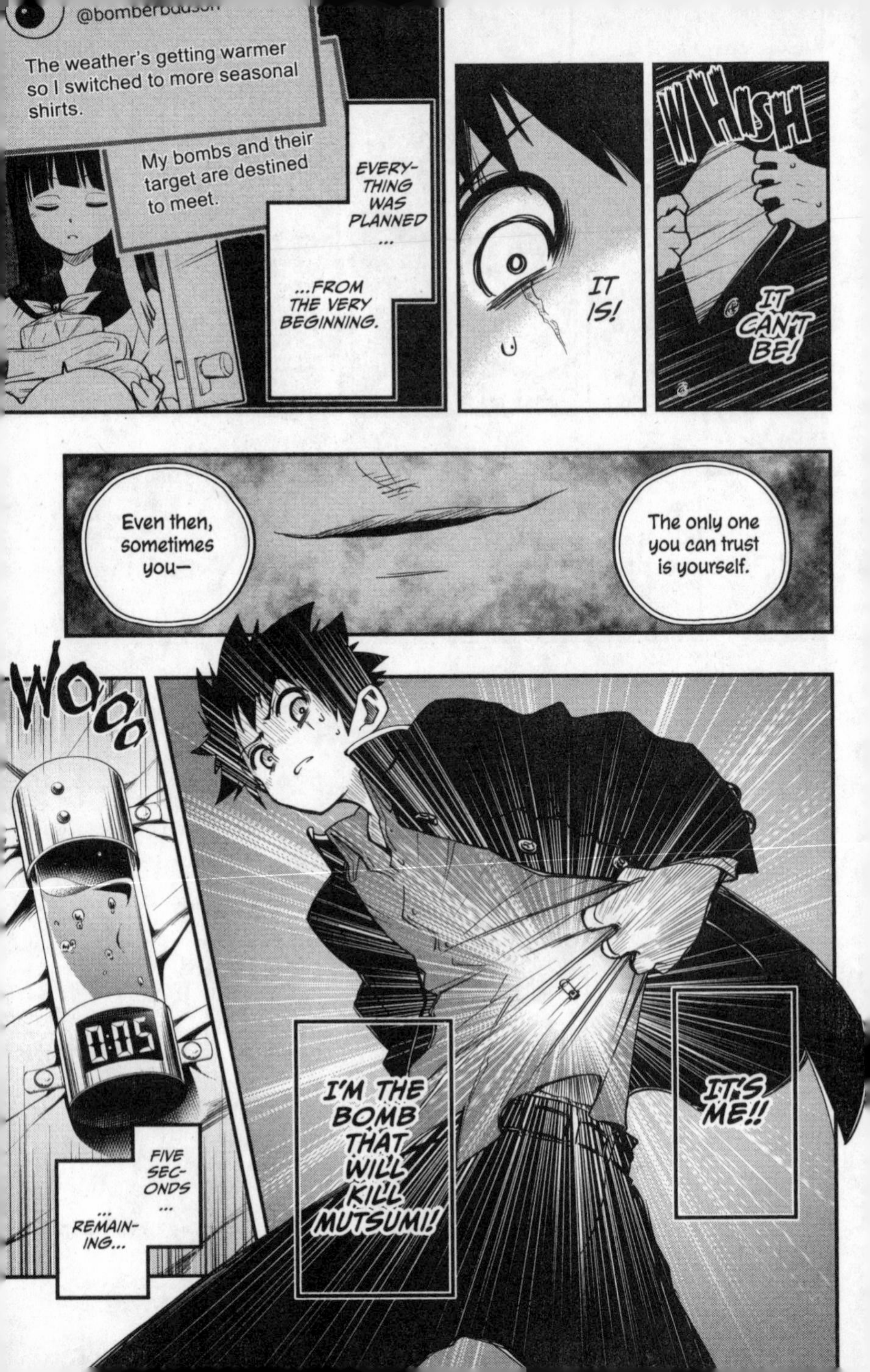

WHISH
IT CAN'T BE!
IT IS!
@bomberbudson
The weather's getting warmer so I switched to more seasonal shirts.
My bombs and their target are destined to meet.
EVERY-THING WAS PLANNED...
...FROM THE VERY BEGINNING.
The only one you can trust is yourself.
Even then, sometimes you—
IT'S ME!!
I'M THE BOMB THAT WILL KILL MUTSUMI!
WOOO
0:05
FIVE SEC-ONDS...
...REMAIN-ING...

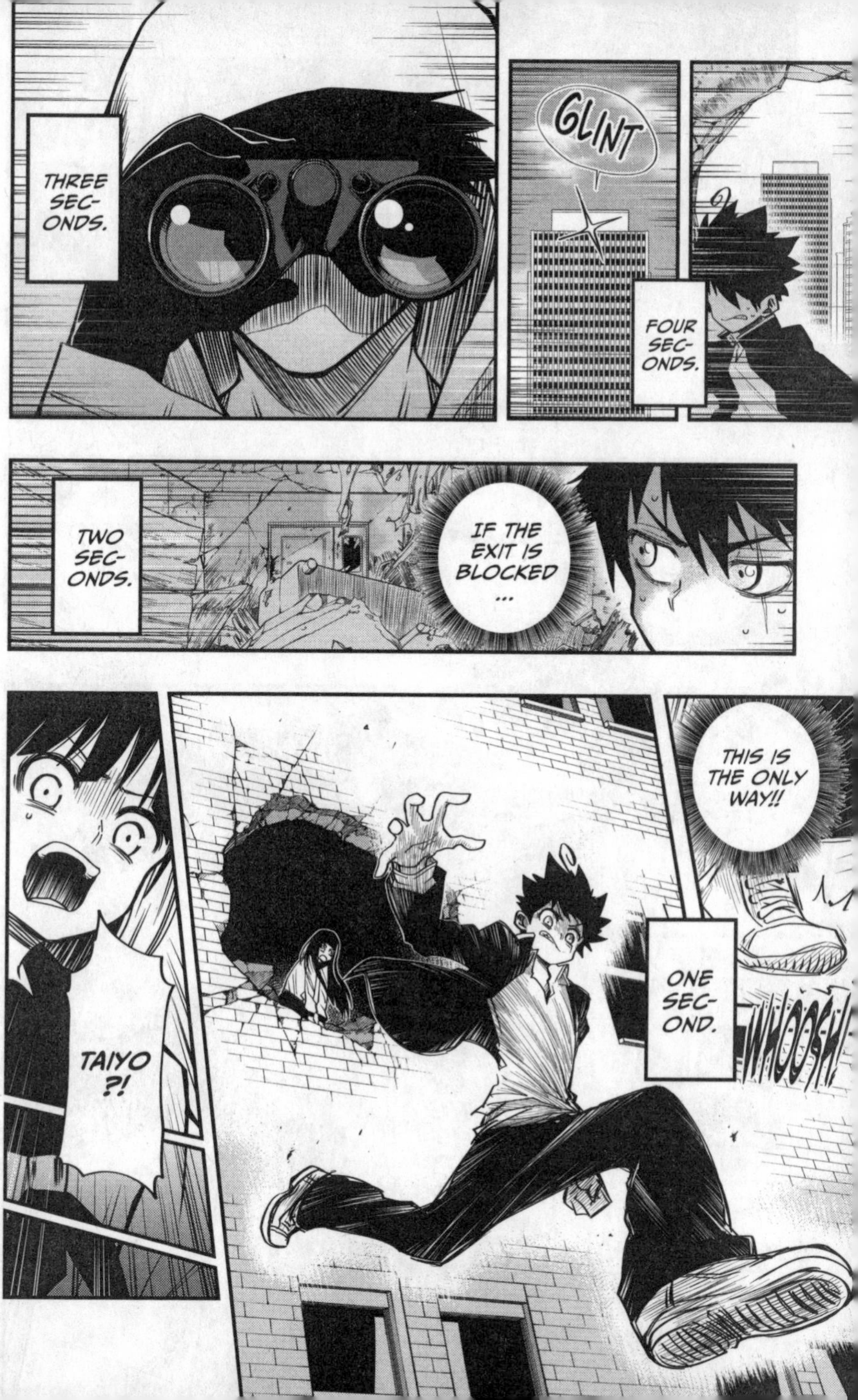
FOUR SEC-ONDS.
GLINT
THREE SEC-ONDS.
IF THE EXIT IS BLOCKED ...
TWO SEC-ONDS.
THIS IS THE ONLY WAY!!
ONE SEC-OND.
WHOOSH!
TAIYO ?!

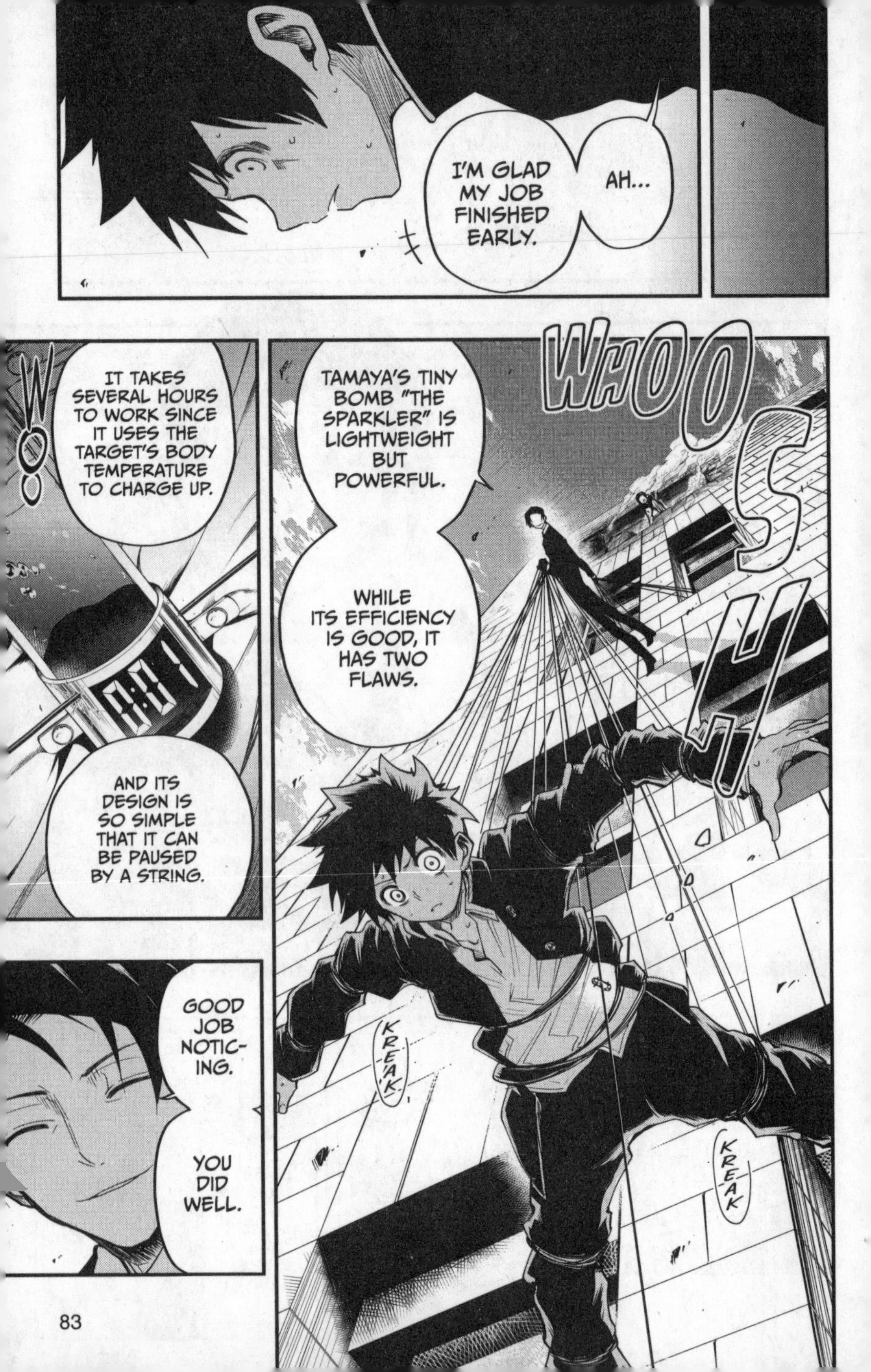
AH...
I'M GLAD MY JOB FINISHED EARLY.
WHOOOSH
TAMAYA'S TINY BOMB "THE SPARKLER" IS LIGHTWEIGHT BUT POWERFUL.
WHILE ITS EFFICIENCY IS GOOD, IT HAS TWO FLAWS.
KREAK
KREAK
IT TAKES SEVERAL HOURS TO WORK SINCE IT USES THE TARGET'S BODY TEMPERATURE TO CHARGE UP.
AND ITS DESIGN IS SO SIMPLE THAT IT CAN BE PAUSED BY A STRING.
GOOD JOB NOTICING.
YOU DID WELL.

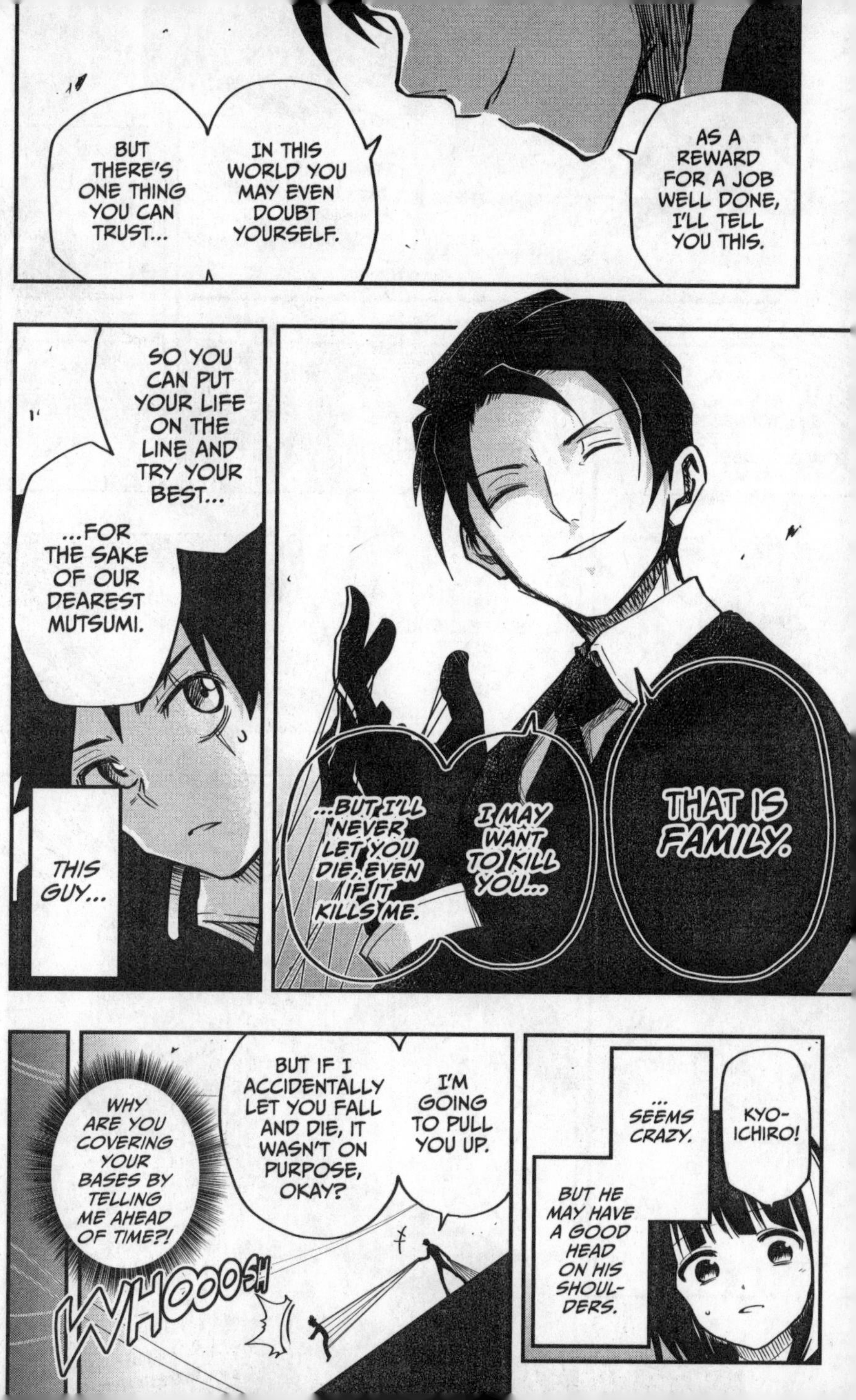
AS A REWARD FOR A JOB WELL DONE, I'LL TELL YOU THIS.
IN THIS WORLD YOU MAY EVEN DOUBT YOURSELF.
BUT THERE'S ONE THING YOU CAN TRUST...
THAT IS FAMILY.
I MAY WANT TO KILL YOU...
...BUT I'LL NEVER LET YOU DIE, EVEN IF IT KILLS ME.
SO YOU CAN PUT YOUR LIFE ON THE LINE AND TRY YOUR BEST...
...FOR THE SAKE OF OUR DEAREST MUTSUMI.
THIS GUY...
KYO-ICHIRO!
...SEEMS CRAZY.
BUT HE MAY HAVE A GOOD HEAD ON HIS SHOUL-DERS.
I'M GOING TO PULL YOU UP.
BUT IF I ACCIDENTALLY LET YOU FALL AND DIE, IT WASN'T ON PURPOSE, OKAY?
WHY ARE YOU COVERING YOUR BASES BY TELLING ME AHEAD OF TIME?!
WHOOOOSH

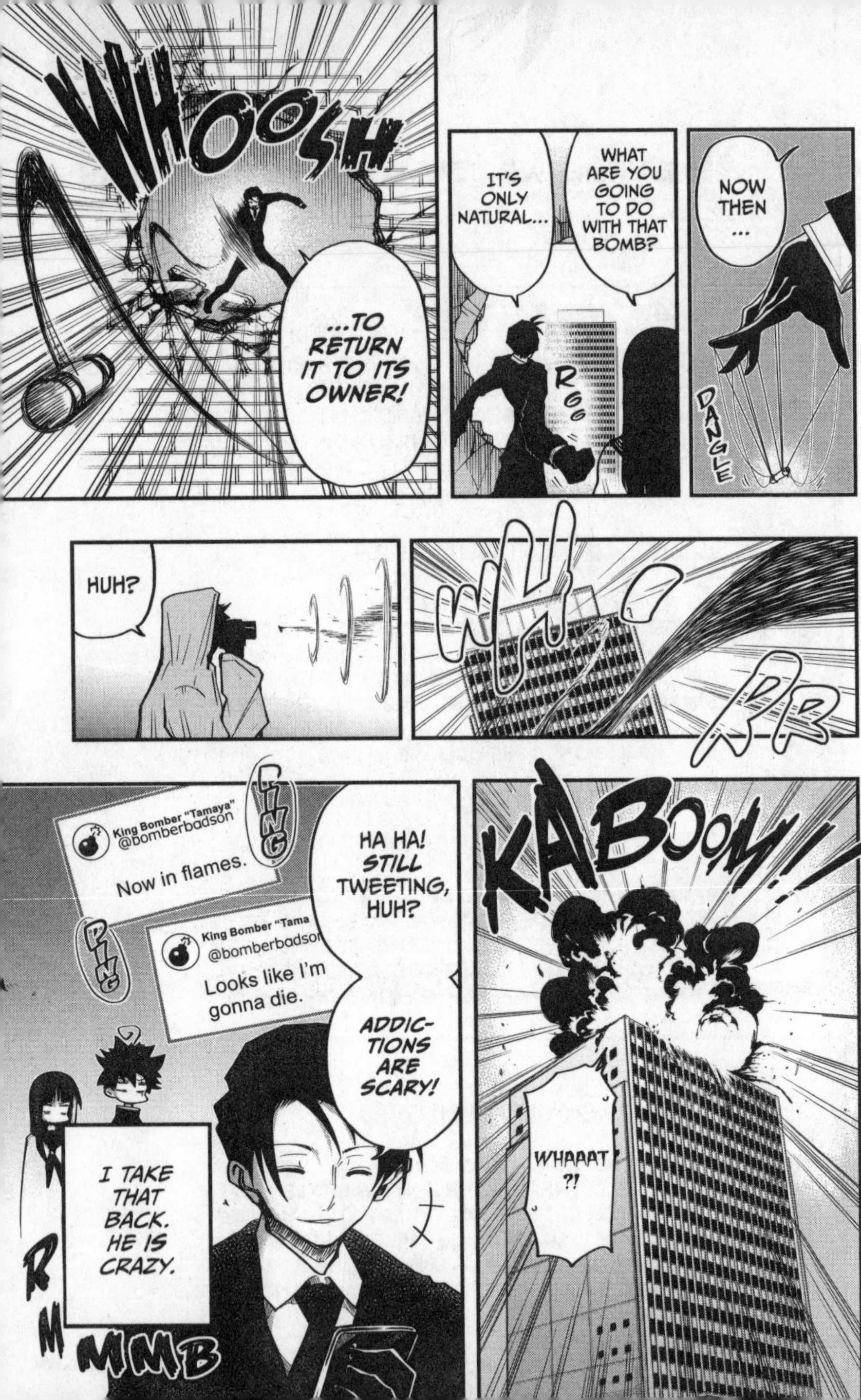
NOW THEN ...
DANGLE
WHAT ARE YOU GOING TO DO WITH THAT BOMB?
IT'S ONLY NATURAL...
RGG
WHOOSH
...TO RETURN IT TO ITS OWNER!
WH
RR
HUH?
KABOOM!!
WHAAAT?!
King Bomber "Tamaya" @bomberbadson
Now in flames.
PING
King Bomber "Tama
@bomberbadson
Looks like I'm gonna die.
PING
HA HA! STILL TWEETING, HUH?
ADDICTIONS ARE SCARY!
I TAKE THAT BACK. HE IS CRAZY.
R M MMB

THE UNDERWORLD'S SOCIAL MEDIA ADDICTS

KING BOMBER "TAMAYA"

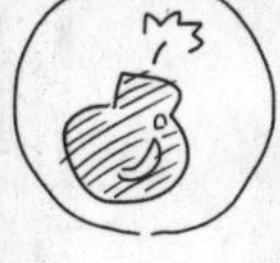

SERIAL BOMBER. CAN DO ANYTHING FROM ASSASSINATIONS TO MAKING FIREWORKS. HE'S BUSY WITH FIREWORK SHOWS DURING THE SUMMER. IT IS SAID THAT COUPLES WHO SEE TAMAYA'S FIREWORKS WILL BLOW UP HAPPILY EVER AFTERWARD.

COVER-UP HEADQUARTERS

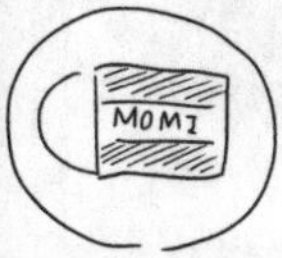
MOMI

HE WILL STUB OUT ANYTHING FROM CIGARETTE BUTTS TO STATE SECRET DOCUMENTS. WHEN HE WAS A STUDENT, HE LOANED A BRAND-NEW ERASER TO MR. A, WHO ENDED UP USING EVERY SINGLE CORNER. HIS RAGE WAS SO GREAT THAT HE WANTED TO ERASE MR. A FROM SOCIETY, THEREBY STUMBLING ONTO HIS CALLING IN LIFE.

ESCAPE MAN (INCARCERATED)

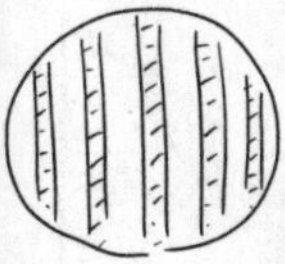

BACK WHEN HE USED TO BE A RESPECTABLE MEMBER OF SOCIETY, HE WAS AN ESCAPE ARTIST. THE SUFFIX OF HIS INTERNET HANDLE CHANGES ACCORDING TO HIS CURRENT STATUS—(ESCAPED), (GOING TO TURN HIMSELF IN), (ON A DIET), ETC.

KYOICHIRO (MUTSUMILOVE)

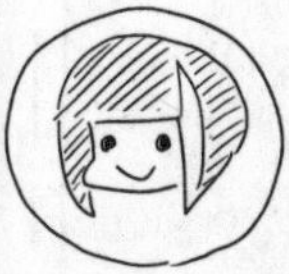

A GROSS ACCOUNT THAT CONSTANTLY GOES ON ABOUT ITS OWNER'S LOVE FOR HIS LITTLE SISTER. IT'S SO NAUSEATING THAT IT REPEATEDLY STIRS UP A FLAME WAR, CAUSING THE OWNER TO GO ON A REVENGE SPREE AGAINST THOSE WHO SEND HIM HATEFUL REPLIES. HIS TOLERANCE FOR PROVOCATION IS LOW.

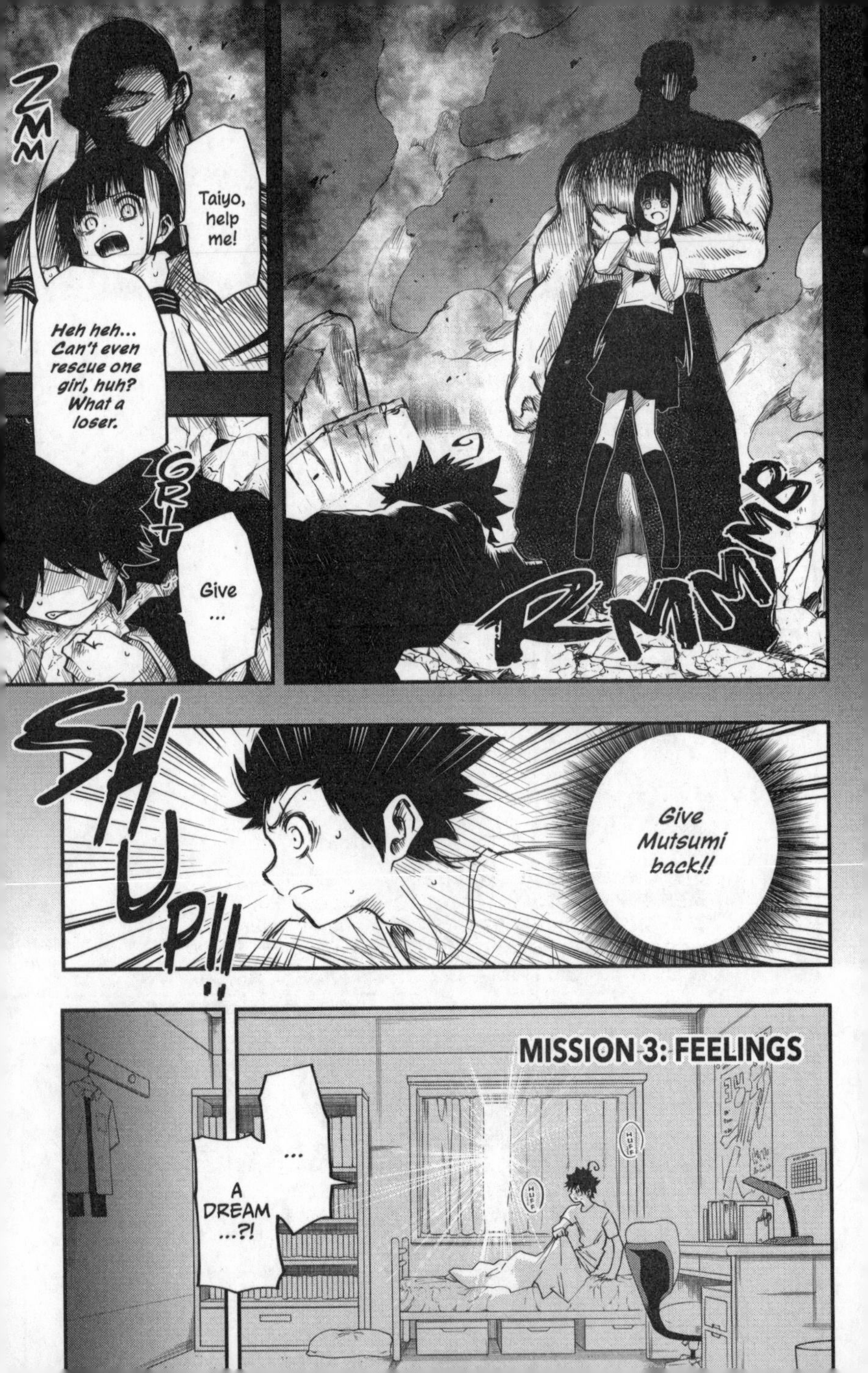
RMMMB
Taiyo, help me!
Heh heh... Can't even rescue one girl, huh? What a loser.
ZMM
GRIT
Give...
Give Mutsumi back!!
SHUP!!
MISSION 3: FEELINGS
HUFF
HUFF
...
A DREAM ...?!

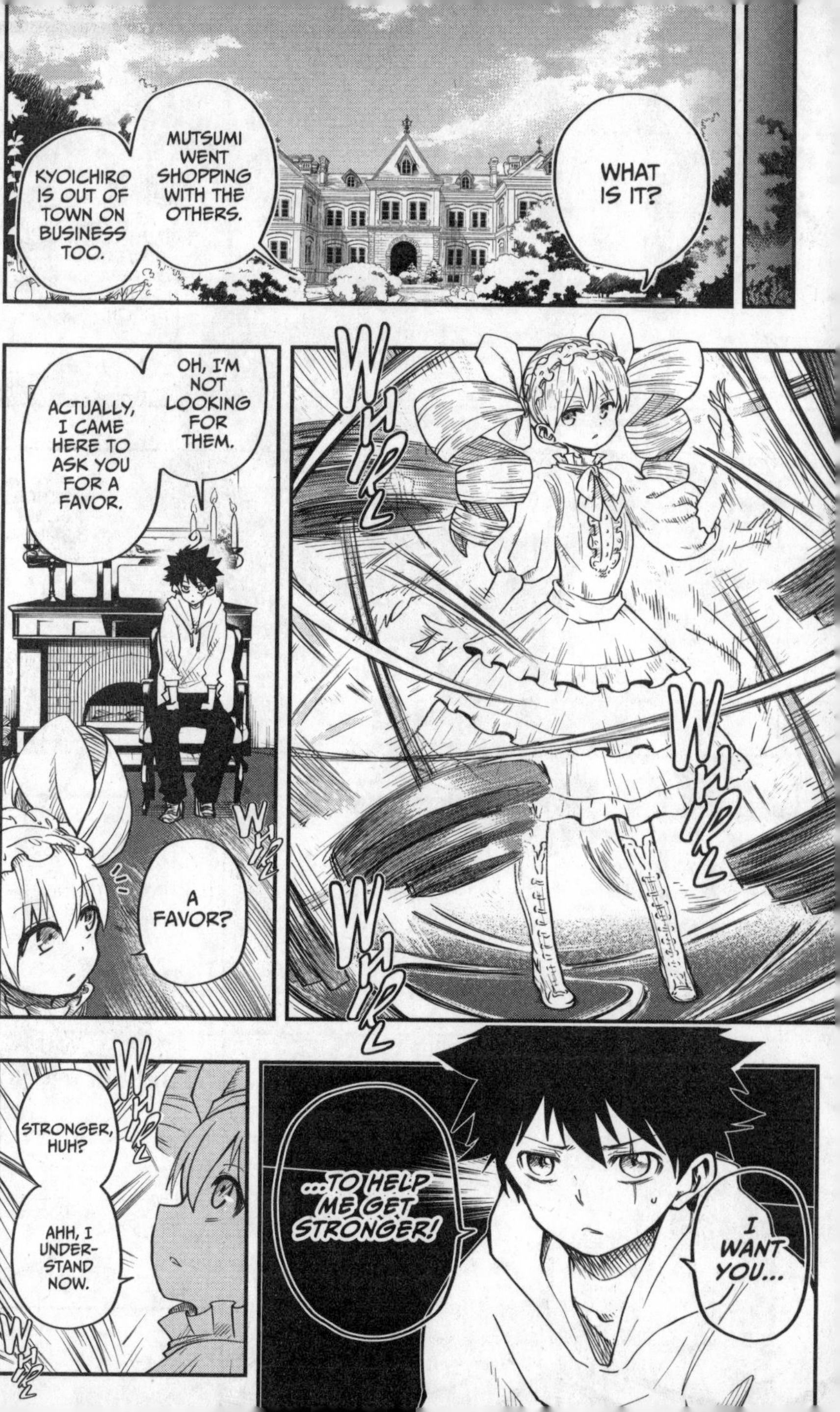
WHAT IS IT?
MUTSUMI WENT SHOPPING WITH THE OTHERS.
KYOICHIRO IS OUT OF TOWN ON BUSINESS TOO.
WHIRL
WHIRL
WHIRL
OH, I'M NOT LOOKING FOR THEM.
ACTUALLY, I CAME HERE TO ASK YOU FOR A FAVOR.
A FAVOR?
I WANT YOU...
...TO HELP ME GET STRONGER!
STRONGER, HUH?
AHH, I UNDERSTAND NOW.

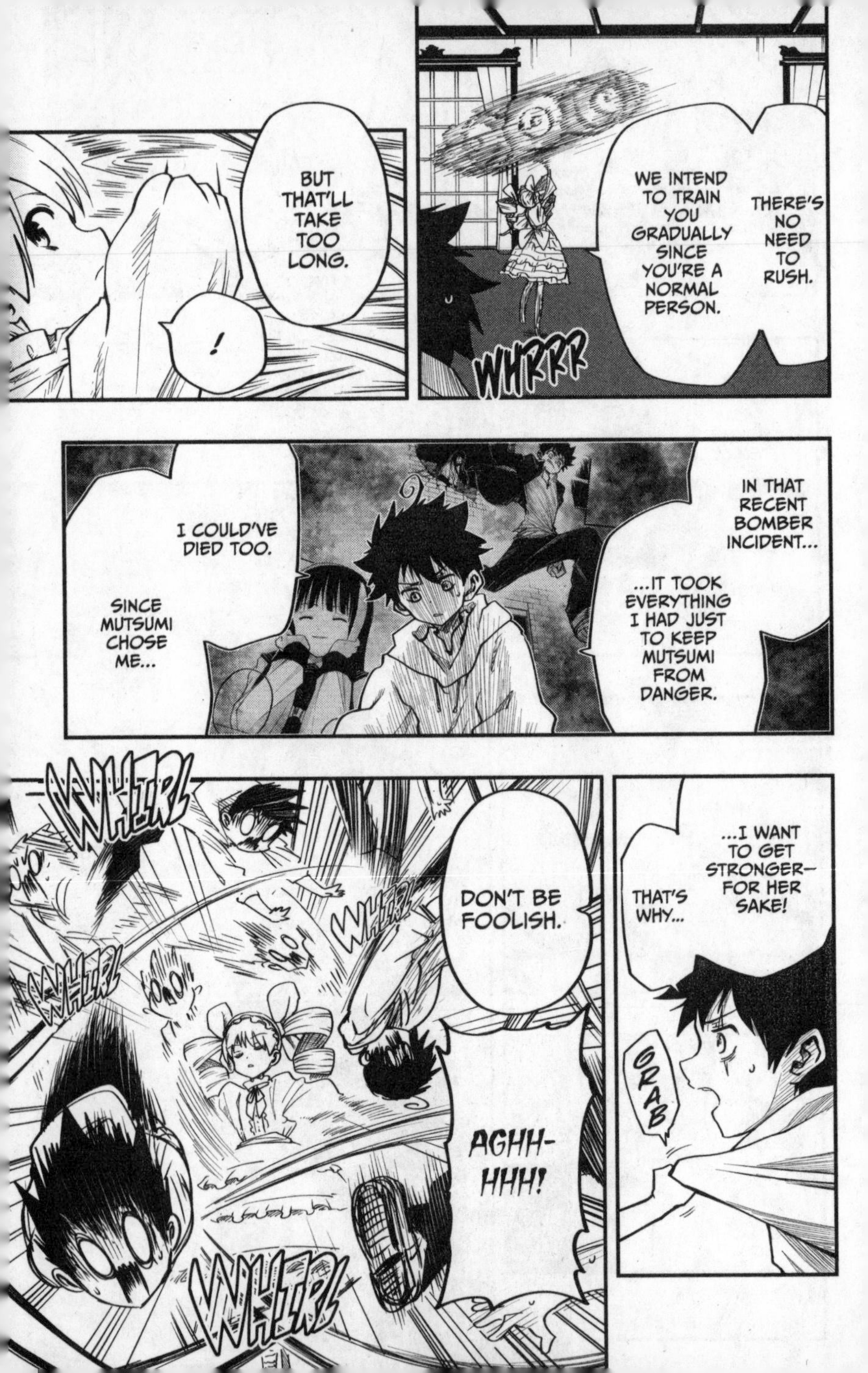
THERE'S NO NEED TO RUSH.
WE INTEND TO TRAIN YOU GRADUALLY SINCE YOU'RE A NORMAL PERSON.
WHRRR
BUT THAT'LL TAKE TOO LONG.
!
IN THAT RECENT BOMBER INCIDENT...
...IT TOOK EVERYTHING I HAD JUST TO KEEP MUTSUMI FROM DANGER.
I COULD'VE DIED TOO.
SINCE MUTSUMI CHOSE ME...
...I WANT TO GET STRONGER— FOR HER SAKE!
THAT'S WHY...
GRAB
DON'T BE FOOLISH.
WHIRL
AGHH-HHH!
WHIRL
WHIRL
WHIRL

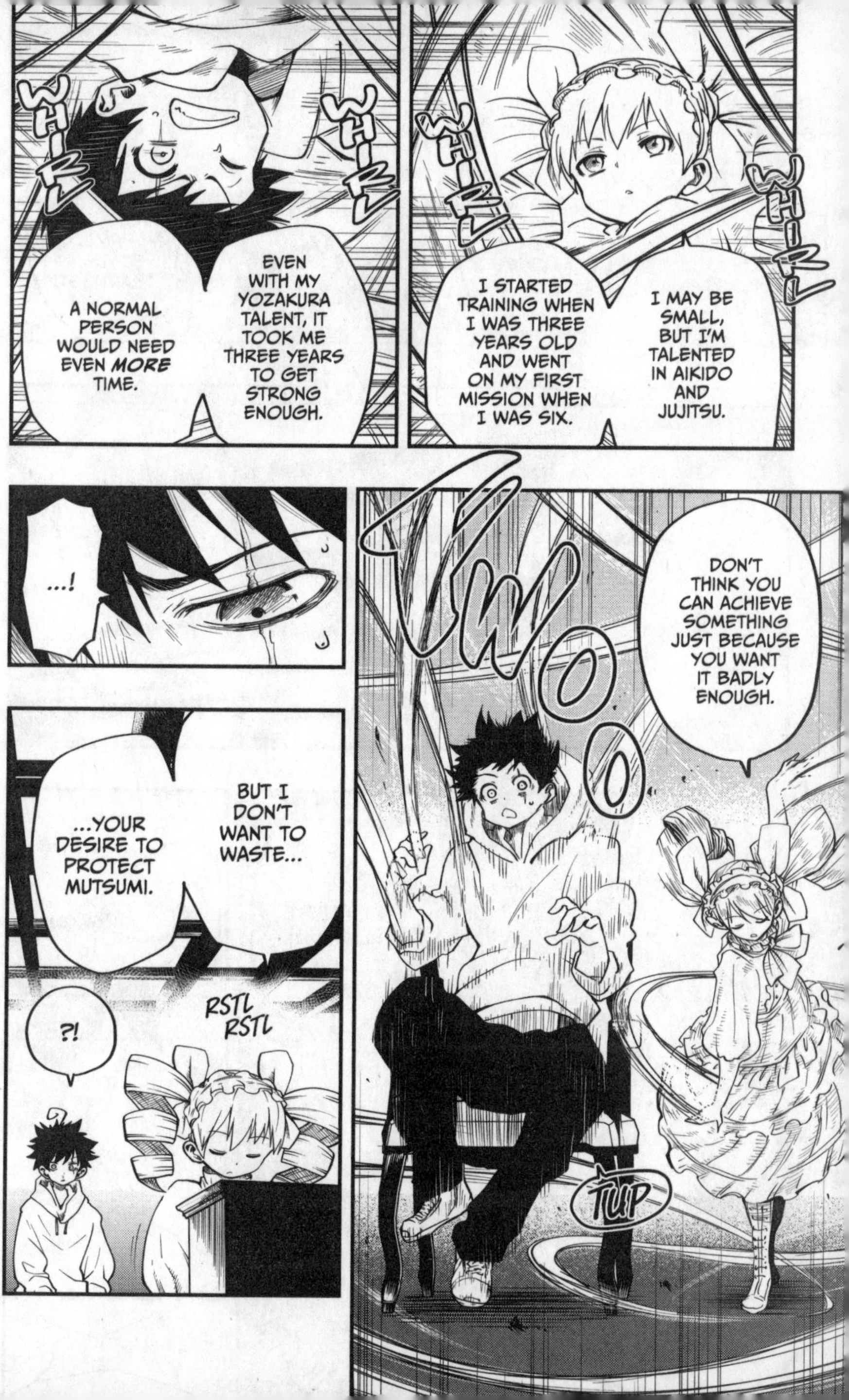
WHIRL
WHIRL
I MAY BE SMALL, BUT I'M TALENTED IN AIKIDO AND JUJITSU.
I STARTED TRAINING WHEN I WAS THREE YEARS OLD AND WENT ON MY FIRST MISSION WHEN I WAS SIX.
WHIRL
WHIRL
EVEN WITH MY YOZAKURA TALENT, IT TOOK ME THREE YEARS TO GET STRONG ENOUGH.
A NORMAL PERSON WOULD NEED EVEN *MORE* TIME.
DON'T THINK YOU CAN ACHIEVE SOMETHING JUST BECAUSE YOU WANT IT BADLY ENOUGH.
WHOOO
TUP
...!
BUT I DON'T WANT TO WASTE...
...YOUR DESIRE TO PROTECT MUTSUMI.
RSTL RSTL
?!

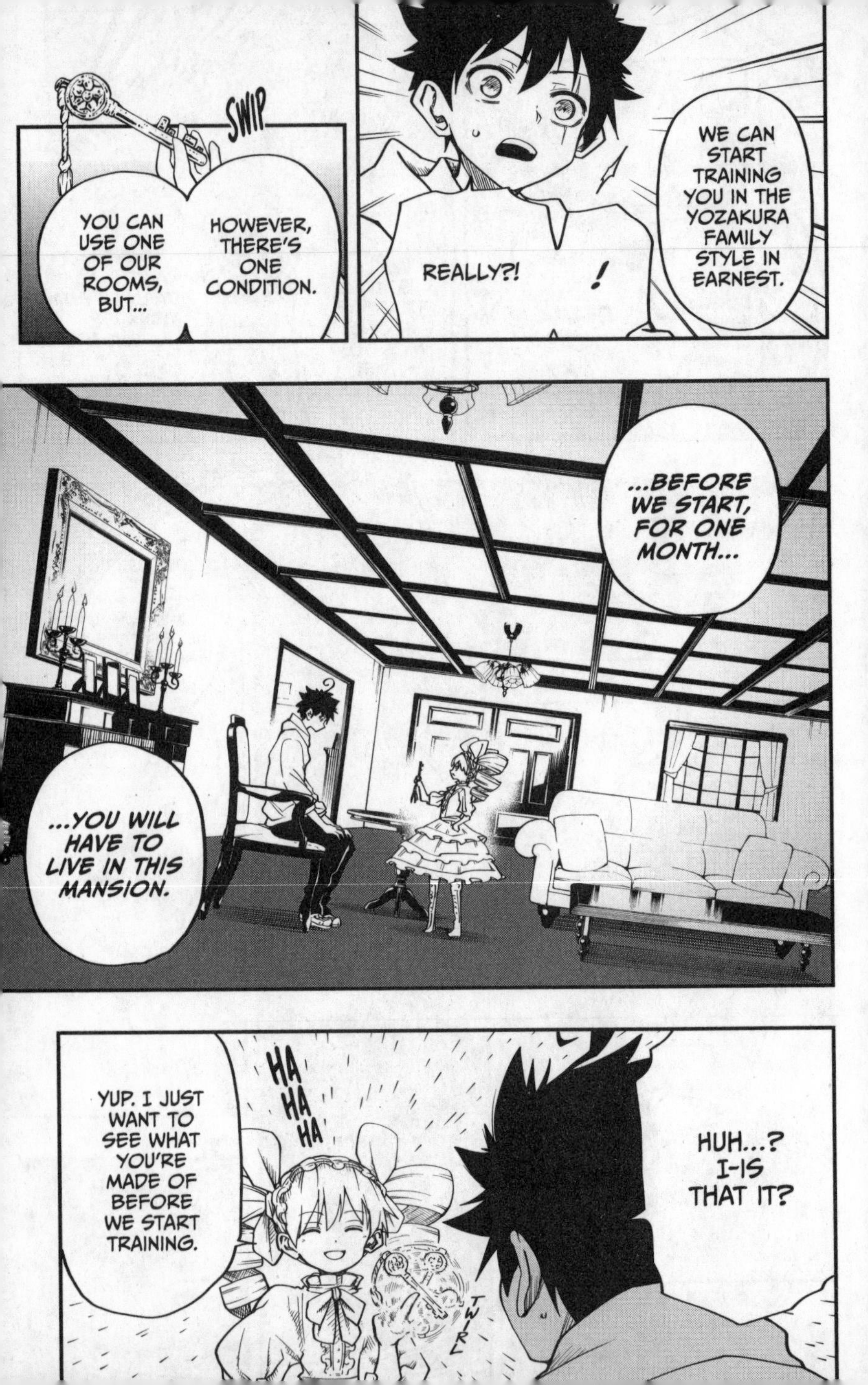
WE CAN START TRAINING YOU IN THE YOZAKURA FAMILY STYLE IN EARNEST.
!
REALLY?!
SWIP
HOWEVER, THERE'S ONE CONDITION.
YOU CAN USE ONE OF OUR ROOMS, BUT...
...BEFORE WE START, FOR ONE MONTH...
...YOU WILL HAVE TO LIVE IN THIS MANSION.
HUH...? I-IS THAT IT?
HA HA HA HA
YUP. I JUST WANT TO SEE WHAT YOU'RE MADE OF BEFORE WE START TRAINING.
TWIRL

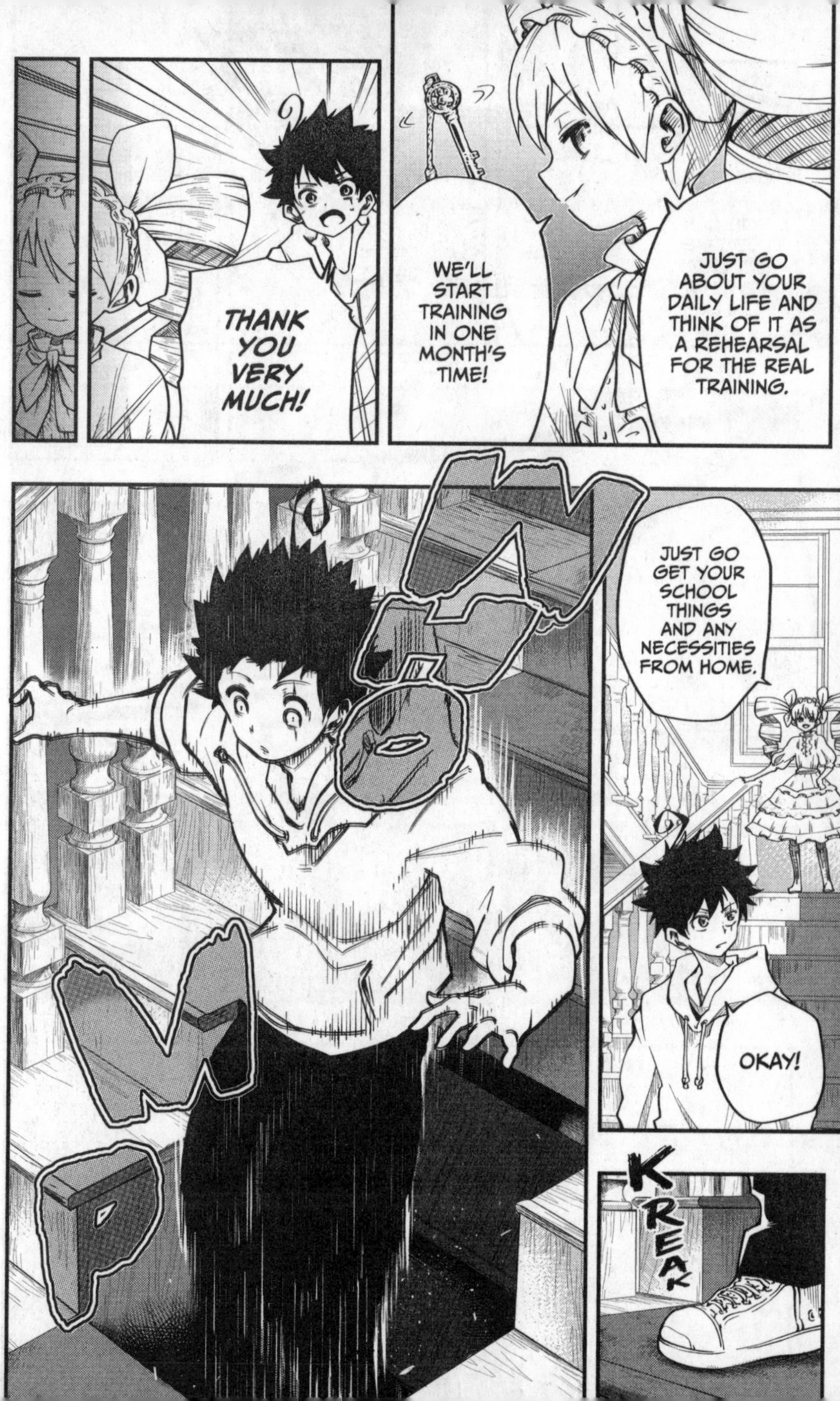
JUST GO ABOUT YOUR DAILY LIFE AND THINK OF IT AS A REHEARSAL FOR THE REAL TRAINING.
WE'LL START TRAINING IN ONE MONTH'S TIME!
THANK YOU VERY MUCH!
JUST GO GET YOUR SCHOOL THINGS AND ANY NECESSITIES FROM HOME.
OKAY!
KREAK

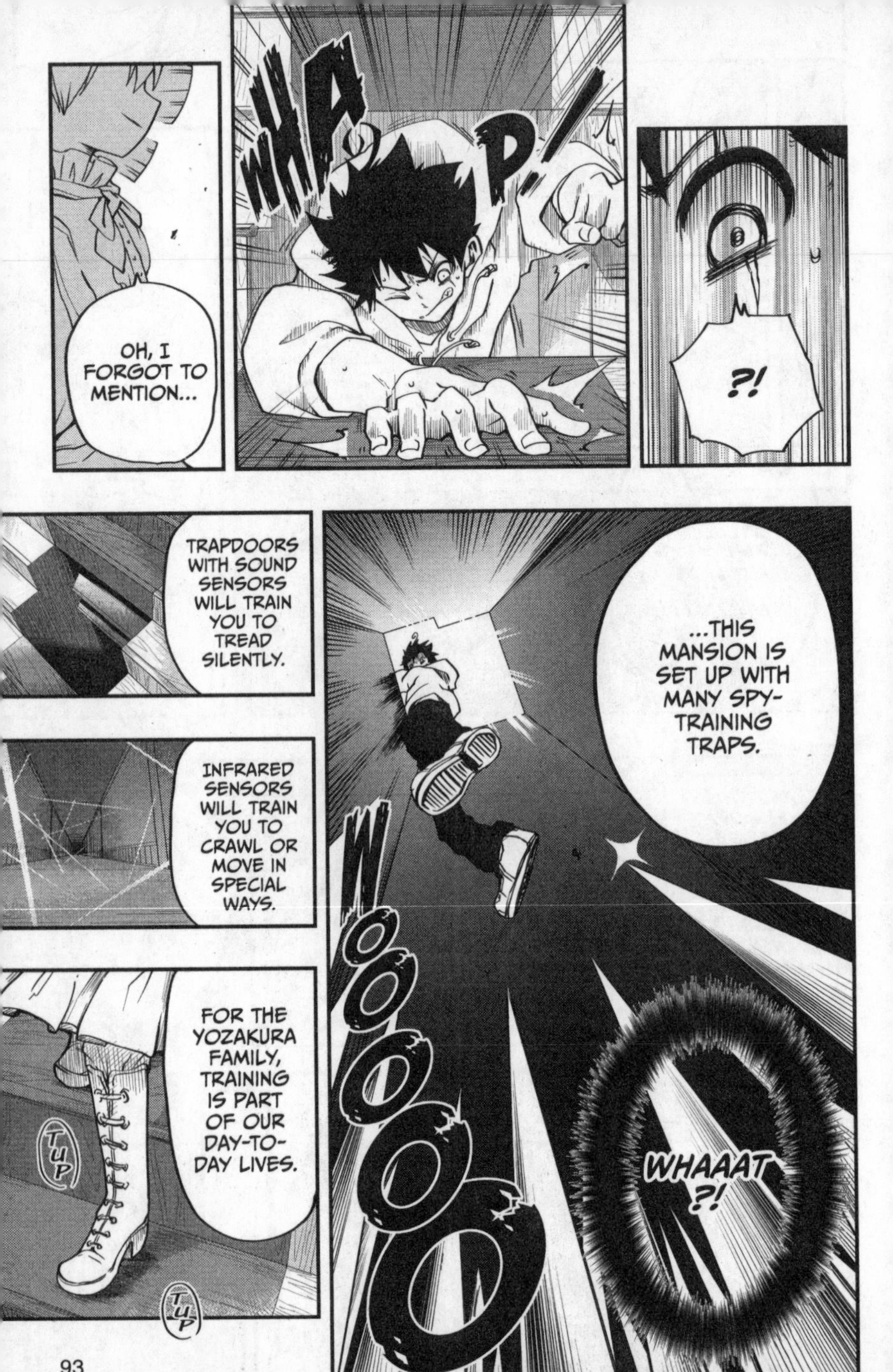
?!
WHAP!
OH, I FORGOT TO MENTION...
...THIS MANSION IS SET UP WITH MANY SPY-TRAINING TRAPS.
WOOOOO
WHAAAT?!
TRAPDOORS WITH SOUND SENSORS WILL TRAIN YOU TO TREAD SILENTLY.
INFRARED SENSORS WILL TRAIN YOU TO CRAWL OR MOVE IN SPECIAL WAYS.
FOR THE YOZAKURA FAMILY, TRAINING IS PART OF OUR DAY-TO-DAY LIVES.
TUP
TUP

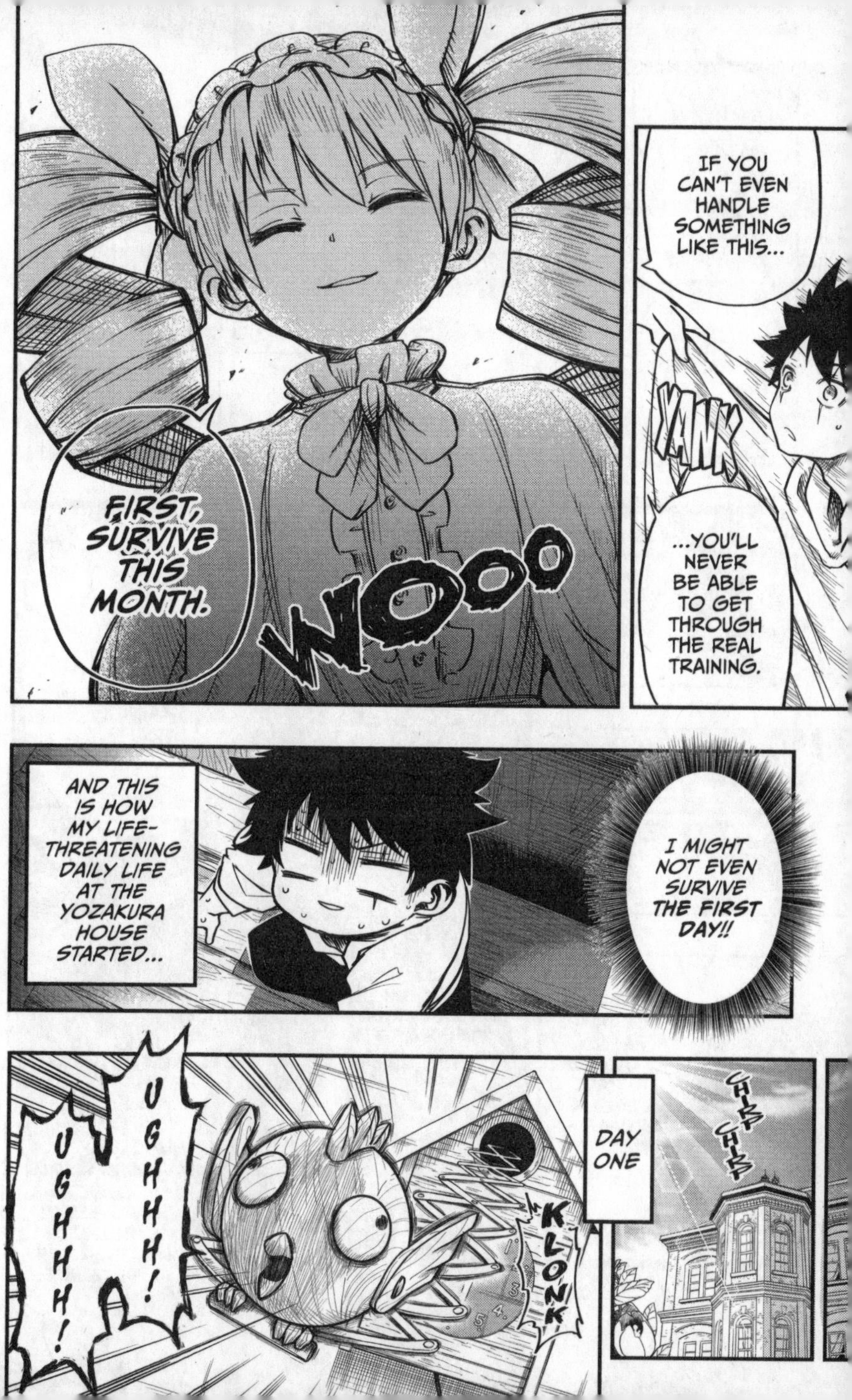
IF YOU CAN'T EVEN HANDLE SOMETHING LIKE THIS...
YANK
...YOU'LL NEVER BE ABLE TO GET THROUGH THE REAL TRAINING.
FIRST, SURVIVE THIS MONTH.
WOOO
I MIGHT NOT EVEN SURVIVE THE FIRST DAY!!
AND THIS IS HOW MY LIFE-THREATENING DAILY LIFE AT THE YOZAKURA HOUSE STARTED...
CHIRP CHIRP
DAY ONE
UGHHH!
UGHHH!
KLONK

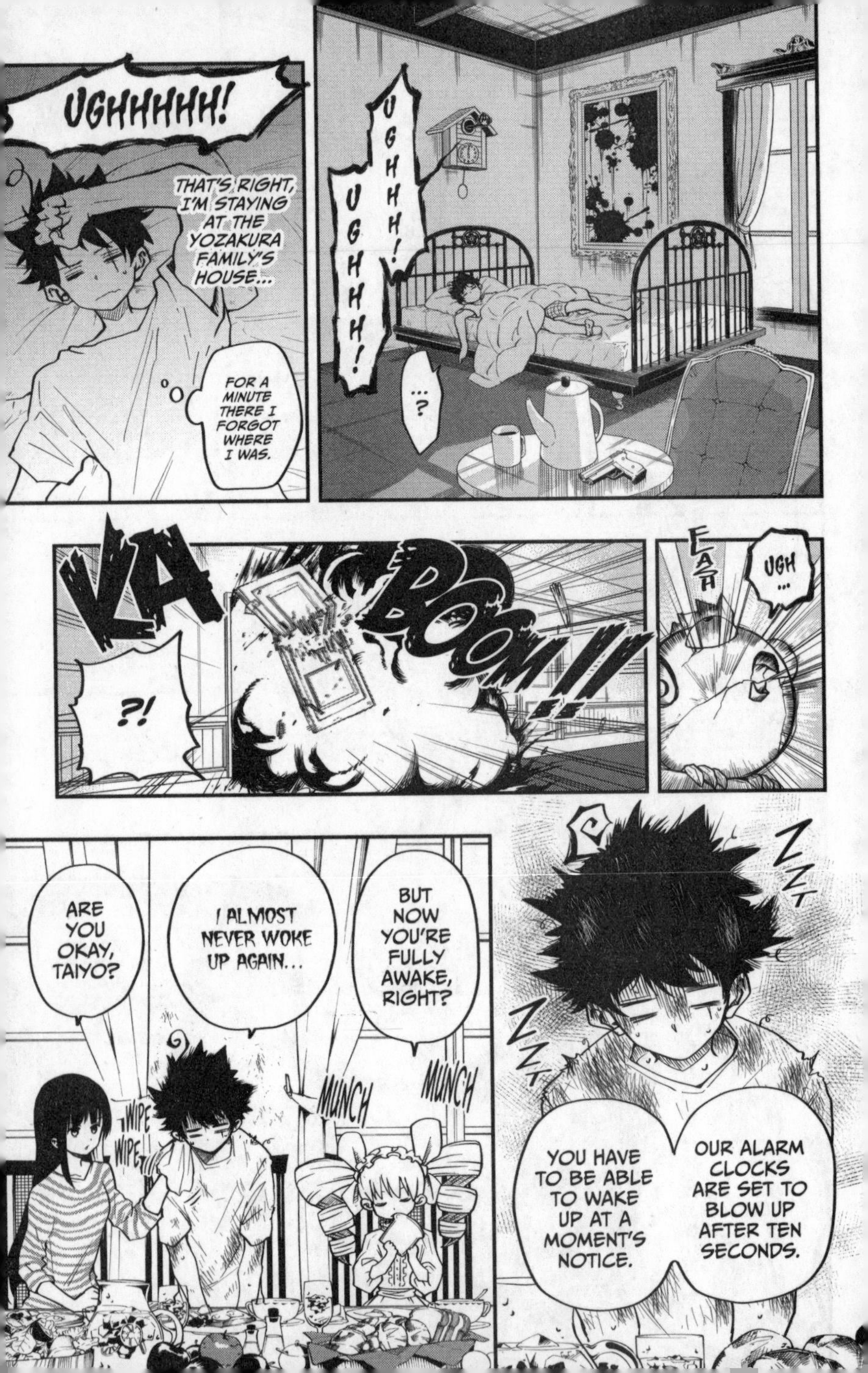
UGHHH!
UGHHHH!
...?
UGHHHHH!
THAT'S RIGHT, I'M STAYING AT THE YOZAKURA FAMILY'S HOUSE...
FOR A MINUTE THERE I FORGOT WHERE I WAS.
FLASH
UGH ...
KA BOOM!!
?!
ZZZ
OUR ALARM CLOCKS ARE SET TO BLOW UP AFTER TEN SECONDS.
YOU HAVE TO BE ABLE TO WAKE UP AT A MOMENT'S NOTICE.
ZZZ
BUT NOW YOU'RE FULLY AWAKE, RIGHT?
MUNCH
MUNCH
I ALMOST NEVER WOKE UP AGAIN...
ARE YOU OKAY, TAIYO?
WIPE
WIPE

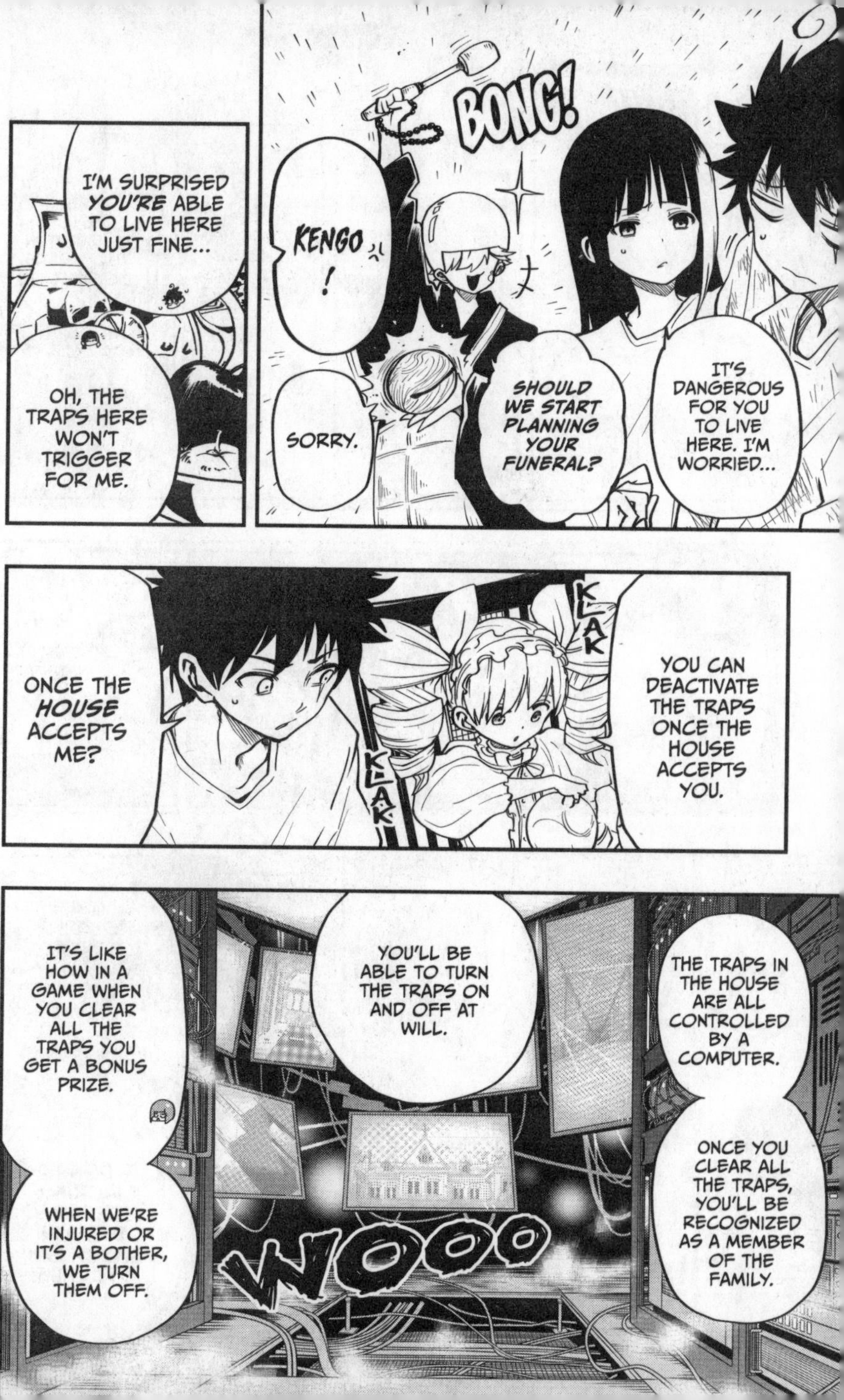
BONG!
IT'S DANGEROUS FOR YOU TO LIVE HERE. I'M WORRIED...
SHOULD WE START PLANNING YOUR FUNERAL?
KENGO!
SORRY.
I'M SURPRISED *YOU'RE* ABLE TO LIVE HERE JUST FINE...
OH, THE TRAPS HERE WON'T TRIGGER FOR ME.
YOU CAN DEACTIVATE THE TRAPS ONCE THE HOUSE ACCEPTS YOU.
KLAK
KLAK
ONCE THE *HOUSE* ACCEPTS ME?
THE TRAPS IN THE HOUSE ARE ALL CONTROLLED BY A COMPUTER.
ONCE YOU CLEAR ALL THE TRAPS, YOU'LL BE RECOGNIZED AS A MEMBER OF THE FAMILY.
YOU'LL BE ABLE TO TURN THE TRAPS ON AND OFF AT WILL.
WOOO
IT'S LIKE HOW IN A GAME WHEN YOU CLEAR ALL THE TRAPS YOU GET A BONUS PRIZE.
WHEN WE'RE INJURED OR IT'S A BOTHER, WE TURN THEM OFF.

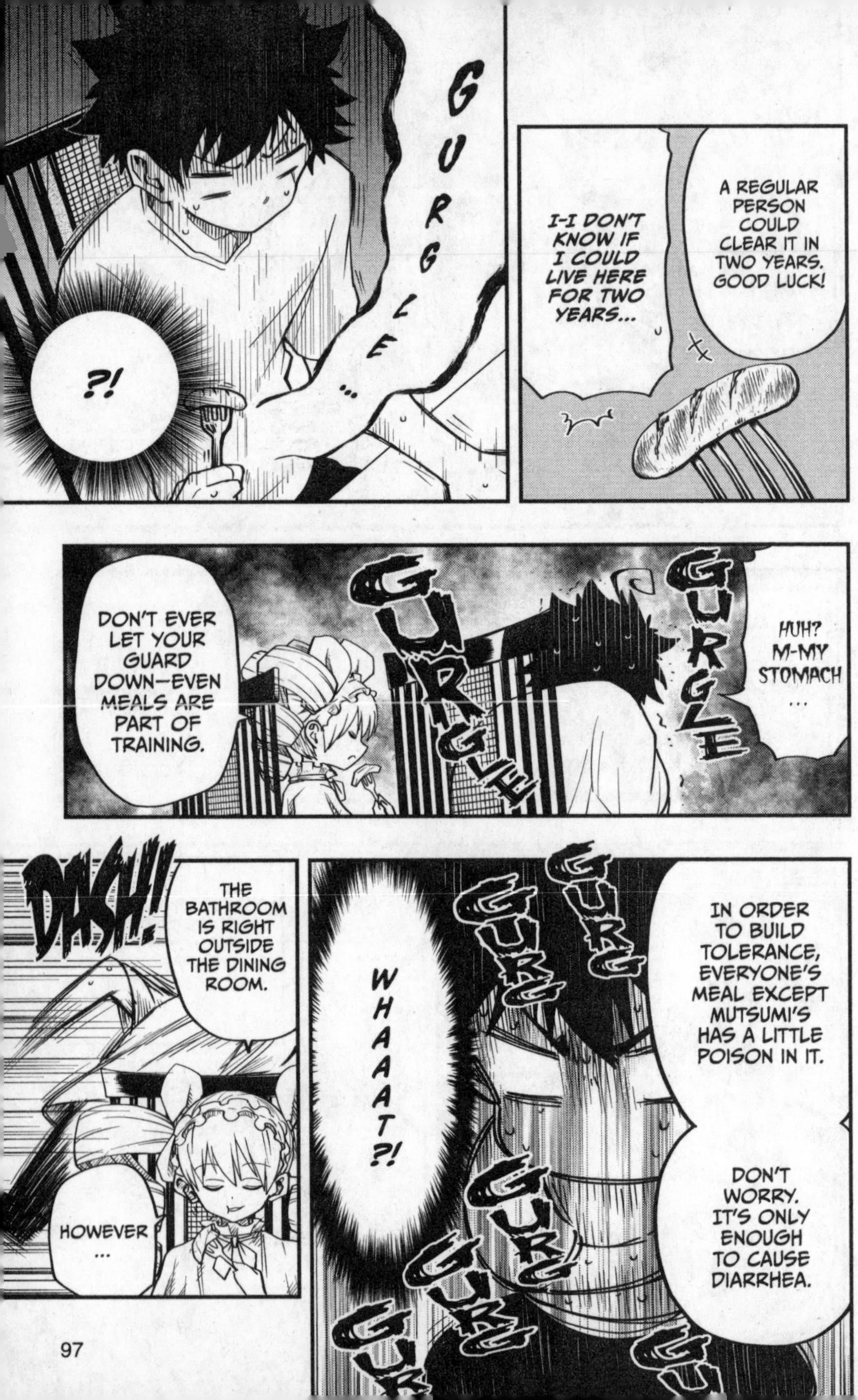

A REGULAR PERSON COULD CLEAR IT IN TWO YEARS. GOOD LUCK!
I-I DON'T KNOW IF I COULD LIVE HERE FOR TWO YEARS...
GURGLE...
?!
HUH? M-MY STOMACH...
GURGLE
GURGLE
DON'T EVER LET YOUR GUARD DOWN—EVEN MEALS ARE PART OF TRAINING.
IN ORDER TO BUILD TOLERANCE, EVERYONE'S MEAL EXCEPT MUTSUMI'S HAS A LITTLE POISON IN IT.
GURG GURG
WHAAAAT?!
DON'T WORRY. IT'S ONLY ENOUGH TO CAUSE DIARRHEA.
GURG GURG
THE BATHROOM IS RIGHT OUTSIDE THE DINING ROOM.
DASH!
HOWEVER...

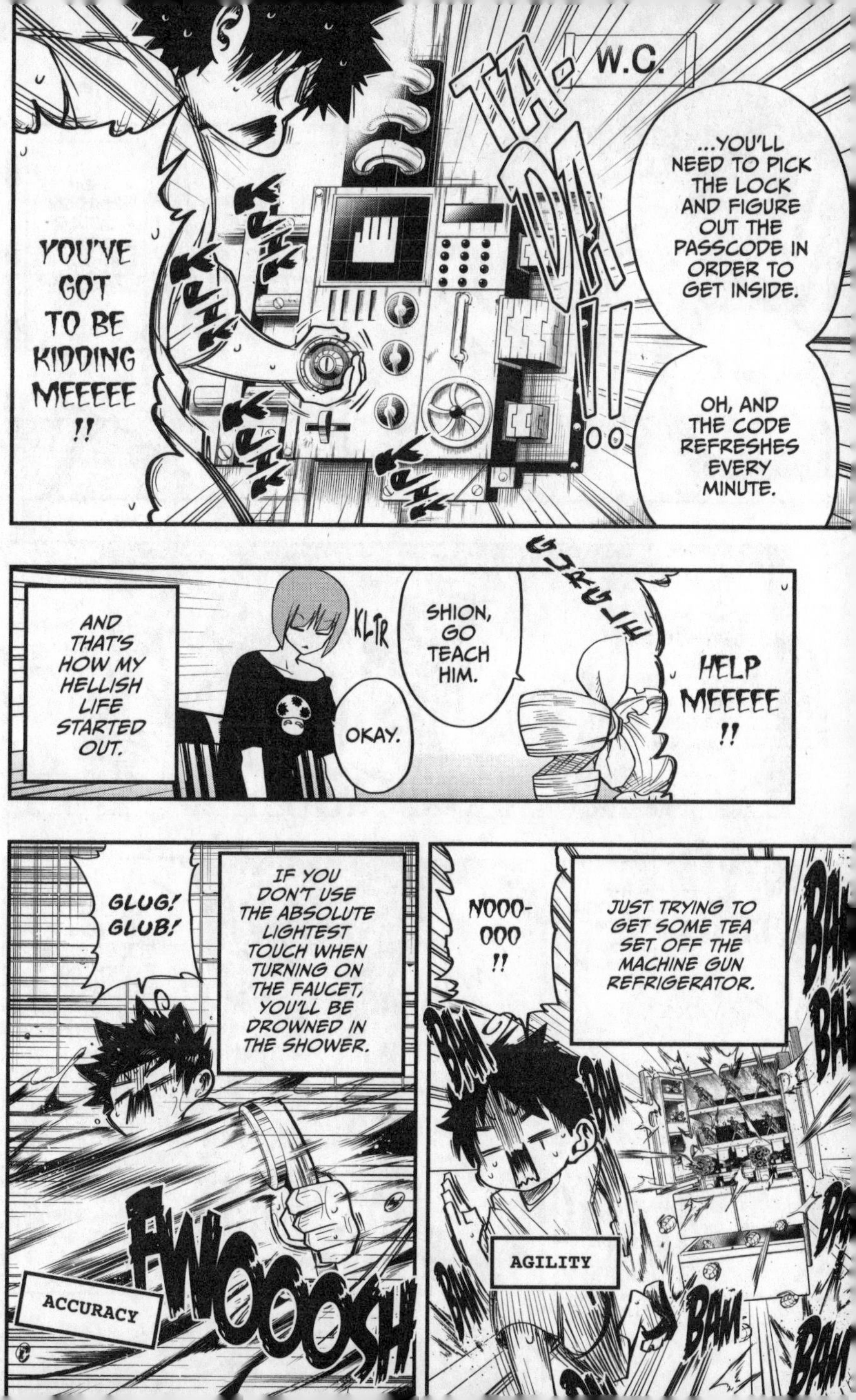
W.C.
...YOU'LL NEED TO PICK THE LOCK AND FIGURE OUT THE PASSCODE IN ORDER TO GET INSIDE.
OH, AND THE CODE REFRESHES EVERY MINUTE.
TA-DA!!
YOU'VE GOT TO BE KIDDING MEEEEE!!
GURGLE
HELP MEEEEE!!
SHION, GO TEACH HIM.
KLTR
OKAY.
AND THAT'S HOW MY HELLISH LIFE STARTED OUT.
JUST TRYING TO GET SOME TEA SET OFF THE MACHINE GUN REFRIGERATOR.
NOOO-OOO!!
BAM
AGILITY
IF YOU DON'T USE THE ABSOLUTE LIGHTEST TOUCH WHEN TURNING ON THE FAUCET, YOU'LL BE DROWNED IN THE SHOWER.
GLUG! GLUB!
WOOOSH
ACCURACY

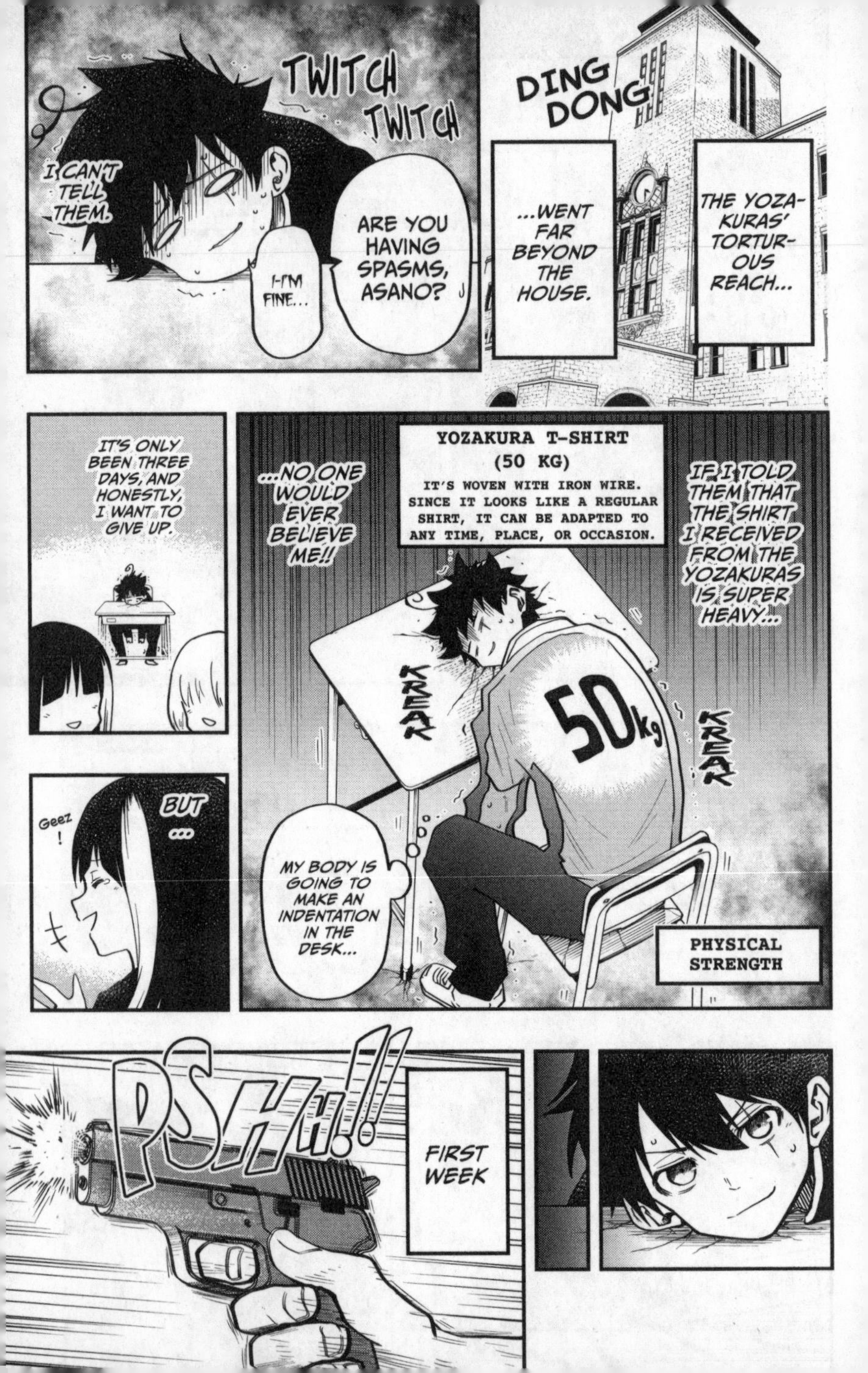
DING DONG
THE YOZAKURAS' TORTUROUS REACH...
...WENT FAR BEYOND THE HOUSE.
TWITCH TWITCH
ARE YOU HAVING SPASMS, ASANO?
I-I'M FINE...
I CAN'T TELL THEM.
IF I TOLD THEM THAT THE SHIRT I RECEIVED FROM THE YOZAKURAS IS SUPER HEAVY...
YOZAKURA T-SHIRT
(50 KG)
IT'S WOVEN WITH IRON WIRE. SINCE IT LOOKS LIKE A REGULAR SHIRT, IT CAN BE ADAPTED TO ANY TIME, PLACE, OR OCCASION.
...NO ONE WOULD EVER BELIEVE ME!!
KREAK
50kg
KREAK
MY BODY IS GOING TO MAKE AN INDENTATION IN THE DESK...
PHYSICAL STRENGTH
IT'S ONLY BEEN THREE DAYS, AND HONESTLY, I WANT TO GIVE UP.
BUT...
Geez!
FIRST WEEK
PSHH!!

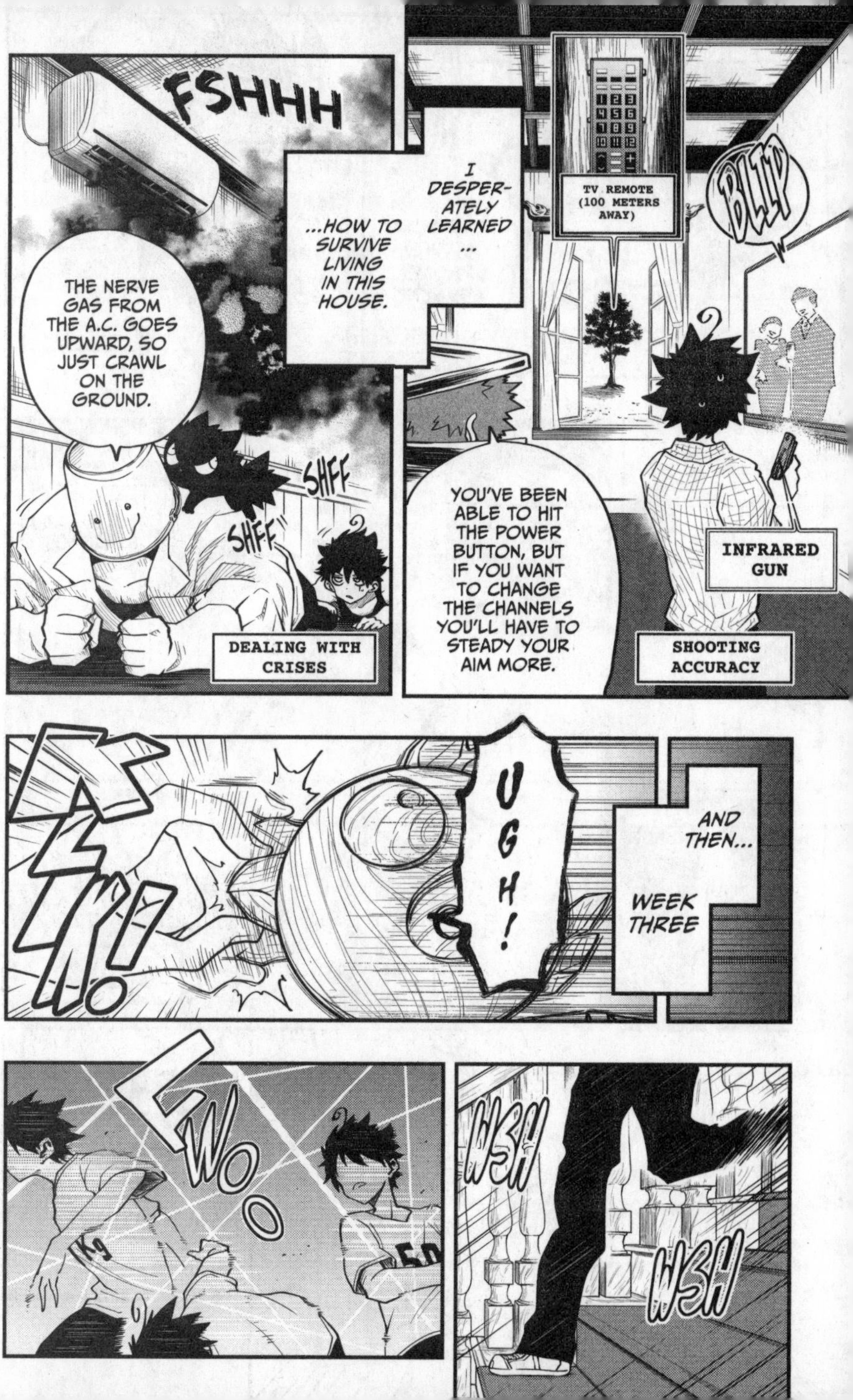

I DESPERATELY LEARNED...
...HOW TO SURVIVE LIVING IN THIS HOUSE.
TV REMOTE (100 METERS AWAY)
BLIP
YOU'VE BEEN ABLE TO HIT THE POWER BUTTON, BUT IF YOU WANT TO CHANGE THE CHANNELS YOU'LL HAVE TO STEADY YOUR AIM MORE.
INFRARED GUN
SHOOTING ACCURACY
FSHHH
THE NERVE GAS FROM THE A.C. GOES UPWARD, SO JUST CRAWL ON THE GROUND.
SHFF
SHFF
DEALING WITH CRISES
AND THEN...
WEEK THREE
UGH!
WSH
WSH
FWOO

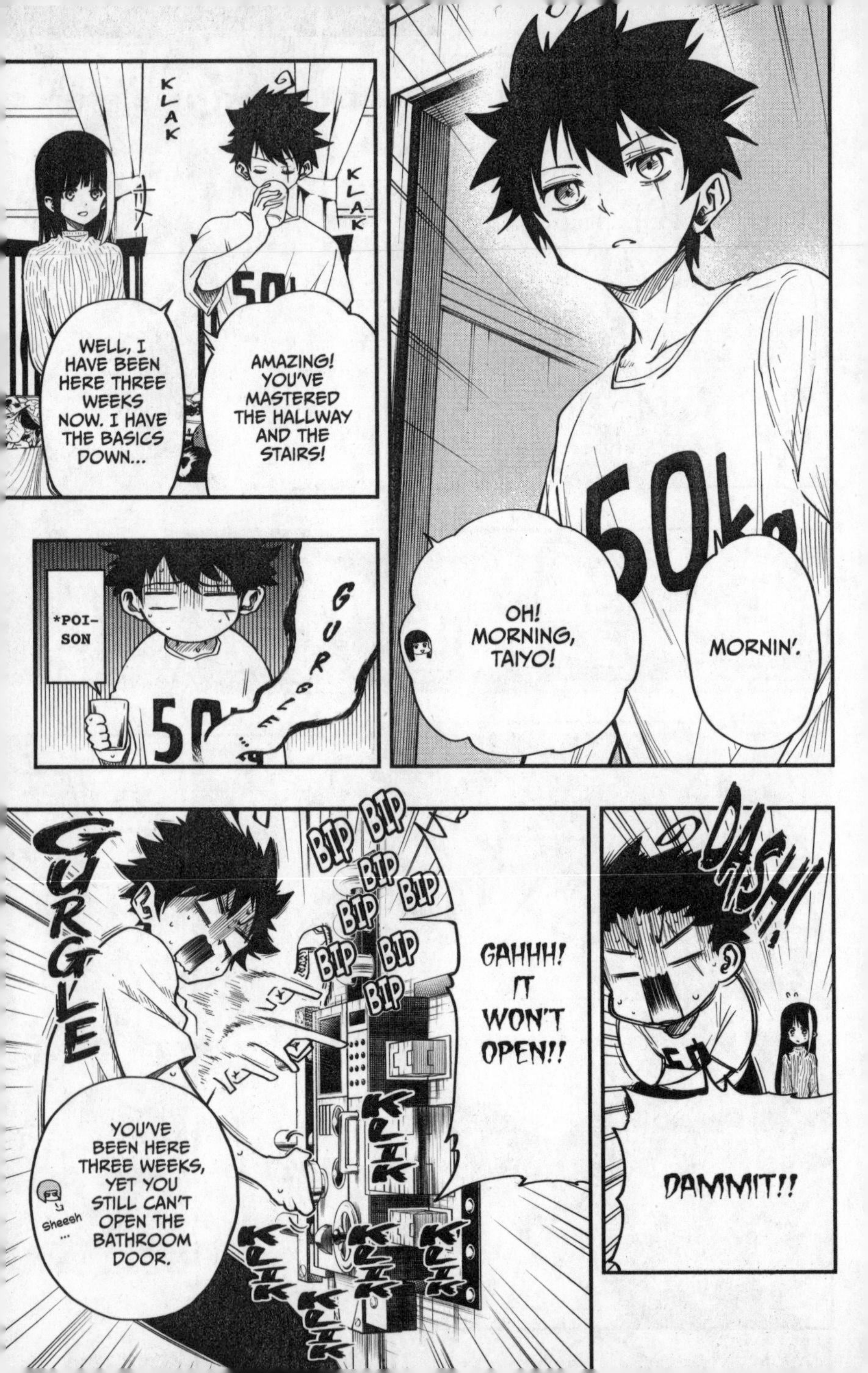
MORNIN'.
OH! MORNING, TAIYO!
KLAK KLAK
AMAZING! YOU'VE MASTERED THE HALLWAY AND THE STAIRS!
WELL, I HAVE BEEN HERE THREE WEEKS NOW. I HAVE THE BASICS DOWN...
GURGLE...
*POI-SON
DASH!
DAMMIT!!
BIP BIP BIP BIP BIP BIP BIP BIP
GAHHH! IT WON'T OPEN!!
GURGLE
YOU'VE BEEN HERE THREE WEEKS, YET YOU STILL CAN'T OPEN THE BATHROOM DOOR.
Sheesh...
KLIK KLIK KLIK KLIK KLIK

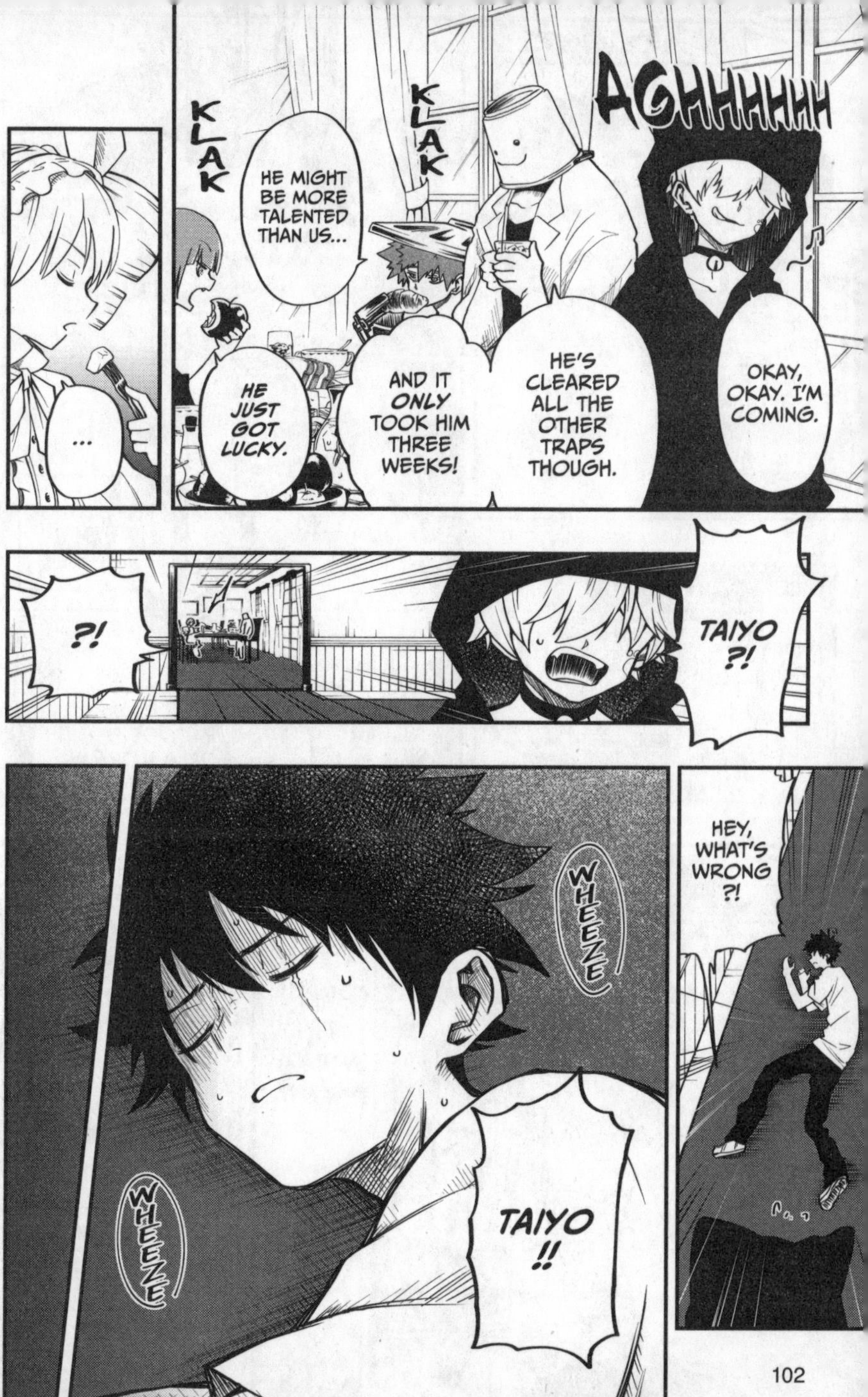

AGHHHHHH
OKAY, OKAY. I'M COMING.
HE'S CLEARED ALL THE OTHER TRAPS THOUGH.
AND IT ONLY TOOK HIM THREE WEEKS!
KLAK
HE MIGHT BE MORE TALENTED THAN US...
KLAK
HE JUST GOT LUCKY.
...
TAIYO ?!
?!
HEY, WHAT'S WRONG ?!
WHEEZE
TAIYO !!
WHEEZE

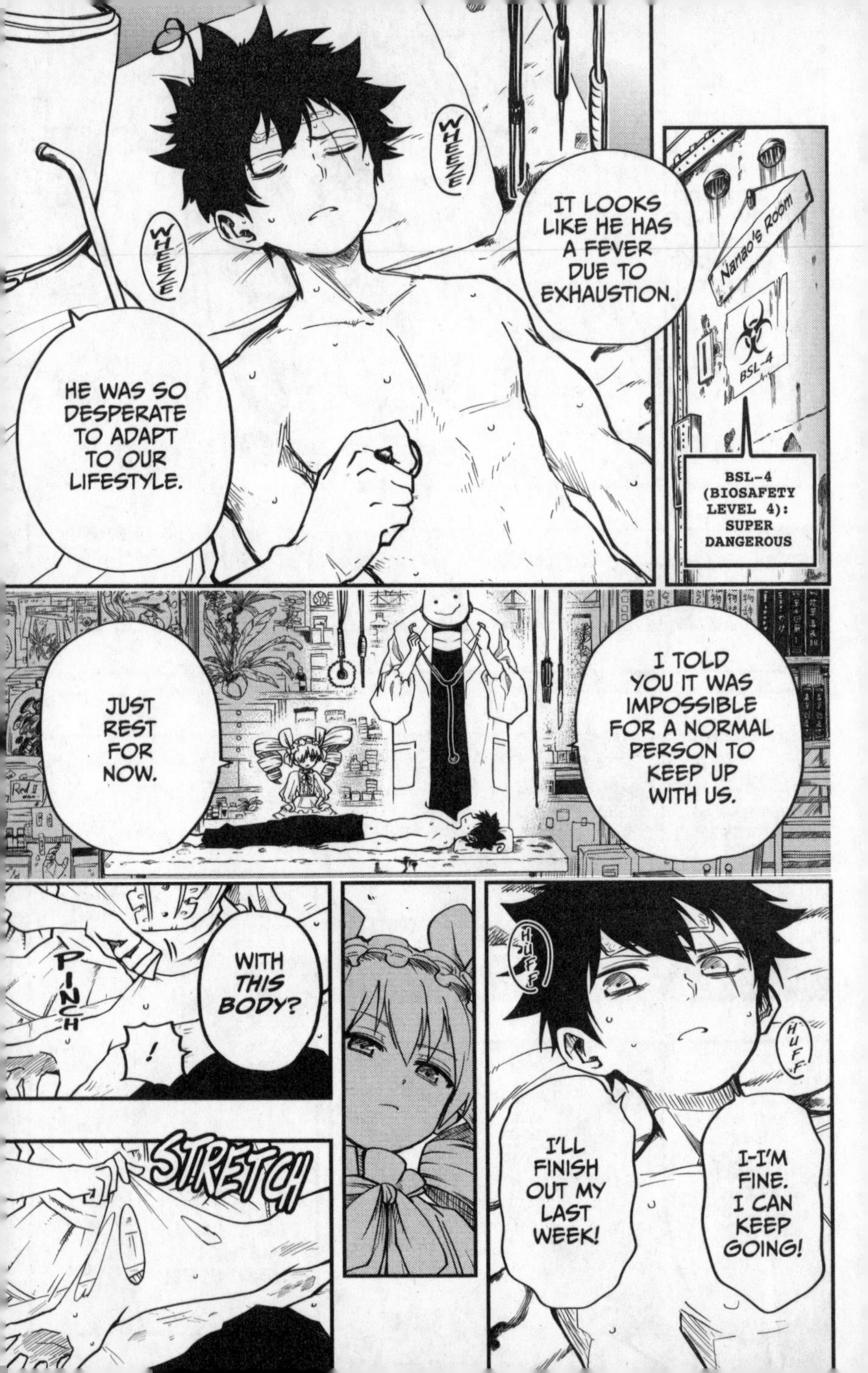
Nanao's Room
BSL-4
BSL-4 (BIOSAFETY LEVEL 4): SUPER DANGEROUS
WHEEZE
WHEEZE
IT LOOKS LIKE HE HAS A FEVER DUE TO EXHAUSTION.
HE WAS SO DESPERATE TO ADAPT TO OUR LIFESTYLE.
I TOLD YOU IT WAS IMPOSSIBLE FOR A NORMAL PERSON TO KEEP UP WITH US.
JUST REST FOR NOW.
HUFF
HUFF
I-I'M FINE. I CAN KEEP GOING!
I'LL FINISH OUT MY LAST WEEK!
WITH THIS BODY?
PINCH
!
STRETCH

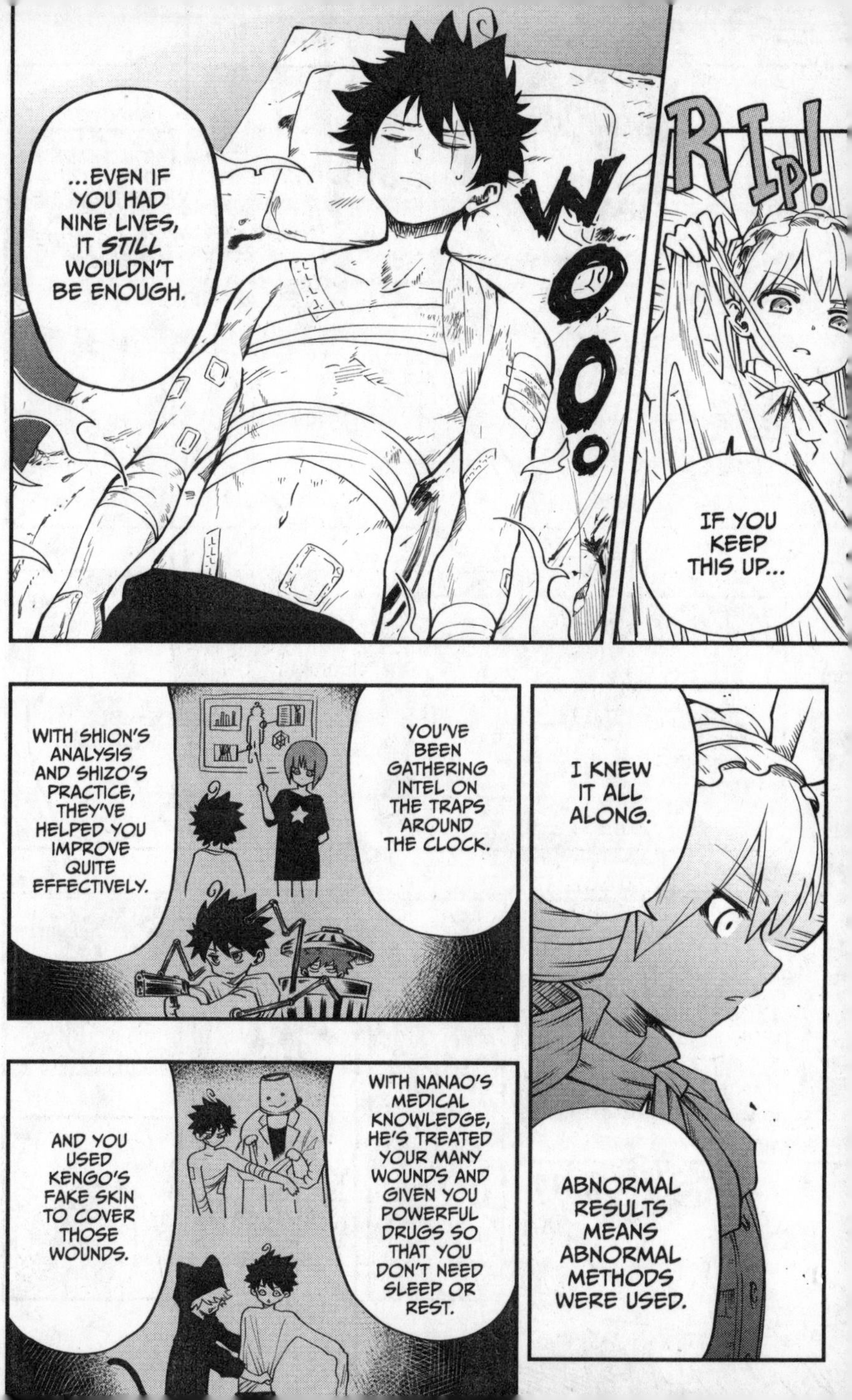
RIP!
IF YOU KEEP THIS UP...
WOOOO
...EVEN IF YOU HAD NINE LIVES, IT *STILL* WOULDN'T BE ENOUGH.
I KNEW IT ALL ALONG.
ABNORMAL RESULTS MEANS ABNORMAL METHODS WERE USED.
YOU'VE BEEN GATHERING INTEL ON THE TRAPS AROUND THE CLOCK.
WITH SHION'S ANALYSIS AND SHIZO'S PRACTICE, THEY'VE HELPED YOU IMPROVE QUITE EFFECTIVELY.
WITH NANAO'S MEDICAL KNOWLEDGE, HE'S TREATED YOUR MANY WOUNDS AND GIVEN YOU POWERFUL DRUGS SO THAT YOU DON'T NEED SLEEP OR REST.
AND YOU USED KENGO'S FAKE SKIN TO COVER THOSE WOUNDS.

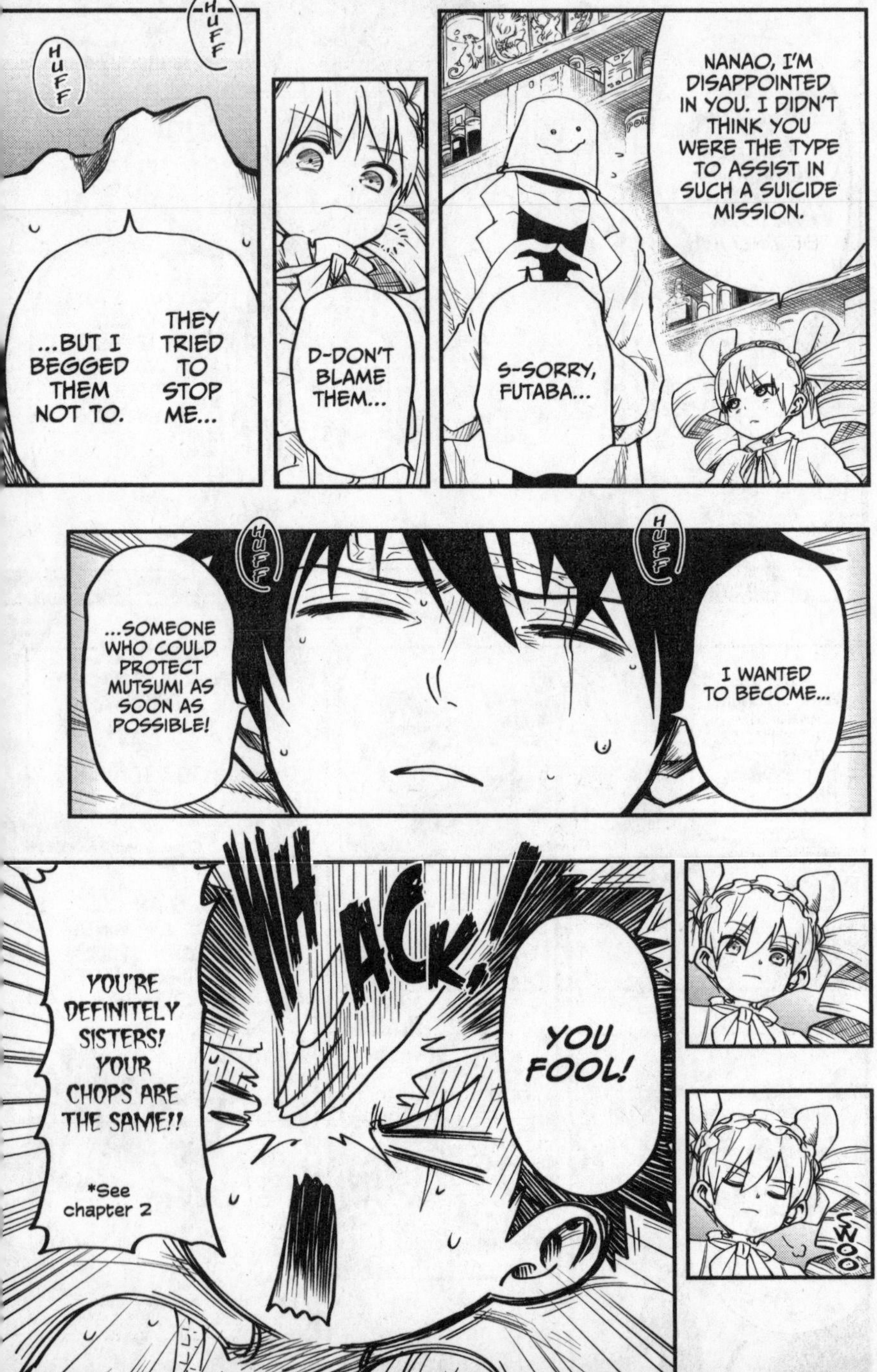
NANAO, I'M DISAPPOINTED IN YOU. I DIDN'T THINK YOU WERE THE TYPE TO ASSIST IN SUCH A SUICIDE MISSION.
S-SORRY, FUTABA...
D-DON'T BLAME THEM...
HUFF
HUFF
THEY TRIED TO STOP ME...
...BUT I BEGGED THEM NOT TO.
HUFF
I WANTED TO BECOME...
HUFF
...SOMEONE WHO COULD PROTECT MUTSUMI AS SOON AS POSSIBLE!
SWOO
WHACK!
YOU FOOL!
YOU'RE DEFINITELY SISTERS! YOUR CHOPS ARE THE SAME!!
*See chapter 2

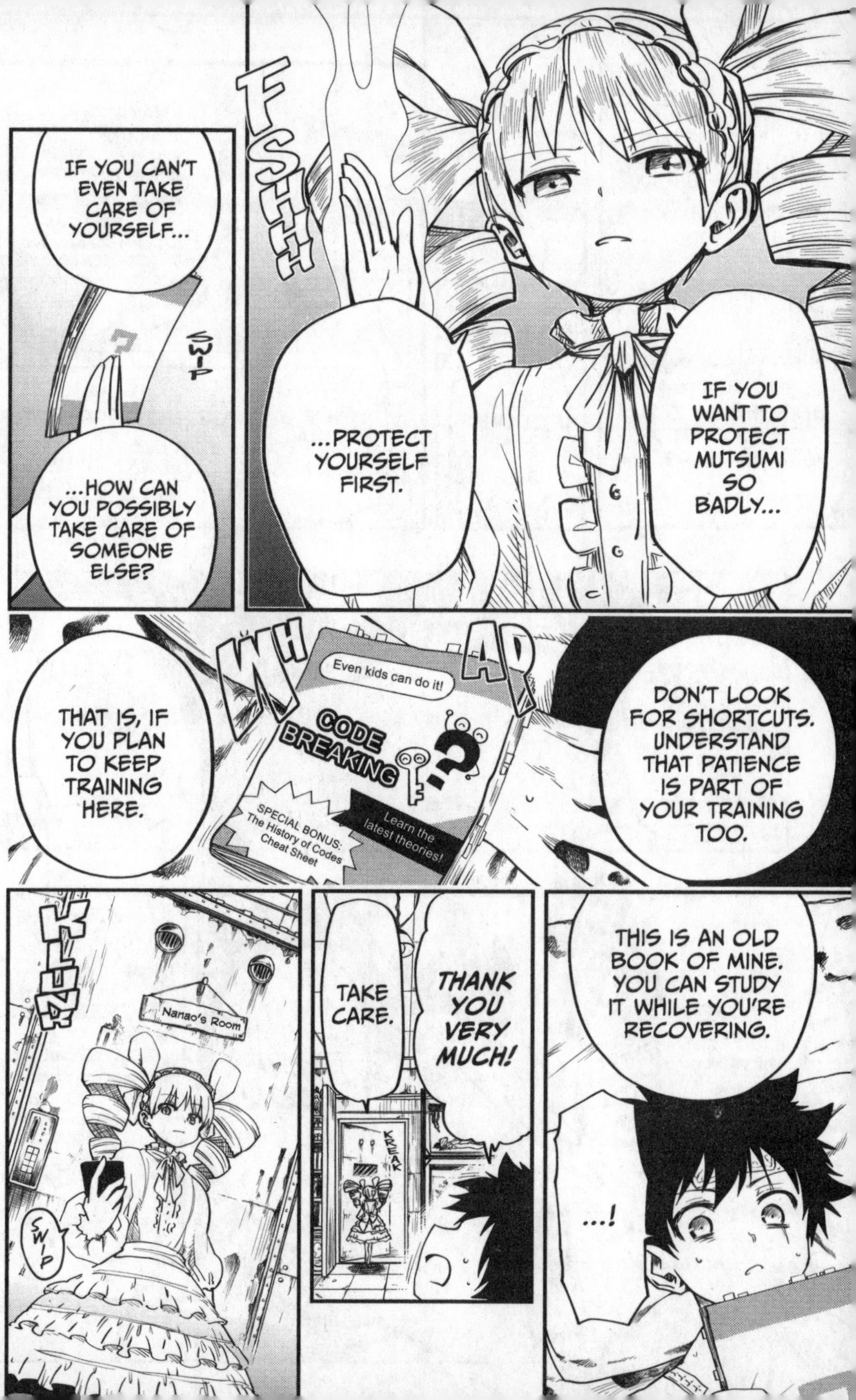
FSHHH
IF YOU WANT TO PROTECT MUTSUMI SO BADLY...
...PROTECT YOURSELF FIRST.
IF YOU CAN'T EVEN TAKE CARE OF YOURSELF...
SWIP
...HOW CAN YOU POSSIBLY TAKE CARE OF SOMEONE ELSE?
DON'T LOOK FOR SHORTCUTS. UNDERSTAND THAT PATIENCE IS PART OF YOUR TRAINING TOO.
WHAP
Even kids can do it!
CODE BREAKING
Learn the latest theories!
SPECIAL BONUS: The History of Codes Cheat Sheet
THAT IS, IF YOU PLAN TO KEEP TRAINING HERE.
THIS IS AN OLD BOOK OF MINE. YOU CAN STUDY IT WHILE YOU'RE RECOVERING.
...!
THANK YOU VERY MUCH!
TAKE CARE.
KREAK
KLUNK
Nanao's Room
SWIP

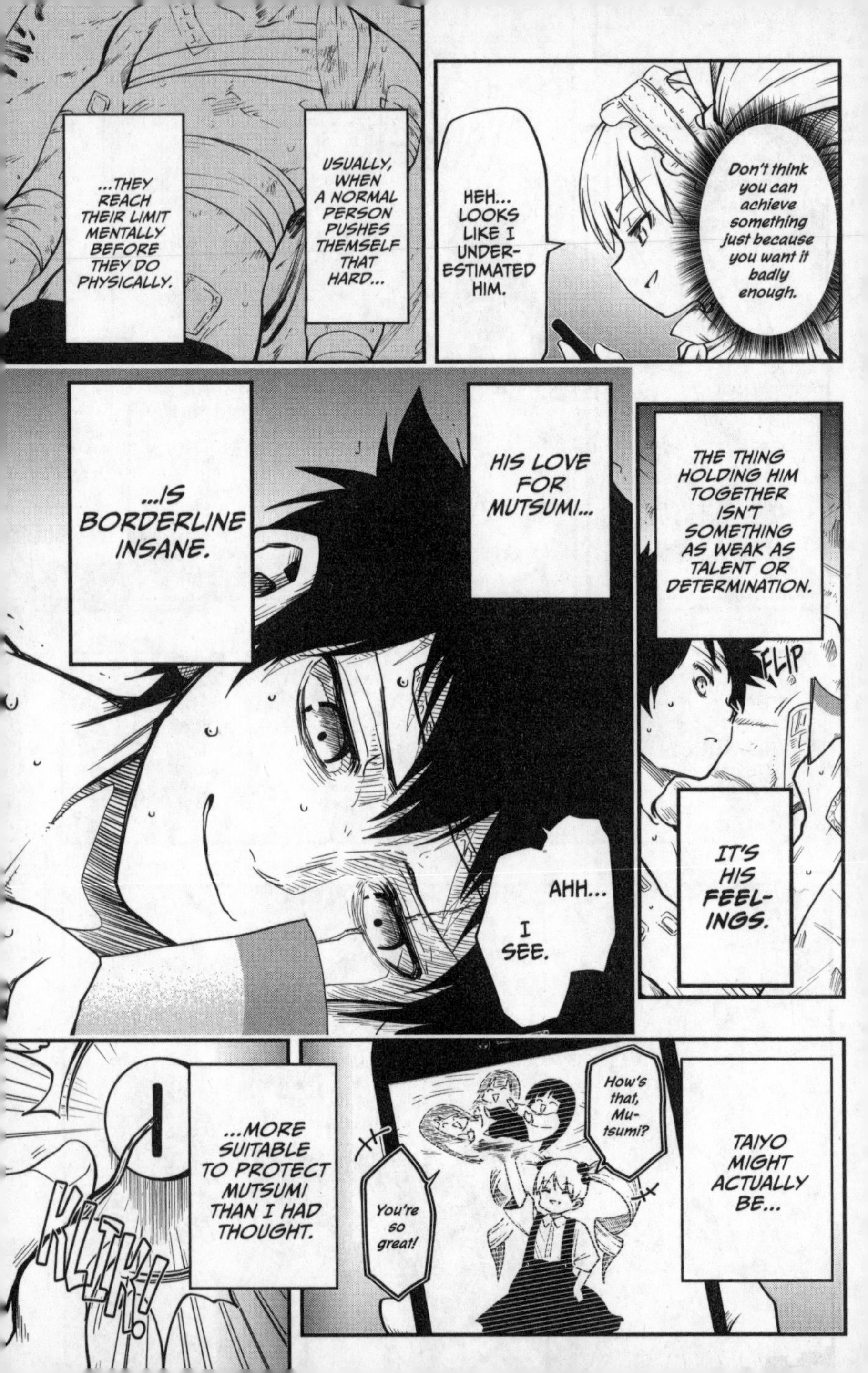
Don't think you can achieve something just because you want it badly enough.
HEH... LOOKS LIKE I UNDER-ESTIMATED HIM.
USUALLY, WHEN A NORMAL PERSON PUSHES THEMSELF THAT HARD...
...THEY REACH THEIR LIMIT MENTALLY BEFORE THEY DO PHYSICALLY.
THE THING HOLDING HIM TOGETHER ISN'T SOMETHING AS WEAK AS TALENT OR DETERMINATION.
FLIP
IT'S HIS FEEL-INGS.
HIS LOVE FOR MUTSUMI...
...IS BORDERLINE INSANE.
AHH... I SEE.
TAIYO MIGHT ACTUALLY BE...
How's that, Mu-tsumi?
You're so great!
...MORE SUITABLE TO PROTECT MUTSUMI THAN I HAD THOUGHT.
KLIK!

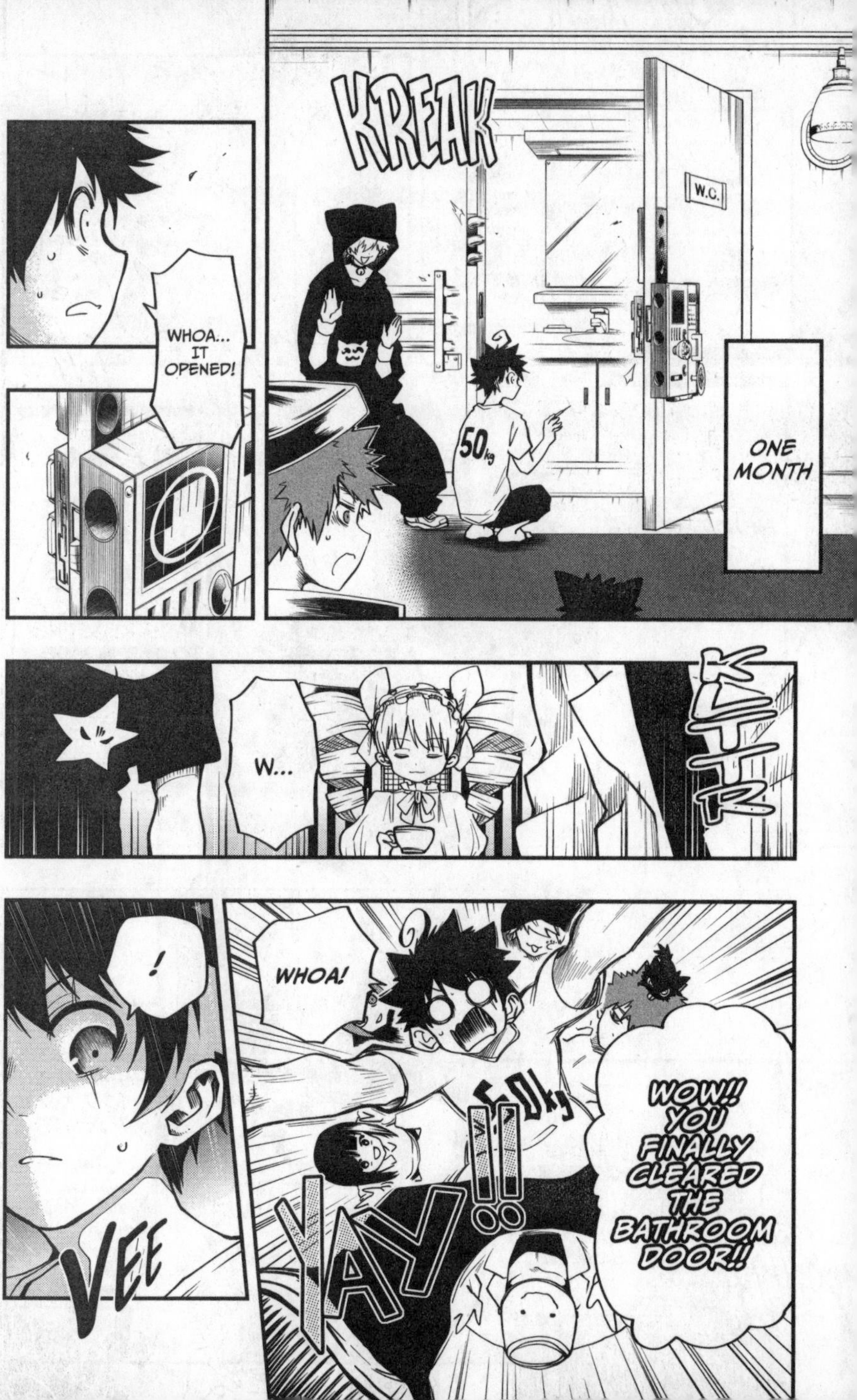
KREAK
W.C.
ONE MONTH
50kg
WHOA... IT OPENED!
KLTTR
W...
WOW!! YOU FINALLY CLEARED THE BATHROOM DOOR!!
50kg
YAY!!
WHOA!
!
VEE

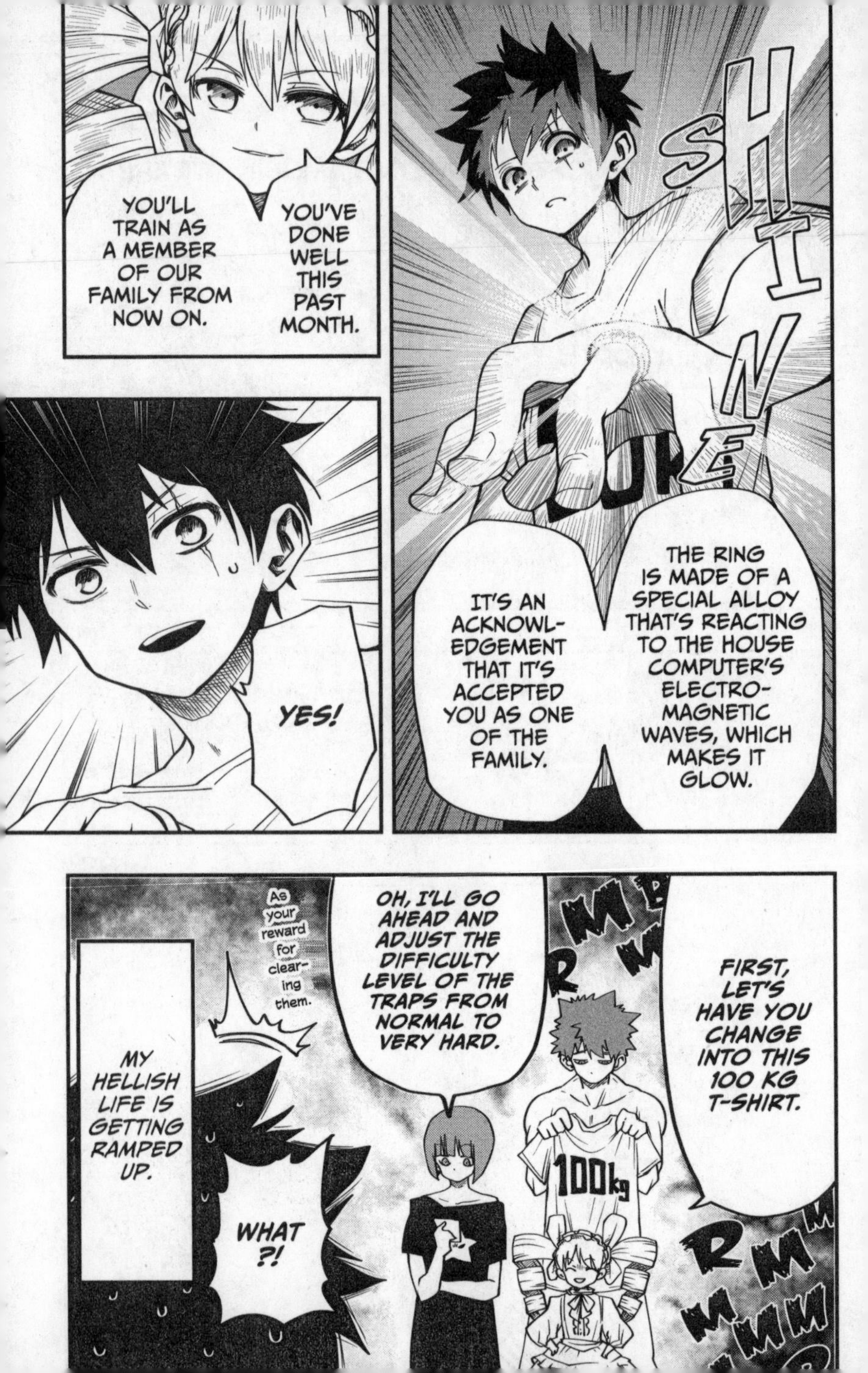

SHINE
THE RING IS MADE OF A SPECIAL ALLOY THAT'S REACTING TO THE HOUSE COMPUTER'S ELECTRO-MAGNETIC WAVES, WHICH MAKES IT GLOW.
IT'S AN ACKNOWL-EDGEMENT THAT IT'S ACCEPTED YOU AS ONE OF THE FAMILY.
YOU'VE DONE WELL THIS PAST MONTH.
YOU'LL TRAIN AS A MEMBER OF OUR FAMILY FROM NOW ON.
YES!
FIRST, LET'S HAVE YOU CHANGE INTO THIS 100 KG T-SHIRT.
100kg
OH, I'LL GO AHEAD AND ADJUST THE DIFFICULTY LEVEL OF THE TRAPS FROM NORMAL TO VERY HARD.
As your reward for clear-ing them.
WHAT ?!
MY HELLISH LIFE IS GETTING RAMPED UP.

and training Items

THE YOZAKURA MANSION'S AMUSING TRAPS

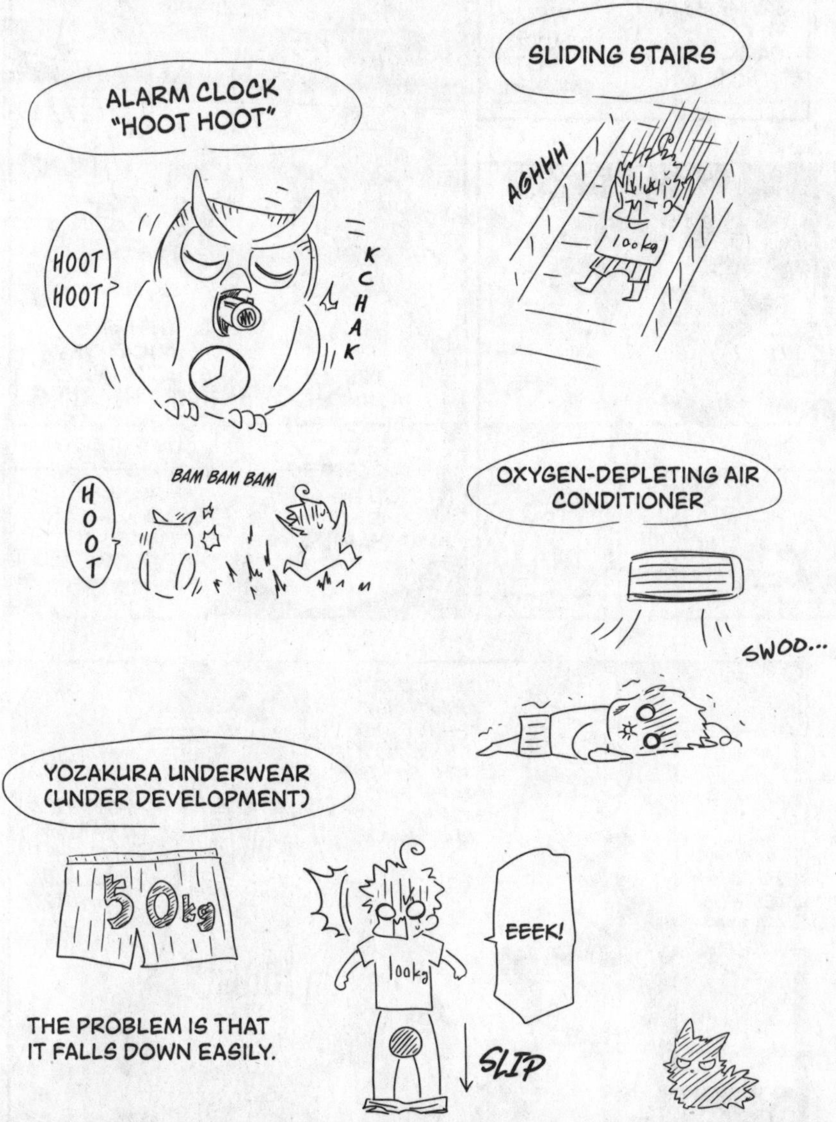
SLIDING STAIRS
AGHHH
100kg
ALARM CLOCK "HOOT HOOT"
HOOT HOOT
KCHAK
BAM BAM BAM
HOOT
OXYGEN-DEPLETING AIR CONDITIONER
SWOO...
YOZAKURA UNDERWEAR (UNDER DEVELOPMENT)
50kg
EEEK!
100kg
SLIP
THE PROBLEM IS THAT IT FALLS DOWN EASILY.

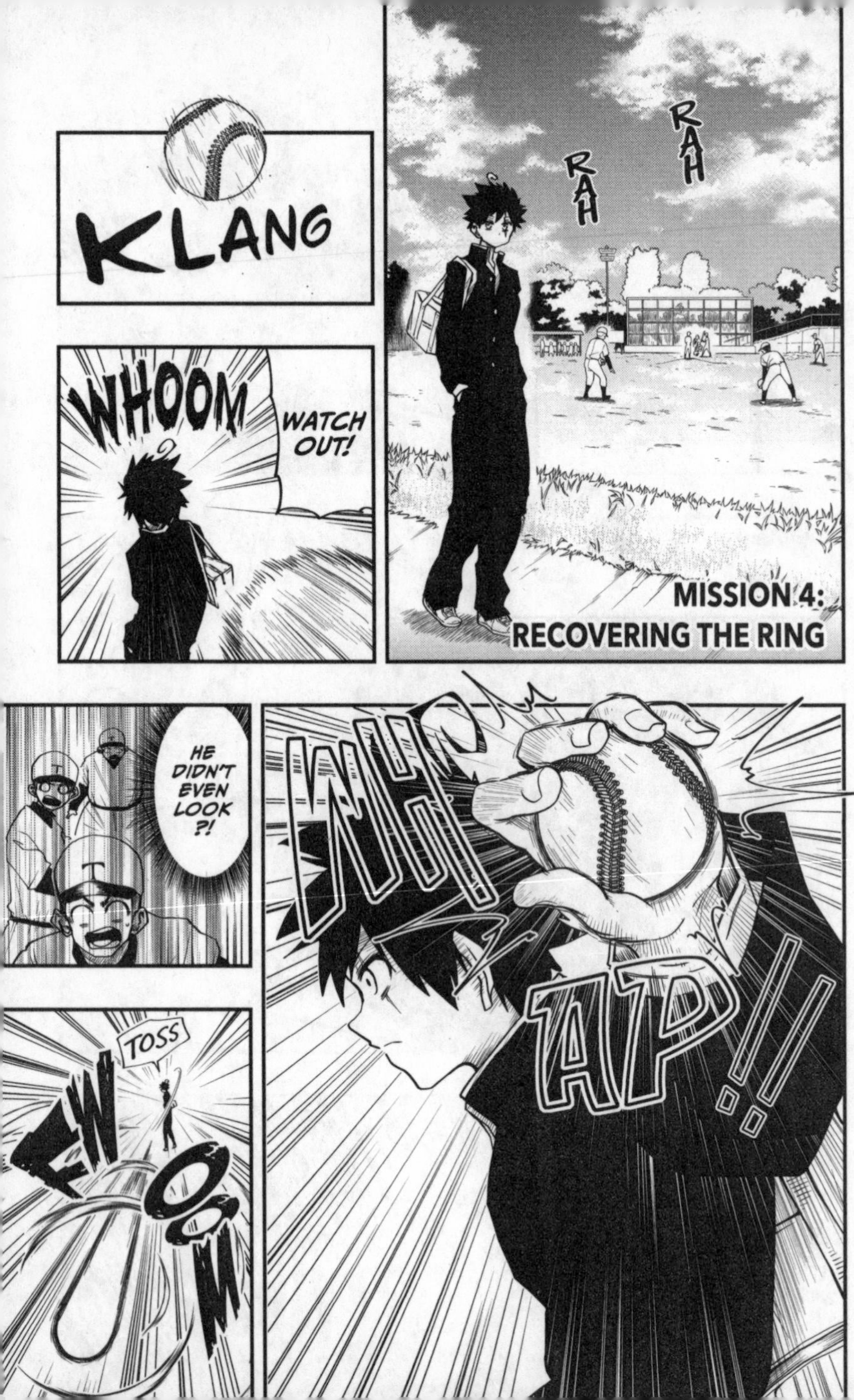
RAH
RAH
MISSION 4:
RECOVERING THE RING
KLANG
WHOOM
WATCH OUT!
WHAP!!
HE DIDN'T EVEN LOOK?!
TOSS
FWOOM

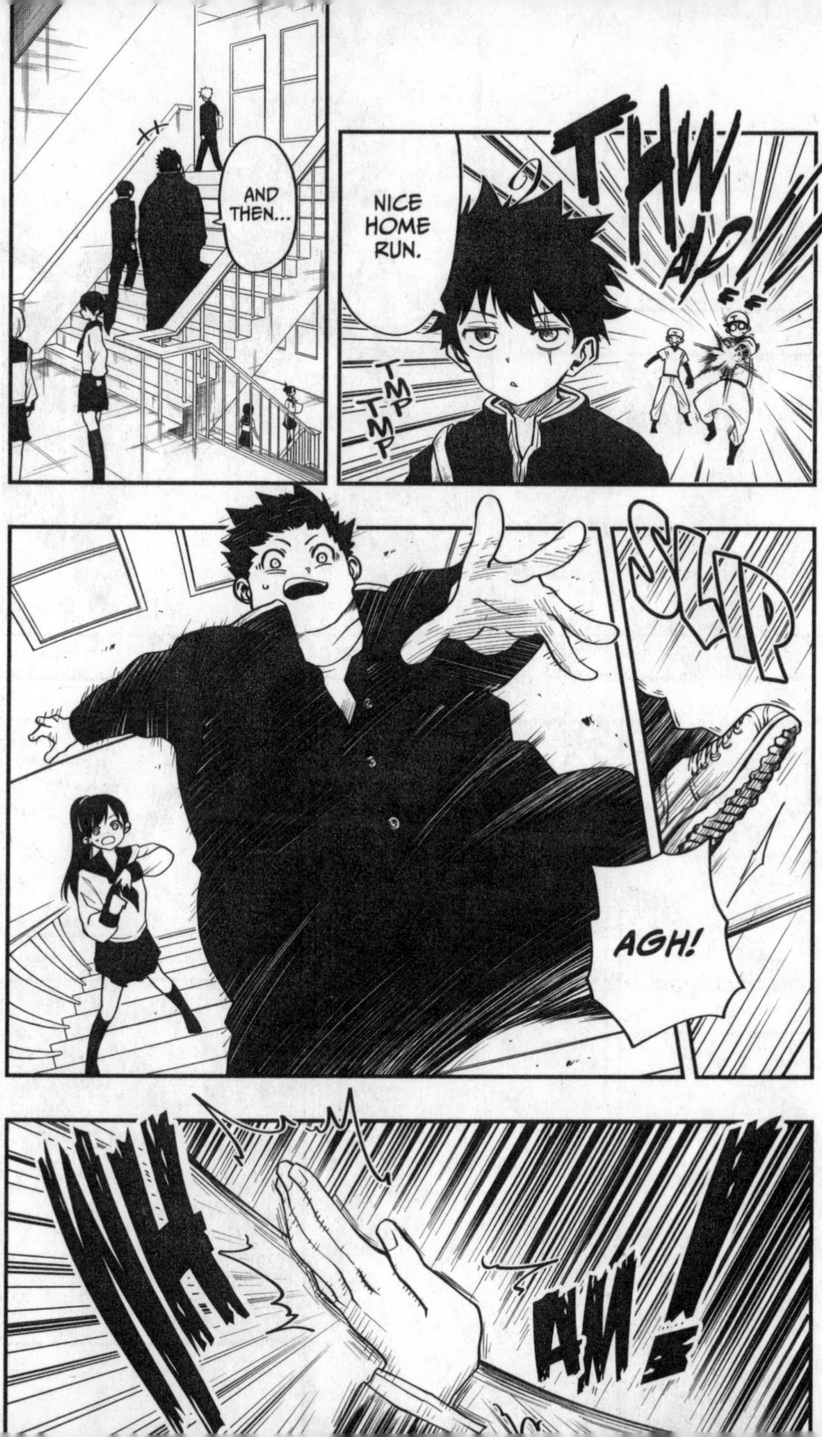
THWAP!!
NICE HOME RUN.
TMP TMP
AND THEN...
SLIP
AGH!
WHAM!

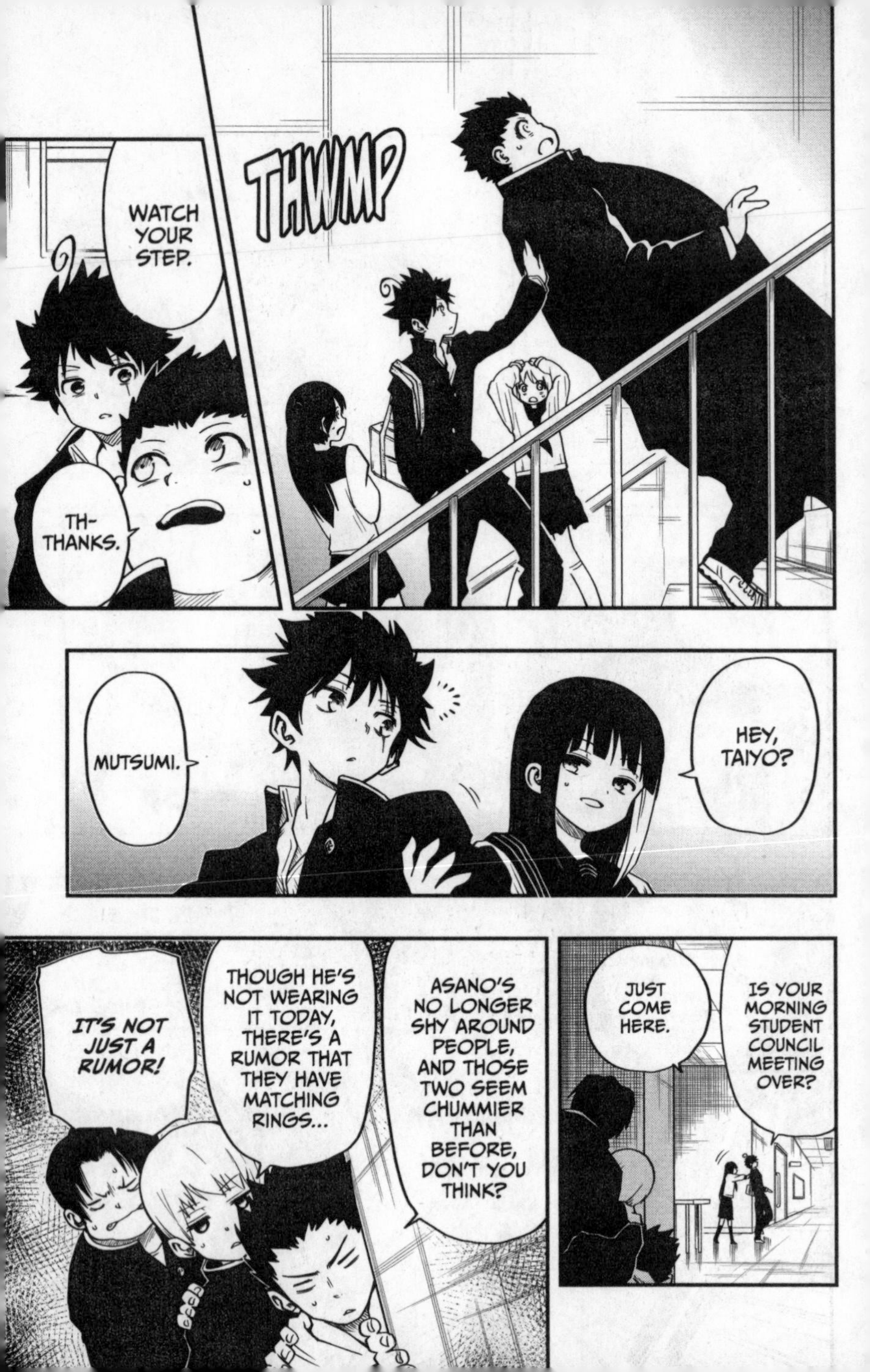
THWMP
WATCH YOUR STEP.
TH- THANKS.
HEY, TAIYO?
MUTSUMI.
IS YOUR MORNING STUDENT COUNCIL MEETING OVER?
JUST COME HERE.
ASANO'S NO LONGER SHY AROUND PEOPLE, AND THOSE TWO SEEM CHUMMIER THAN BEFORE, DON'T YOU THINK?
THOUGH HE'S NOT WEARING IT TODAY, THERE'S A RUMOR THAT THEY HAVE MATCHING RINGS...
IT'S NOT JUST A RUMOR!

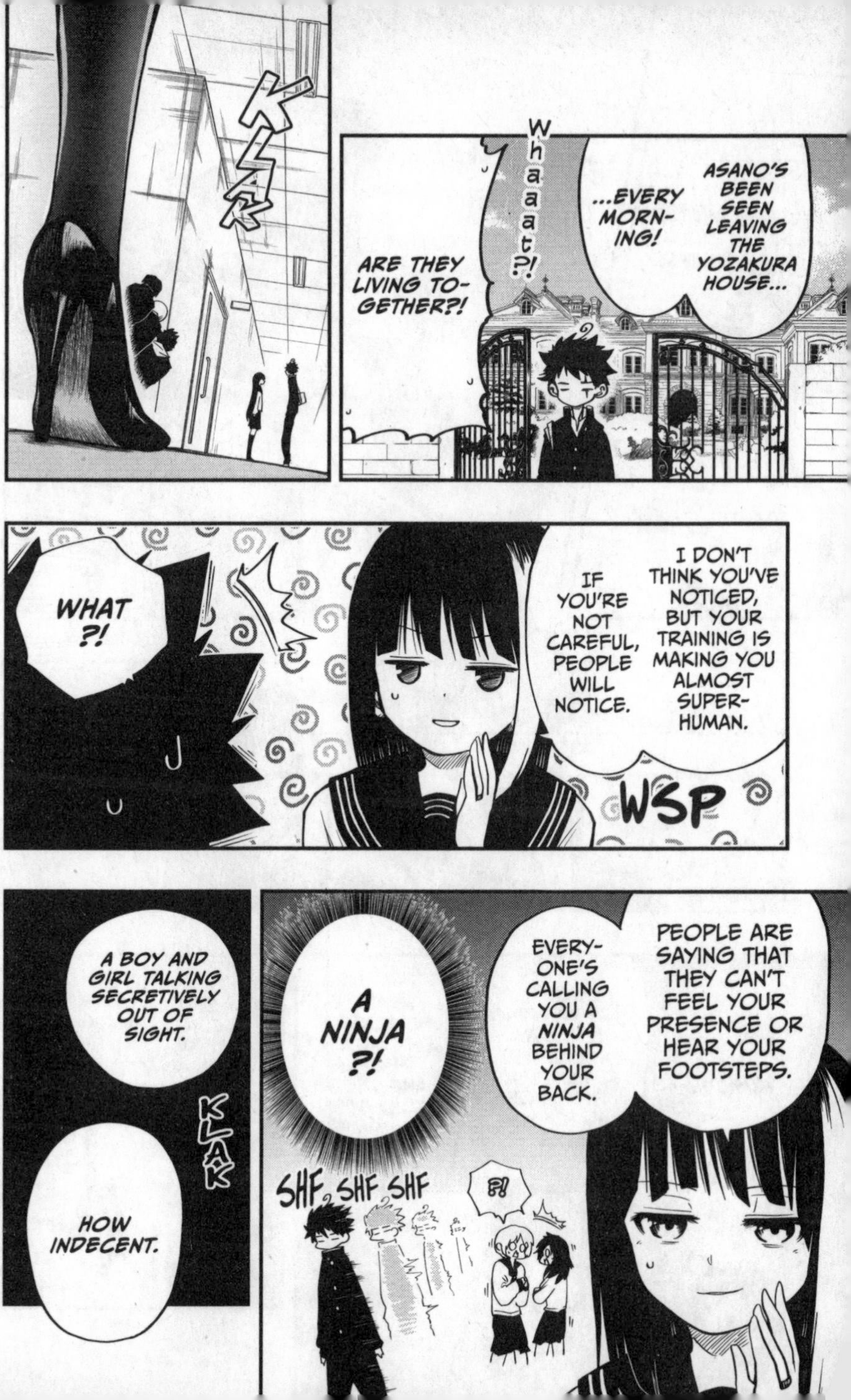
ASANO'S BEEN SEEN LEAVING THE YOZAKURA HOUSE...
...EVERY MORNING!
Whaaat?!
ARE THEY LIVING TOGETHER?!
KLAK
I DON'T THINK YOU'VE NOTICED, BUT YOUR TRAINING IS MAKING YOU ALMOST SUPERHUMAN.
IF YOU'RE NOT CAREFUL, PEOPLE WILL NOTICE.
WSP
WHAT ?!
PEOPLE ARE SAYING THAT THEY CAN'T FEEL YOUR PRESENCE OR HEAR YOUR FOOTSTEPS.
EVERYONE'S CALLING YOU A NINJA BEHIND YOUR BACK.
A NINJA ?!
SHF SHF SHF
?!
A BOY AND GIRL TALKING SECRETIVELY OUT OF SIGHT.
KLAK
HOW INDECENT.

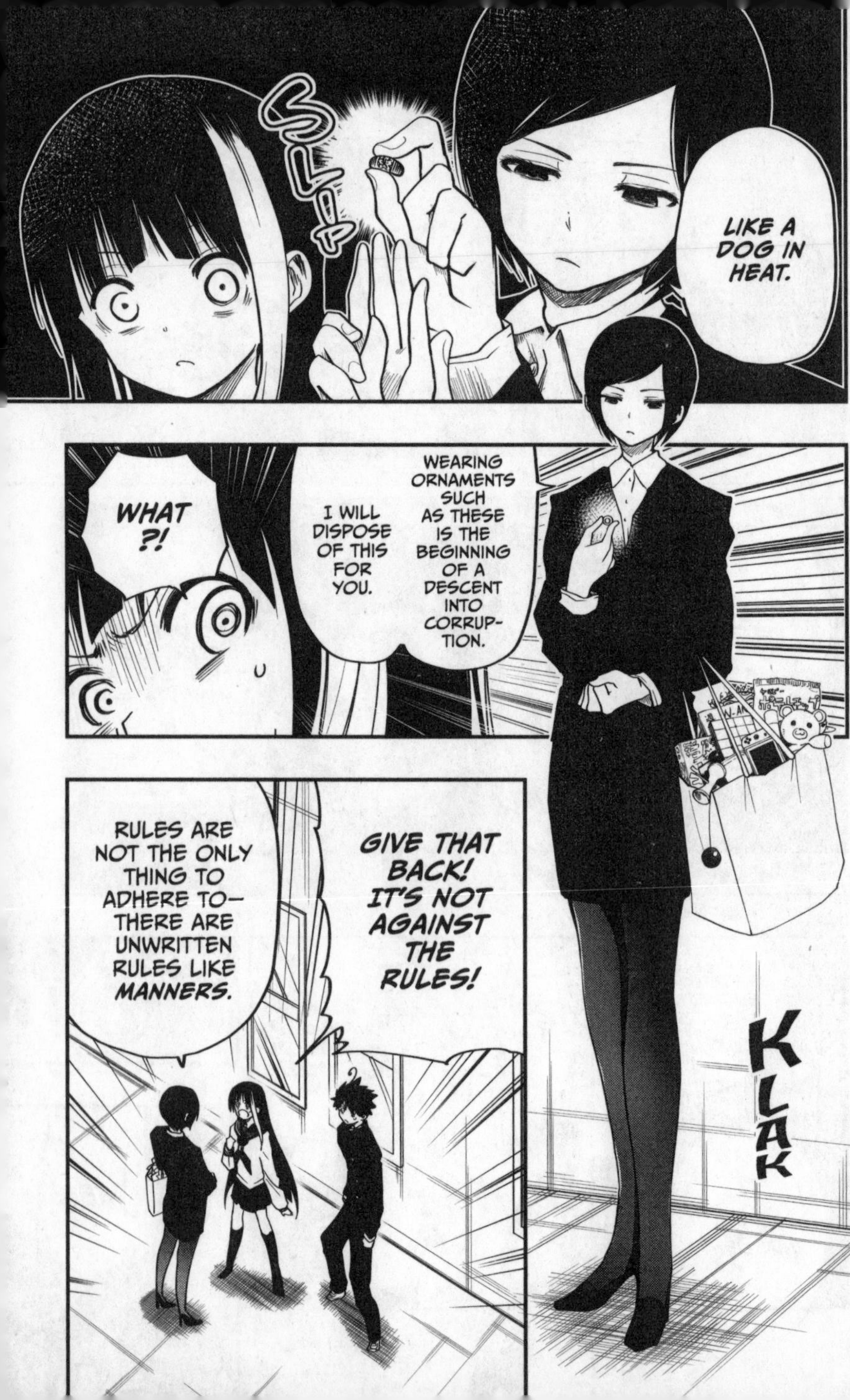
LIKE A DOG IN HEAT.
SLIP
KLAK
WEARING ORNAMENTS SUCH AS THESE IS THE BEGINNING OF A DESCENT INTO CORRUP-TION.
I WILL DISPOSE OF THIS FOR YOU.
WHAT ?!
GIVE THAT BACK! IT'S NOT AGAINST THE RULES!
RULES ARE NOT THE ONLY THING TO ADHERE TO—THERE ARE UNWRITTEN RULES LIKE *MANNERS.*

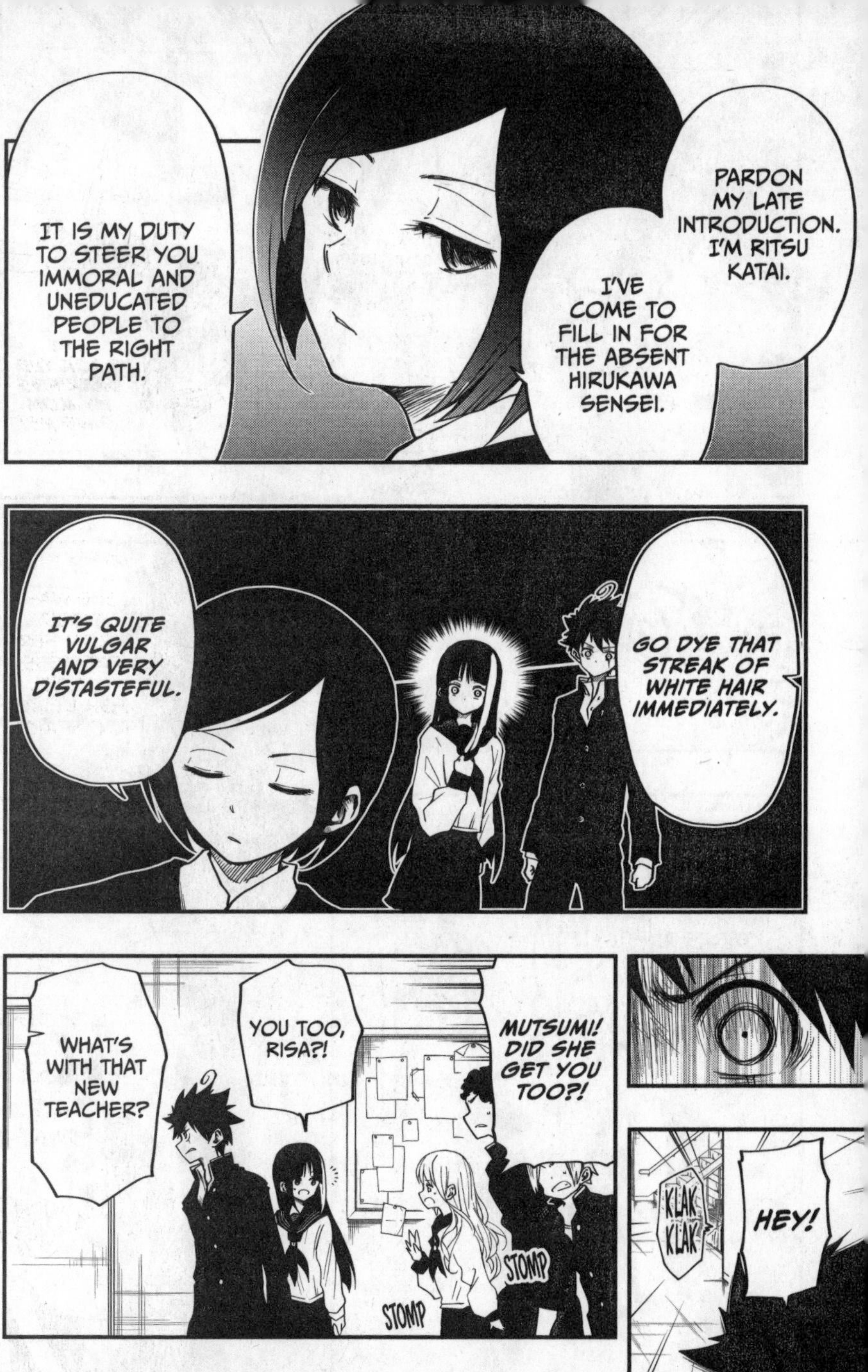
PARDON MY LATE INTRODUCTION. I'M RITSU KATAI.
I'VE COME TO FILL IN FOR THE ABSENT HIRUKAWA SENSEI.
IT IS MY DUTY TO STEER YOU IMMORAL AND UNEDUCATED PEOPLE TO THE RIGHT PATH.
GO DYE THAT STREAK OF WHITE HAIR IMMEDIATELY.
IT'S QUITE VULGAR AND VERY DISTASTEFUL.
KLAK KLAK
HEY!
MUTSUMI! DID SHE GET YOU TOO?!
STOMP
STOMP
YOU TOO, RISA?!
WHAT'S WITH THAT NEW TEACHER?

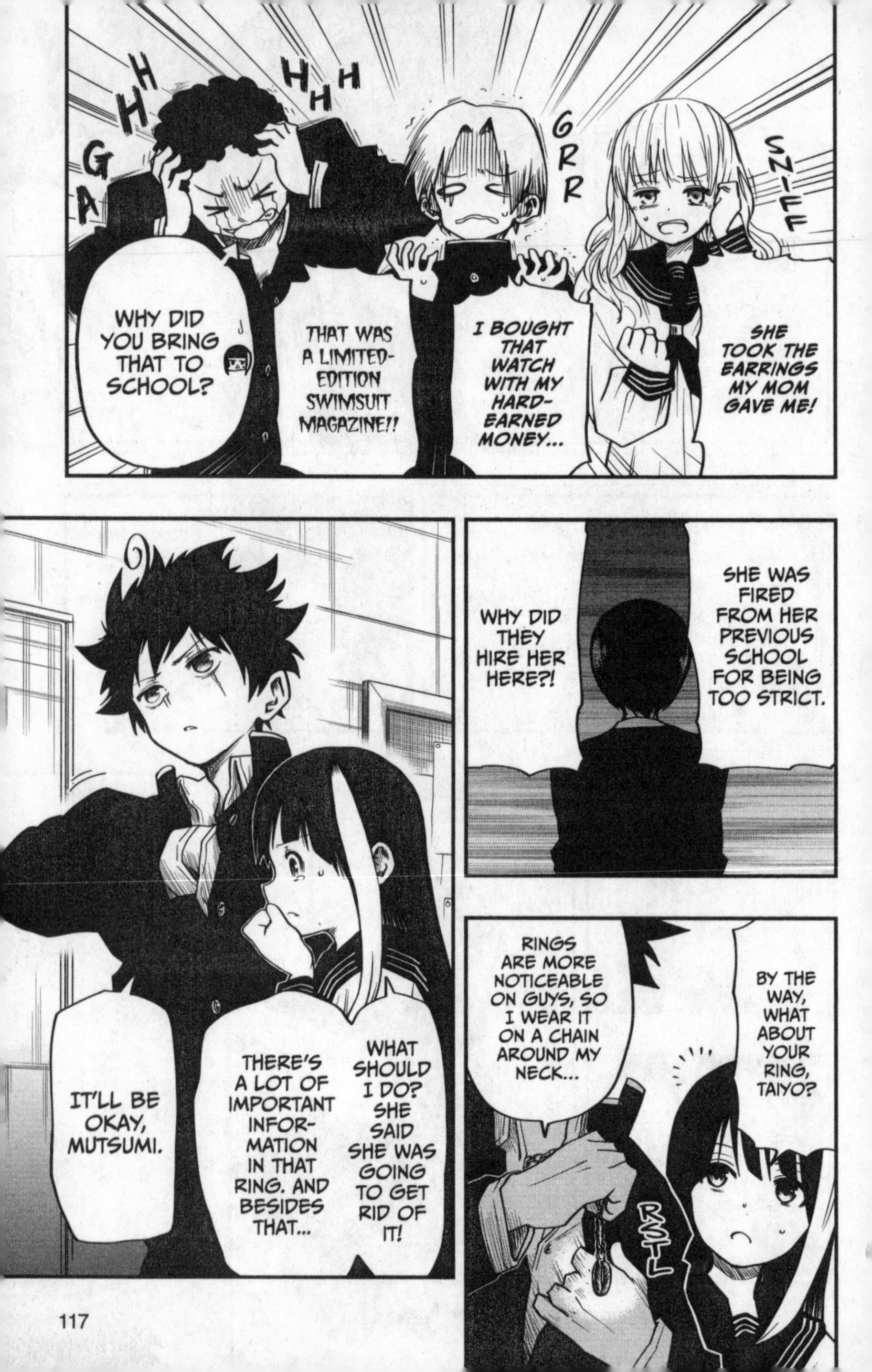
SNIFF
SHE TOOK THE EARRINGS MY MOM GAVE ME!
GRR
I BOUGHT THAT WATCH WITH MY HARD-EARNED MONEY...
THAT WAS A LIMITED-EDITION SWIMSUIT MAGAZINE!!
GAHHHHH
WHY DID YOU BRING THAT TO SCHOOL?
SHE WAS FIRED FROM HER PREVIOUS SCHOOL FOR BEING TOO STRICT.
WHY DID THEY HIRE HER HERE?!
BY THE WAY, WHAT ABOUT YOUR RING, TAIYO?
RINGS ARE MORE NOTICEABLE ON GUYS, SO I WEAR IT ON A CHAIN AROUND MY NECK...
RSTL
WHAT SHOULD I DO? SHE SAID SHE WAS GOING TO GET RID OF IT!
THERE'S A LOT OF IMPORTANT INFOR-MATION IN THAT RING. AND BESIDES THAT...
IT'LL BE OKAY, MUTSUMI.

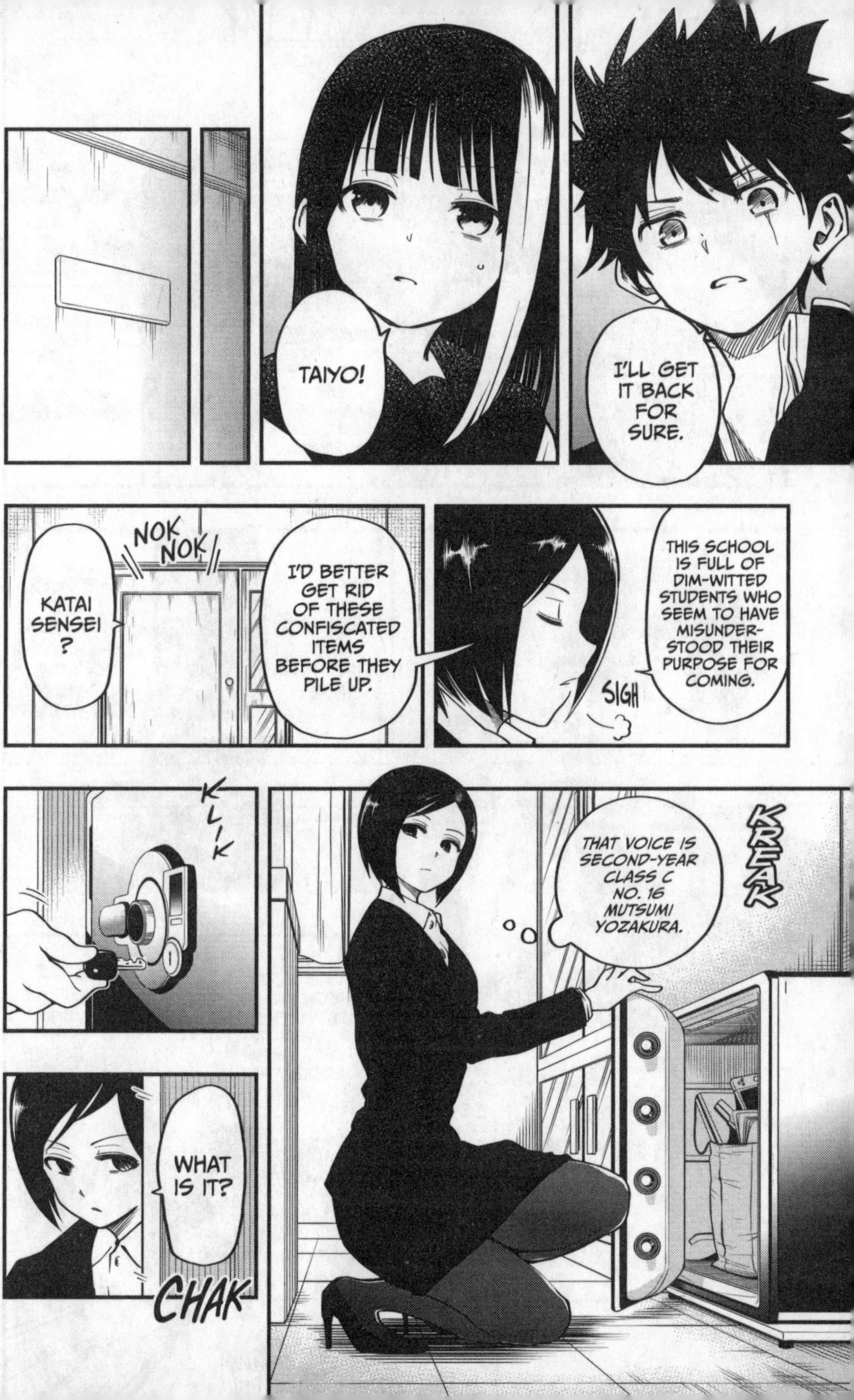
I'LL GET IT BACK FOR SURE.
TAIYO!
THIS SCHOOL IS FULL OF DIM-WITTED STUDENTS WHO SEEM TO HAVE MISUNDERSTOOD THEIR PURPOSE FOR COMING.
SIGH
I'D BETTER GET RID OF THESE CONFISCATED ITEMS BEFORE THEY PILE UP.
NOK NOK
KATAI SENSEI?
KREAK
THAT VOICE IS SECOND-YEAR CLASS C NO. 16 MUTSUMI YOZAKURA.
KLIK
WHAT IS IT?
CHAK

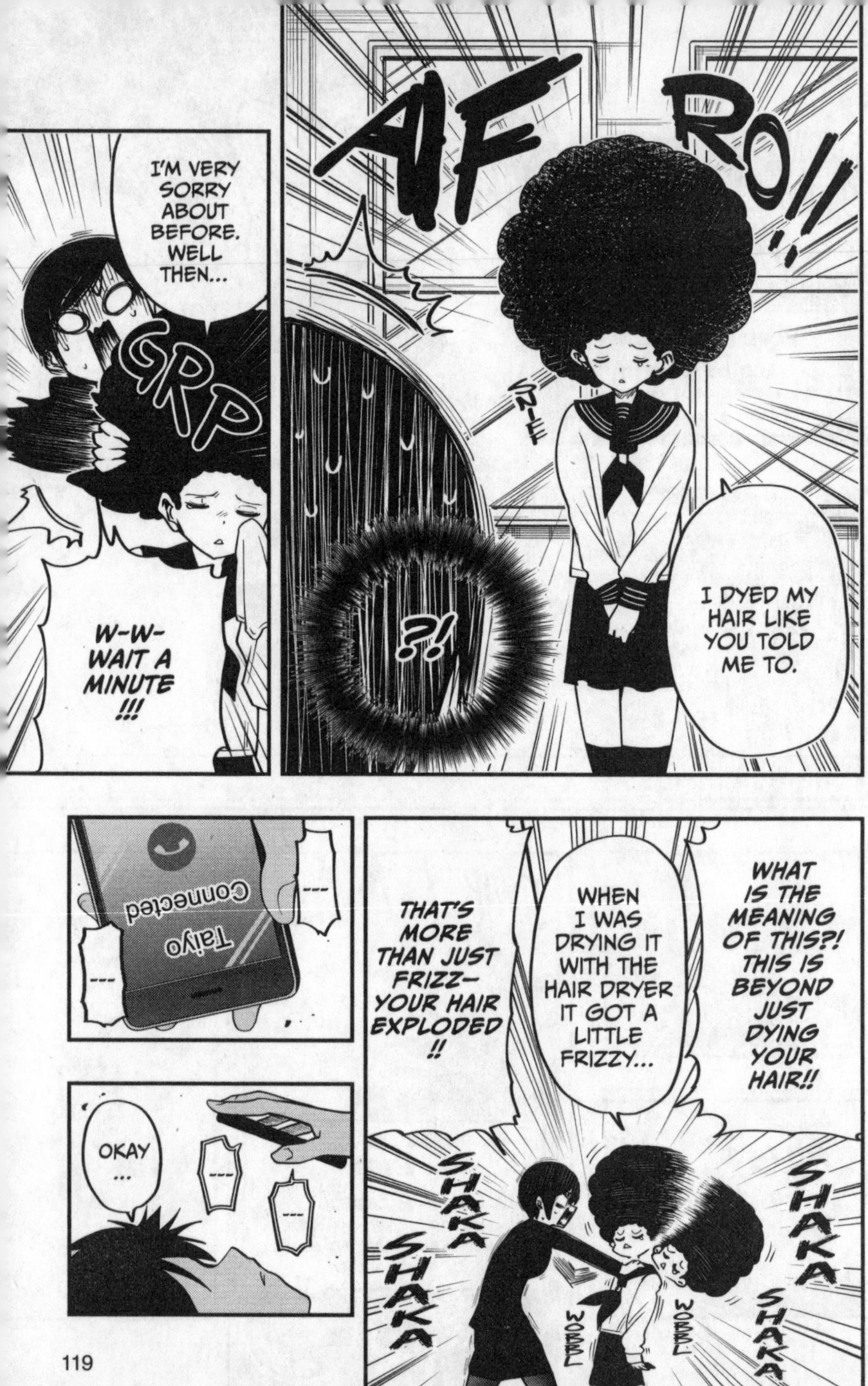
AFRO!!
SNIFF
I DYED MY HAIR LIKE YOU TOLD ME TO.
?!
I'M VERY SORRY ABOUT BEFORE. WELL THEN...
GRP
W-W-WAIT A MINUTE!!!
WHAT IS THE MEANING OF THIS?! THIS IS BEYOND JUST DYING YOUR HAIR!!
WHEN I WAS DRYING IT WITH THE HAIR DRYER IT GOT A LITTLE FRIZZY...
THAT'S MORE THAN JUST FRIZZ—YOUR HAIR EXPLODED!!
SHAKA SHAKA
WOBBL
WOBBL
SHAKA SHAKA
Taiyo
Connected

OKAY...

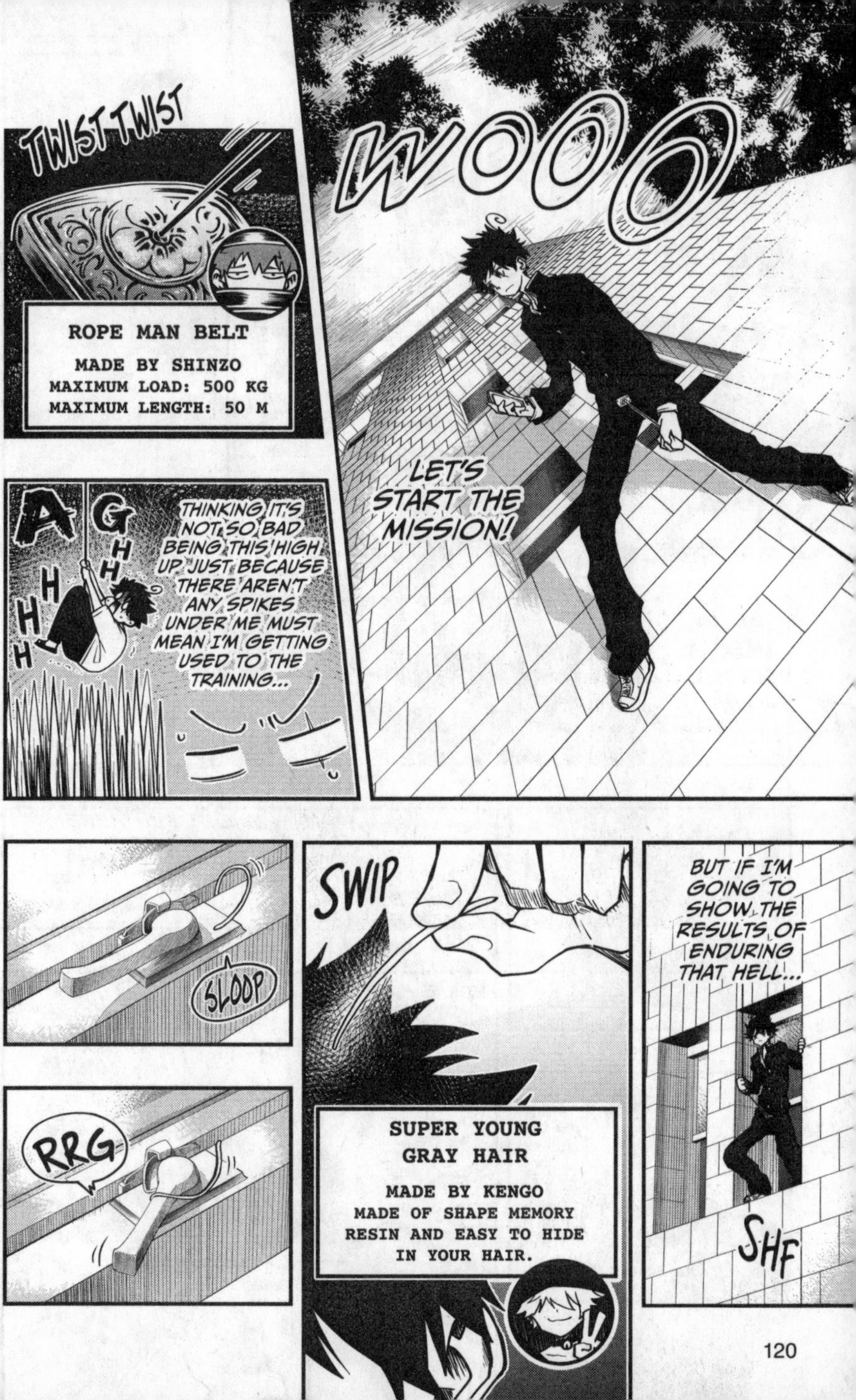
WOOO
LET'S START THE MISSION!
TWIST TWIST
ROPE MAN BELT
MADE BY SHINZO
MAXIMUM LOAD: 500 KG
MAXIMUM LENGTH: 50 M
AGHHHHH
THINKING IT'S NOT SO BAD BEING THIS HIGH UP JUST BECAUSE THERE AREN'T ANY SPIKES UNDER ME MUST MEAN I'M GETTING USED TO THE TRAINING...
BUT IF I'M GOING TO SHOW THE RESULTS OF ENDURING THAT HELL...
SHF
SWIP
SUPER YOUNG GRAY HAIR
MADE BY KENGO
MADE OF SHAPE MEMORY RESIN AND EASY TO HIDE IN YOUR HAIR.
SLOOP
RRG

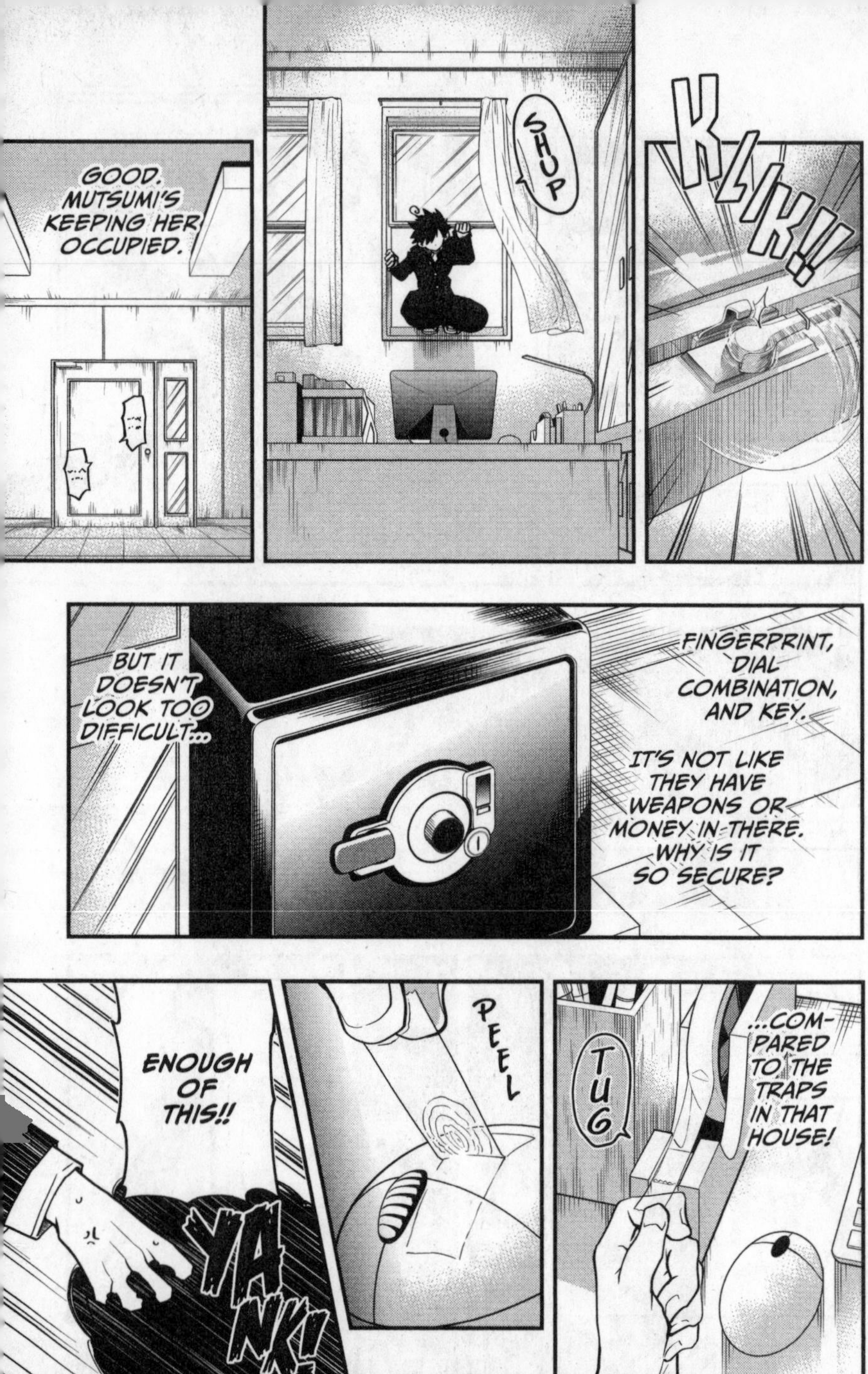
KLIK!!
SHUP
GOOD. MUTSUMI'S KEEPING HER OCCUPIED.
FINGERPRINT, DIAL COMBINATION, AND KEY.
IT'S NOT LIKE THEY HAVE WEAPONS OR MONEY IN THERE. WHY IS IT SO SECURE?
BUT IT DOESN'T LOOK TOO DIFFICULT...
TUG
...COM-PARED TO THE TRAPS IN THAT HOUSE!
PEEL
ENOUGH OF THIS!!
YANK!!

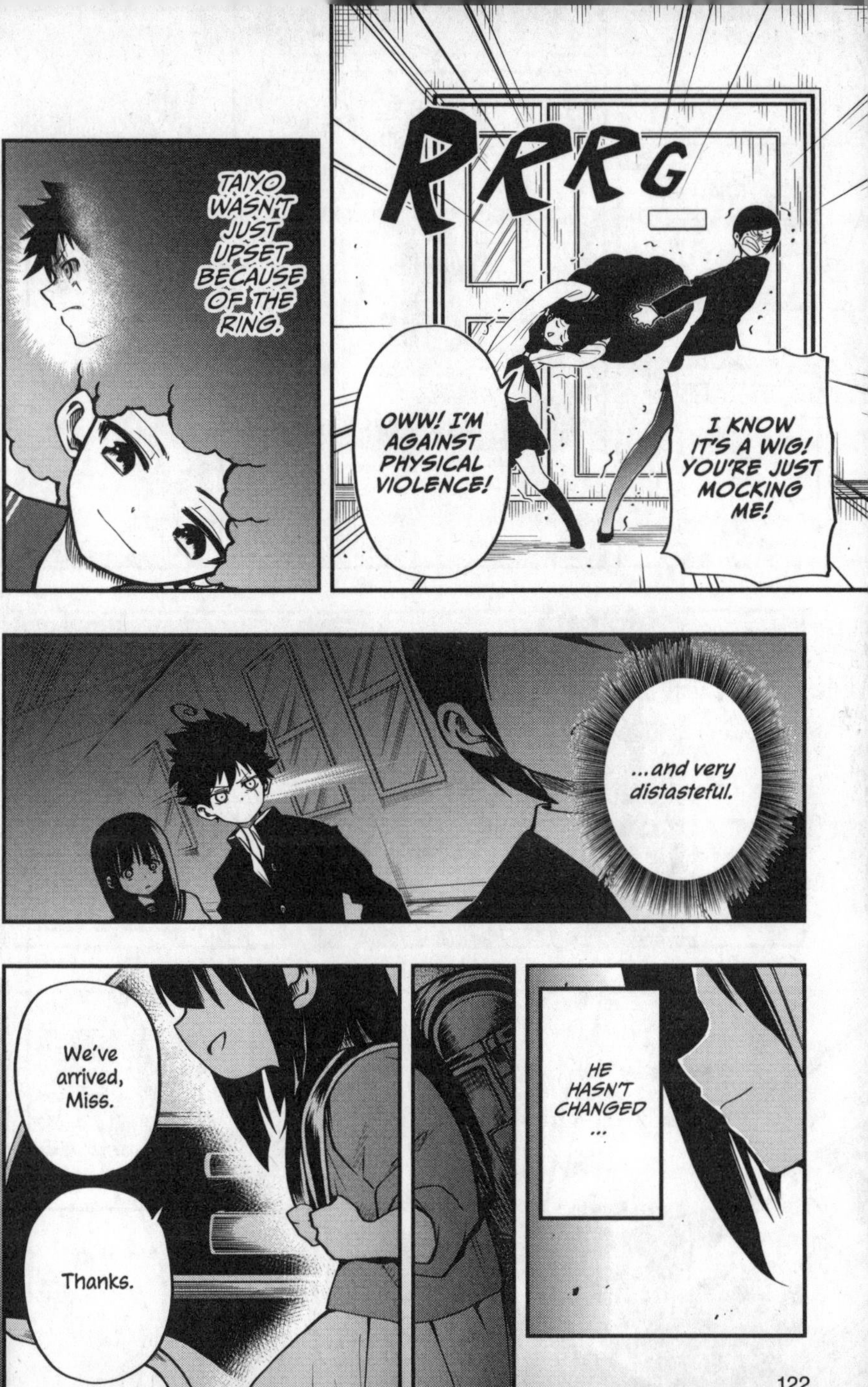
RRRG
I KNOW IT'S A WIG! YOU'RE JUST MOCKING ME!
OWW! I'M AGAINST PHYSICAL VIOLENCE!
TAIYO WASN'T JUST UPSET BECAUSE OF THE RING.
...and very distasteful.
HE HASN'T CHANGED ...
We've arrived, Miss.
Thanks.

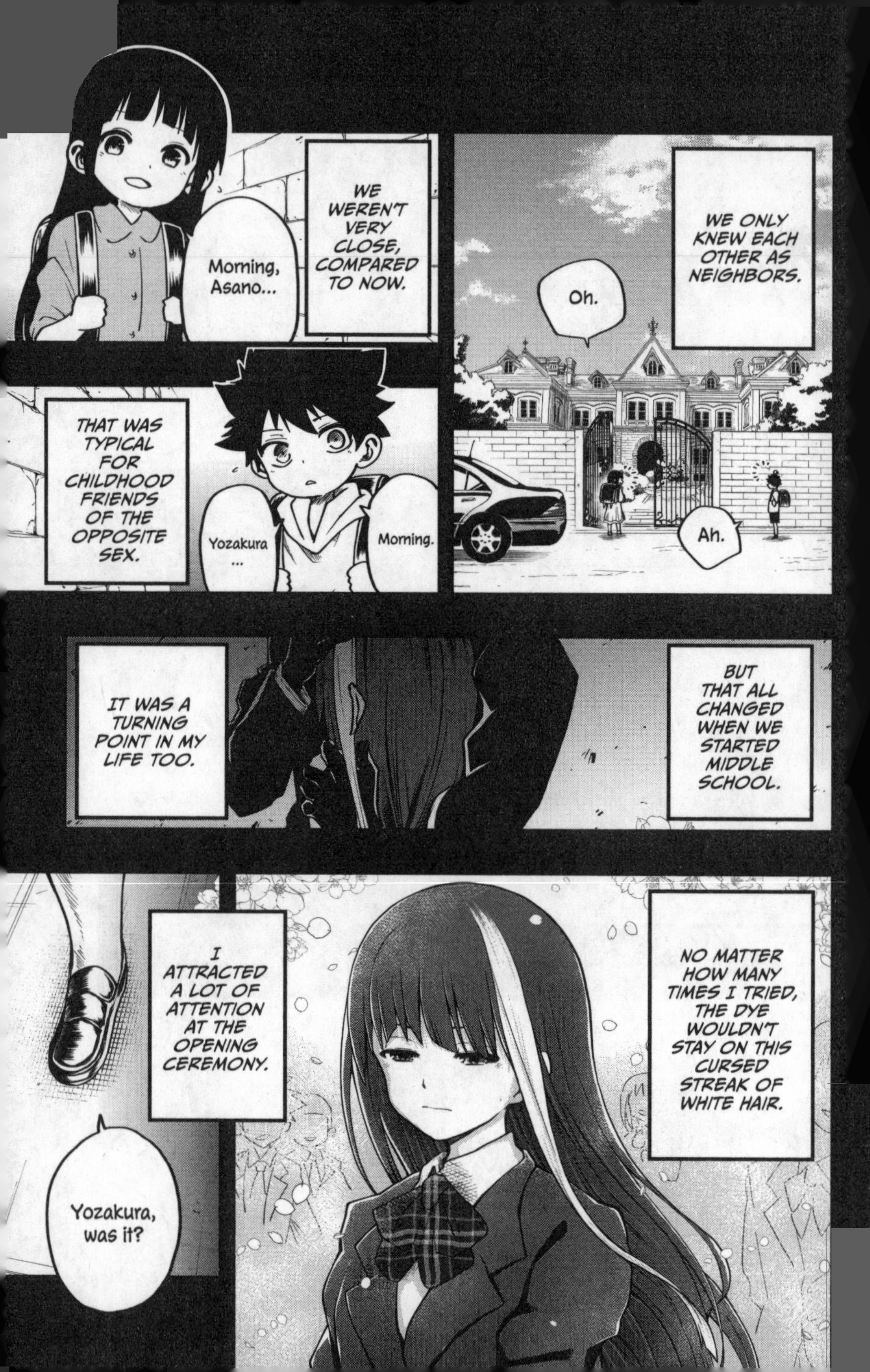
WE ONLY KNEW EACH OTHER AS NEIGHBORS.
Oh.
Ah.
WE WEREN'T VERY CLOSE, COMPARED TO NOW.
Morning, Asano...
THAT WAS TYPICAL FOR CHILDHOOD FRIENDS OF THE OPPOSITE SEX.
Morning.
Yozakura ...
BUT THAT ALL CHANGED WHEN WE STARTED MIDDLE SCHOOL.
IT WAS A TURNING POINT IN MY LIFE TOO.
NO MATTER HOW MANY TIMES I TRIED, THE DYE WOULDN'T STAY ON THIS CURSED STREAK OF WHITE HAIR.
I ATTRACTED A LOT OF ATTENTION AT THE OPENING CEREMONY.
Yozakura, was it?

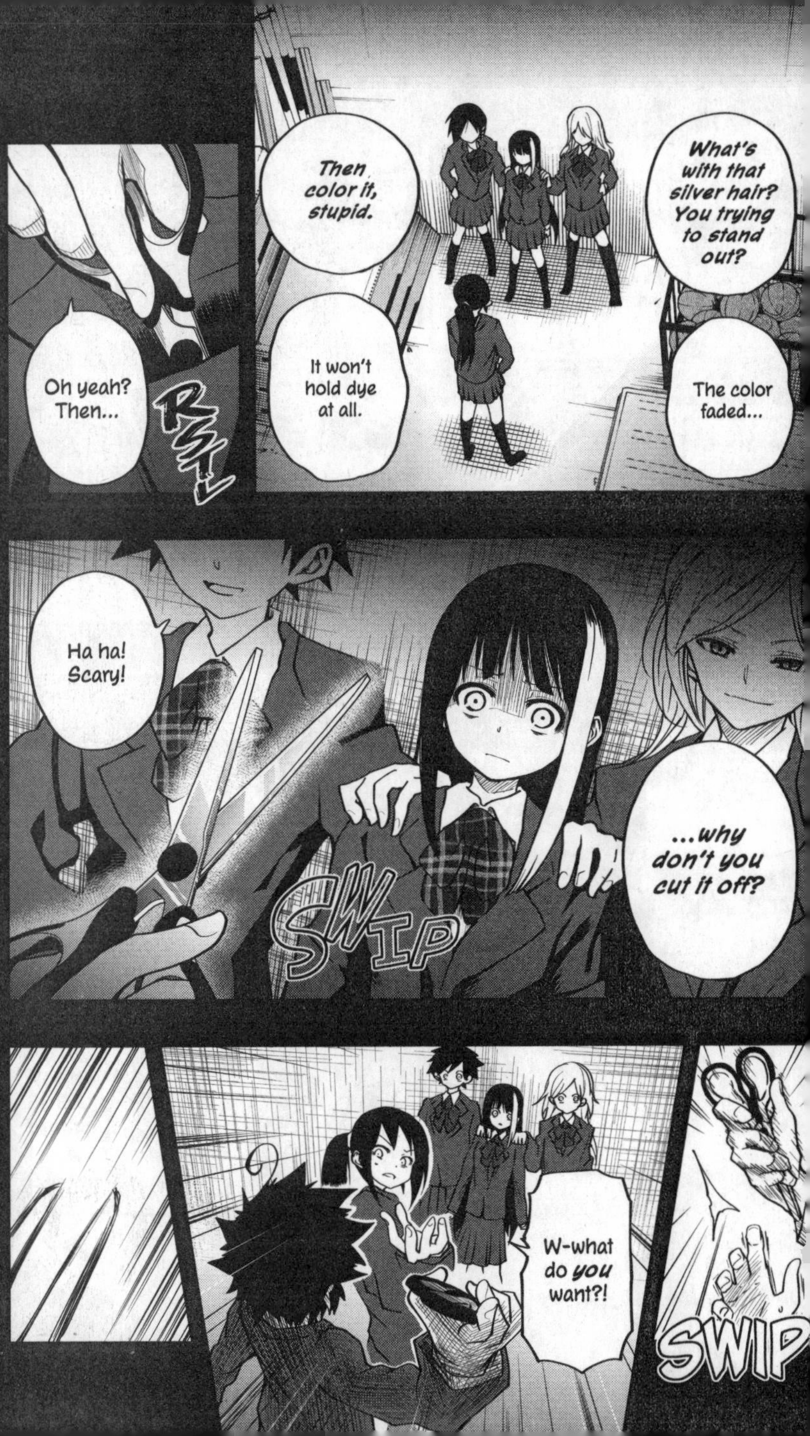
What's with that silver hair? You trying to stand out?
Then color it, stupid.
The color faded...
It won't hold dye at all.
Oh yeah? Then...
RSTL
...why don't you cut it off?
Ha ha! Scary!
SWIP
SWIP
W-what do you want?!

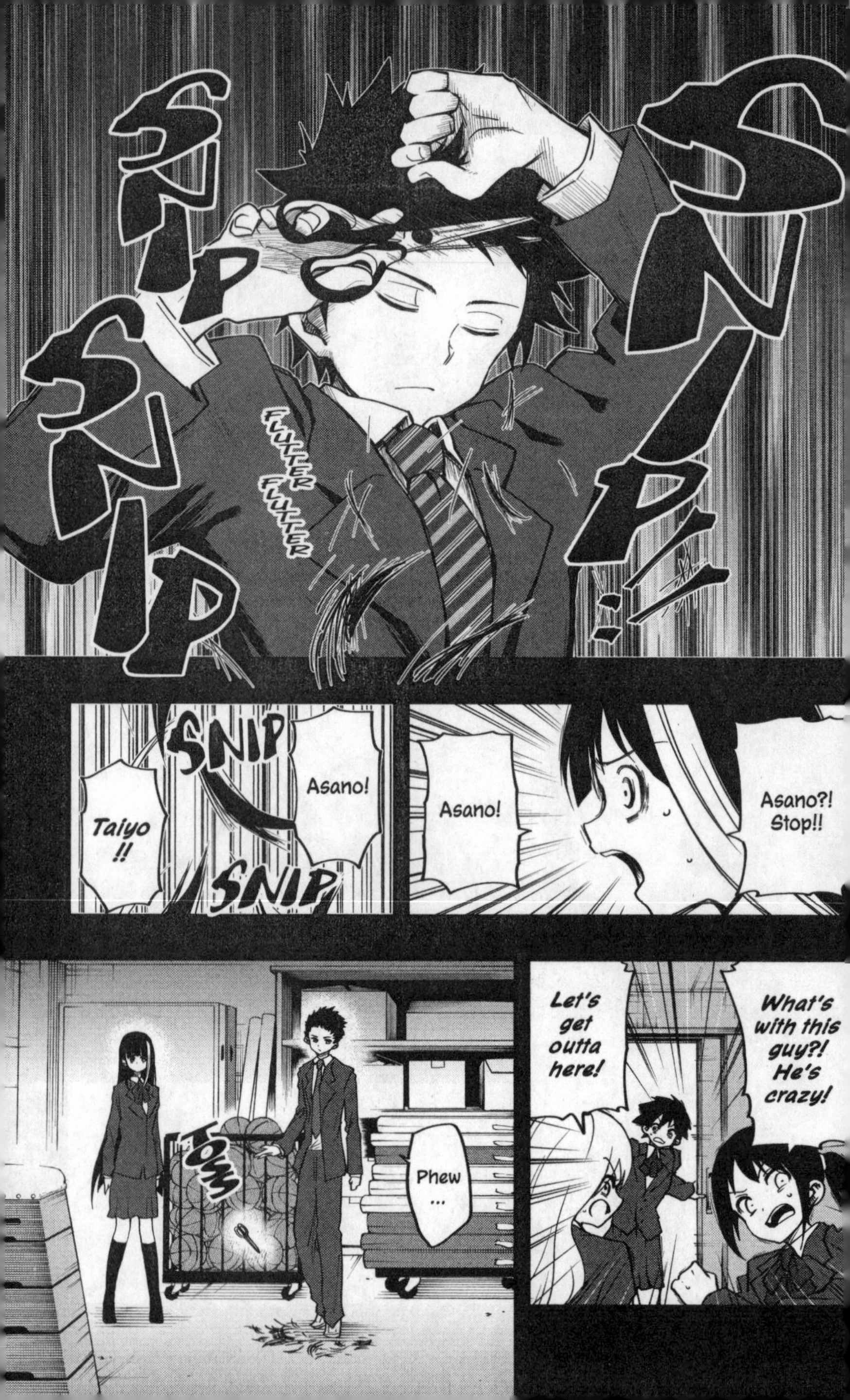
SNIP!!
SNIP SNIP
FLUTTER FLUTTER
Asano?! Stop!!
Asano!
SNIP
Asano!
Taiyo !!
SNIP
What's with this guy?! He's crazy!
Let's get outta here!
TOMM
Phew ...

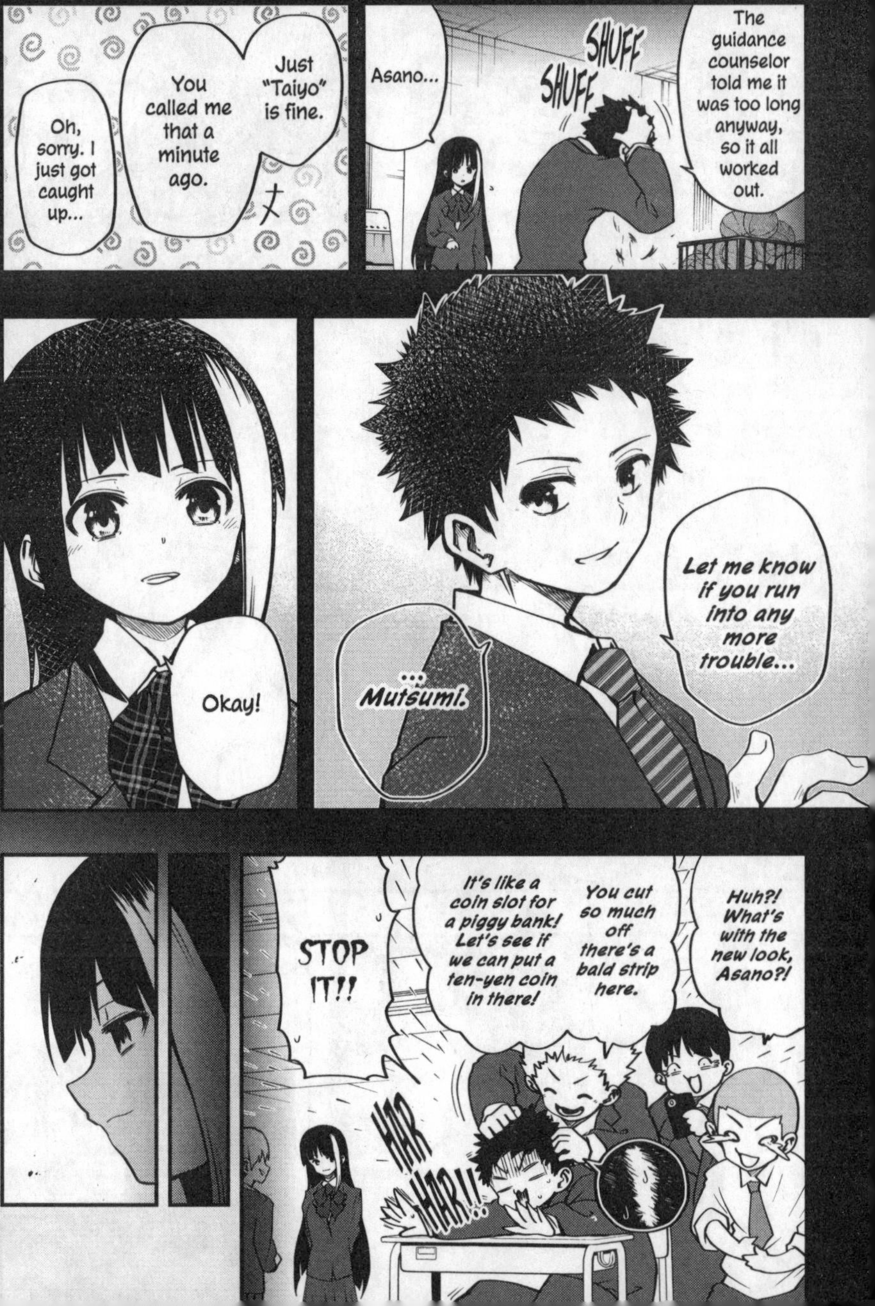
The guidance counselor told me it was too long anyway, so it all worked out.
SHUFF
SHUFF
Asano...
Just "Taiyo" is fine.
You called me that a minute ago.
Oh, sorry. I just got caught up...
Let me know if you run into any more trouble...
... Mutsumi.
Okay!
Huh?! What's with the new look, Asano?!
You cut so much off there's a bald strip here.
It's like a coin slot for a piggy bank! Let's see if we can put a ten-yen coin in there!
STOP IT!!
HAR HAR!!

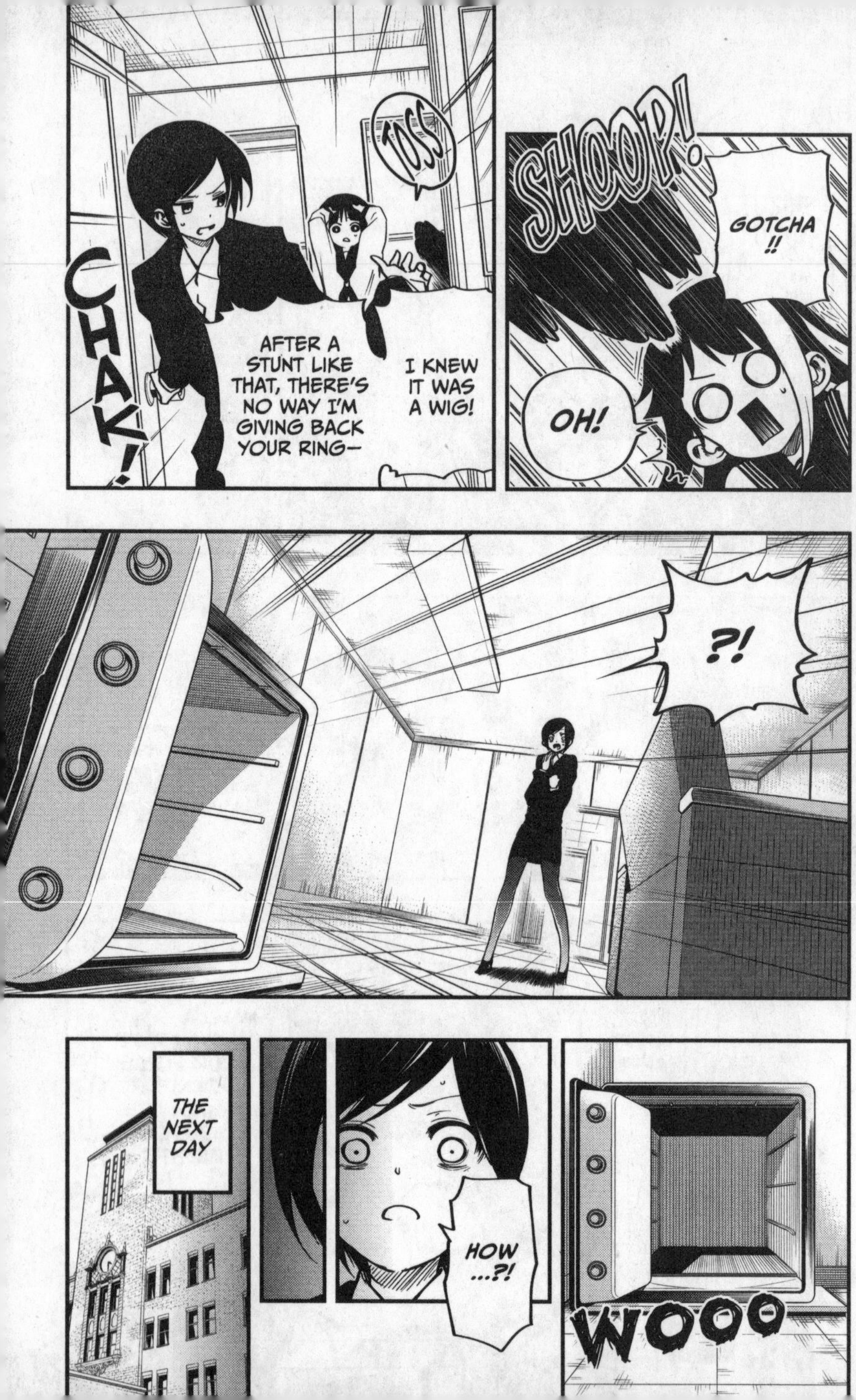
SHOOP!
GOTCHA !!
OH!
TOSS
I KNEW IT WAS A WIG!
AFTER A STUNT LIKE THAT, THERE'S NO WAY I'M GIVING BACK YOUR RING—
CHAK!
?!
WOOO
HOW ...?!
THE NEXT DAY

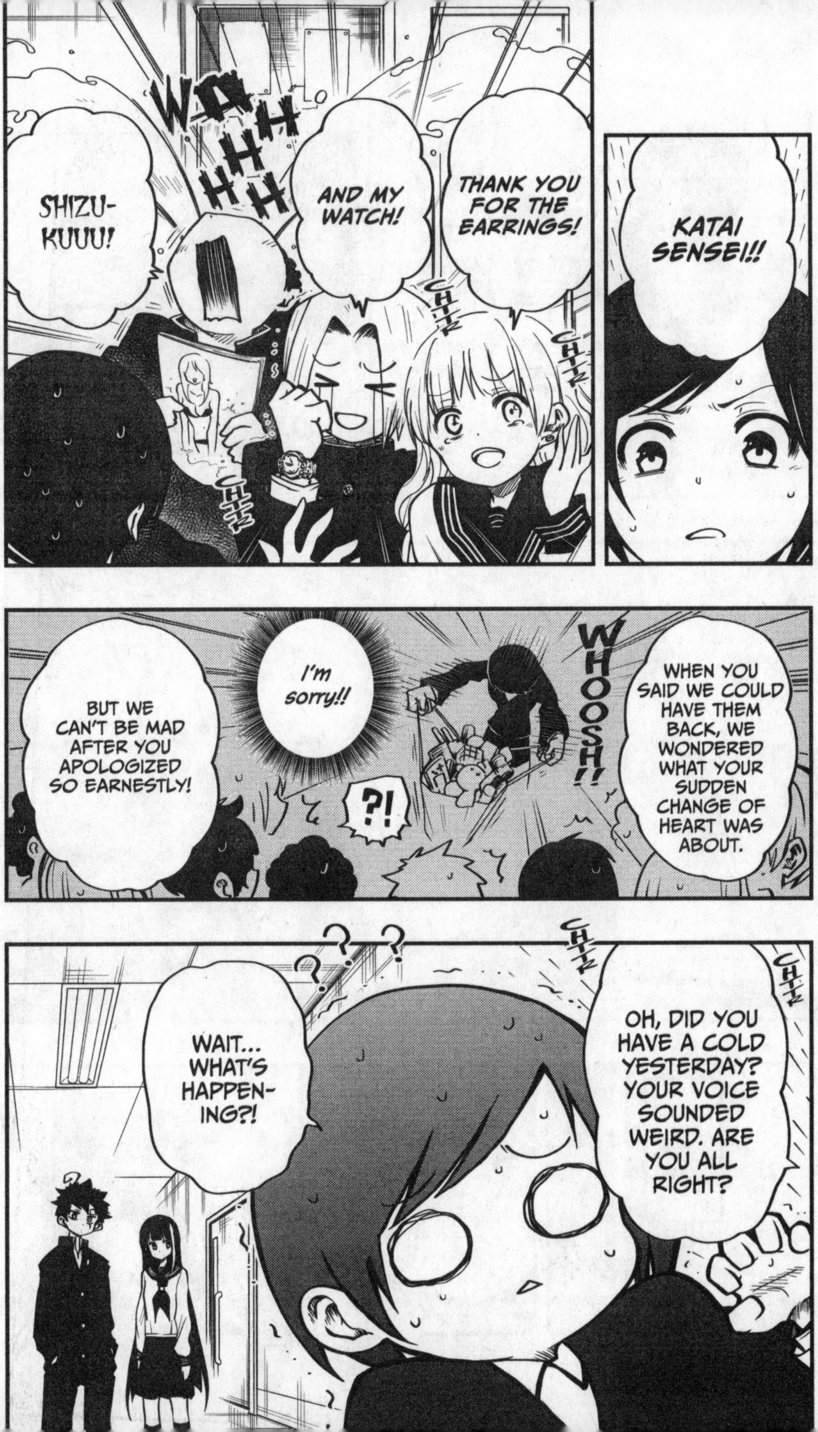
KATAI SENSEI!!
THANK YOU FOR THE EARRINGS!
CHTIR
CHTIR
AND MY WATCH!
WAHHHHH
SHIZU-KUUU!
CHTIR
WHEN YOU SAID WE COULD HAVE THEM BACK, WE WONDERED WHAT YOUR SUDDEN CHANGE OF HEART WAS ABOUT.
WHOOSH!!
I'm sorry!!
?!
BUT WE CAN'T BE MAD AFTER YOU APOLOGIZED SO EARNESTLY!
CHTIR
CHTIR
OH, DID YOU HAVE A COLD YESTERDAY? YOUR VOICE SOUNDED WEIRD. ARE YOU ALL RIGHT?
WAIT... WHAT'S HAPPEN-ING?!
???

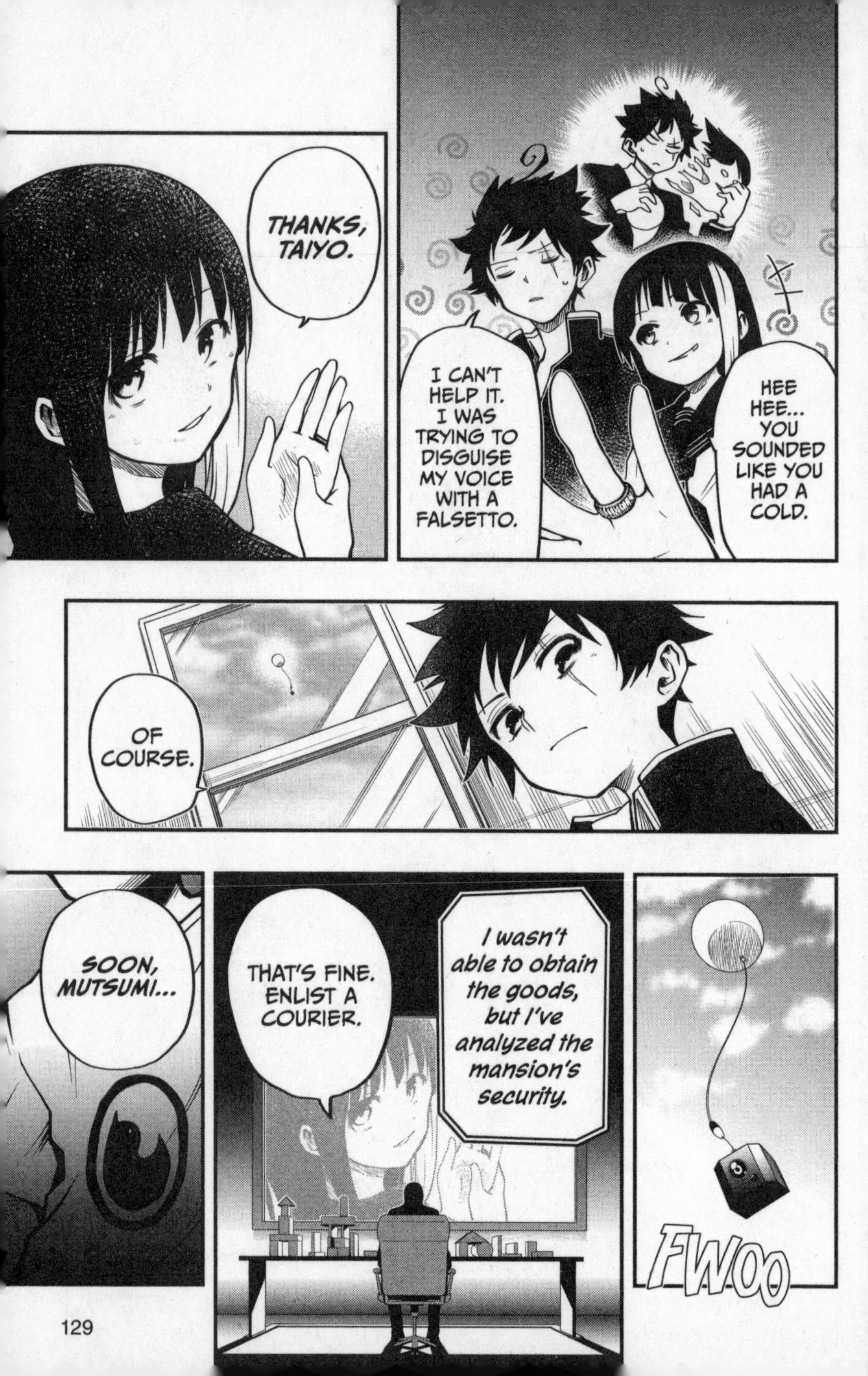
HEE HEE... YOU SOUNDED LIKE YOU HAD A COLD.
I CAN'T HELP IT. I WAS TRYING TO DISGUISE MY VOICE WITH A FALSETTO.
THANKS, TAIYO.
OF COURSE.
FWOO
I wasn't able to obtain the goods, but I've analyzed the mansion's security.
THAT'S FINE. ENLIST A COURIER.
SOON, MUTSUMI...

KATAI'S A PUSHOVER

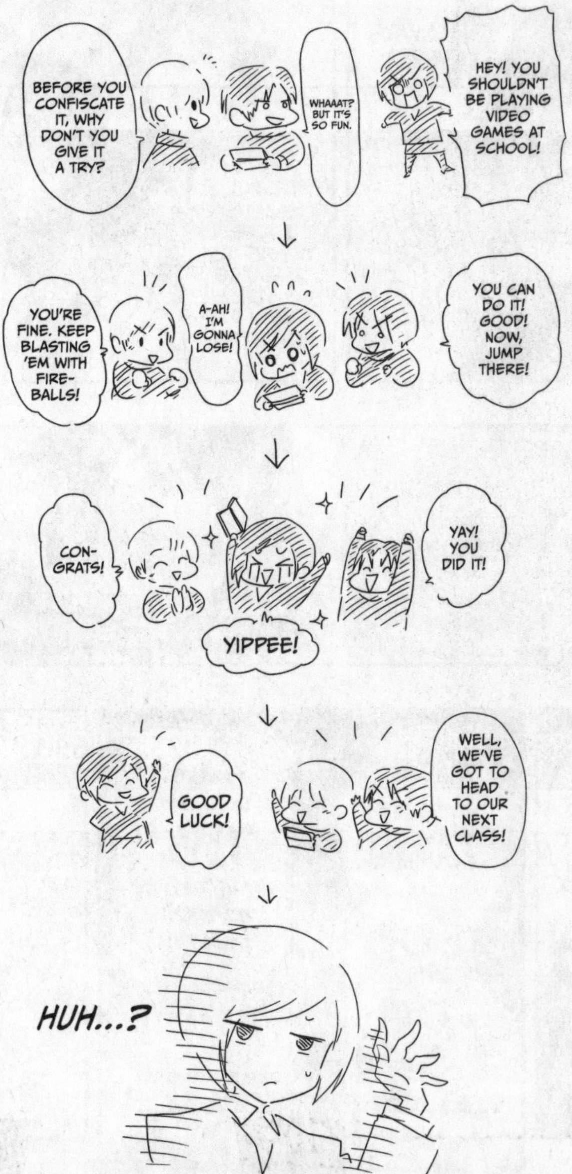
HEY! YOU SHOULDN'T BE PLAYING VIDEO GAMES AT SCHOOL!
WHAAAT? BUT IT'S SO FUN.
BEFORE YOU CONFISCATE IT, WHY DON'T YOU GIVE IT A TRY?
YOU CAN DO IT! GOOD! NOW, JUMP THERE!
A-AH! I'M GONNA LOSE!
YOU'RE FINE. KEEP BLASTING 'EM WITH FIRE-BALLS!
YAY! YOU DID IT!
YIPPEE!
CON-GRATS!
WELL, WE'VE GOT TO HEAD TO OUR NEXT CLASS!
GOOD LUCK!
HUH...?

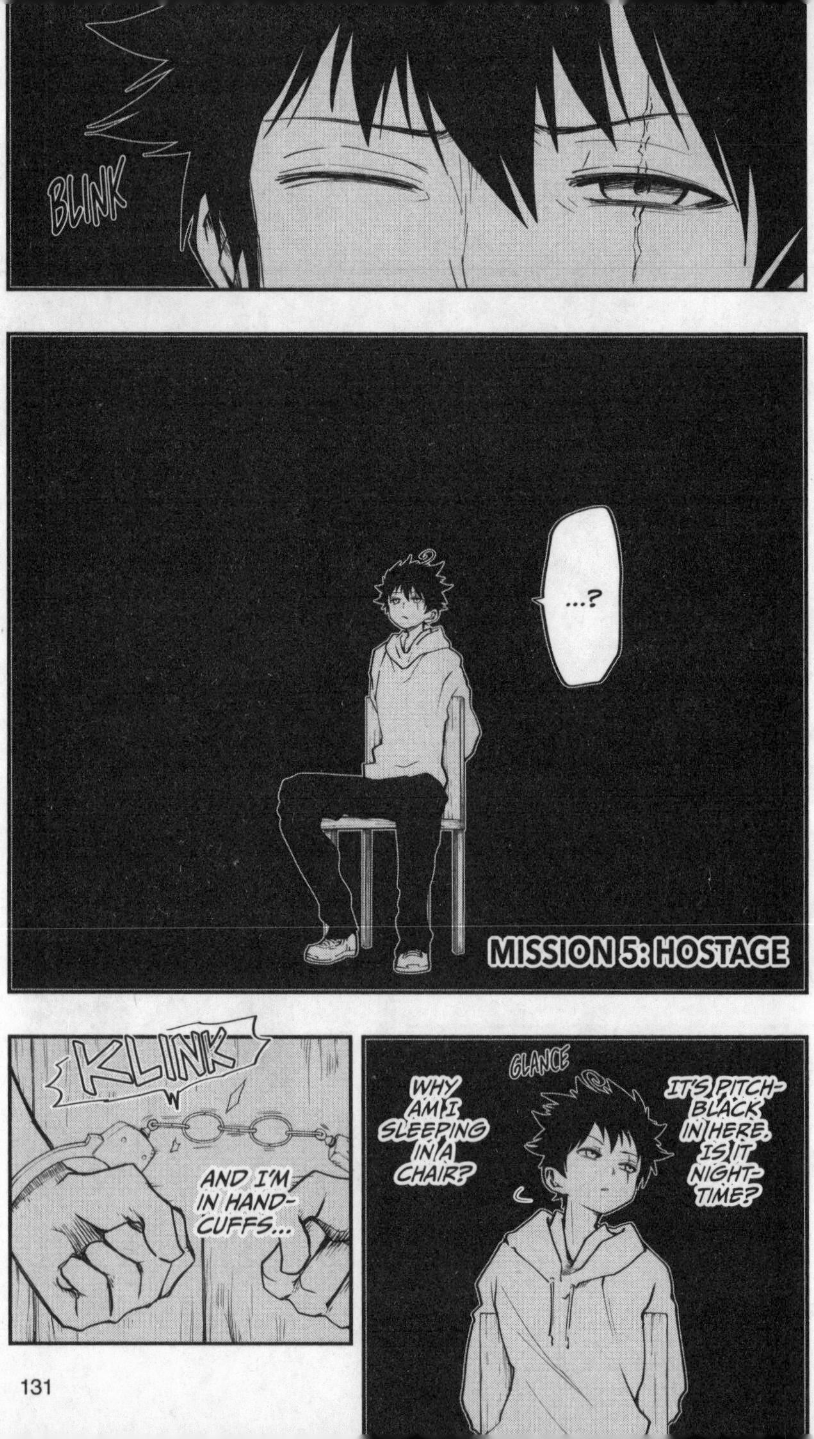
BLINK
...?
MISSION 5: HOSTAGE
GLANCE
IT'S PITCH-BLACK IN HERE. IS IT NIGHT-TIME?
WHY AM I SLEEPING IN A CHAIR?
KLINK
AND I'M IN HAND-CUFFS...

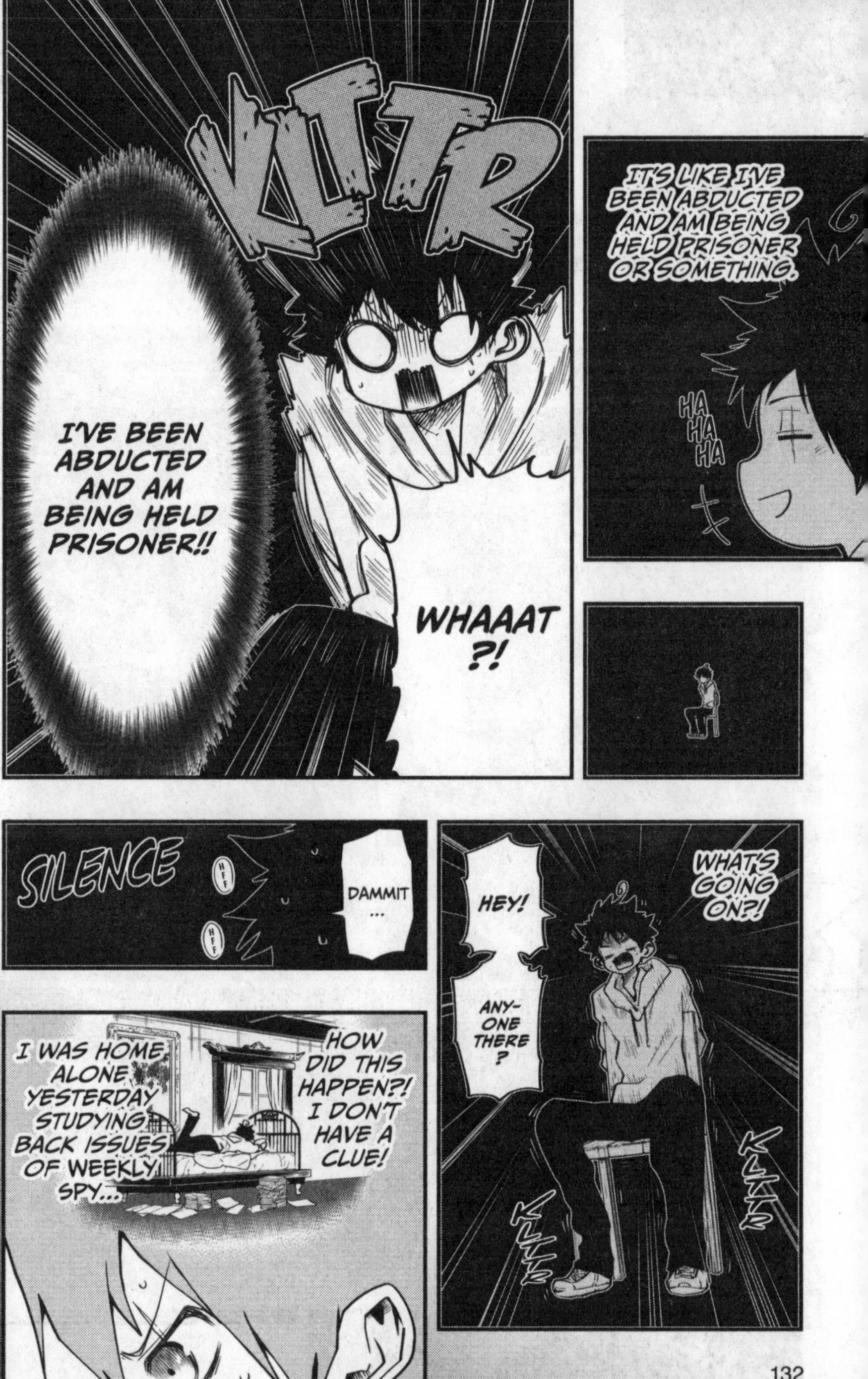
IT'S LIKE I'VE BEEN ABDUCTED AND AM BEING HELD PRISONER OR SOMETHING.
HA HA HA
KLTTR
WHAAAT?!
I'VE BEEN ABDUCTED AND AM BEING HELD PRISONER!!
WHAT'S GOING ON?!
HEY!
ANY-ONE THERE?
KLTTR
KLTTR
DAMMIT...
HFF
HFF
SILENCE
HOW DID THIS HAPPEN?! I DON'T HAVE A CLUE!
I WAS HOME ALONE YESTERDAY STUDYING BACK ISSUES OF WEEKLY SPY...

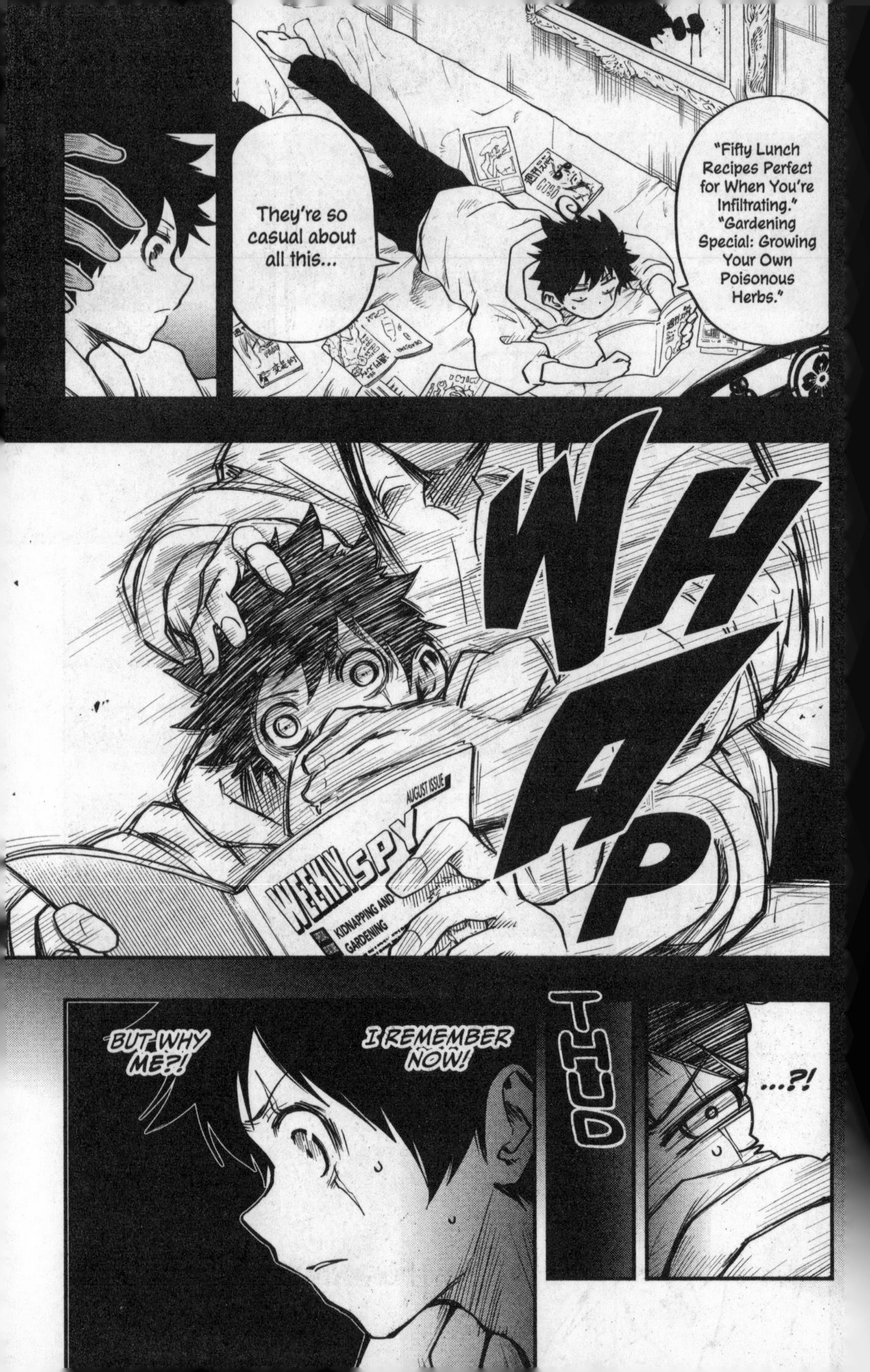
"Fifty Lunch Recipes Perfect for When You're Infiltrating." "Gardening Special: Growing Your Own Poisonous Herbs."
They're so casual about all this...
WHAP
AUGUST ISSUE
WEEKL SPY
KIDNAPPING AND GARDENING
...?!
THUD
I REMEMBER NOW!
BUT WHY ME?!

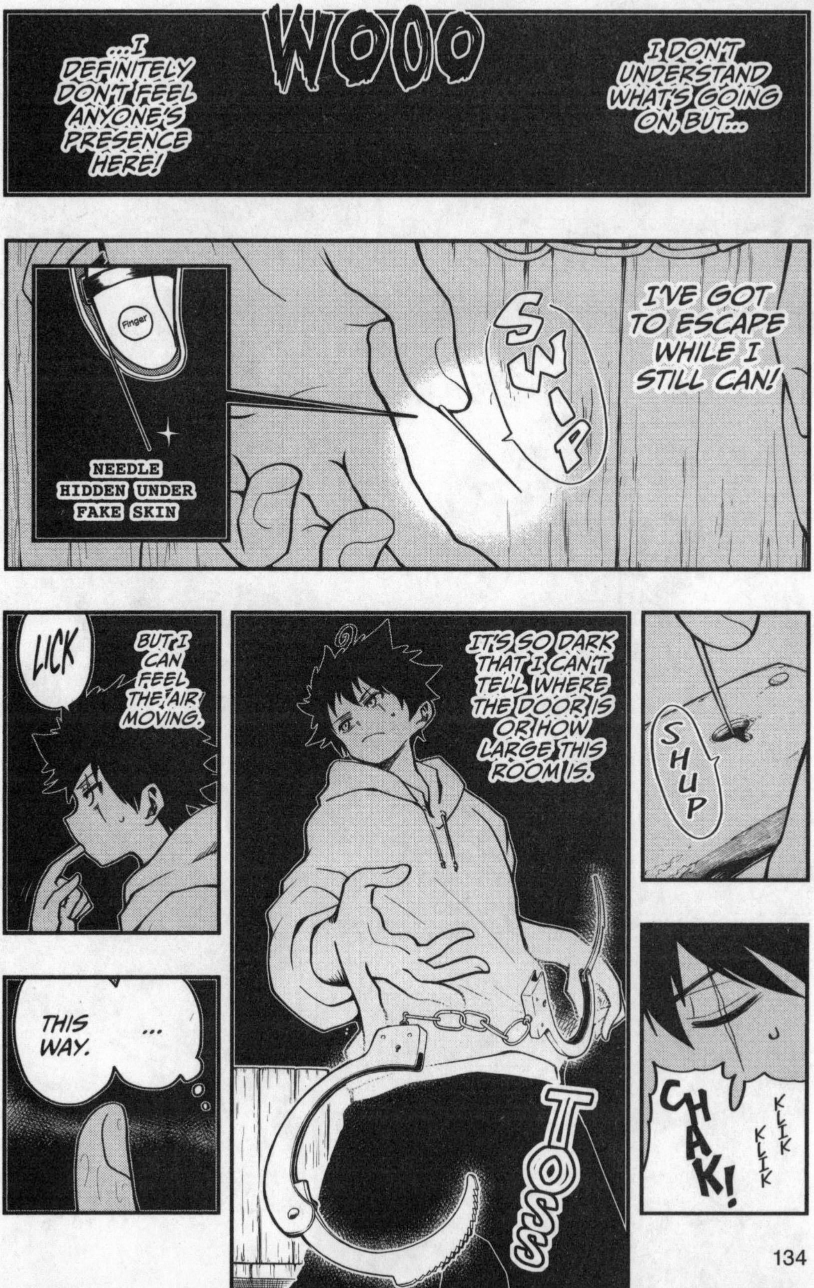
I DON'T UNDERSTAND WHAT'S GOING ON, BUT...
WOOO
...I DEFINITELY DON'T FEEL ANYONE'S PRESENCE HERE!
I'VE GOT TO ESCAPE WHILE I STILL CAN!
SWIP
Finger
NEEDLE HIDDEN UNDER FAKE SKIN
SHUP
CHAK!
KLIK KLIK
IT'S SO DARK THAT I CAN'T TELL WHERE THE DOOR IS OR HOW LARGE THIS ROOM IS.
TOSS
BUT I CAN FEEL THE AIR MOVING.
LICK
...
THIS WAY.

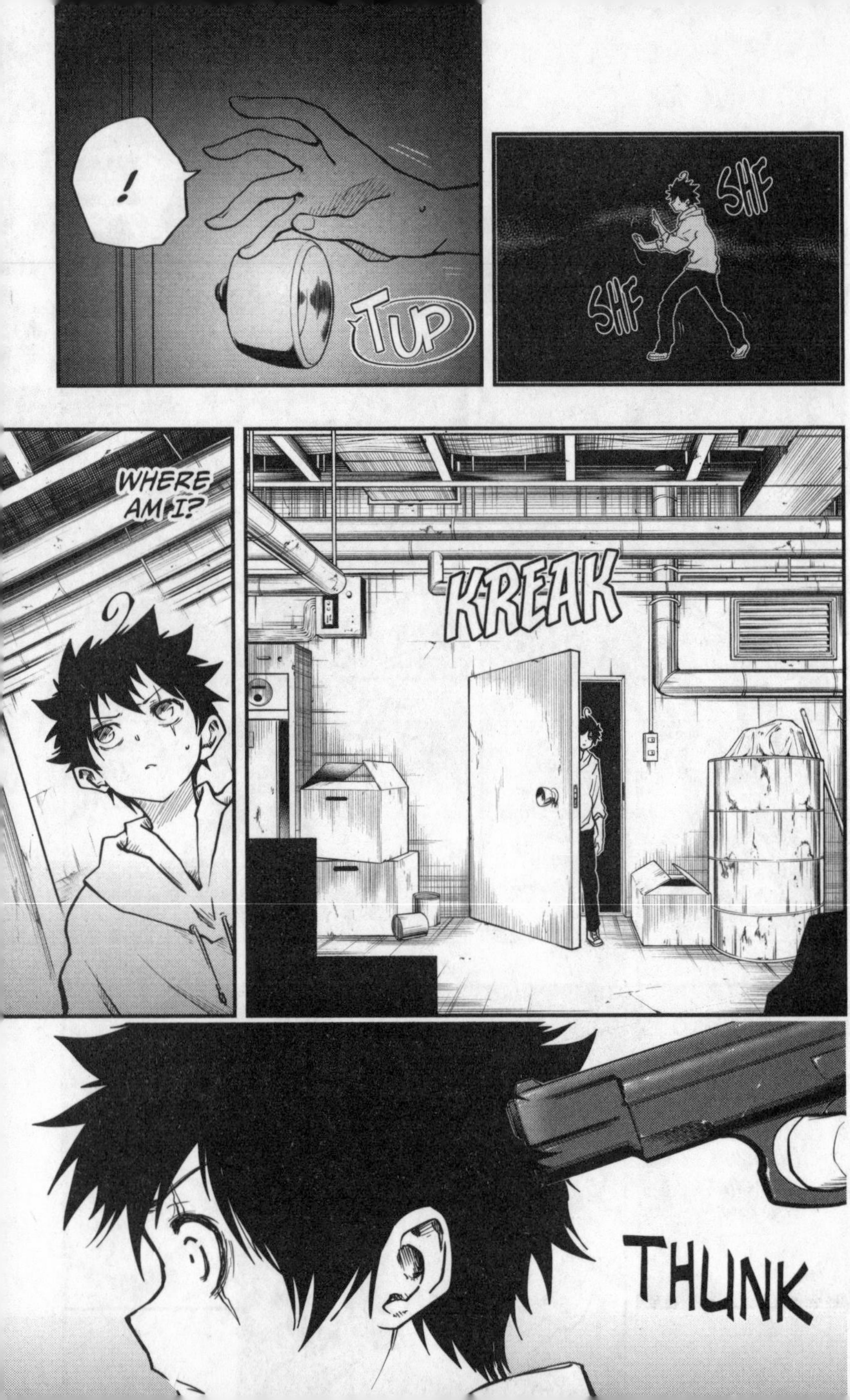
SHF
SHF
!
TUP
KREAK
WHERE AM I?
THUNK

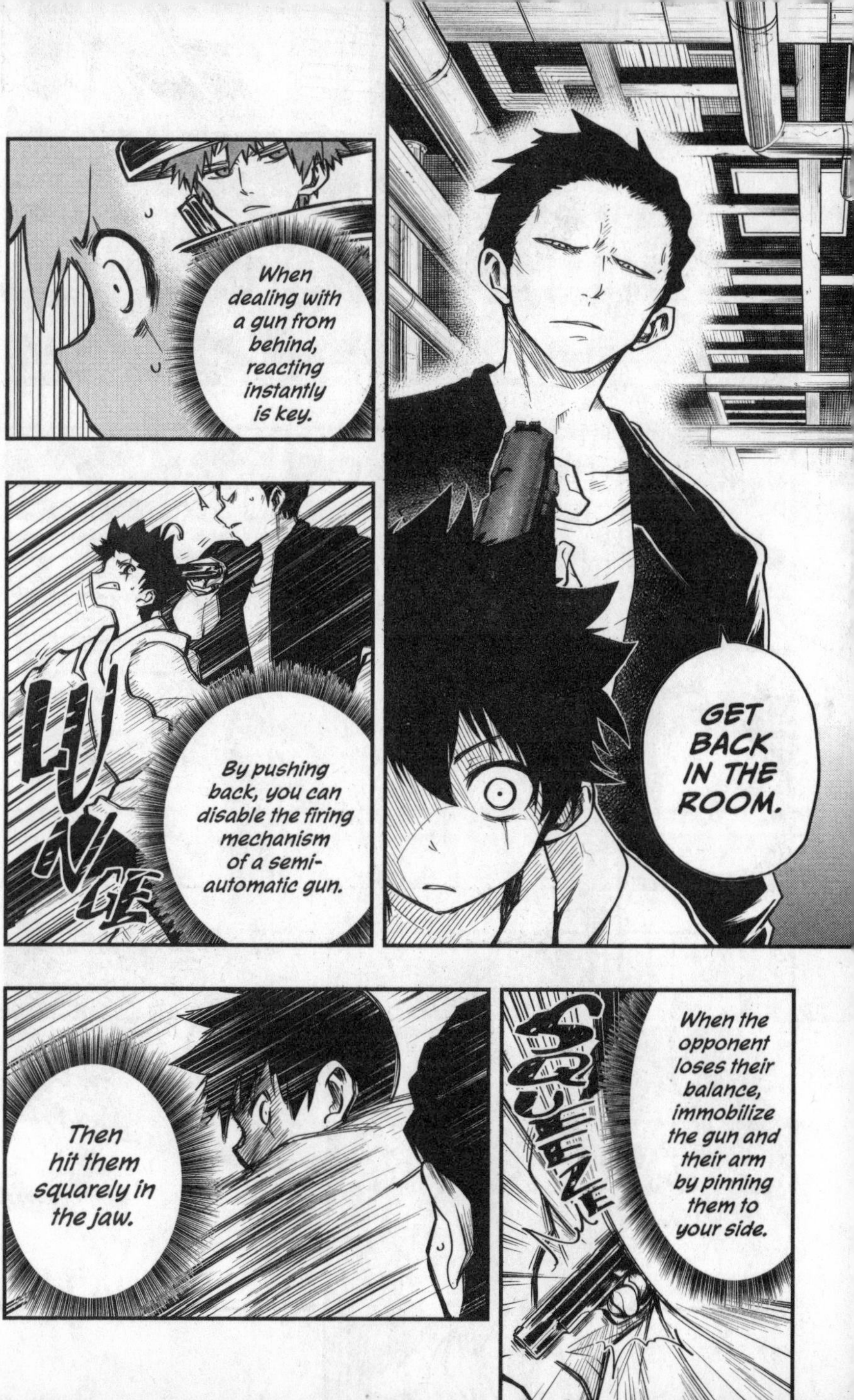
GET BACK IN THE ROOM.
When dealing with a gun from behind, reacting instantly is key.
LUNGE
By pushing back, you can disable the firing mechanism of a semi-automatic gun.
SQUEEZE
When the opponent loses their balance, immobilize the gun and their arm by pinning them to your side.
Then hit them squarely in the jaw.

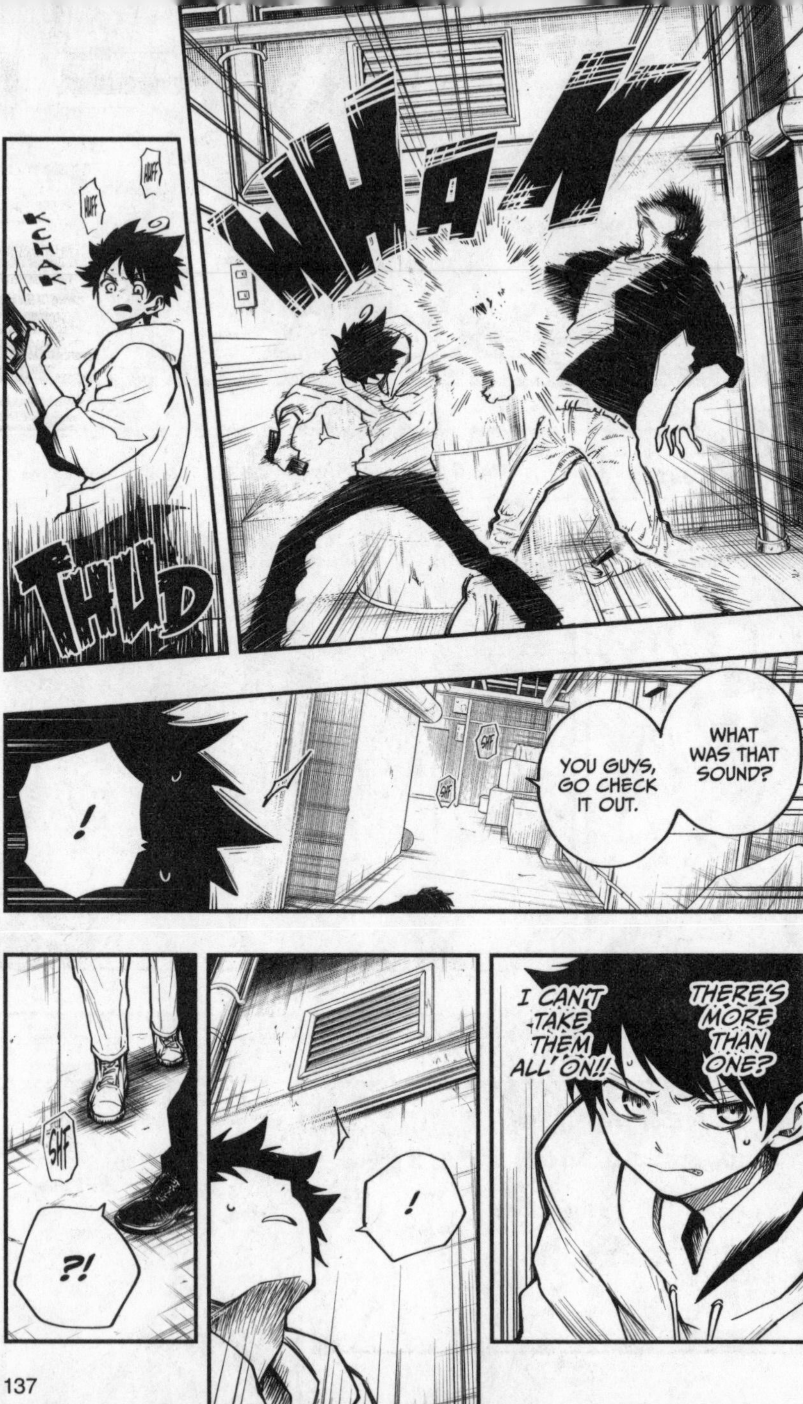
WHAK
HUFF
HUFF
KCHAK
THUD
WHAT WAS THAT SOUND?
YOU GUYS, GO CHECK IT OUT.
SHF
SHF
!
THERE'S MORE THAN ONE?
I CAN'T TAKE THEM ALL ON!!
!
SHF
?!

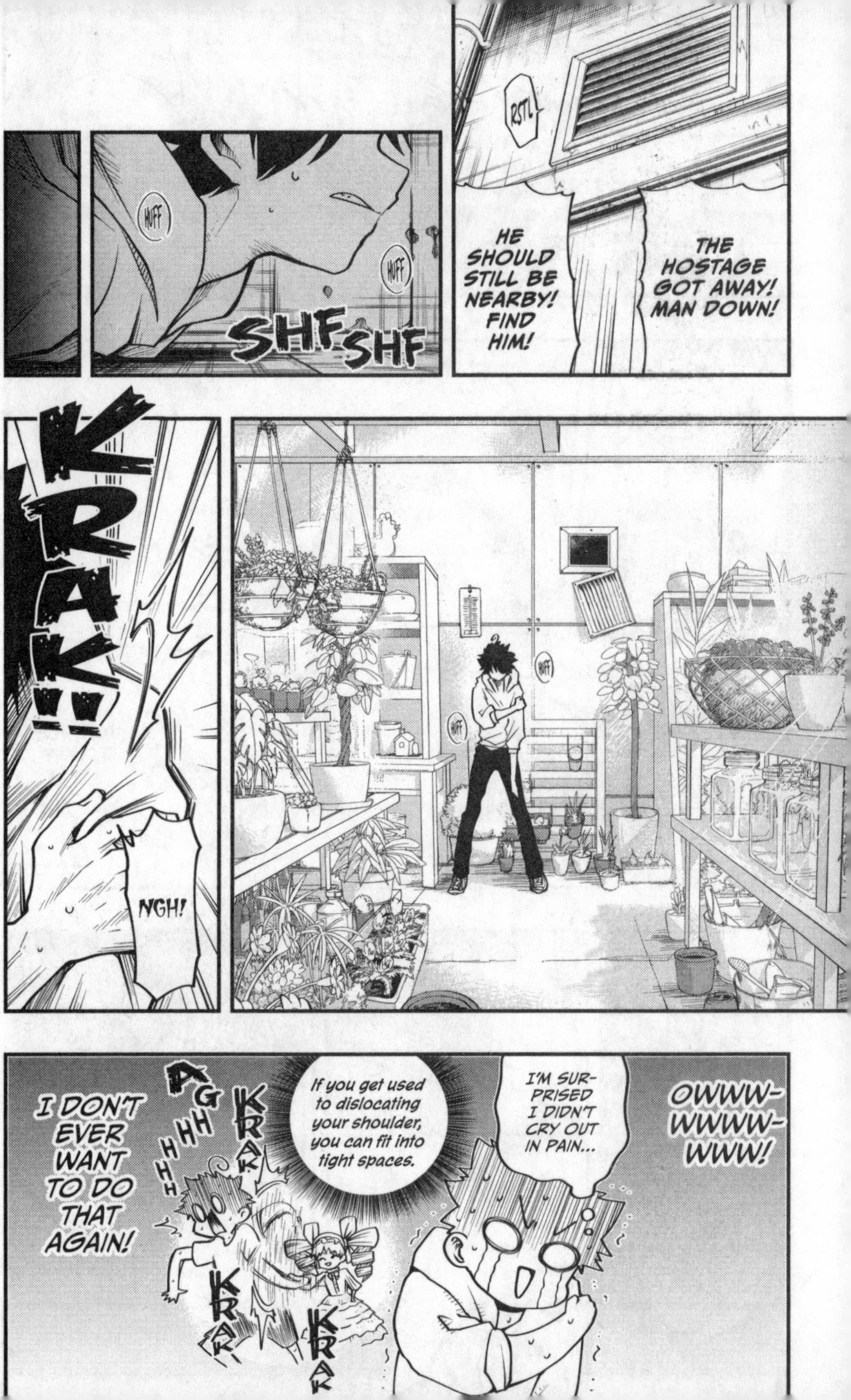
RSTL
THE HOSTAGE GOT AWAY! MAN DOWN!
HE SHOULD STILL BE NEARBY! FIND HIM!
HUFF
HUFF
SHF SHF
HUFF
HUFF
KRAK!!
NGH!
OWWW-WWWW-WWW!
I'M SURPRISED I DIDN'T CRY OUT IN PAIN...
If you get used to dislocating your shoulder, you can fit into tight spaces.
KRAK
AGHHHHH
I DON'T EVER WANT TO DO THAT AGAIN!
KRAK
KRAK

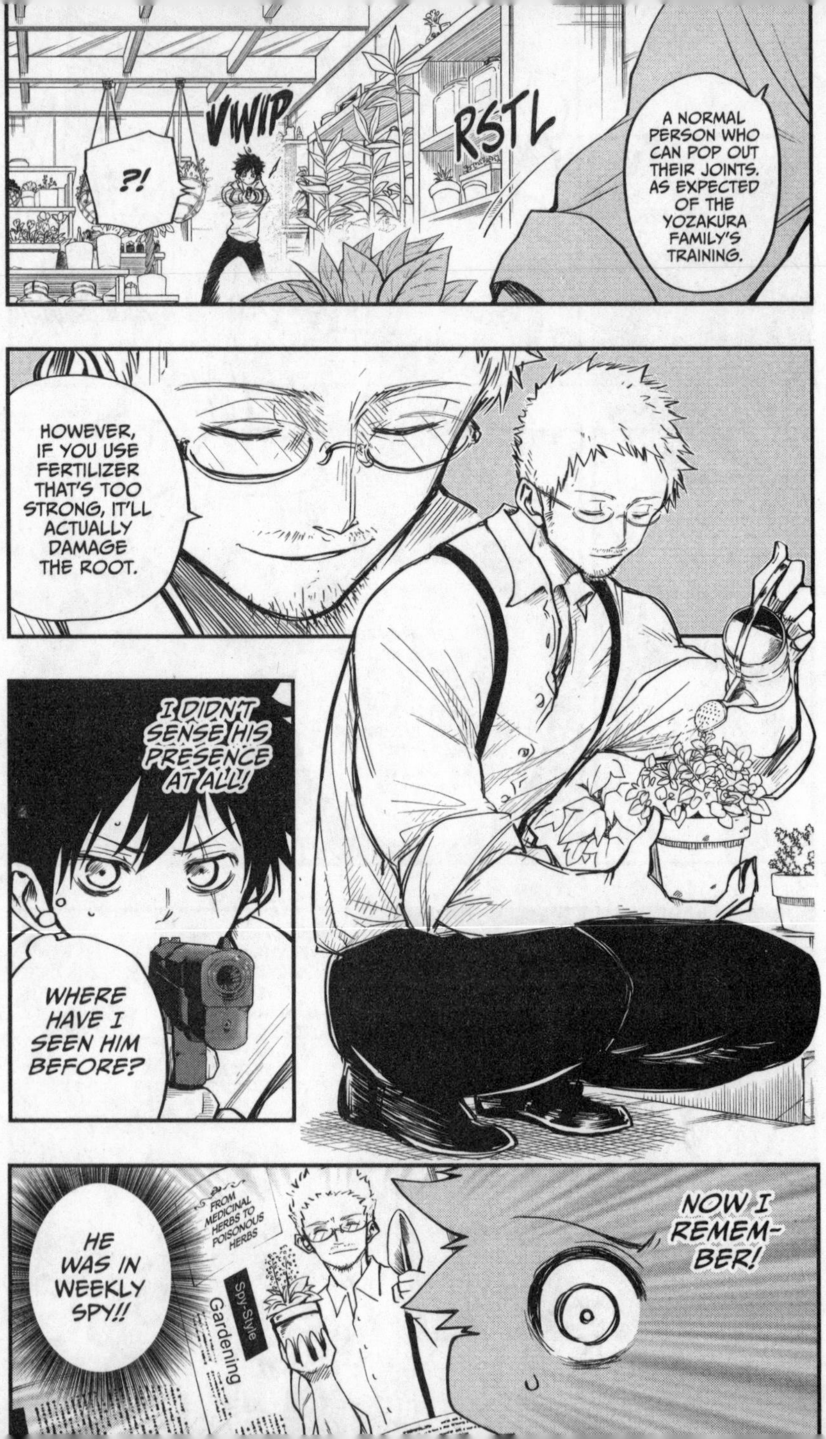
A NORMAL PERSON WHO CAN POP OUT THEIR JOINTS. AS EXPECTED OF THE YOZAKURA FAMILY'S TRAINING.
RSTL
VWIP
?!
HOWEVER, IF YOU USE FERTILIZER THAT'S TOO STRONG, IT'LL ACTUALLY DAMAGE THE ROOT.
I DIDN'T SENSE HIS PRESENCE AT ALL!
WHERE HAVE I SEEN HIM BEFORE?
NOW I REMEM-BER!
FROM MEDICINAL HERBS TO POISONOUS HERBS
Spy-Style
Gardening
HE WAS IN WEEKLY SPY!!

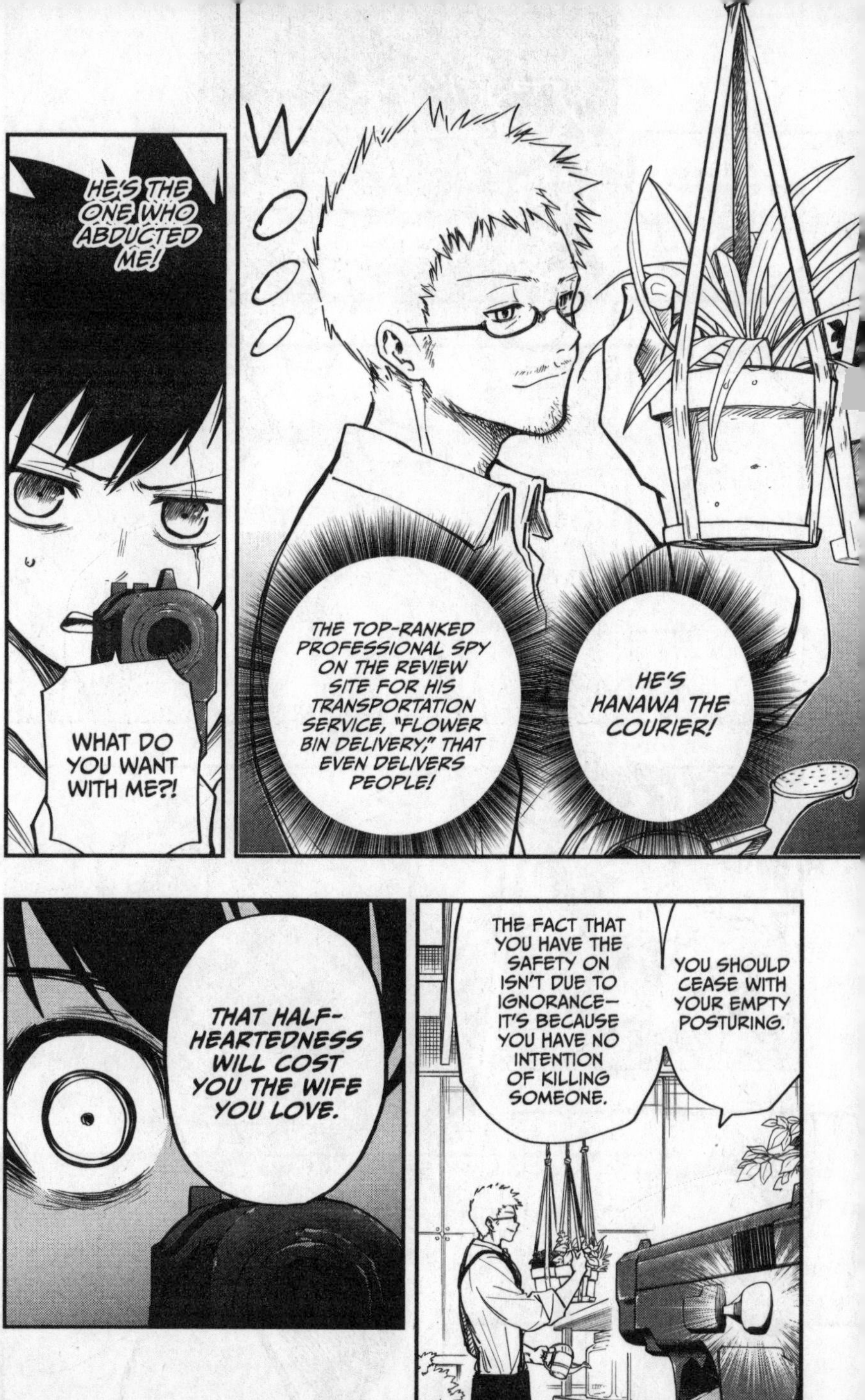
WOOO
HE'S HANAWA THE COURIER!
THE TOP-RANKED PROFESSIONAL SPY ON THE REVIEW SITE FOR HIS TRANSPORTATION SERVICE, "FLOWER BIN DELIVERY," THAT EVEN DELIVERS PEOPLE!
HE'S THE ONE WHO ABDUCTED ME!
WHAT DO YOU WANT WITH ME?!
YOU SHOULD CEASE WITH YOUR EMPTY POSTURING.
THE FACT THAT YOU HAVE THE SAFETY ON ISN'T DUE TO IGNORANCE—IT'S BECAUSE YOU HAVE NO INTENTION OF KILLING SOMEONE.
THAT HALF-HEARTEDNESS WILL COST YOU THE WIFE YOU LOVE.

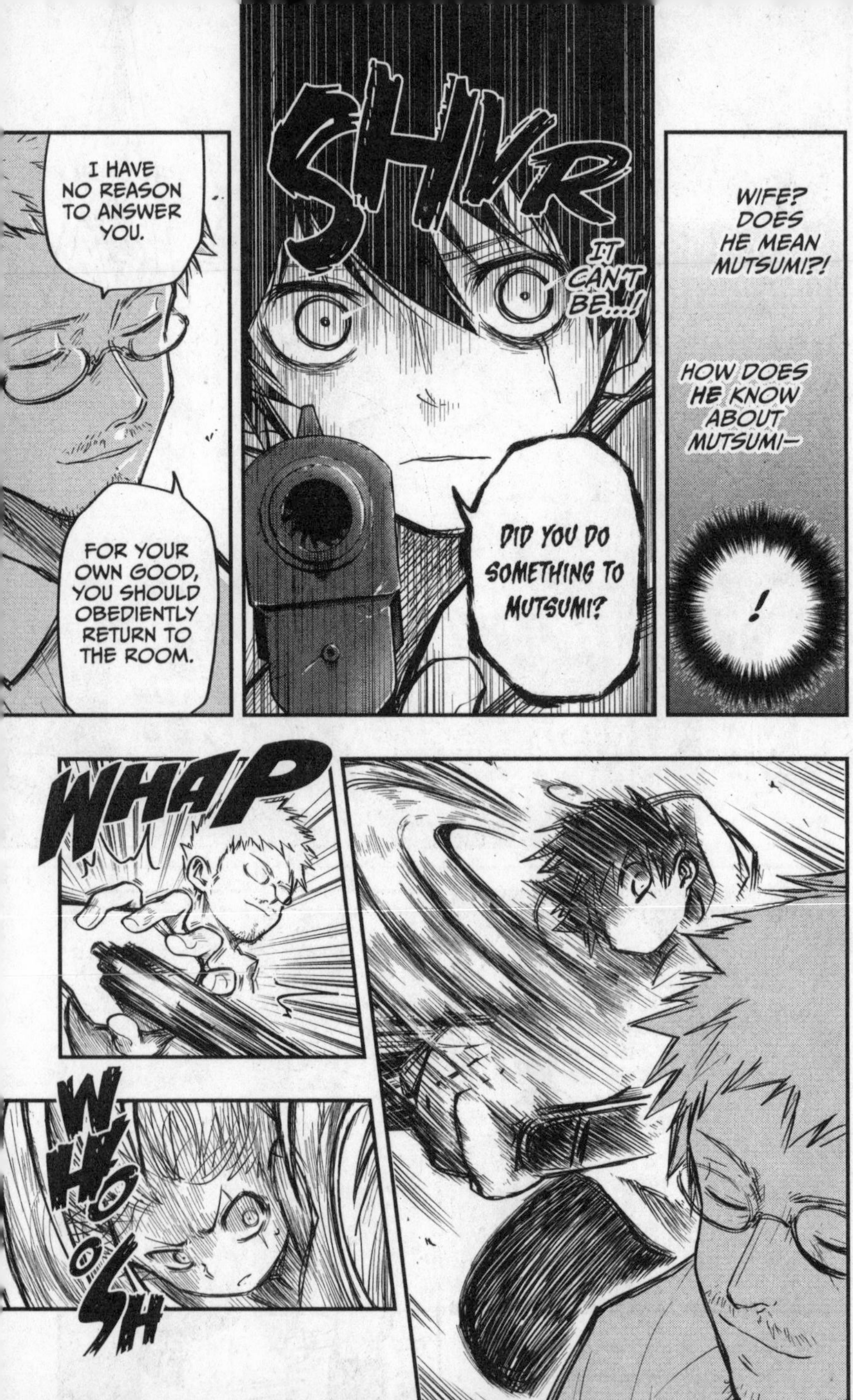
WIFE? DOES HE MEAN MUTSUMI?!
HOW DOES HE KNOW ABOUT MUTSUMI—
!
SHVR
IT CAN'T BE...!
DID YOU DO SOMETHING TO MUTSUMI?
I HAVE NO REASON TO ANSWER YOU.
FOR YOUR OWN GOOD, YOU SHOULD OBEDIENTLY RETURN TO THE ROOM.
WHAP
WHOOSH

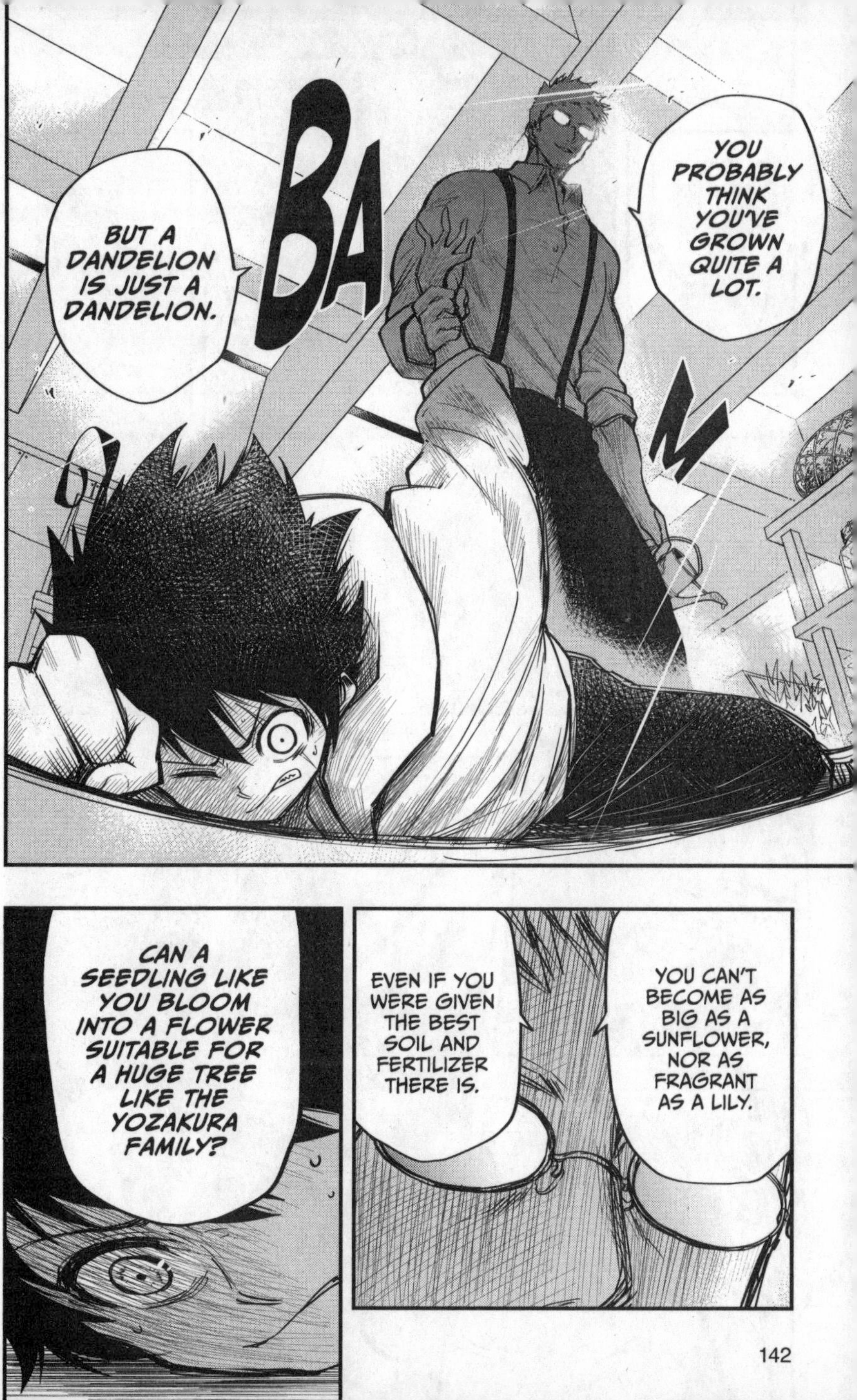
YOU PROBABLY THINK YOU'VE GROWN QUITE A LOT.
BAM
BUT A DANDELION IS JUST A DANDELION.
YOU CAN'T BECOME AS BIG AS A SUNFLOWER, NOR AS FRAGRANT AS A LILY.
EVEN IF YOU WERE GIVEN THE BEST SOIL AND FERTILIZER THERE IS.
CAN A SEEDLING LIKE YOU BLOOM INTO A FLOWER SUITABLE FOR A HUGE TREE LIKE THE YOZAKURA FAMILY?

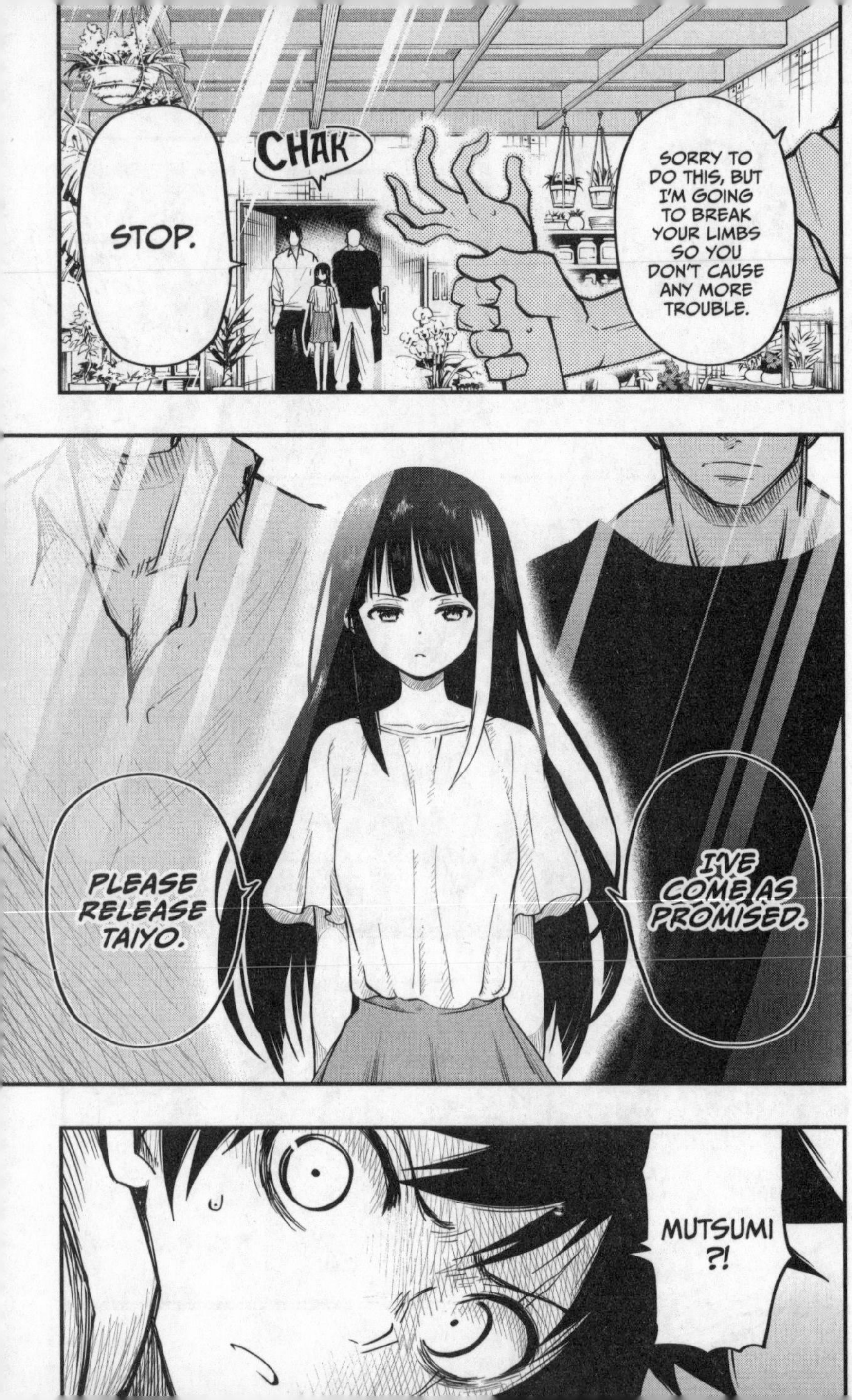
SORRY TO DO THIS, BUT I'M GOING TO BREAK YOUR LIMBS SO YOU DON'T CAUSE ANY MORE TROUBLE.
CHAK
STOP.
I'VE COME AS PROMISED.
PLEASE RELEASE TAIYO.
MUTSUMI?!

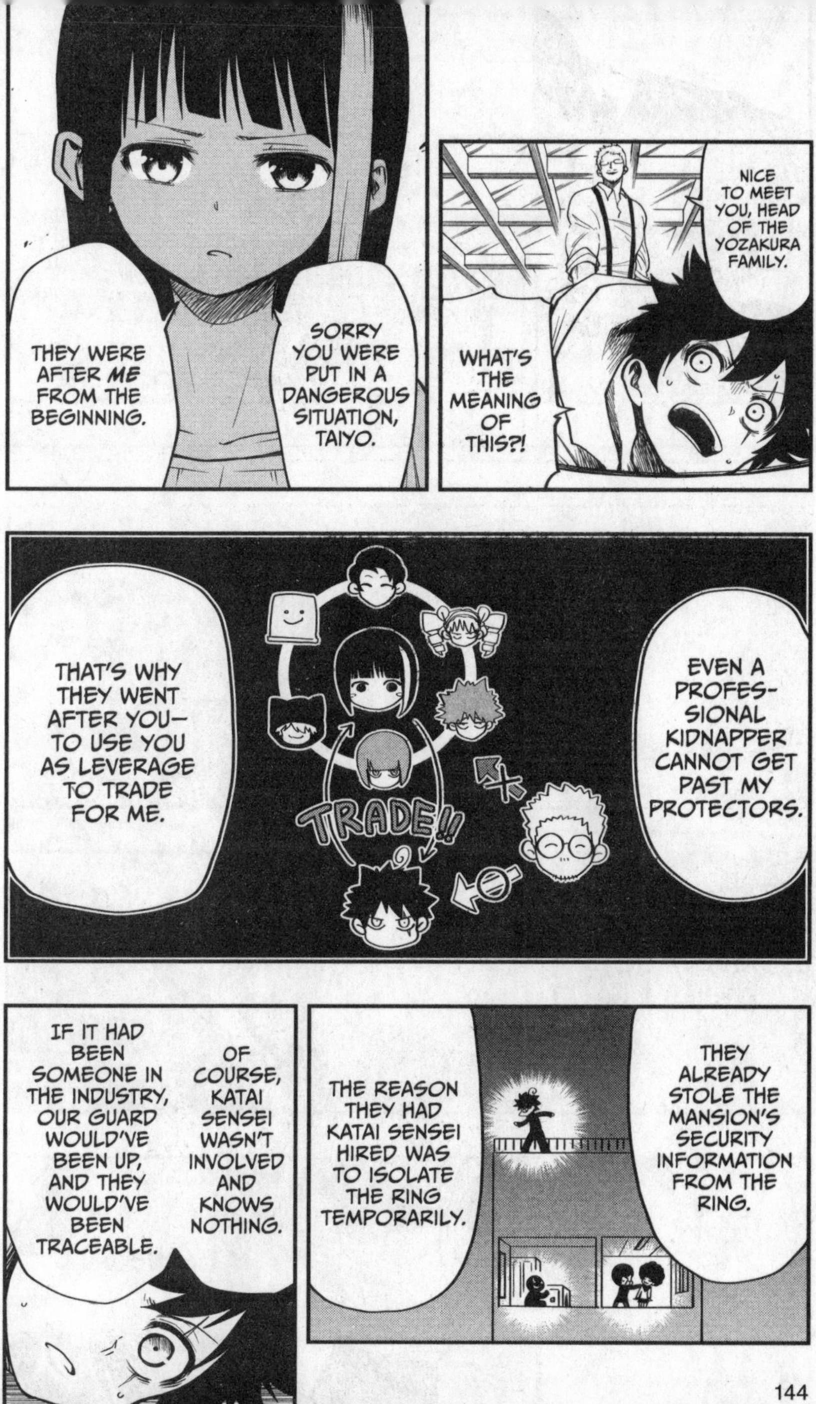
NICE TO MEET YOU, HEAD OF THE YOZAKURA FAMILY.
WHAT'S THE MEANING OF THIS?!
SORRY YOU WERE PUT IN A DANGEROUS SITUATION, TAIYO.
THEY WERE AFTER *ME* FROM THE BEGINNING.
EVEN A PROFES-SIONAL KIDNAPPER CANNOT GET PAST MY PROTECTORS.
THAT'S WHY THEY WENT AFTER YOU—TO USE YOU AS LEVERAGE TO TRADE FOR ME.
TRADE!!
THEY ALREADY STOLE THE MANSION'S SECURITY INFORMATION FROM THE RING.
THE REASON THEY HAD KATAI SENSEI HIRED WAS TO ISOLATE THE RING TEMPORARILY.
OF COURSE, KATAI SENSEI WASN'T INVOLVED AND KNOWS NOTHING.
IF IT HAD BEEN SOMEONE IN THE INDUSTRY, OUR GUARD WOULD'VE BEEN UP, AND THEY WOULD'VE BEEN TRACEABLE.

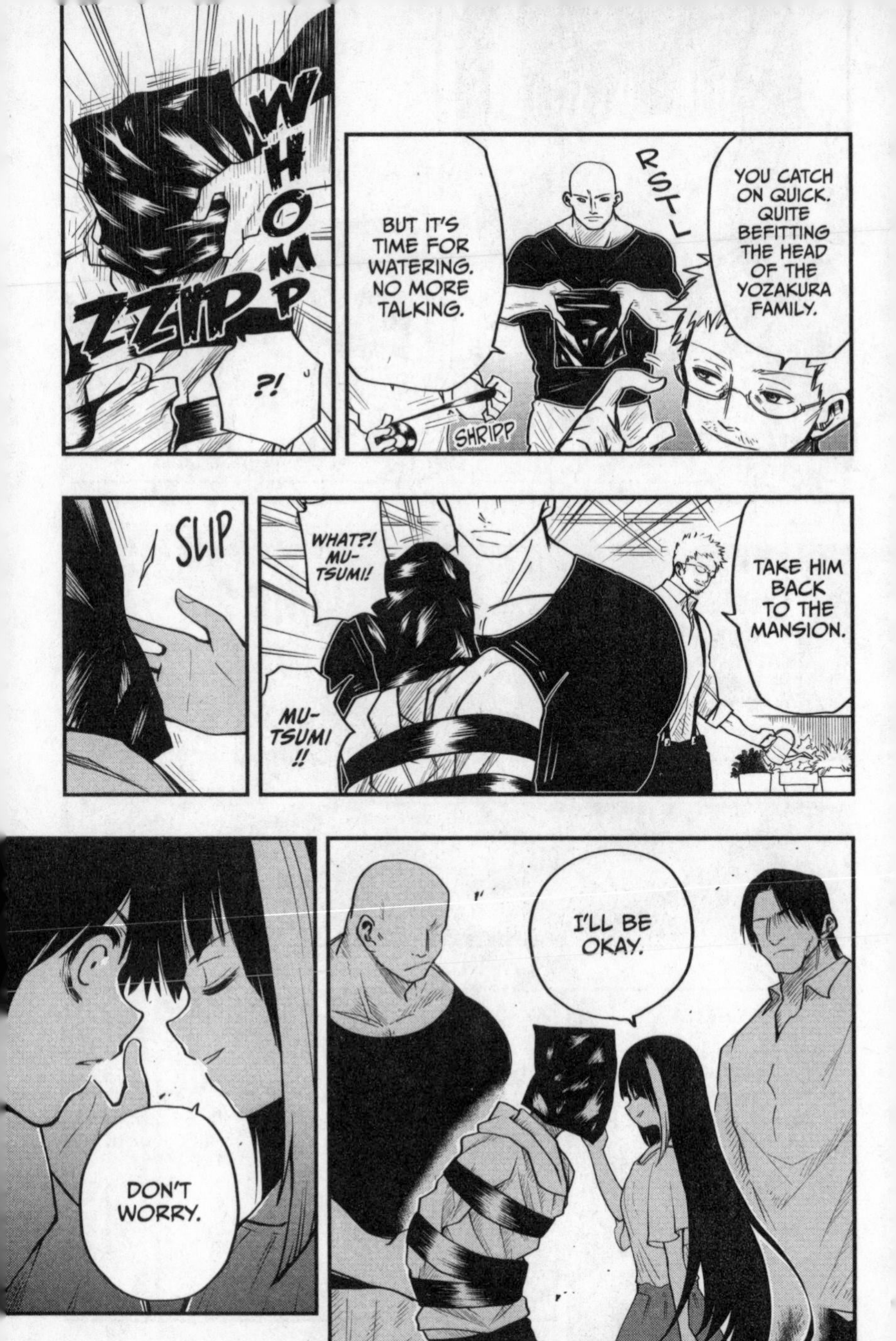
RSTL
YOU CATCH ON QUICK. QUITE BEFITTING THE HEAD OF THE YOZAKURA FAMILY.
BUT IT'S TIME FOR WATERING. NO MORE TALKING.
SHRIPP
WHOMP
ZZIP
?!
TAKE HIM BACK TO THE MANSION.
WHAT?! MU-TSUMI!
MU-TSUMI!!
SLIP
I'LL BE OKAY.
DON'T WORRY.

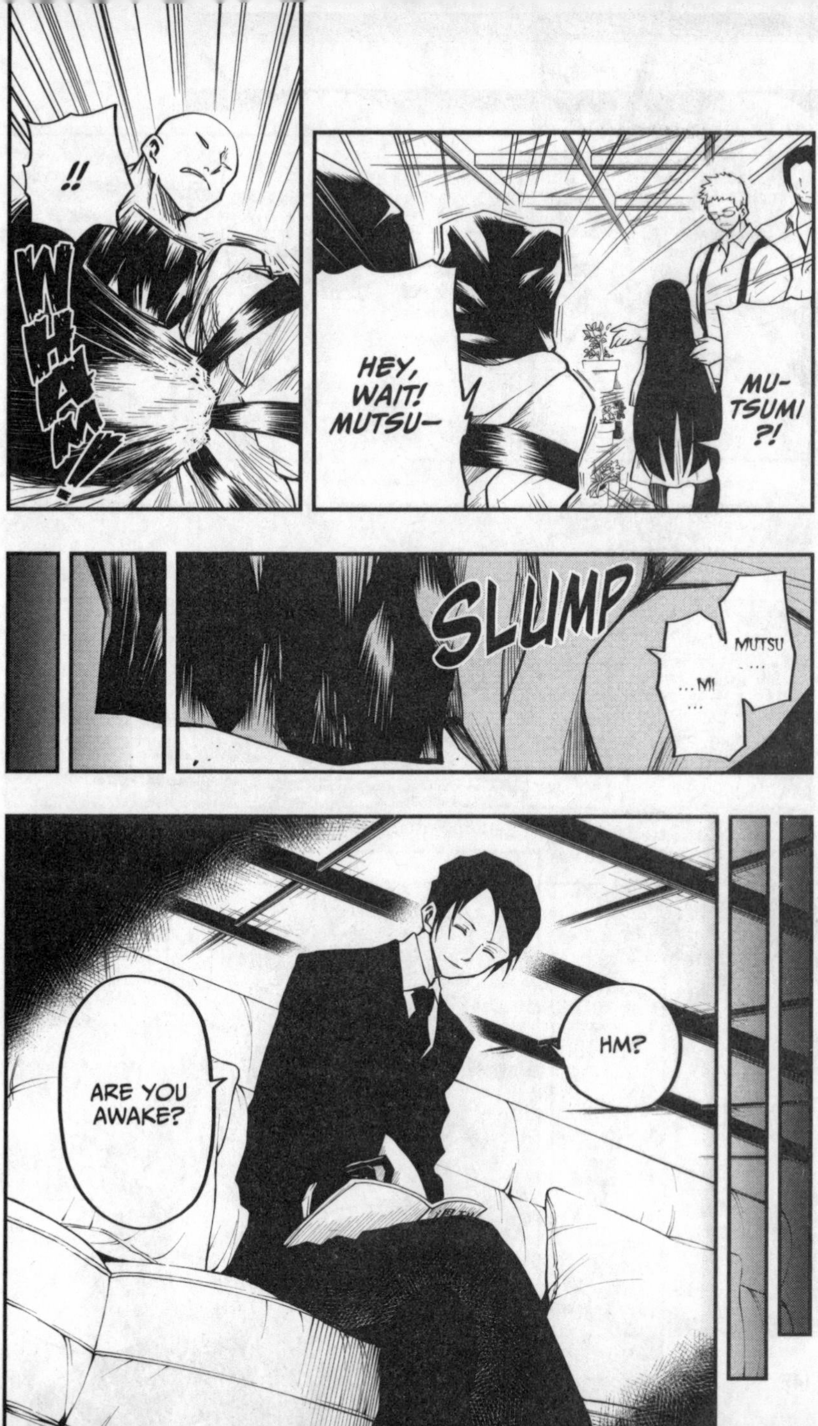
MU-
TSUMI
?!
HEY,
WAIT!
MUTSU—
!!
WHAM!
MUTSU
...
...MI
...
SLUMP
HM?
ARE YOU
AWAKE?

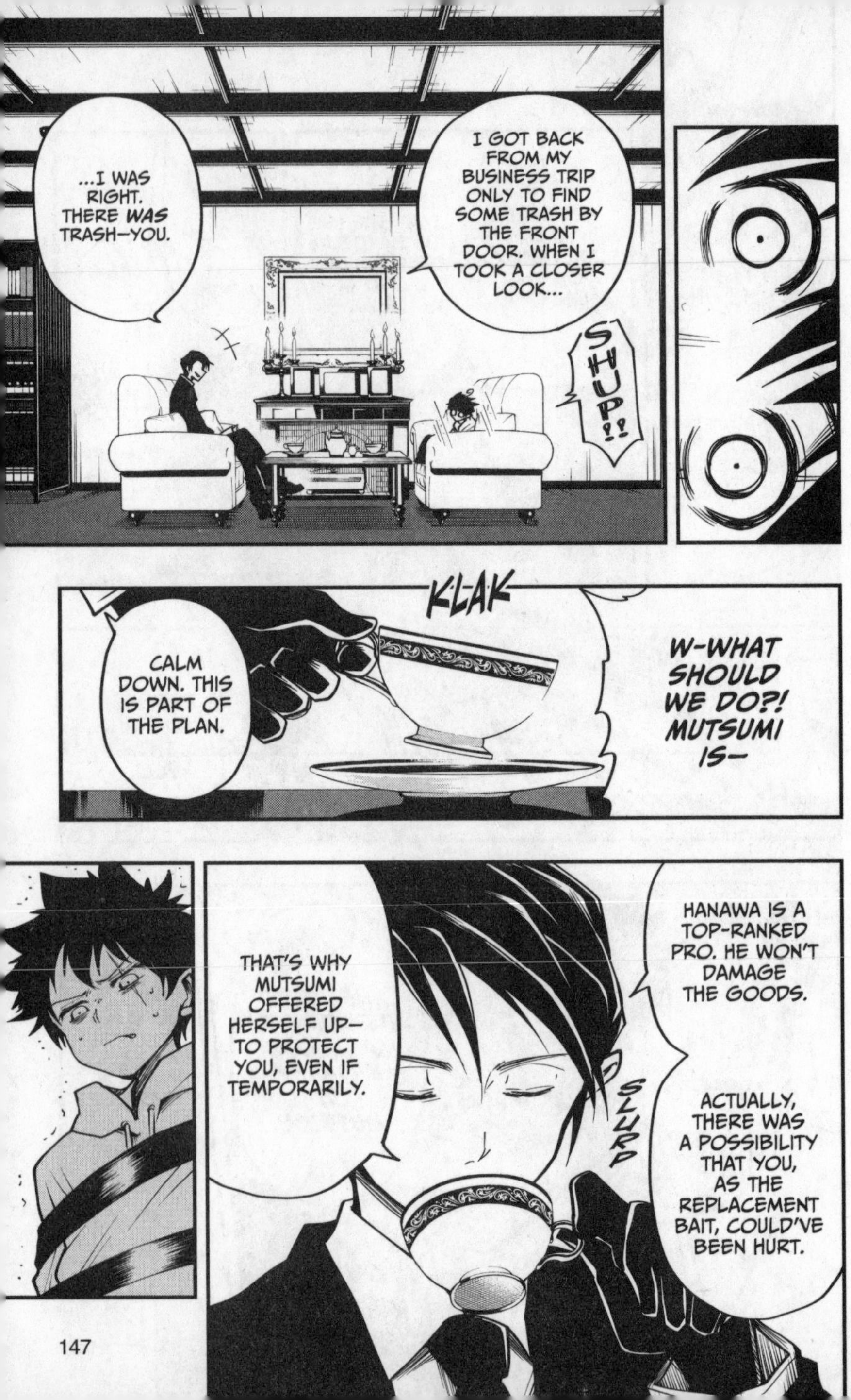

I GOT BACK FROM MY BUSINESS TRIP ONLY TO FIND SOME TRASH BY THE FRONT DOOR. WHEN I TOOK A CLOSER LOOK...
...I WAS RIGHT. THERE WAS TRASH—YOU.
SHUP!!
W-WHAT SHOULD WE DO?! MUTSUMI IS—
KLAK
CALM DOWN. THIS IS PART OF THE PLAN.
HANAWA IS A TOP-RANKED PRO. HE WON'T DAMAGE THE GOODS.
SLURP
ACTUALLY, THERE WAS A POSSIBILITY THAT YOU, AS THE REPLACEMENT BAIT, COULD'VE BEEN HURT.
THAT'S WHY MUTSUMI OFFERED HERSELF UP—TO PROTECT YOU, EVEN IF TEMPORARILY.

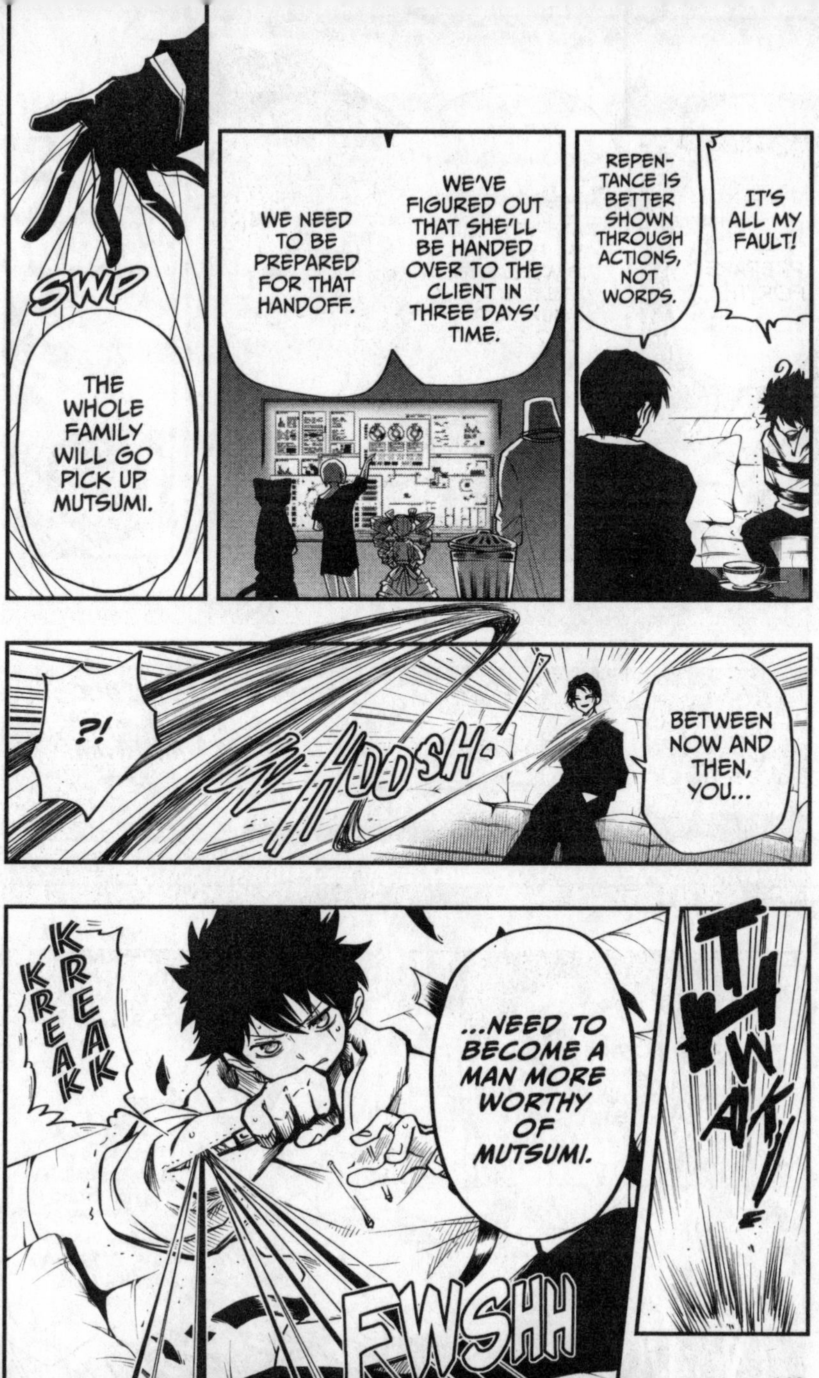
IT'S ALL MY FAULT!
REPEN-TANCE IS BETTER SHOWN THROUGH ACTIONS, NOT WORDS.
WE'VE FIGURED OUT THAT SHE'LL BE HANDED OVER TO THE CLIENT IN THREE DAYS' TIME.
WE NEED TO BE PREPARED FOR THAT HANDOFF.
SWP
THE WHOLE FAMILY WILL GO PICK UP MUTSUMI.
BETWEEN NOW AND THEN, YOU...
WHOOSH
?!
THWAK!
...NEED TO BECOME A MAN MORE WORTHY OF MUTSUMI.
KREAK KREAK
FWSHH

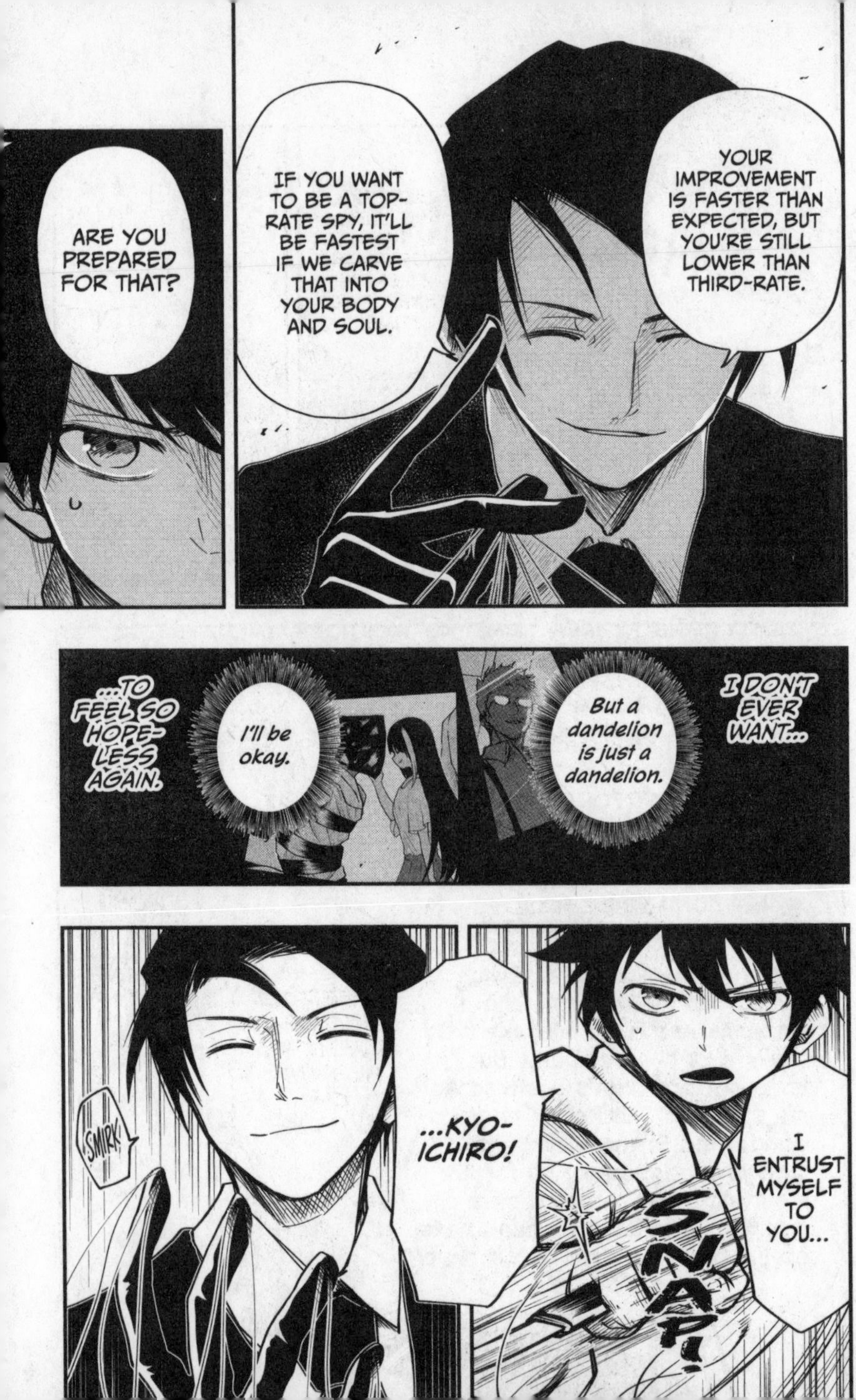
YOUR IMPROVEMENT IS FASTER THAN EXPECTED, BUT YOU'RE STILL LOWER THAN THIRD-RATE.
IF YOU WANT TO BE A TOP-RATE SPY, IT'LL BE FASTEST IF WE CARVE THAT INTO YOUR BODY AND SOUL.
ARE YOU PREPARED FOR THAT?
I DON'T EVER WANT...
But a dandelion is just a dandelion.
I'll be okay.
...TO FEEL SO HOPE-LESS AGAIN.
I ENTRUST MYSELF TO YOU...
SNAP!
...KYO-ICHIRO!
SMIRK

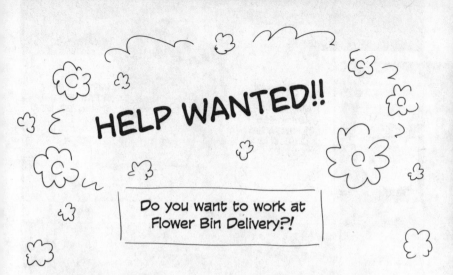

HELP WANTED!!

Do you want to work at
Flower Bin Delivery?!

- NO EXPERIENCE NECESSARY! IT'S A SIMPLE JOB—ALL YOU HAVE TO DO IS PULL THE TRIGGER!

- FAMILY REGISTRY? REAL NAME? NO QUESTIONS ASKED!

- PERFECT FOR THOSE WHO WANT TO WORK WITHOUT BEING BOUND BY LEGAL CONSTRAINTS!

- 99 PERCENT EMPLOYEE RETENTION RATE!

- RECOMMENDED FOR THRILL SEEKERS!

COMMENT FROM MR. B,
A SECOND-YEAR EMPLOYEE

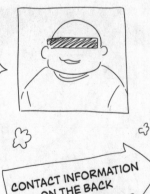

It's a relaxed workplace with a job that feels worthwhile. I once made a huge mistake that really hurt the company, but my superiors didn't get mad at me at all. In fact, they were so concerned for my well-being that they signed me up for life insurance. We're going on a company trip to the ocean next, so I'm really excited about that!

CONTACT INFORMATION
ON THE BACK

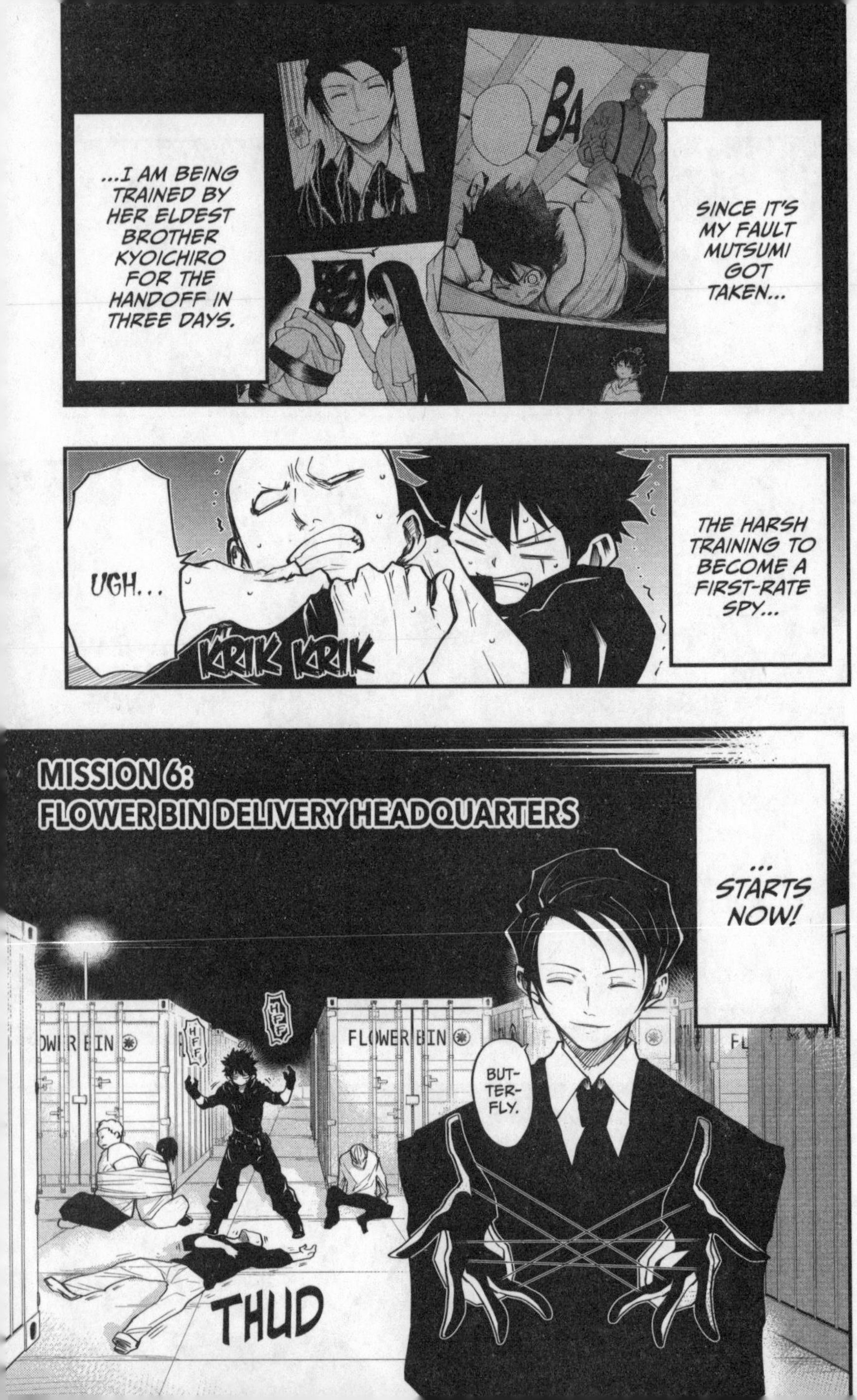
SINCE IT'S MY FAULT MUTSUMI GOT TAKEN...
BA
...I AM BEING TRAINED BY HER ELDEST BROTHER KYOICHIRO FOR THE HANDOFF IN THREE DAYS.
THE HARSH TRAINING TO BECOME A FIRST-RATE SPY...
KRIK KRIK
UGH...
...STARTS NOW!
MISSION 6:
FLOWER BIN DELIVERY HEADQUARTERS
BUT-TER-FLY.
HFF
HFF
FLOWER BIN
THUD

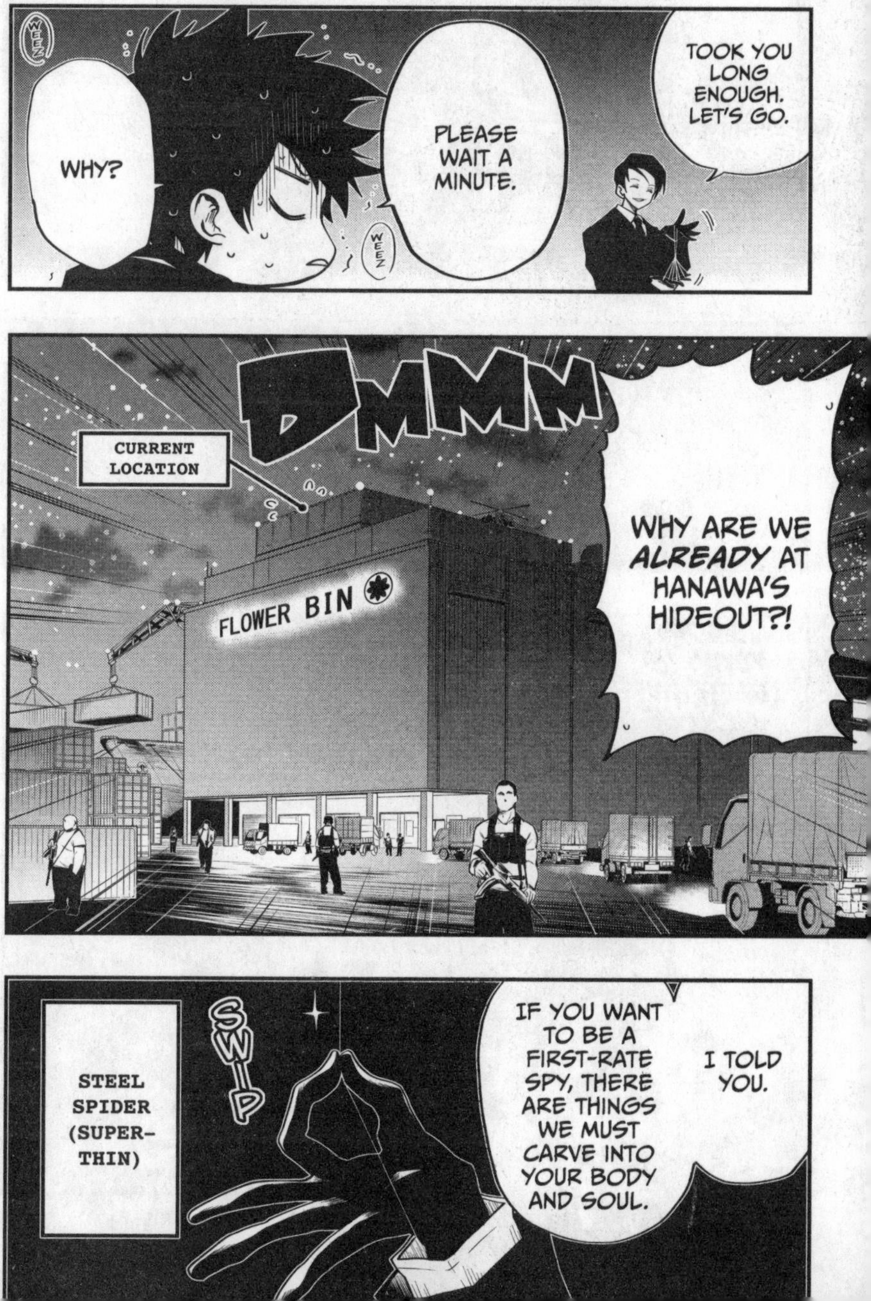
TOOK YOU LONG ENOUGH. LET'S GO.
PLEASE WAIT A MINUTE.
WEEZ
WHY?
WEEZ
DMMM
WHY ARE WE *ALREADY* AT HANAWA'S HIDEOUT?!
FLOWER BIN
CURRENT LOCATION
I TOLD YOU.
IF YOU WANT TO BE A FIRST-RATE SPY, THERE ARE THINGS WE MUST CARVE INTO YOUR BODY AND SOUL.
SWIP
STEEL SPIDER (SUPER-THIN)

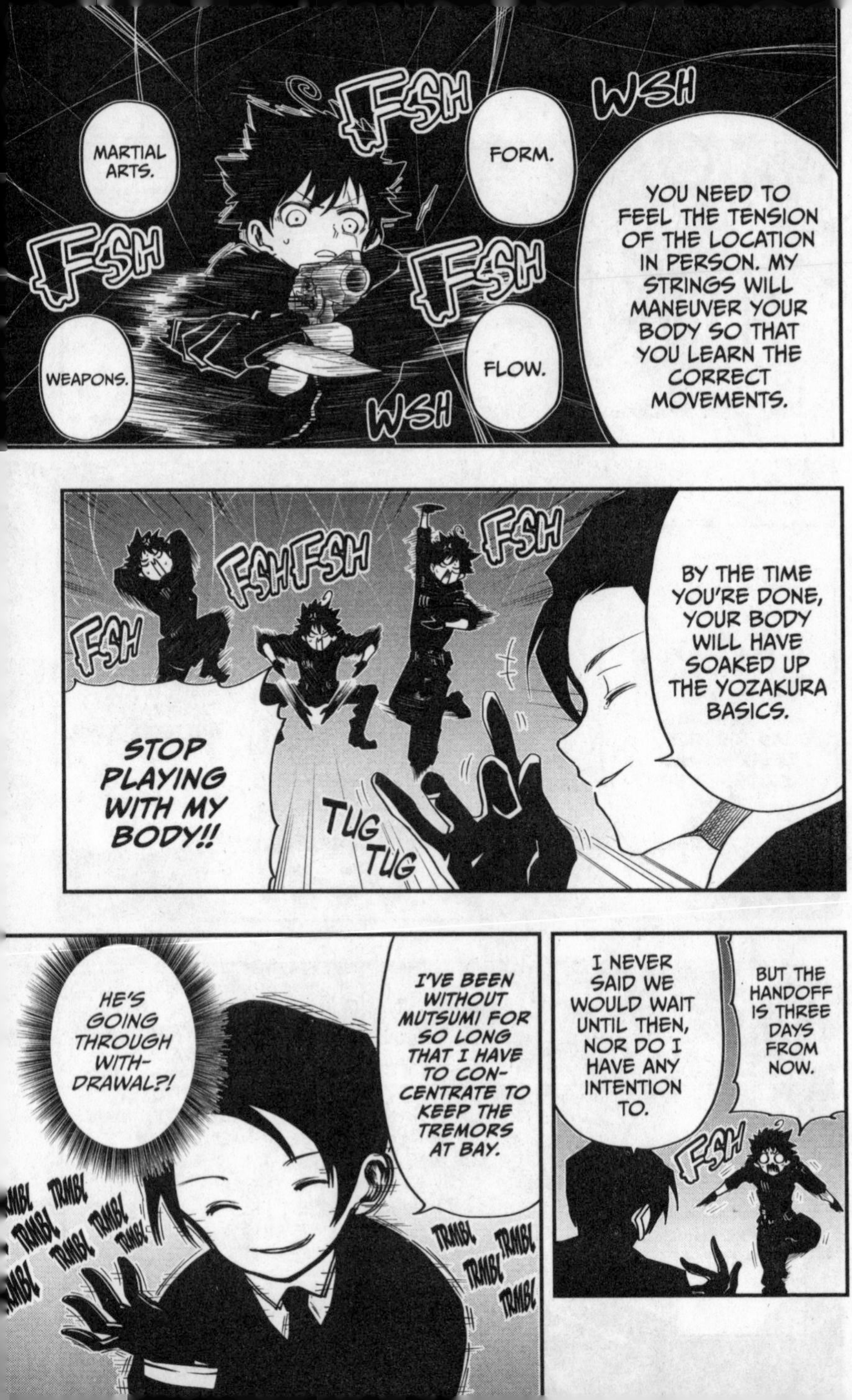
WSH
YOU NEED TO FEEL THE TENSION OF THE LOCATION IN PERSON. MY STRINGS WILL MANEUVER YOUR BODY SO THAT YOU LEARN THE CORRECT MOVEMENTS.
FORM.
FSH
MARTIAL ARTS.
FSH
FSH
FLOW.
WSH
WEAPONS.
BY THE TIME YOU'RE DONE, YOUR BODY WILL HAVE SOAKED UP THE YOZAKURA BASICS.
FSH
FSH FSH
FSH
TUG TUG
STOP PLAYING WITH MY BODY!!
BUT THE HANDOFF IS THREE DAYS FROM NOW.
I NEVER SAID WE WOULD WAIT UNTIL THEN, NOR DO I HAVE ANY INTENTION TO.
FSH
I'VE BEEN WITHOUT MUTSUMI FOR SO LONG THAT I HAVE TO CONCENTRATE TO KEEP THE TREMORS AT BAY.
HE'S GOING THROUGH WITH-DRAWAL?!
TRMBL TRMBL TRMBL TRMBL
TRMBL TRMBL TRMBL TRMBL

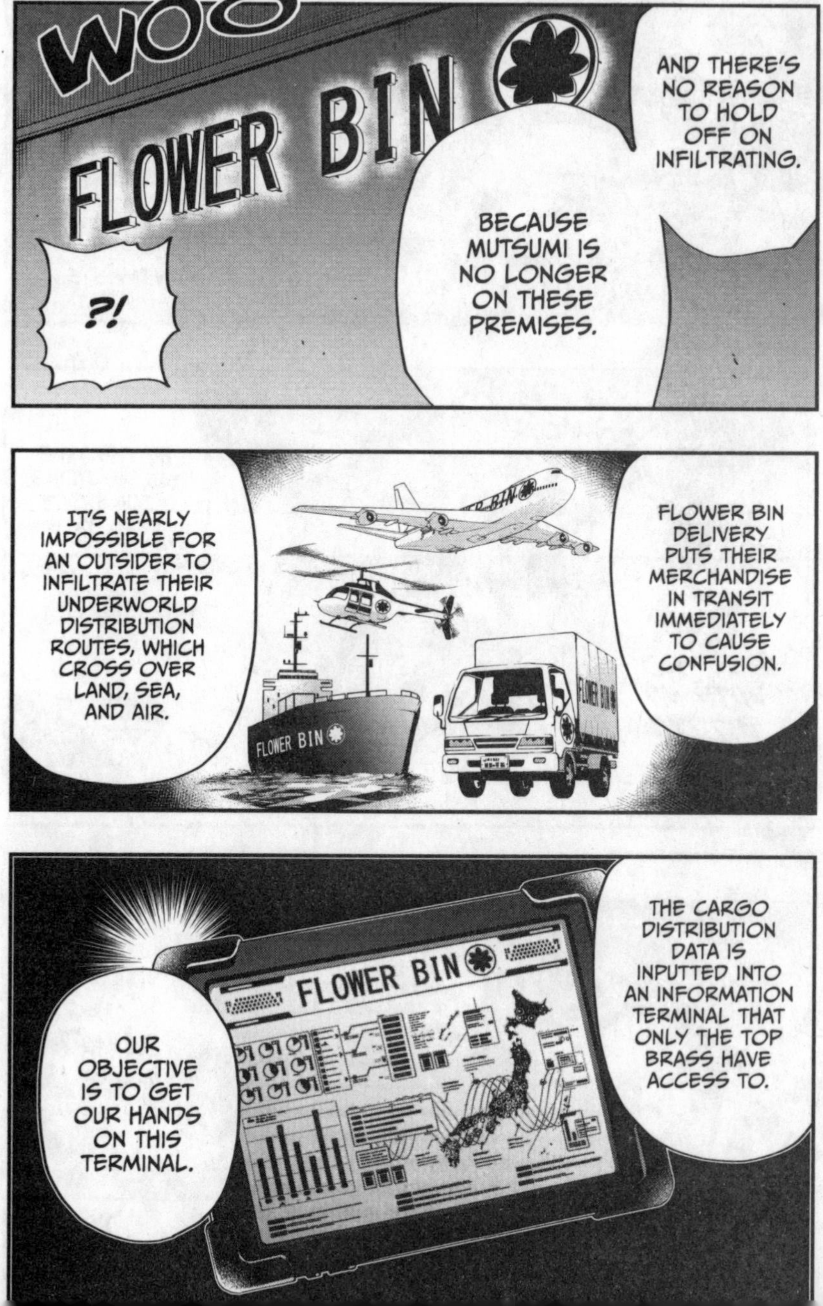
AND THERE'S NO REASON TO HOLD OFF ON INFILTRATING.
WOO
FLOWER BIN
BECAUSE MUTSUMI IS NO LONGER ON THESE PREMISES.
?!
FLOWER BIN DELIVERY PUTS THEIR MERCHANDISE IN TRANSIT IMMEDIATELY TO CAUSE CONFUSION.
FLOWER BIN
FLOWER BIN
IT'S NEARLY IMPOSSIBLE FOR AN OUTSIDER TO INFILTRATE THEIR UNDERWORLD DISTRIBUTION ROUTES, WHICH CROSS OVER LAND, SEA, AND AIR.
THE CARGO DISTRIBUTION DATA IS INPUTTED INTO AN INFORMATION TERMINAL THAT ONLY THE TOP BRASS HAVE ACCESS TO.
FLOWER BIN
OUR OBJECTIVE IS TO GET OUR HANDS ON THIS TERMINAL.

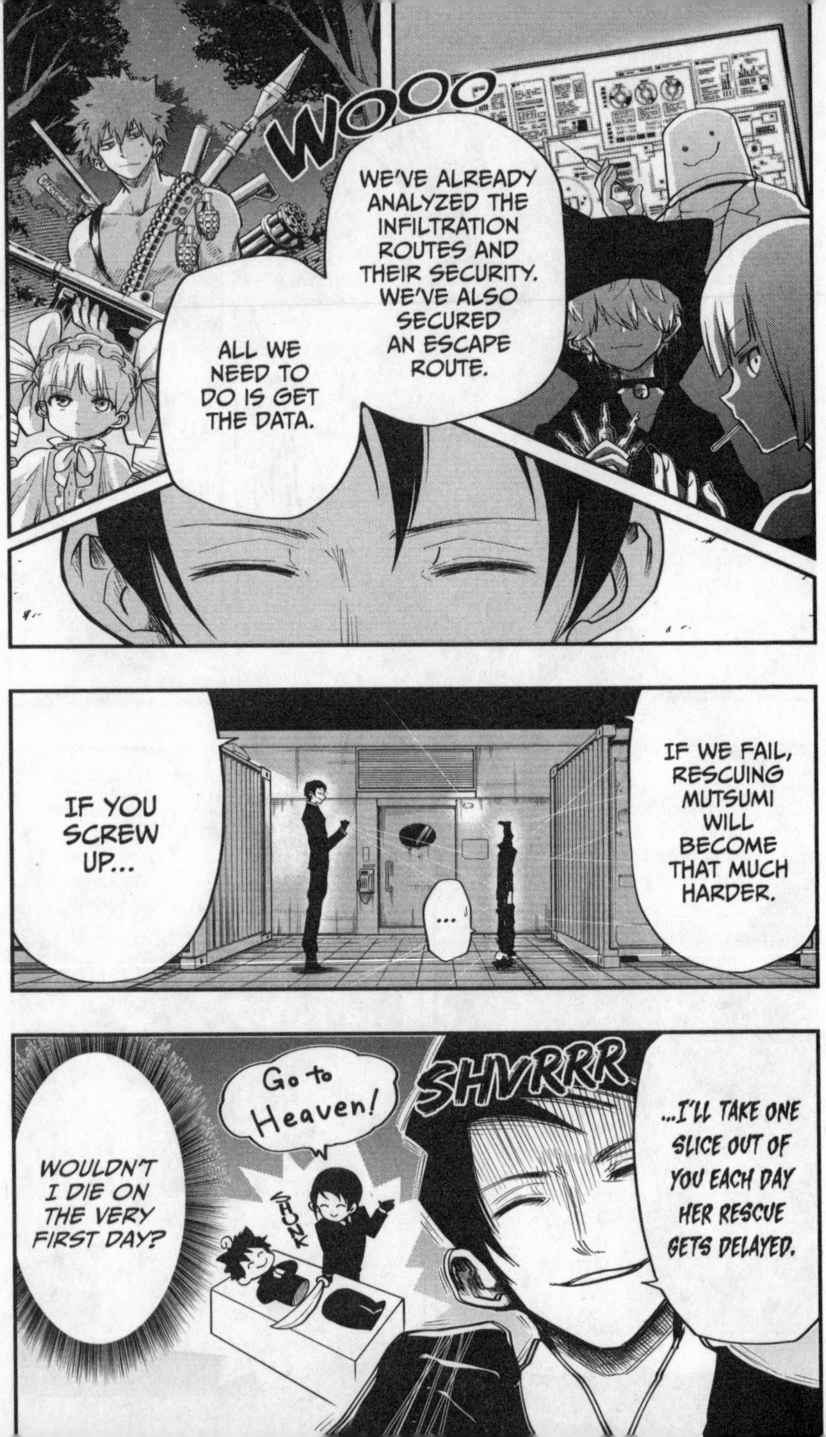
WOOO
WE'VE ALREADY ANALYZED THE INFILTRATION ROUTES AND THEIR SECURITY. WE'VE ALSO SECURED AN ESCAPE ROUTE.
ALL WE NEED TO DO IS GET THE DATA.
IF WE FAIL, RESCUING MUTSUMI WILL BECOME THAT MUCH HARDER.
...
IF YOU SCREW UP...
SHVRRR
...I'LL TAKE ONE SLICE OUT OF YOU EACH DAY HER RESCUE GETS DELAYED.
Go to Heaven!
SHUNK
WOULDN'T I DIE ON THE VERY FIRST DAY?

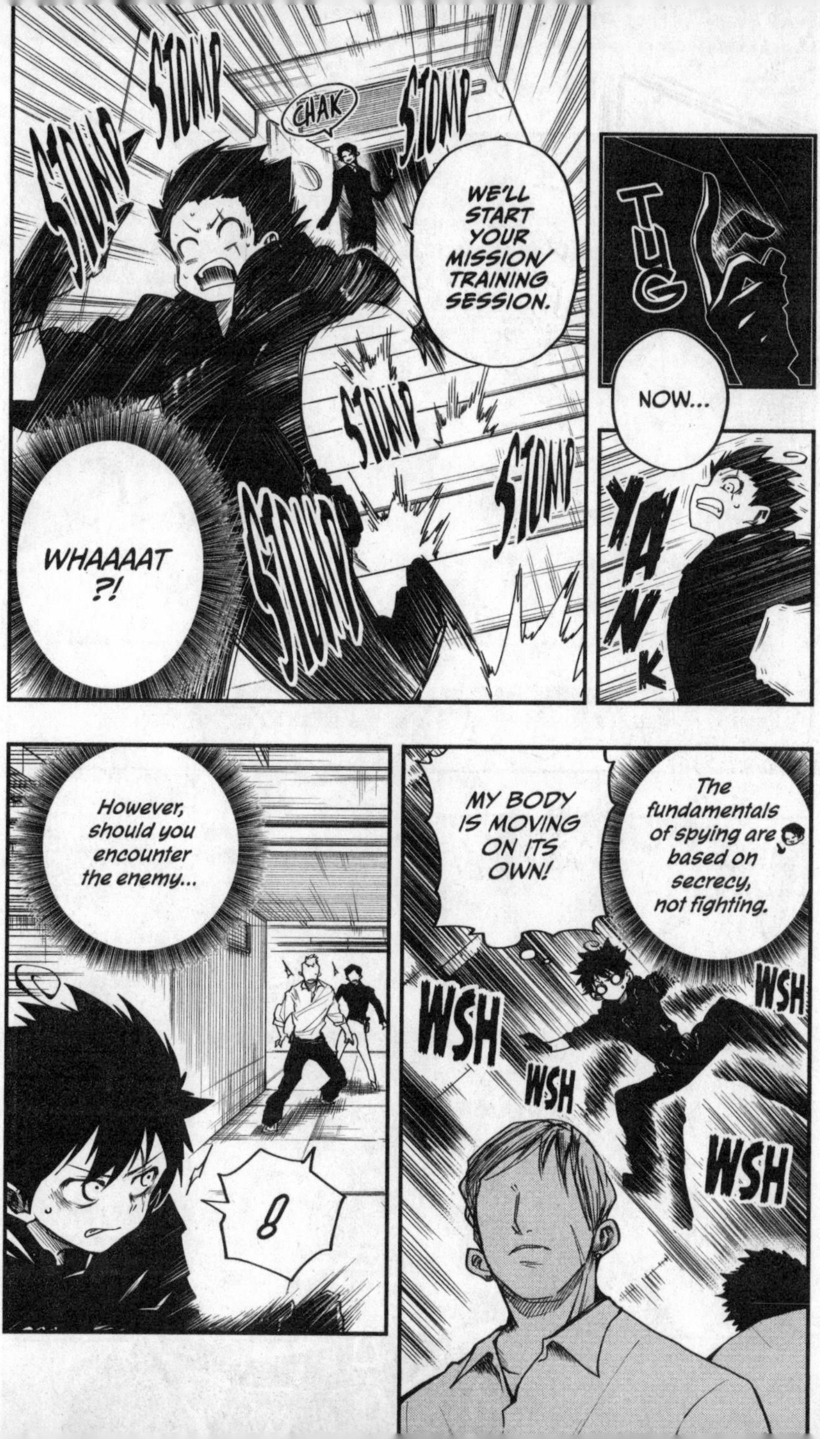
TUG
NOW...
YANK
STOMP
STOMP
STOMP
CHAK
STOMP
WE'LL START YOUR MISSION/ TRAINING SESSION.
STOMP
STOMP
STOMP
WHAAAAT ?!
The fundamentals of spying are based on secrecy, not fighting.
MY BODY IS MOVING ON ITS OWN!
WSH
WSH
WSH
WSH
However, should you encounter the enemy...
!

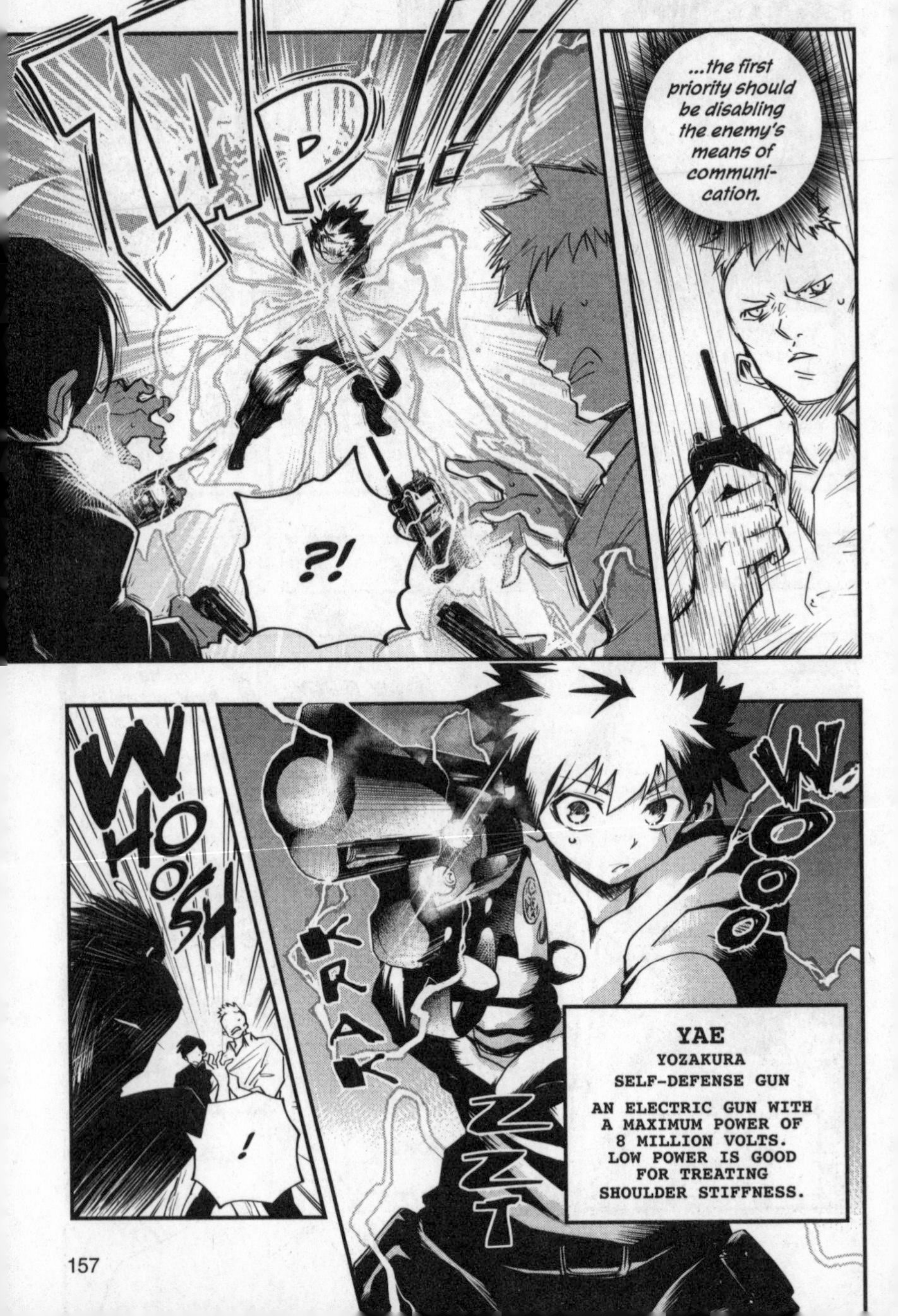
...the first priority should be disabling the enemy's means of communication.
ZAP!!
?!
WOOOO
KRRAK
ZZZT
YAE
YOZAKURA
SELF-DEFENSE GUN
AN ELECTRIC GUN WITH A MAXIMUM POWER OF 8 MILLION VOLTS. LOW POWER IS GOOD FOR TREATING SHOULDER STIFFNESS.
WHOOSH
!

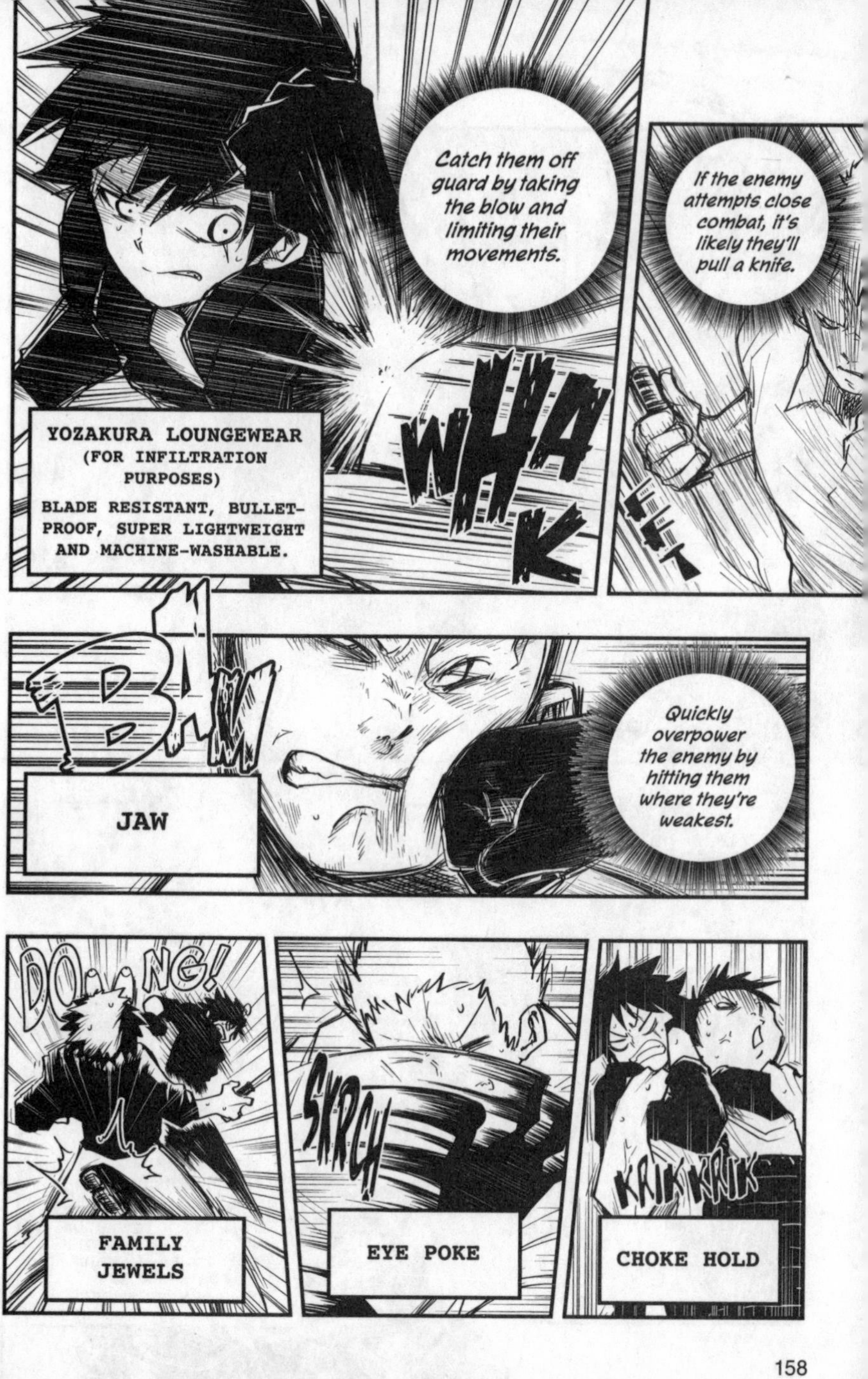

If the enemy attempts close combat, it's likely they'll pull a knife.
FFT
Catch them off guard by taking the blow and limiting their movements.
WHAK
YOZAKURA LOUNGEWEAR (FOR INFILTRATION PURPOSES)
BLADE RESISTANT, BULLET-PROOF, SUPER LIGHTWEIGHT AND MACHINE-WASHABLE.
Quickly overpower the enemy by hitting them where they're weakest.
BAM
JAW
KRIK KRIK
CHOKE HOLD
SKRCH
EYE POKE
DO...NG!
FAMILY JEWELS

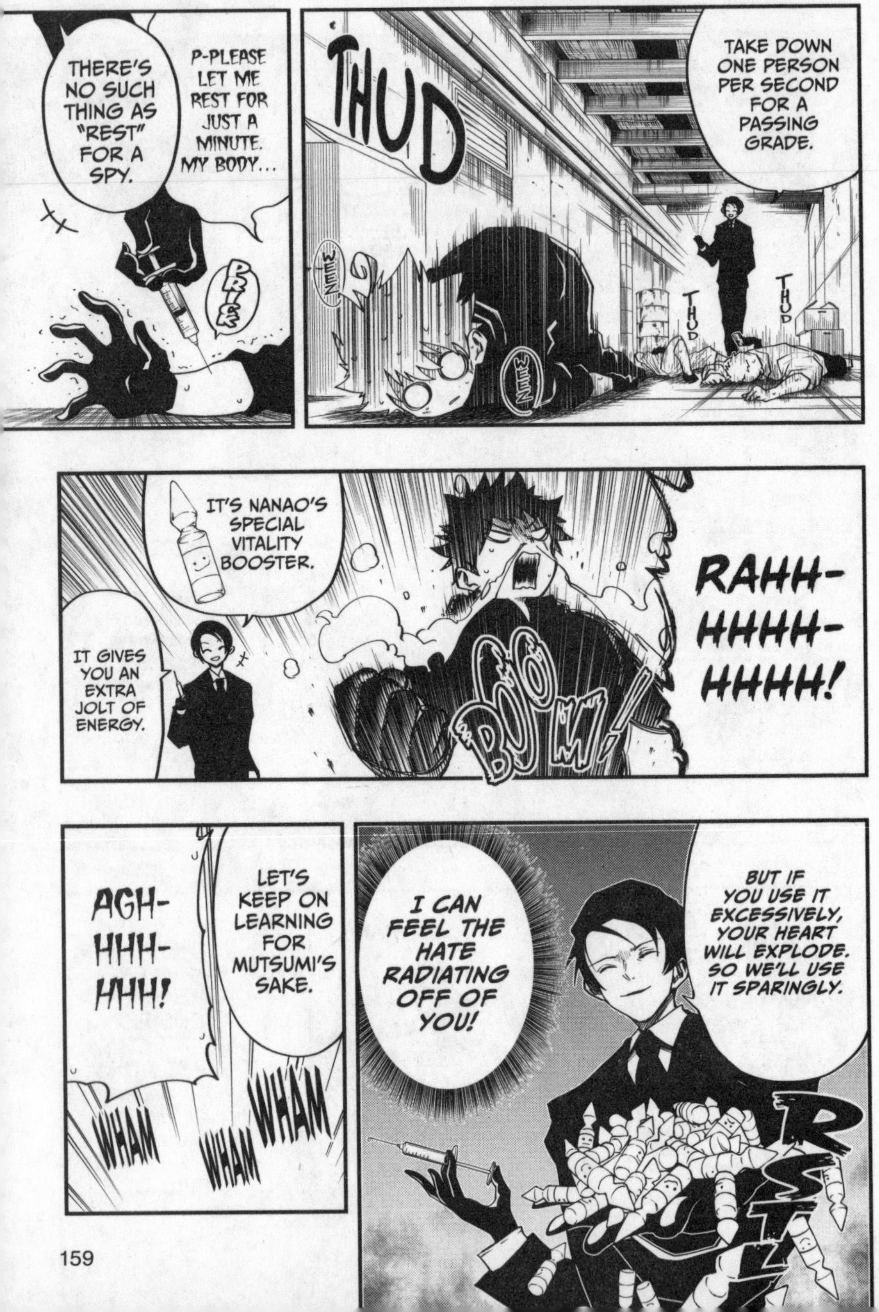
TAKE DOWN ONE PERSON PER SECOND FOR A PASSING GRADE.
THUD
WEEZ
WEEZ
THUD
THUD
P-PLEASE LET ME REST FOR JUST A MINUTE. MY BODY...
THERE'S NO SUCH THING AS "REST" FOR A SPY.
PRICK
RAHH-HHHH-HHHH!
BOOM!
IT'S NANAO'S SPECIAL VITALITY BOOSTER.
IT GIVES YOU AN EXTRA JOLT OF ENERGY.
BUT IF YOU USE IT EXCESSIVELY, YOUR HEART WILL EXPLODE. SO WE'LL USE IT SPARINGLY.
I CAN FEEL THE HATE RADIATING OFF OF YOU!
RST
LET'S KEEP ON LEARNING FOR MUTSUMI'S SAKE.
AGH-HHH-HHH!
WHAM
WHAM
WHAM

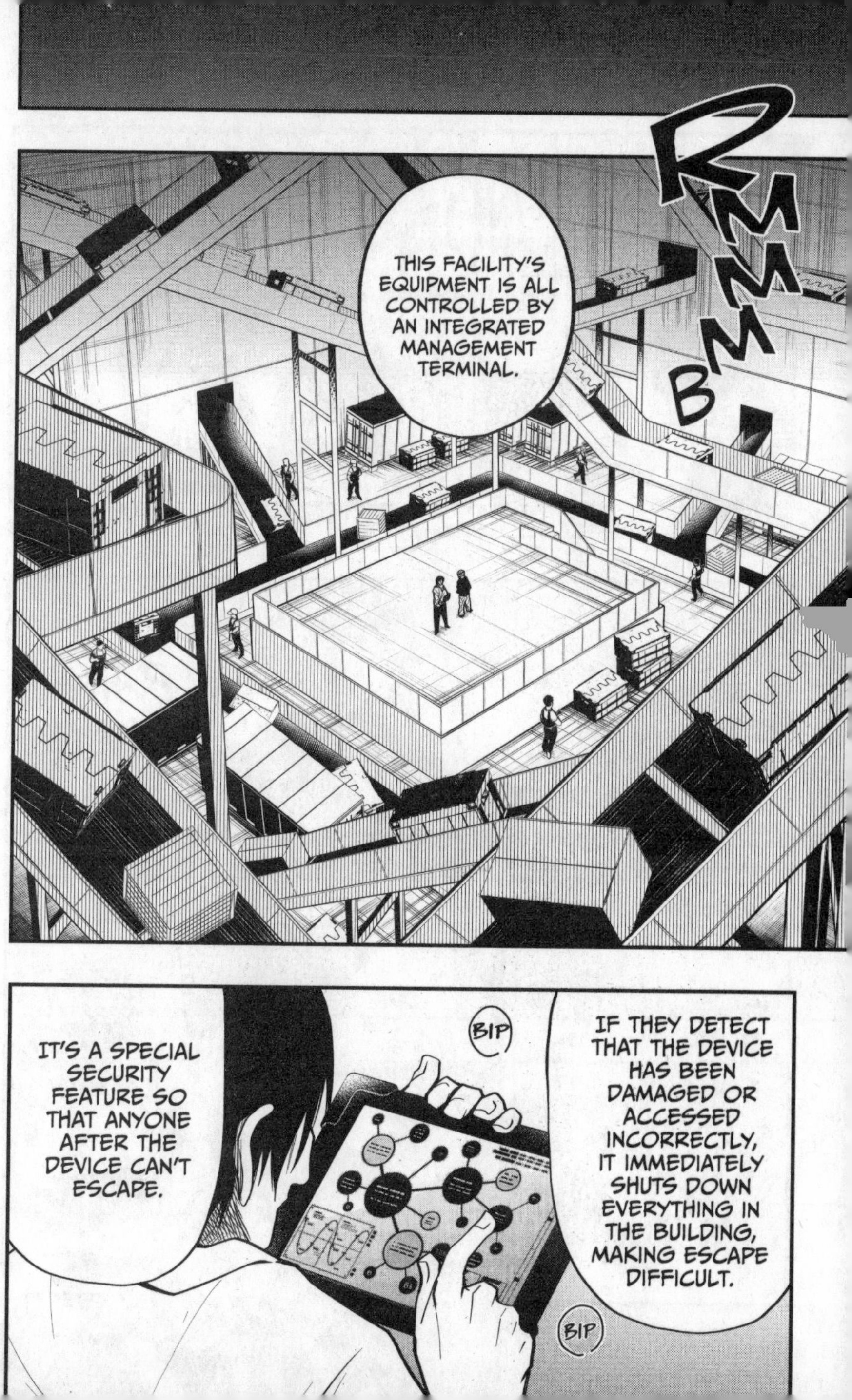
RMMMBM
THIS FACILITY'S EQUIPMENT IS ALL CONTROLLED BY AN INTEGRATED MANAGEMENT TERMINAL.
BIP
IF THEY DETECT THAT THE DEVICE HAS BEEN DAMAGED OR ACCESSED INCORRECTLY, IT IMMEDIATELY SHUTS DOWN EVERYTHING IN THE BUILDING, MAKING ESCAPE DIFFICULT.
IT'S A SPECIAL SECURITY FEATURE SO THAT ANYONE AFTER THE DEVICE CAN'T ESCAPE.
BIP

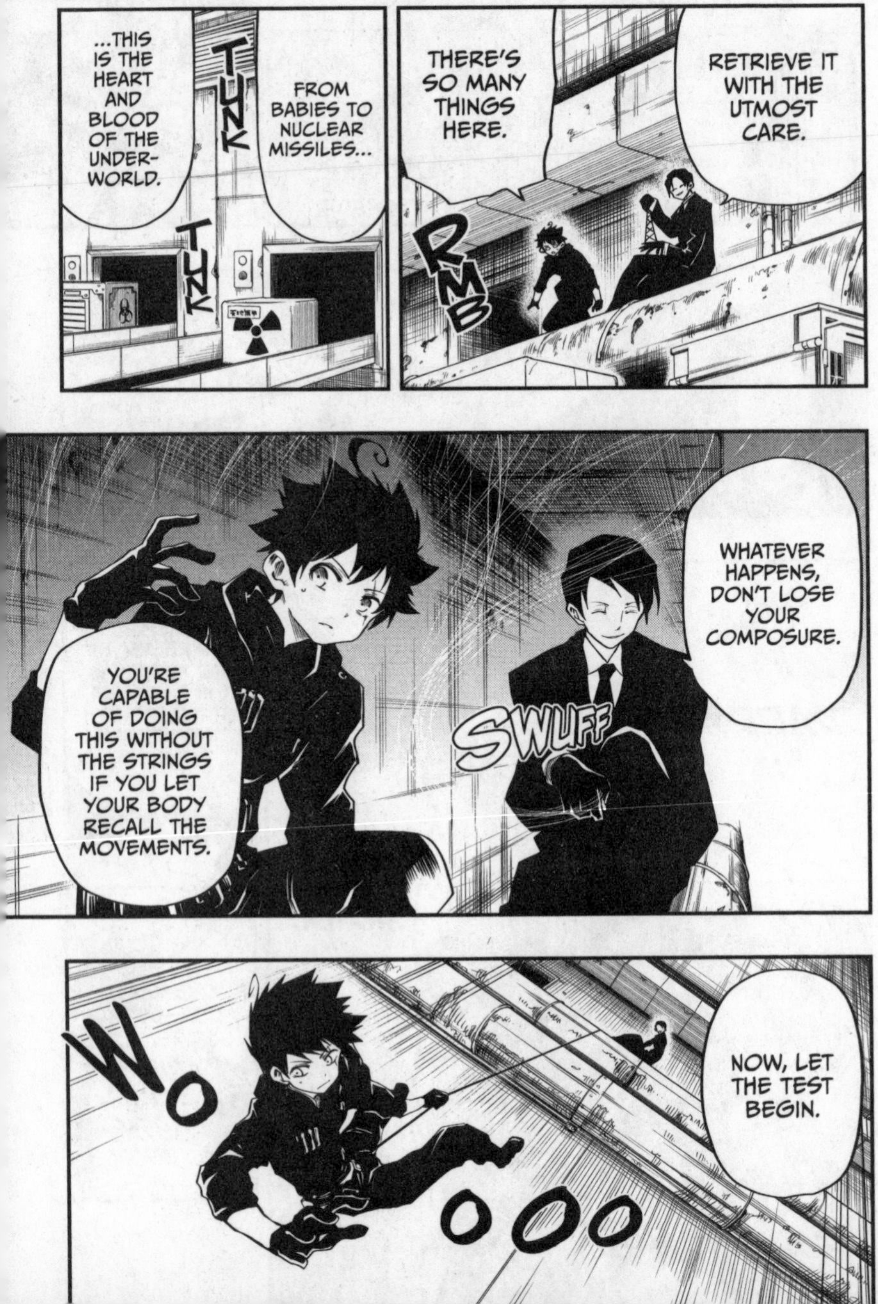
RETRIEVE IT WITH THE UTMOST CARE.
THERE'S SO MANY THINGS HERE.
RMB
FROM BABIES TO NUCLEAR MISSILES...
TUNK
...THIS IS THE HEART AND BLOOD OF THE UNDER-WORLD.
TUNK
WHATEVER HAPPENS, DON'T LOSE YOUR COMPOSURE.
SWUFF
YOU'RE CAPABLE OF DOING THIS WITHOUT THE STRINGS IF YOU LET YOUR BODY RECALL THE MOVEMENTS.
NOW, LET THE TEST BEGIN.
WOOOOO

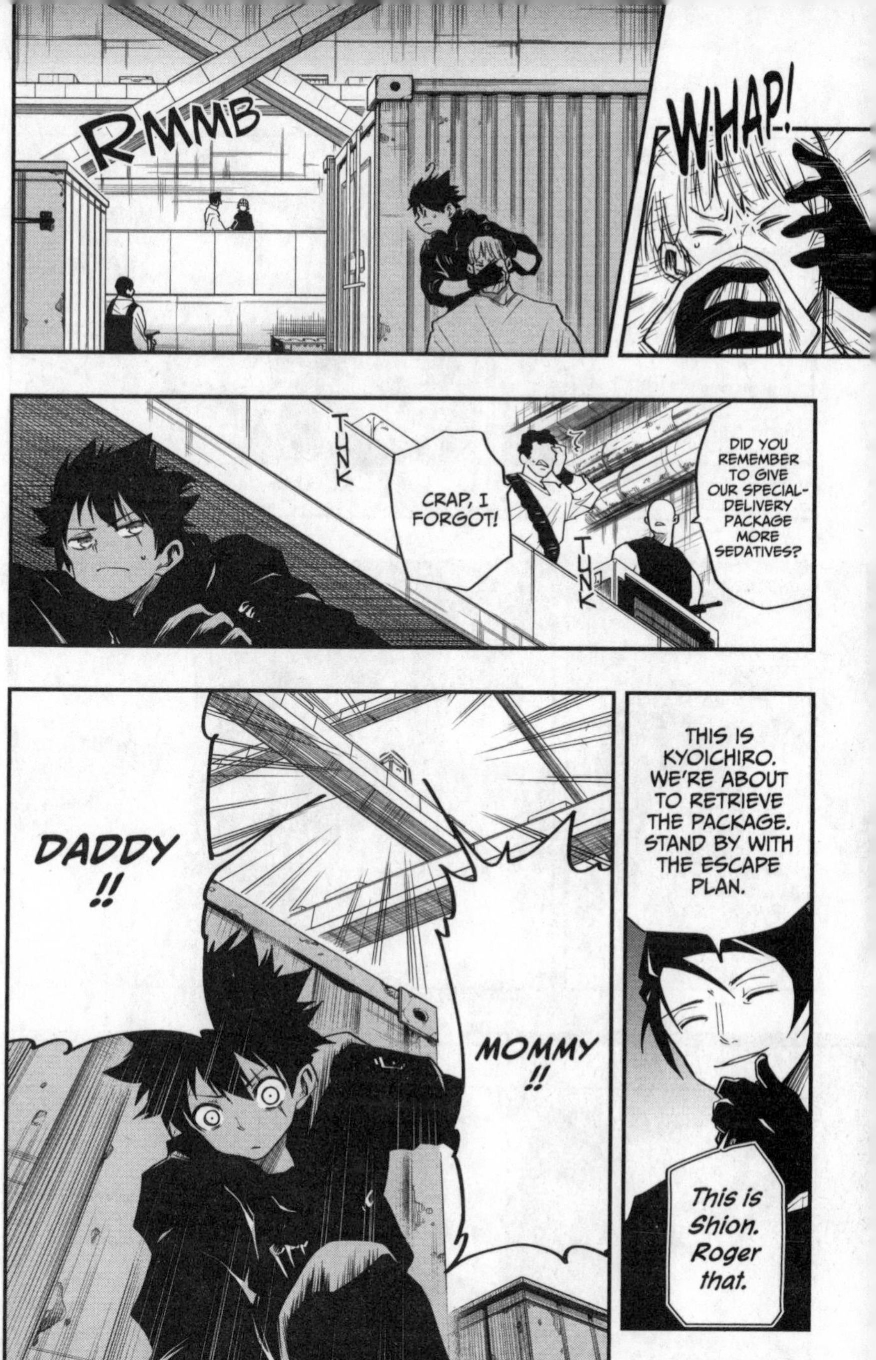
WHAP!
RMMB
DID YOU REMEMBER TO GIVE OUR SPECIAL-DELIVERY PACKAGE MORE SEDATIVES?
TUNK
CRAP, I FORGOT!
TUNK
THIS IS KYOICHIRO. WE'RE ABOUT TO RETRIEVE THE PACKAGE. STAND BY WITH THE ESCAPE PLAN.
This is Shion. Roger that.
DADDY !!
MOMMY !!

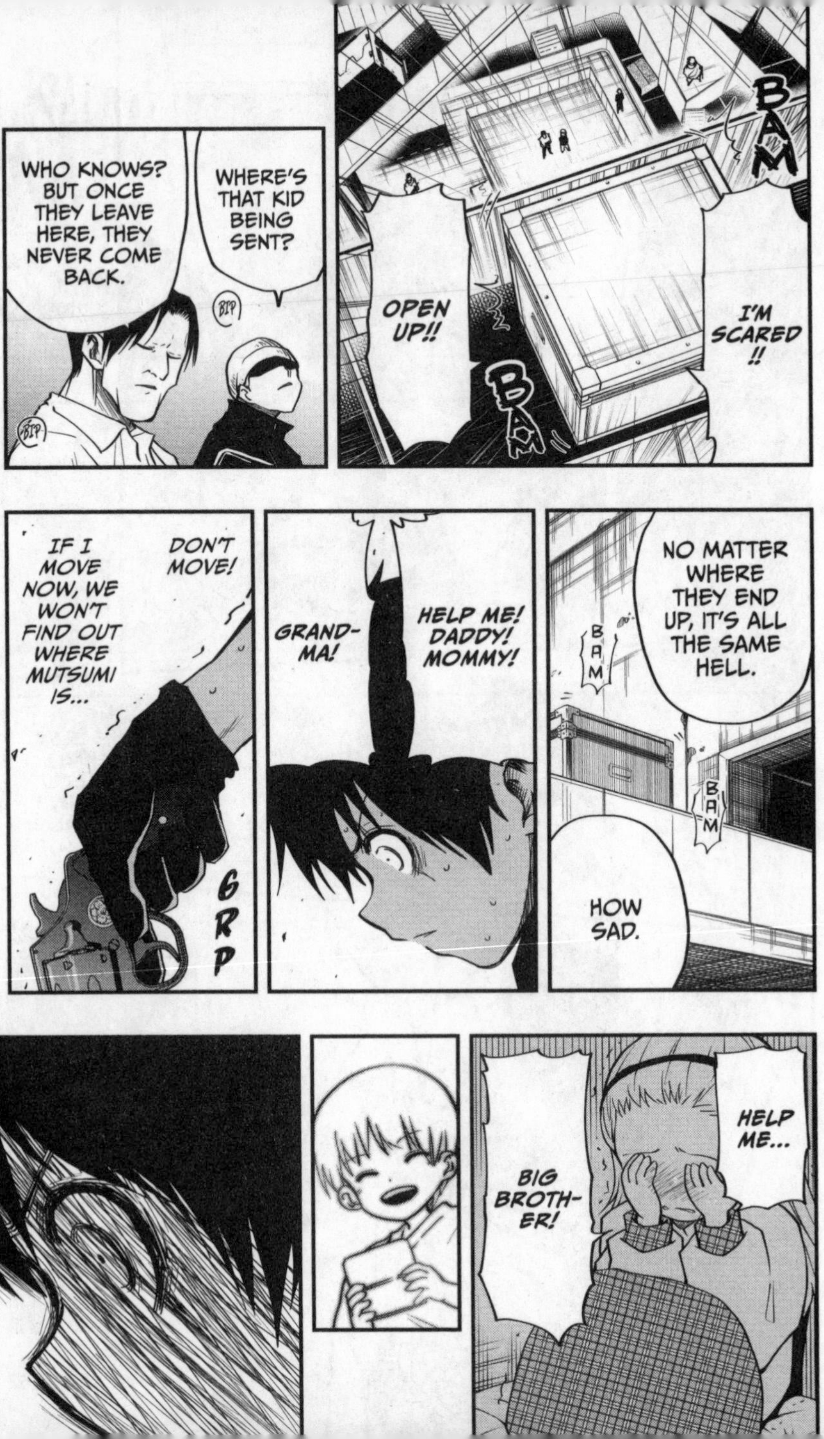
BAM
I'M SCARED!!
OPEN UP!!
BAM
WHERE'S THAT KID BEING SENT?
WHO KNOWS? BUT ONCE THEY LEAVE HERE, THEY NEVER COME BACK.
BIP
BIP
NO MATTER WHERE THEY END UP, IT'S ALL THE SAME HELL.
BAM
BAM
HOW SAD.
HELP ME! DADDY! MOMMY!
GRAND-MA!
DON'T MOVE!
IF I MOVE NOW, WE WON'T FIND OUT WHERE MUTSUMI IS...
GRP
HELP ME...
BIG BROTHER-ER!

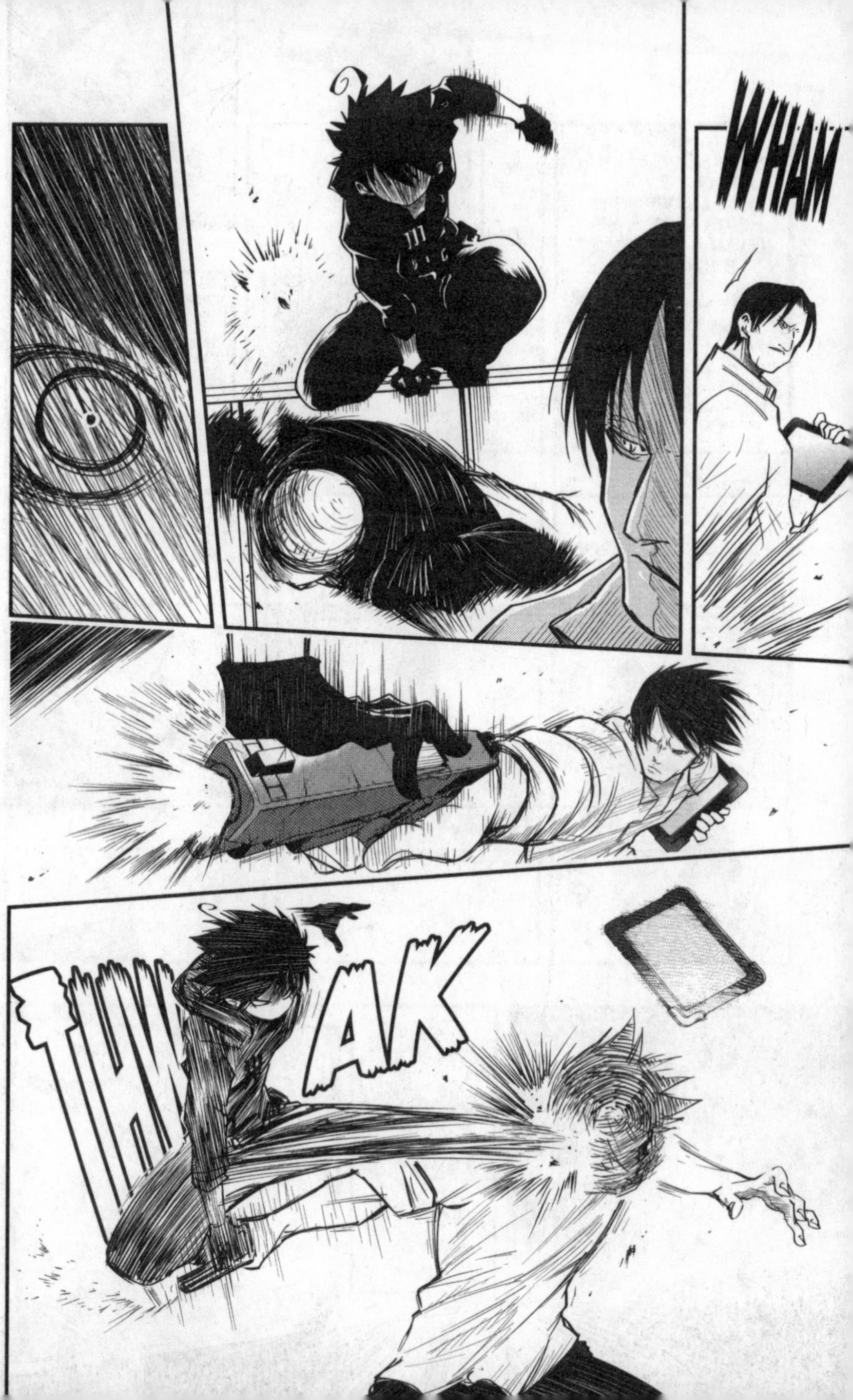
WHAM
THWAK

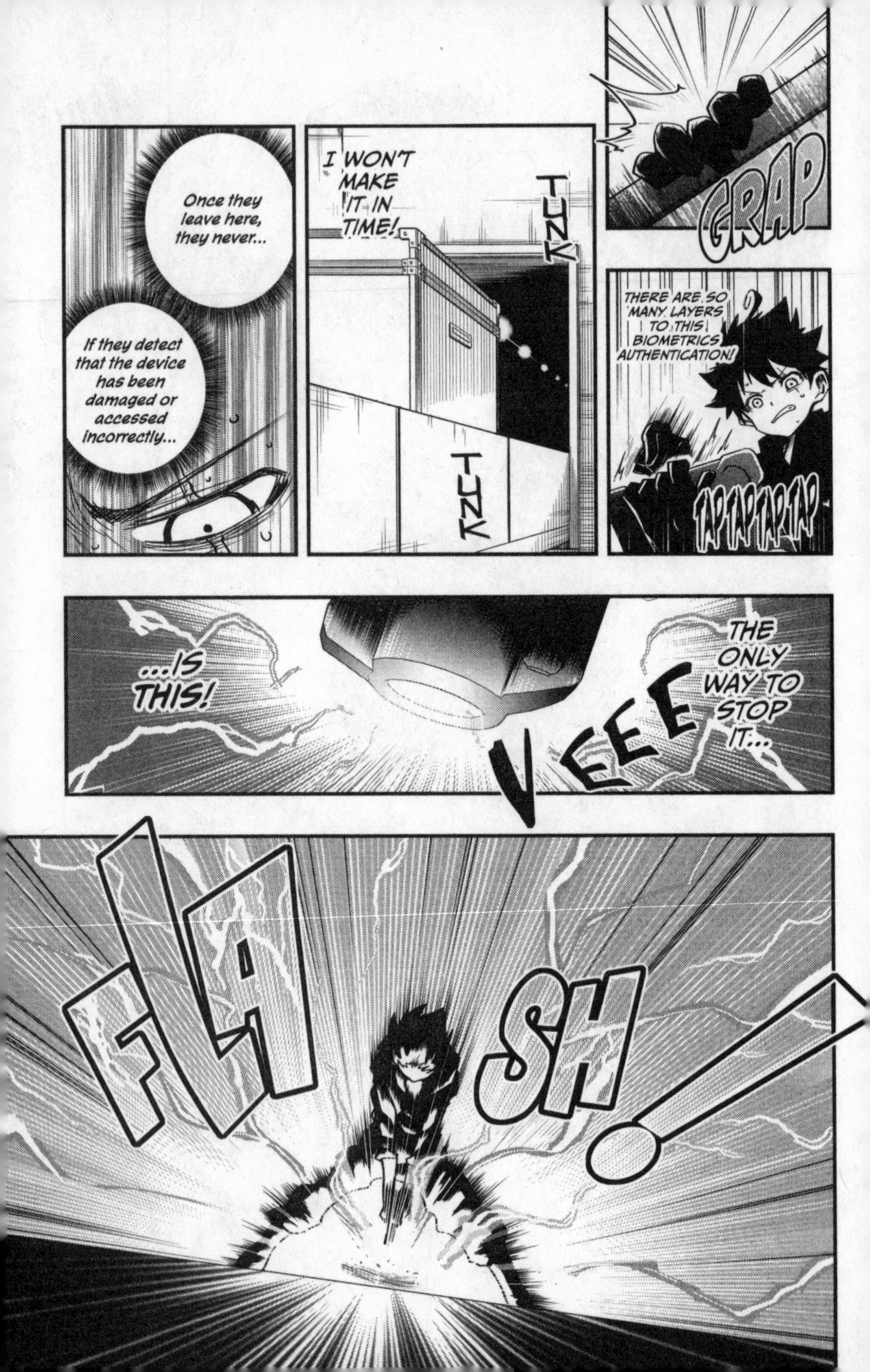
GRAP
THERE ARE SO MANY LAYERS TO THIS BIOMETRICS AUTHENTICATION!
TAP TAP TAP TAP
I WON'T MAKE IT IN TIME!
TUNK
TUNK
Once they leave here, they never...
If they detect that the device has been damaged or accessed incorrectly...
THE ONLY WAY TO STOP IT...
VEEE
...IS THIS!
FLASH!

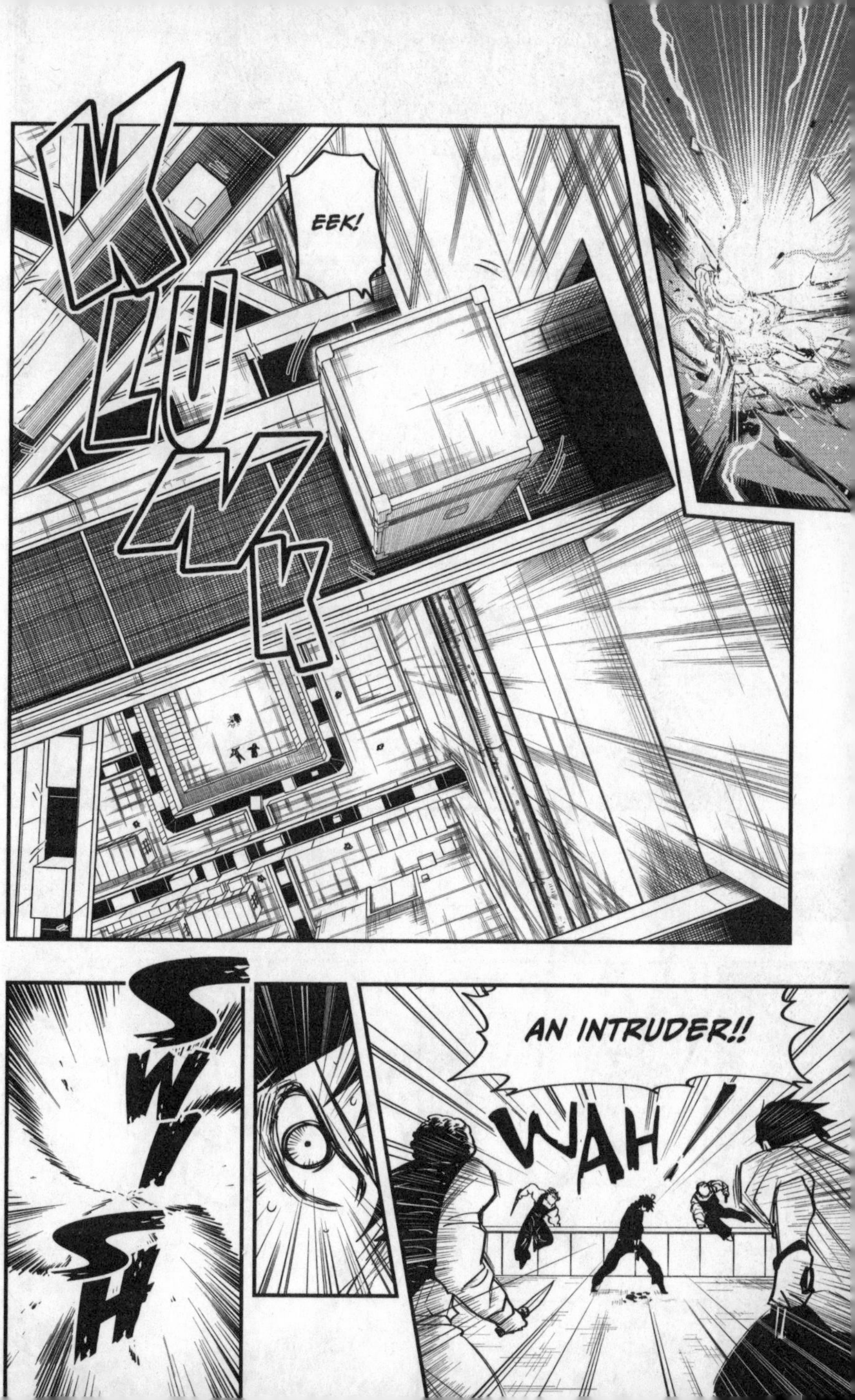
EEK!
KLUNK
AN INTRUDER!!
WAH
SWISH

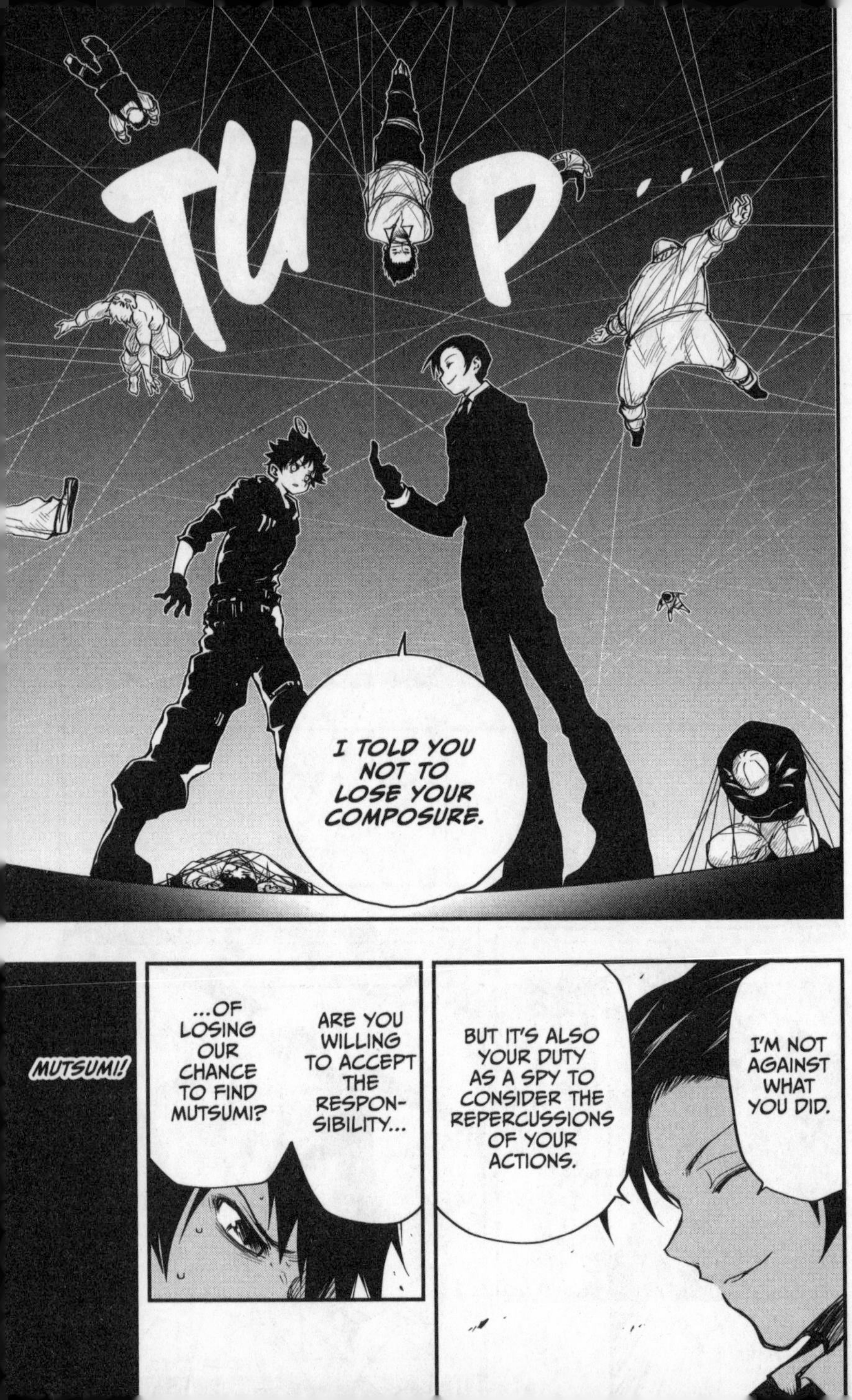
TUP...
I TOLD YOU NOT TO LOSE YOUR COMPOSURE.
I'M NOT AGAINST WHAT YOU DID.
BUT IT'S ALSO YOUR DUTY AS A SPY TO CONSIDER THE REPERCUSSIONS OF YOUR ACTIONS.
ARE YOU WILLING TO ACCEPT THE RESPON-SIBILITY...
...OF LOSING OUR CHANCE TO FIND MUTSUMI?
MUTSUMI!

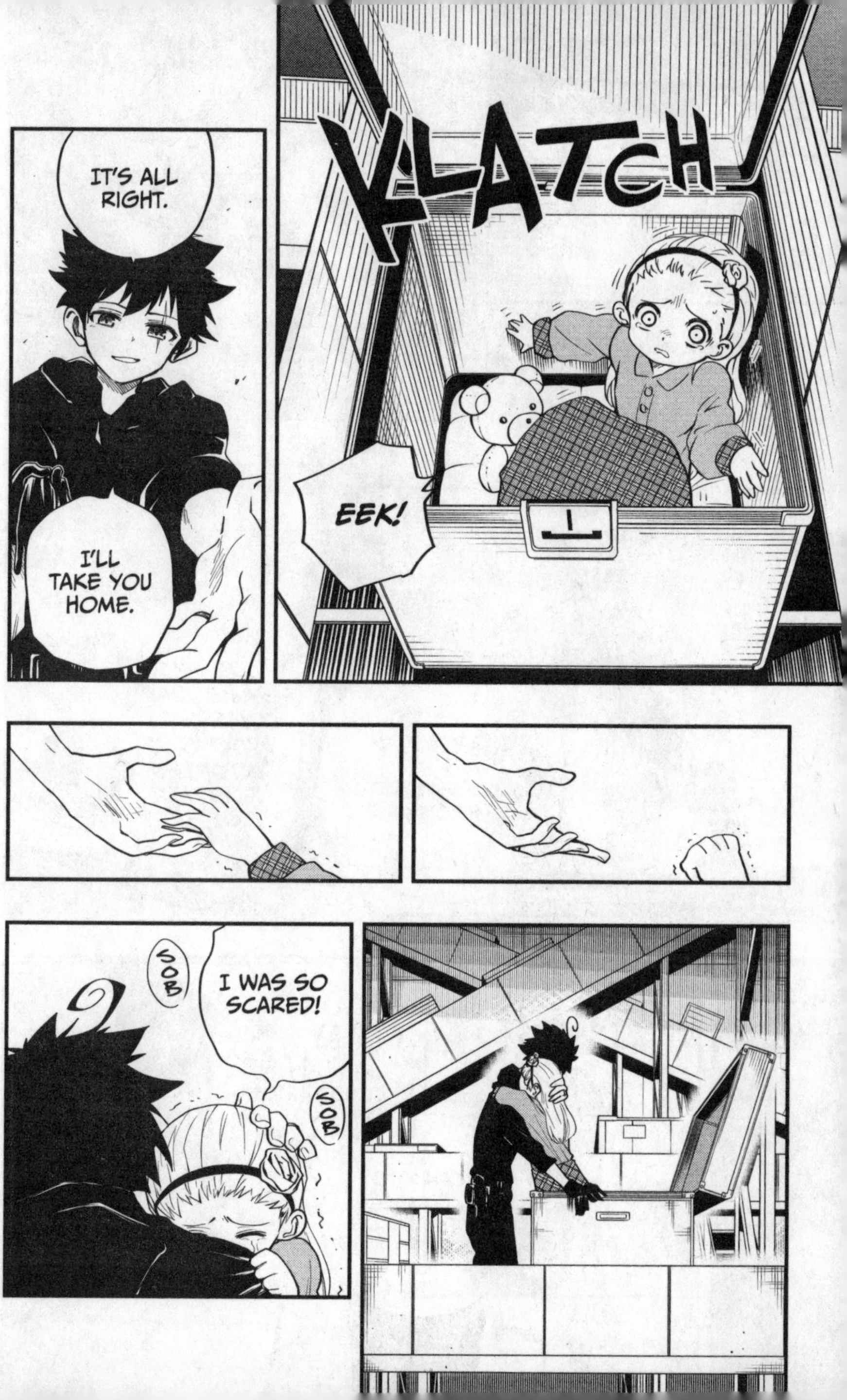
KLATCH
EEK!
IT'S ALL RIGHT.
I'LL TAKE YOU HOME.
SOB
I WAS SO SCARED!
SOB

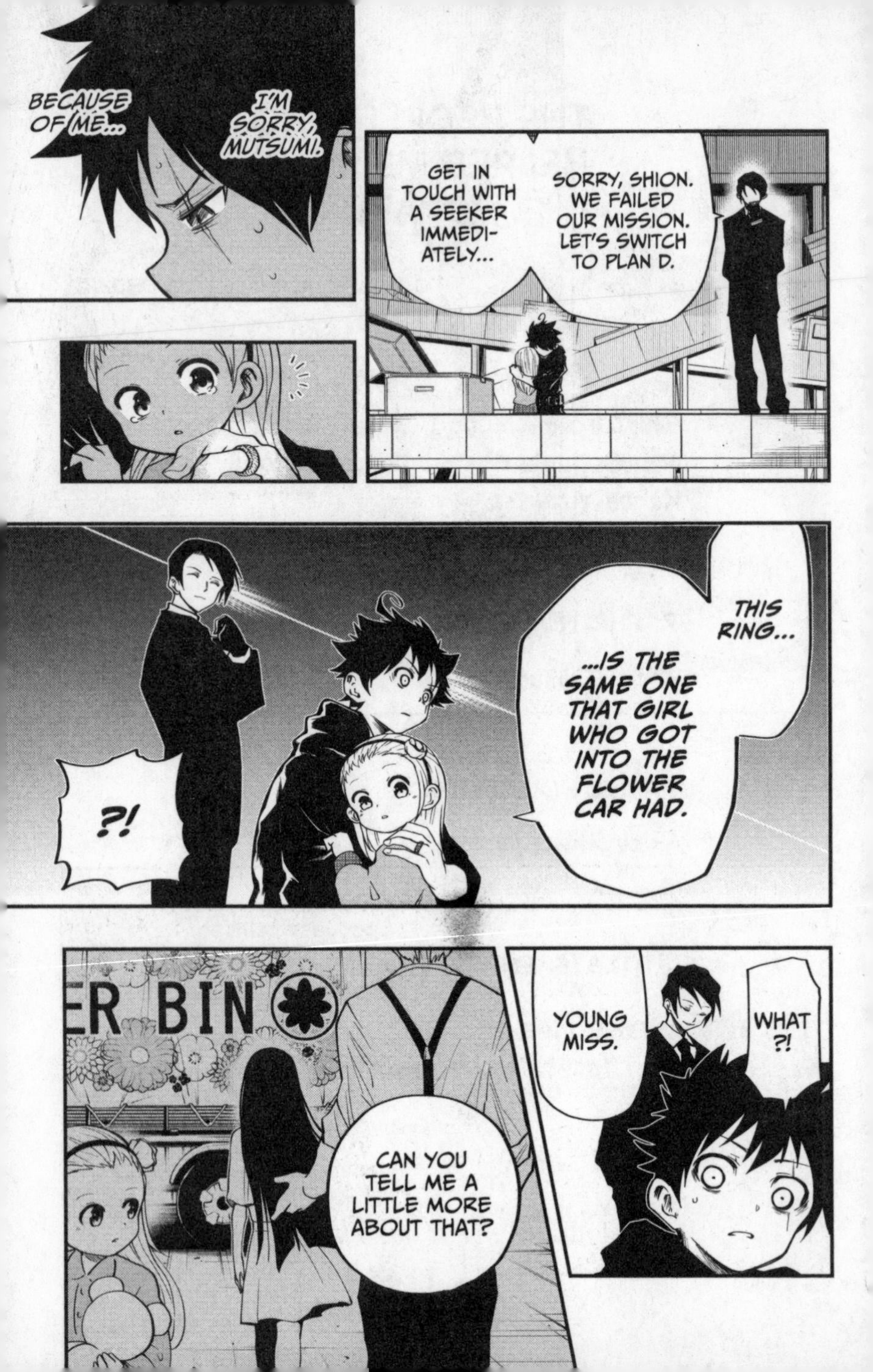
SORRY, SHION. WE FAILED OUR MISSION. LET'S SWITCH TO PLAN D.
GET IN TOUCH WITH A SEEKER IMMEDI- ATELY...
I'M SORRY, MUTSUMI.
BECAUSE OF ME...
THIS RING...
...IS THE SAME ONE THAT GIRL WHO GOT INTO THE FLOWER CAR HAD.
?!
WHAT ?!
YOUNG MISS.
ER BIN
CAN YOU TELL ME A LITTLE MORE ABOUT THAT?

THE PEOPLE WHO HELPED ME MAKE THE "YOZAKURAS"

(*IN ALPHABETICAL ORDER)

○ ASSISTANTS

Shintaro Imamoto   Moe Shinohara
Ryu Segawa   Tomohiro Yagi
Kenta Yuzuriha

○ GRAPHIC NOVEL DESIGNER

Kaori Shimura

○ GRAPHIC NOVEL EDITOR

Akihiro Katayama ←

They are not
actually related!!

○ EDITORS (FRENEMIES)

(First Editor) Takeru Isaka
(Second Editor) Tatsuhiko Katayama

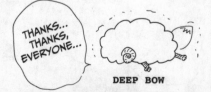

THANKS...
THANKS,
EVERYONE...

DEEP BOW

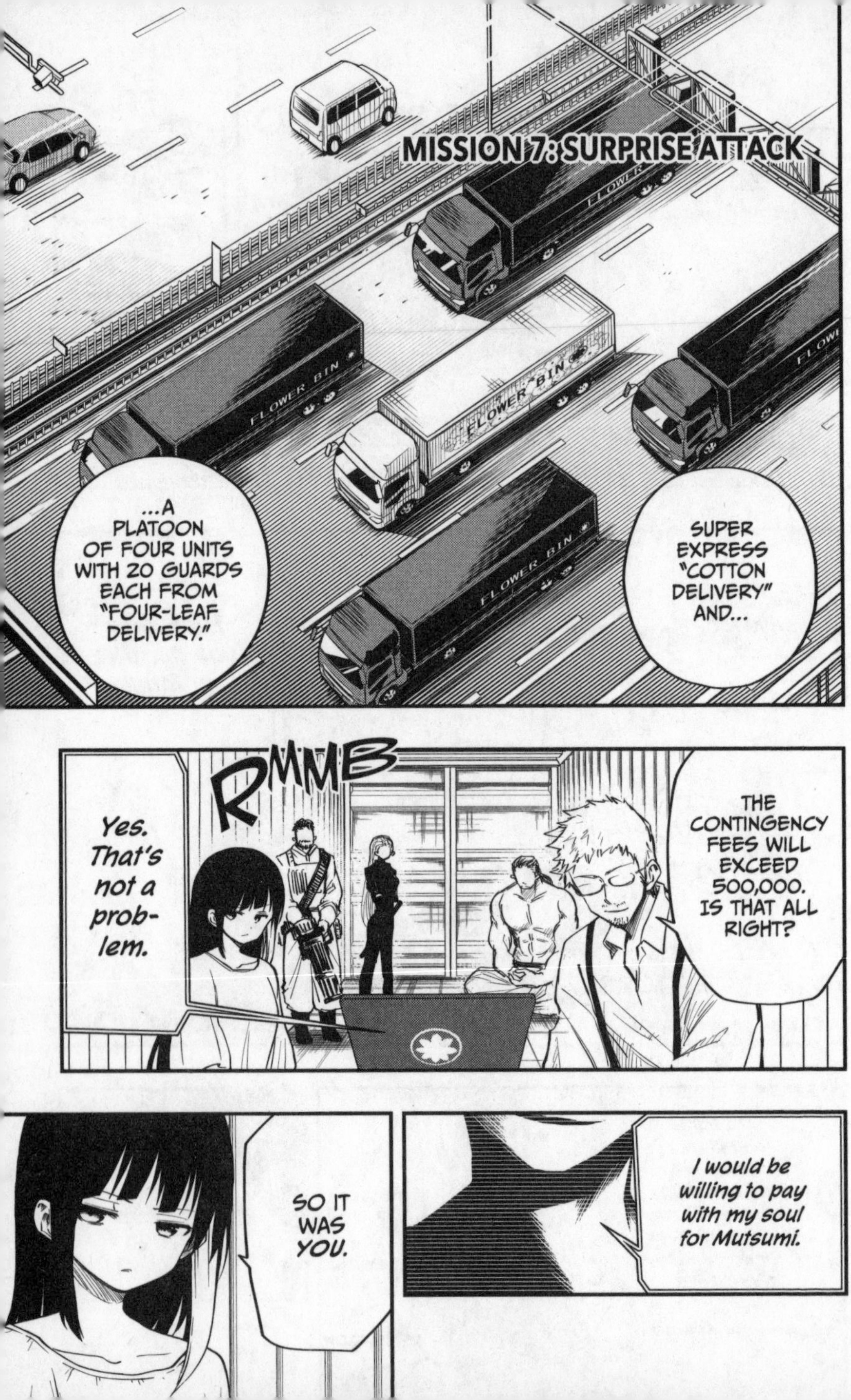
MISSION 7: SURPRISE ATTACK
SUPER EXPRESS "COTTON DELIVERY" AND...
...A PLATOON OF FOUR UNITS WITH 20 GUARDS EACH FROM "FOUR-LEAF DELIVERY."
THE CONTINGENCY FEES WILL EXCEED 500,000. IS THAT ALL RIGHT?
RMMB
Yes. That's not a prob-lem.
I would be willing to pay with my soul for Mutsumi.
SO IT WAS YOU.

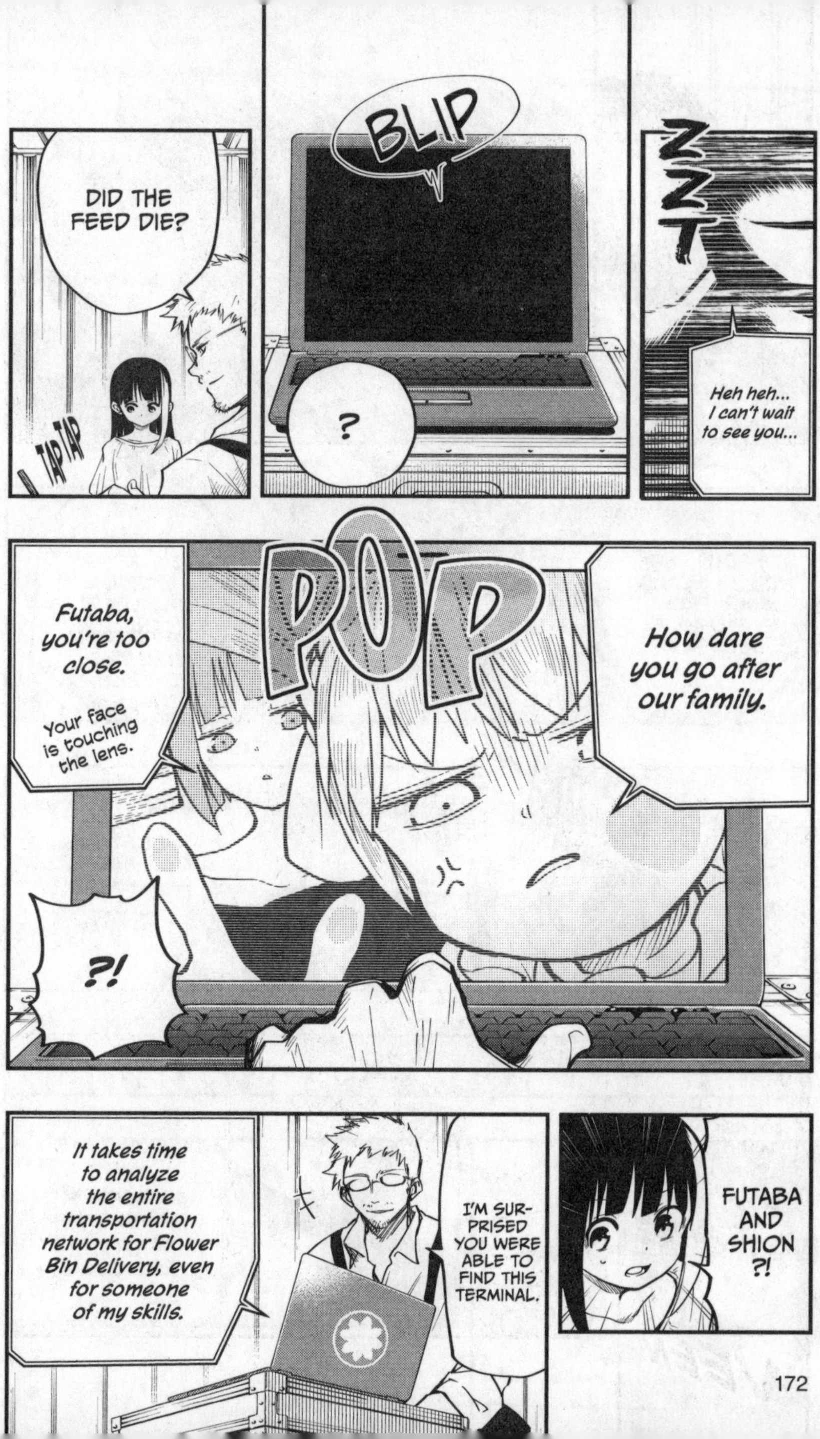
ZZT
Heh heh... I can't wait to see you...
BLIP
?
DID THE FEED DIE?
TAP TAP
POP
How dare you go after our family.
Futaba, you're too close.
Your face is touching the lens.
?!
FUTABA AND SHION ?!
I'M SUR- PRISED YOU WERE ABLE TO FIND THIS TERMINAL.
It takes time to analyze the entire transportation network for Flower Bin Delivery, even for someone of my skills.

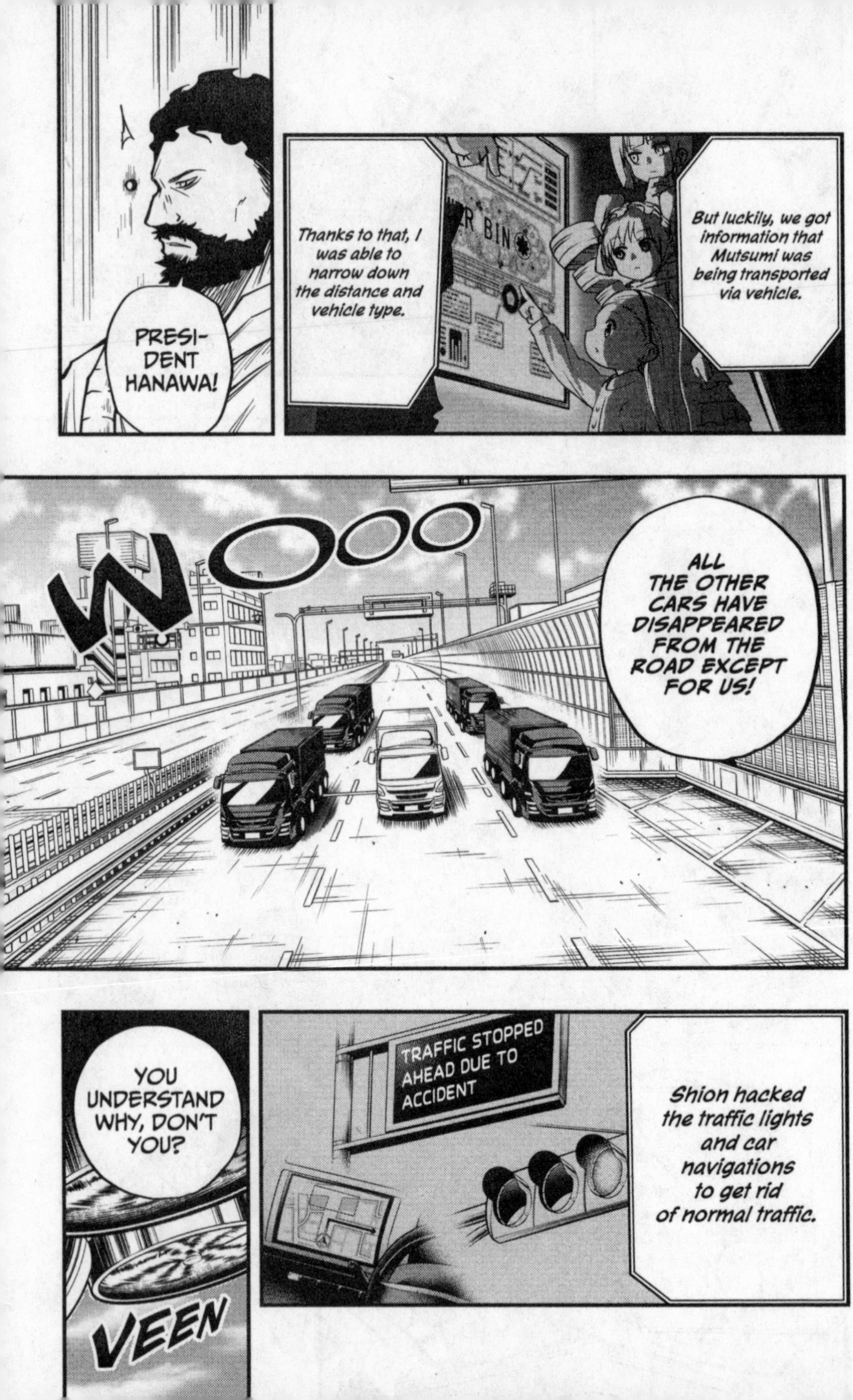
But luckily, we got information that Mutsumi was being transported via vehicle.
Thanks to that, I was able to narrow down the distance and vehicle type.
PRESI-DENT HANAWA!
ALL THE OTHER CARS HAVE DISAPPEARED FROM THE ROAD EXCEPT FOR US!
WOOO
Shion hacked the traffic lights and car navigations to get rid of normal traffic.
TRAFFIC STOPPED AHEAD DUE TO ACCIDENT
YOU UNDERSTAND WHY, DON'T YOU?
VEEN

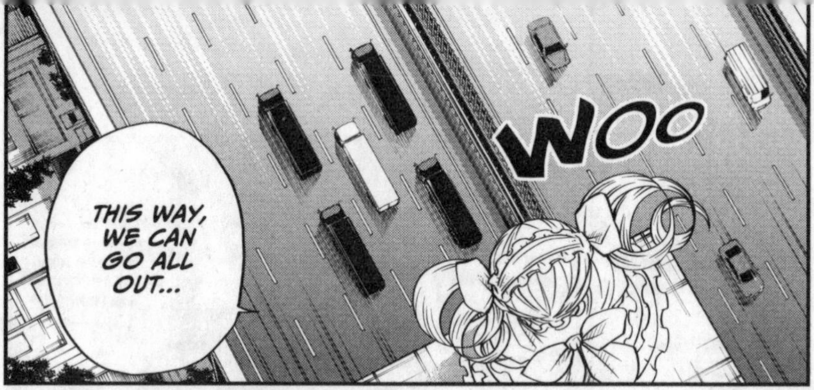
WOO
THIS WAY, WE CAN GO ALL OUT...
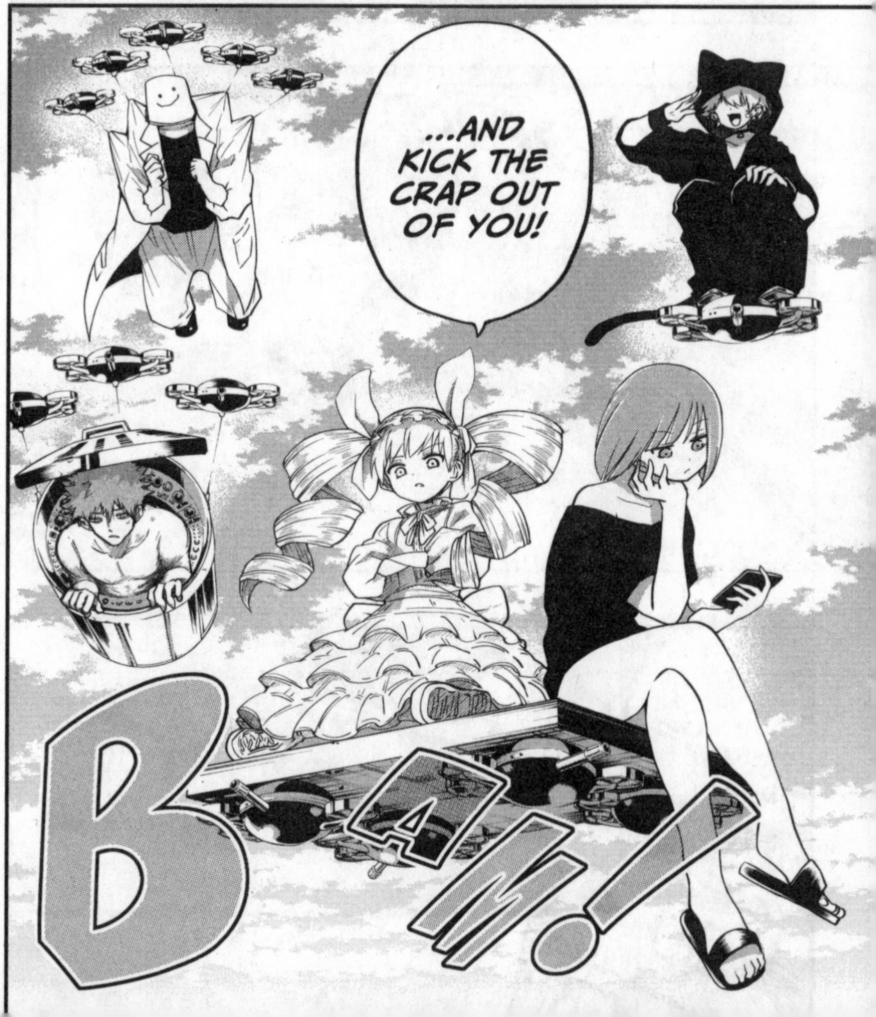
...AND KICK THE CRAP OUT OF YOU!
BAM!!

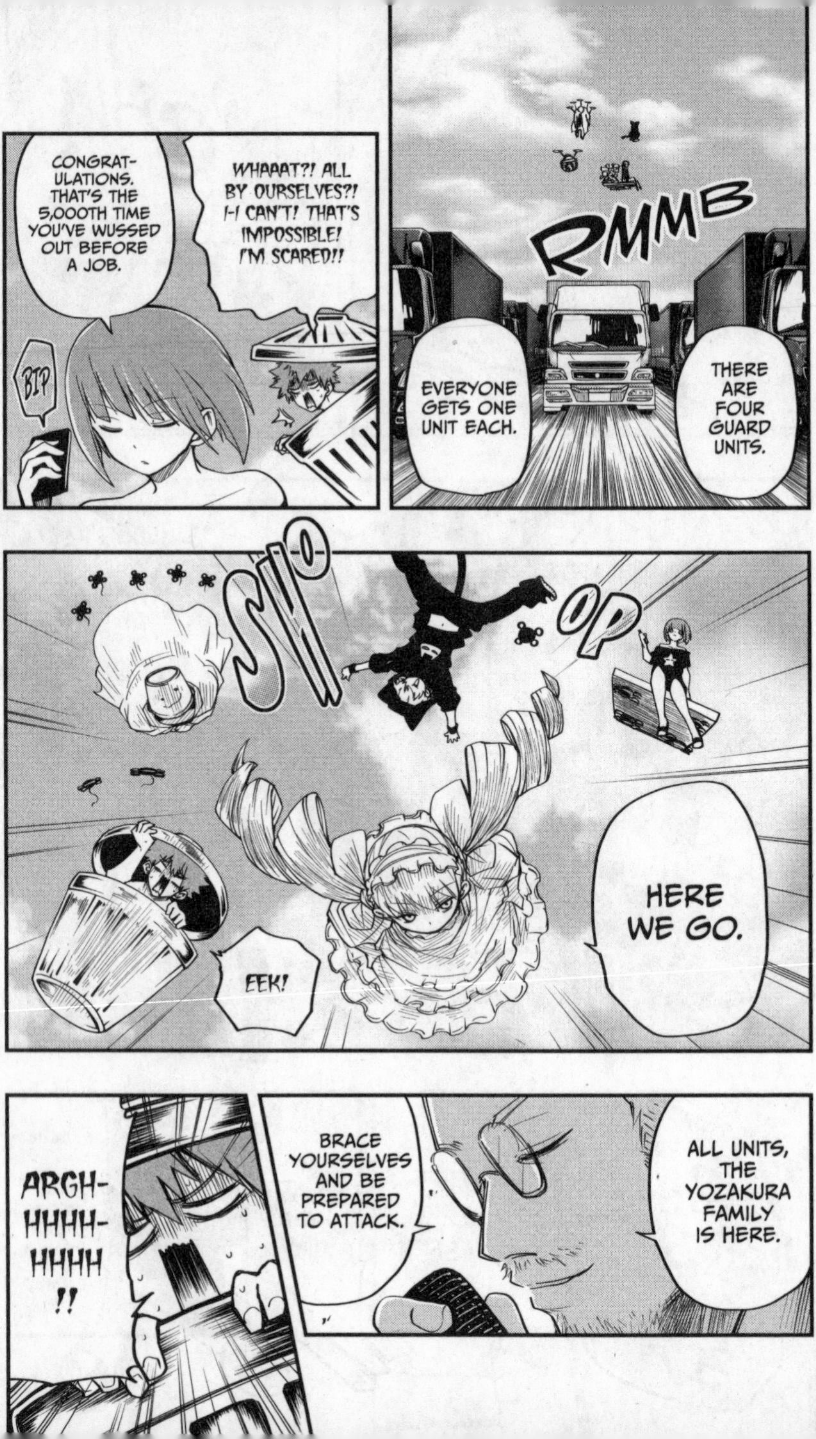
RMMB
THERE ARE FOUR GUARD UNITS.
EVERYONE GETS ONE UNIT EACH.
WHAAAT?! ALL BY OURSELVES?! I-I CAN'T! THAT'S IMPOSSIBLE! I'M SCARED!!
CONGRAT-ULATIONS. THAT'S THE 5,000TH TIME YOU'VE WUSSED OUT BEFORE A JOB.
BIP
SHOOP
HERE WE GO.
EEK!
ALL UNITS, THE YOZAKURA FAMILY IS HERE.
BRACE YOURSELVES AND BE PREPARED TO ATTACK.
ARGH-HHHH-HHHH!!

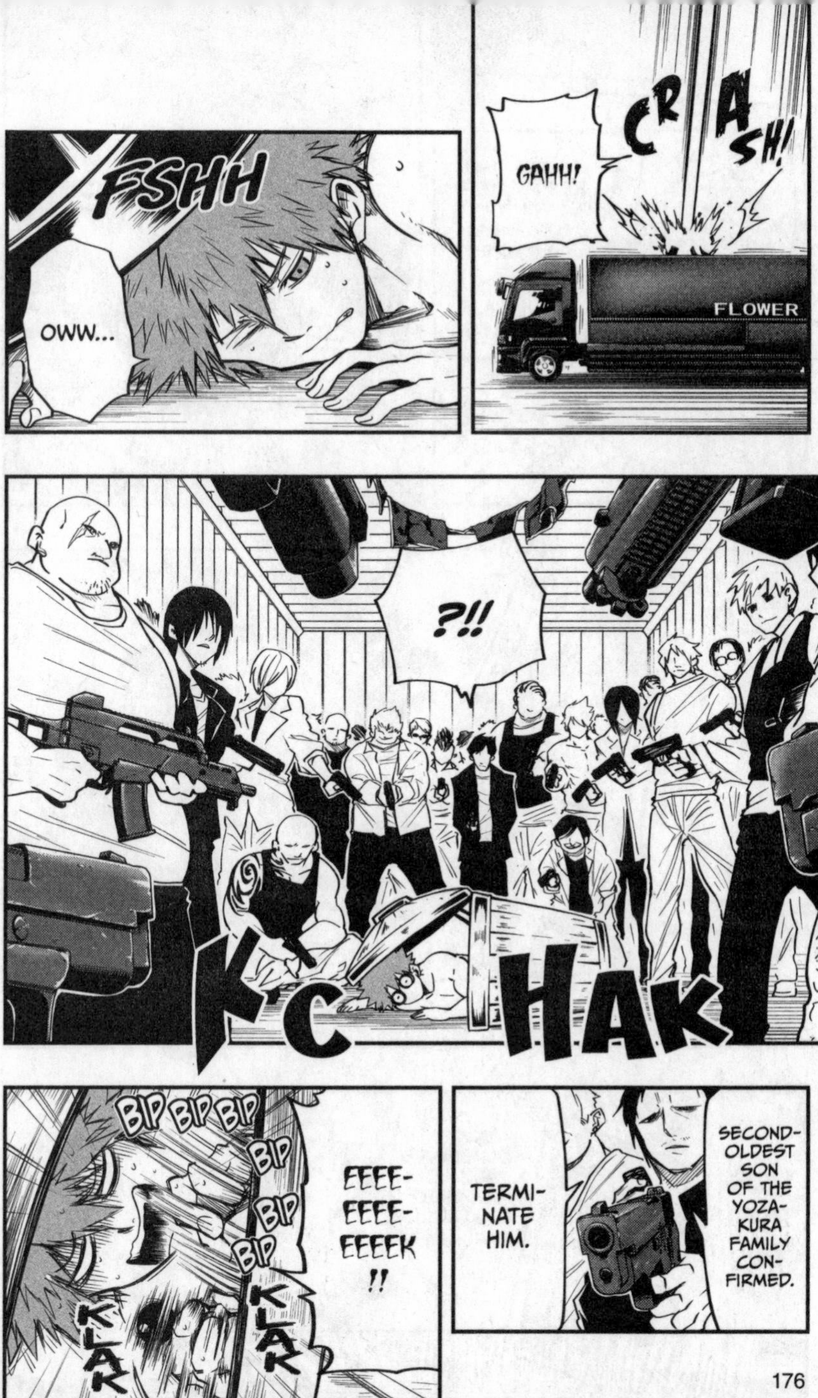

CRASH!
GAHH!
FSHH
OWW...
?!!
K'CHAK
SECOND-OLDEST SON OF THE YOZAKURA FAMILY CONFIRMED.
TERMINATE HIM.
BIP BIP BIP BIP BIP BIP
EEEE-EEEE-EEEEK!!
KLAK KLAK
FLOWER

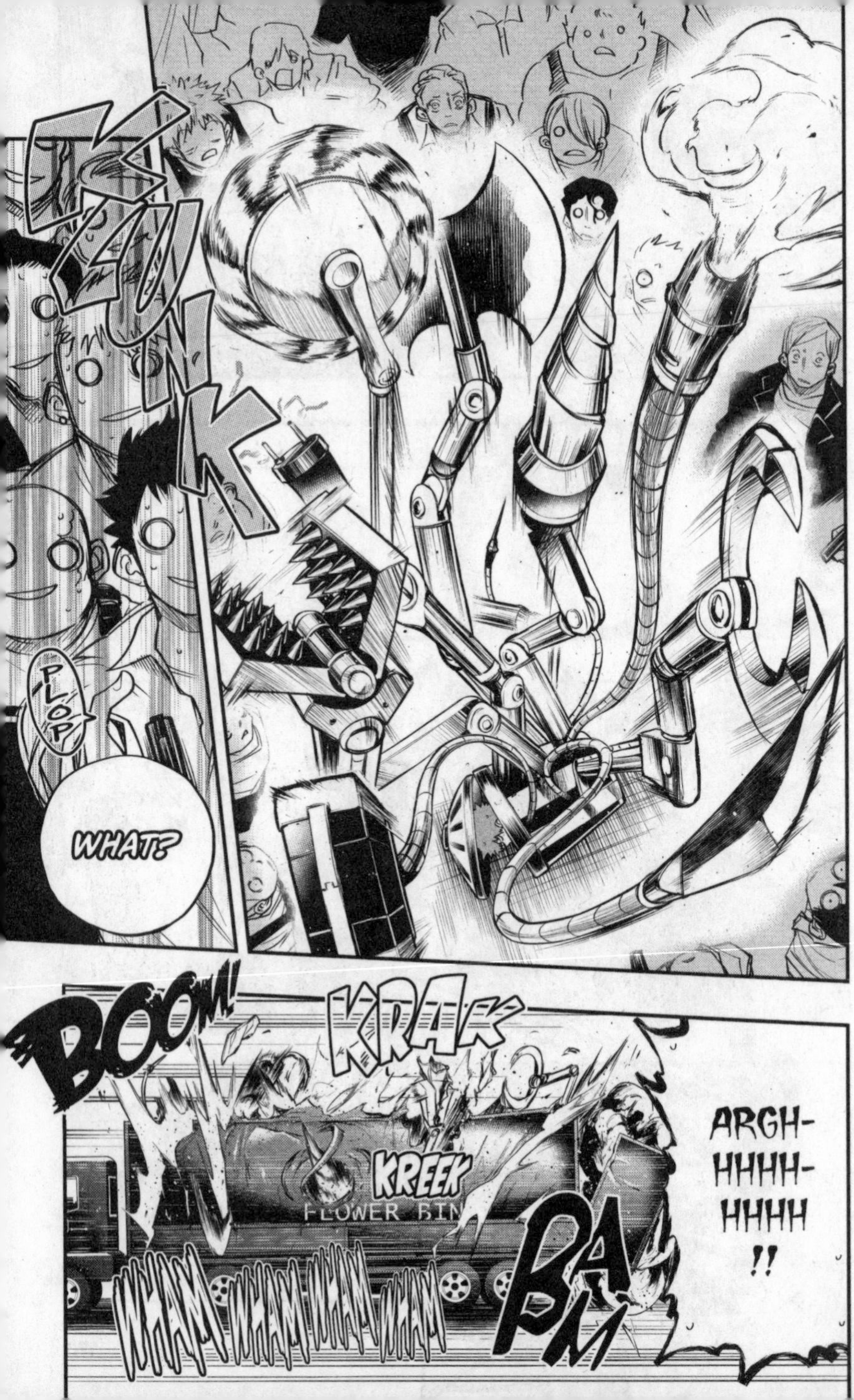
KLUNK
PLOP
WHAT?
ARGH-HHHH-HHHH!!
KRAK
BOOM!
KREEK
BAM
WHAM WHAM WHAM WHAM

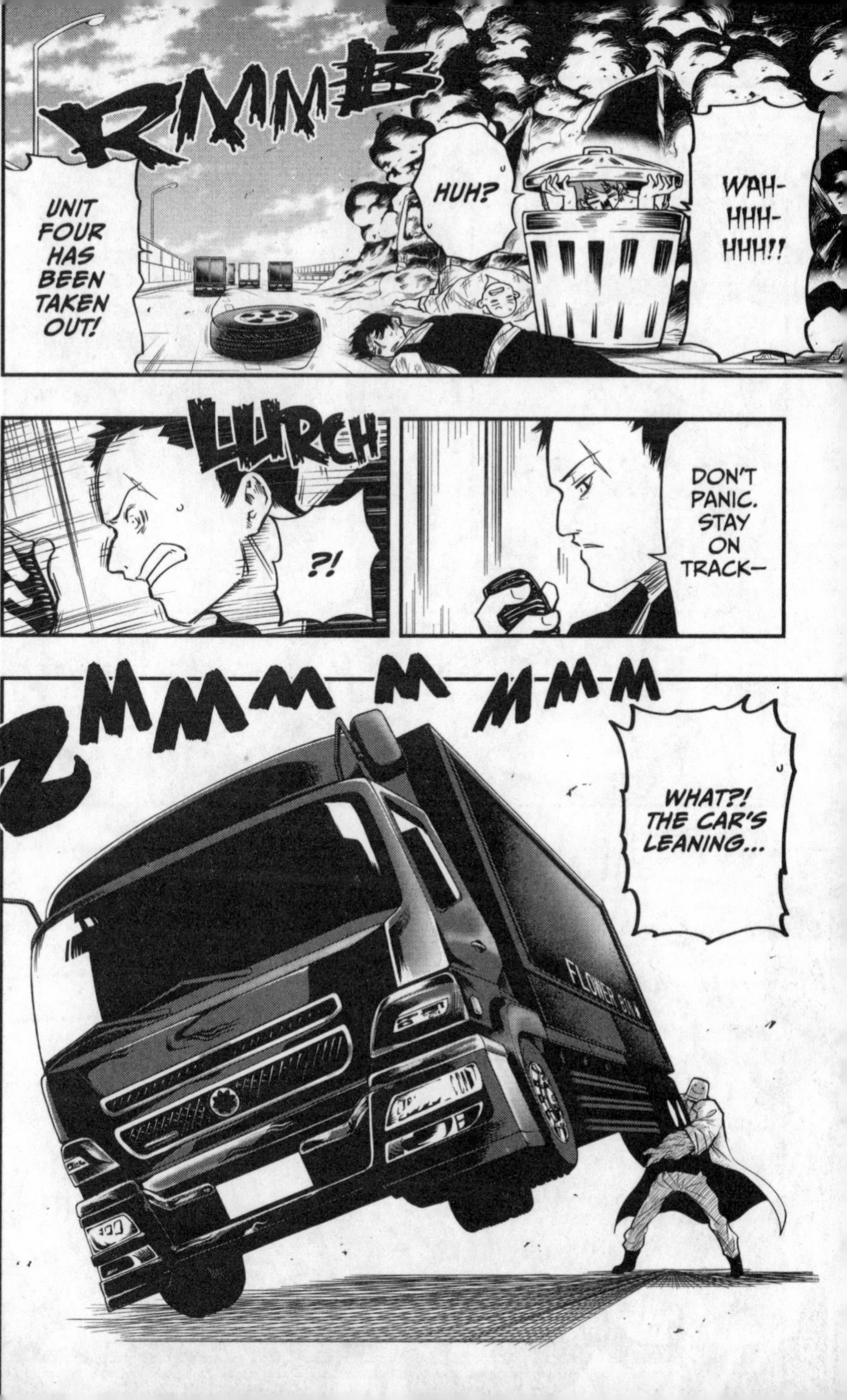
WAH-HHH-HHH!!
HUH?
RMMB
UNIT FOUR HAS BEEN TAKEN OUT!
DON'T PANIC. STAY ON TRACK—
LURCH
?!
WHAT?! THE CAR'S LEANING...
ZMMMM M MMM

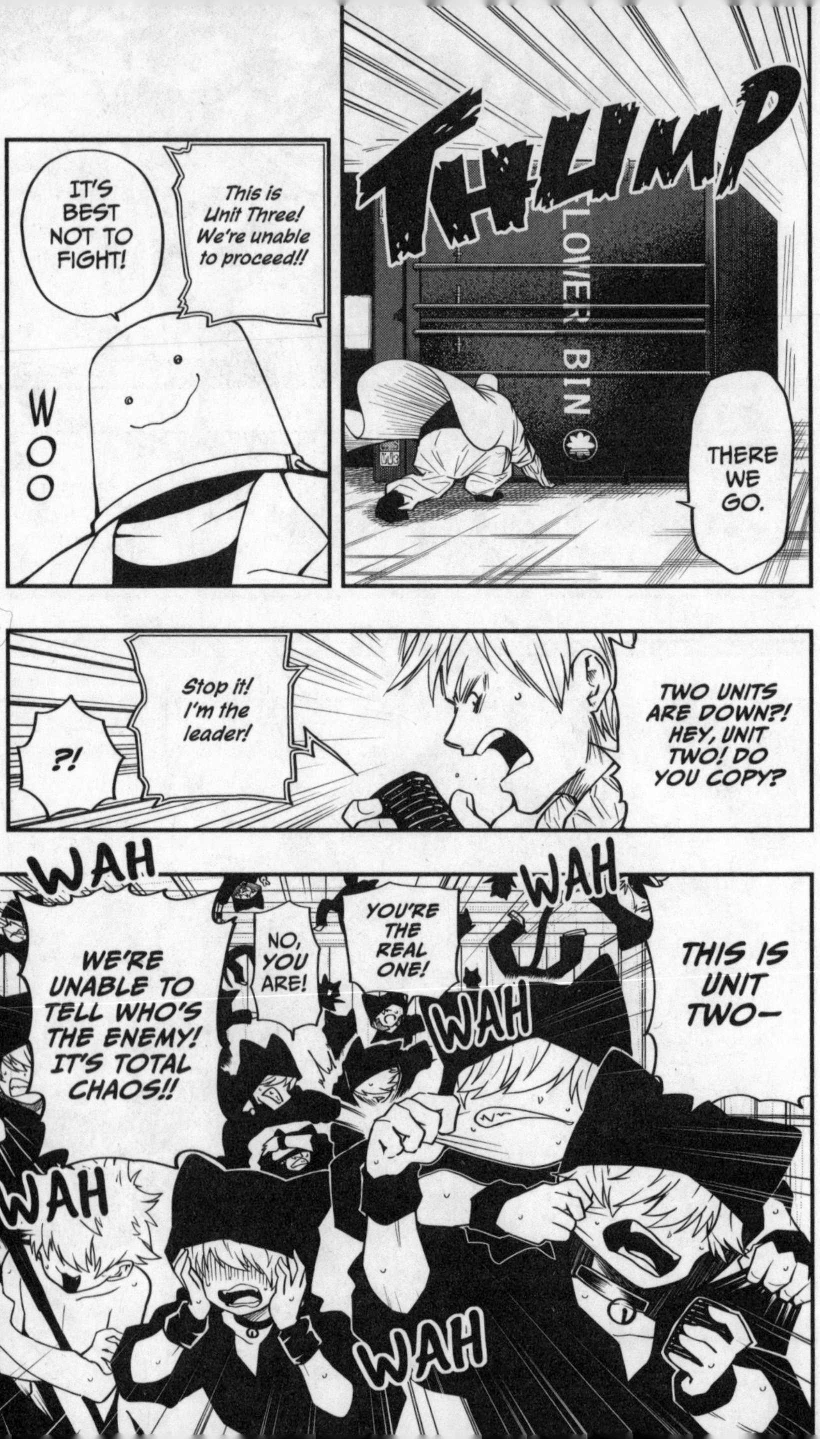
THUMP
THERE WE GO.
LOWER BIN
This is Unit Three! We're unable to proceed!!
IT'S BEST NOT TO FIGHT!
WOO
TWO UNITS ARE DOWN?! HEY, UNIT TWO! DO YOU COPY?
Stop it! I'm the leader!
?!
THIS IS UNIT TWO—
WAH
YOU'RE THE REAL ONE!
NO, YOU ARE!
WAH
WE'RE UNABLE TO TELL WHO'S THE ENEMY! IT'S TOTAL CHAOS!!
WAH
WAH
WAH

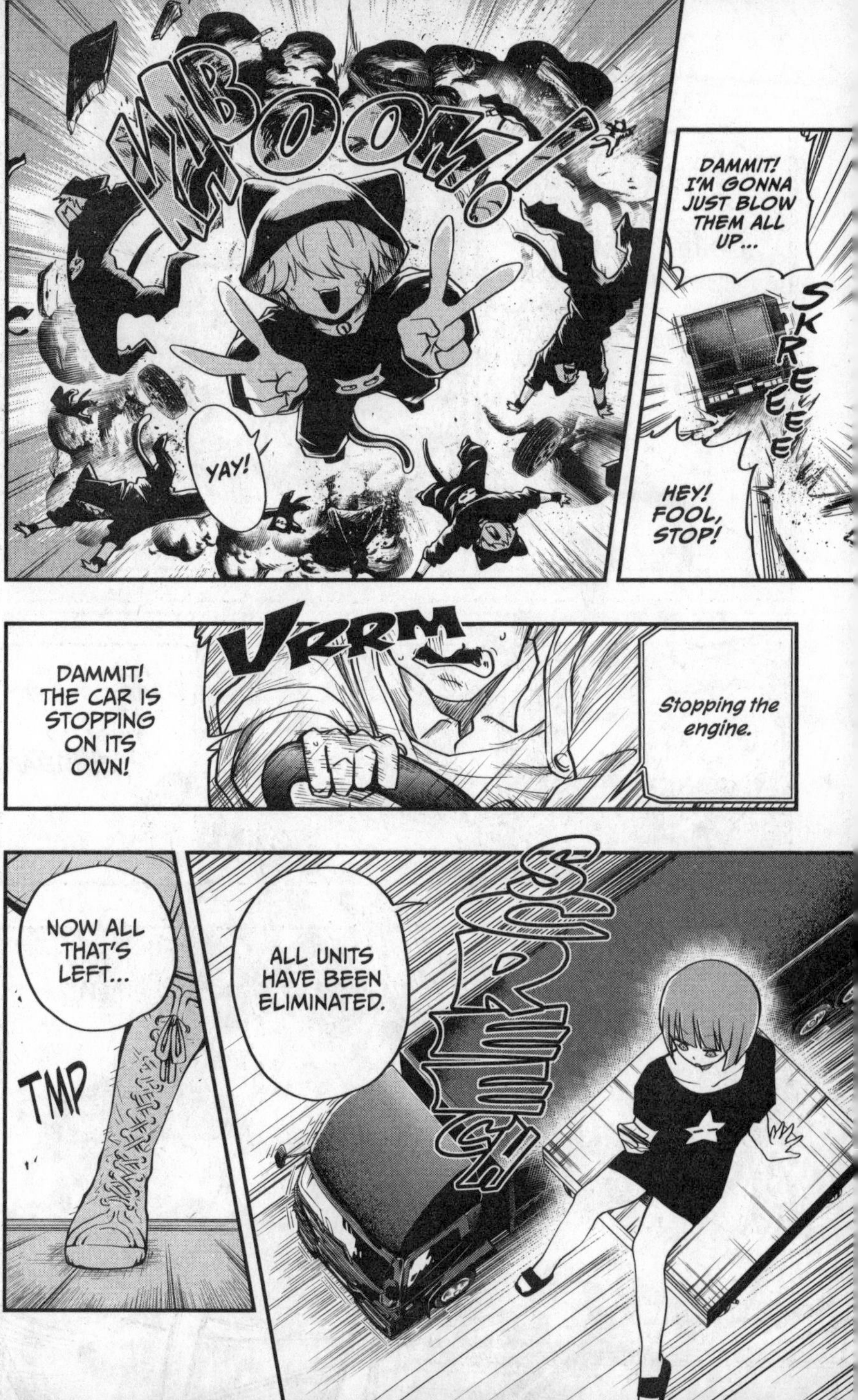
DAMMIT! I'M GONNA JUST BLOW THEM ALL UP...
SKREEEEE
HEY! FOOL, STOP!
KABOOM!
YAY!
Stopping the engine.
VRRM
DAMMIT! THE CAR IS STOPPING ON ITS OWN!
SCREECH!
ALL UNITS HAVE BEEN ELIMINATED.
NOW ALL THAT'S LEFT...
TMP

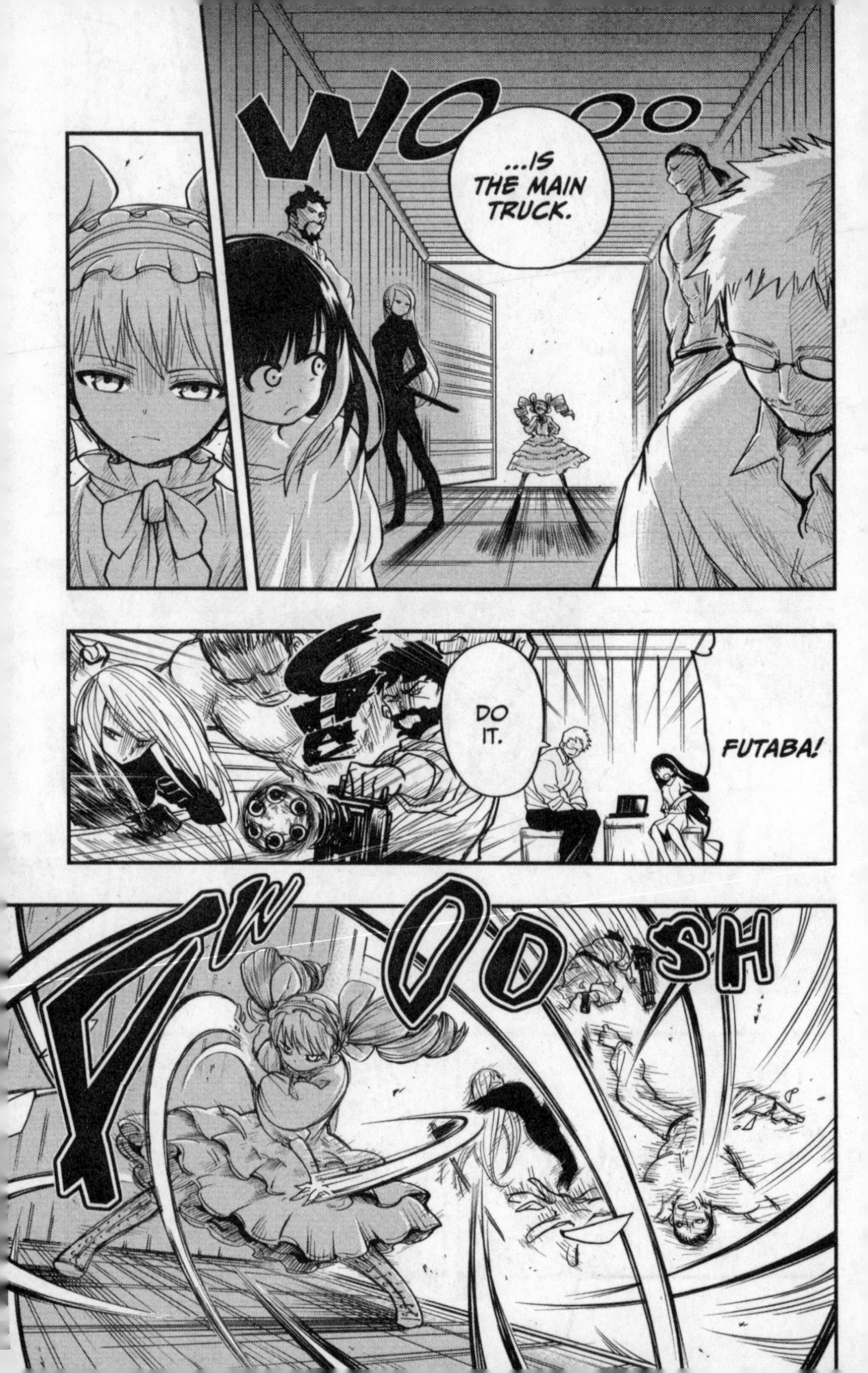
WOooo
...IS THE MAIN TRUCK.
FUTABA!
DO IT.

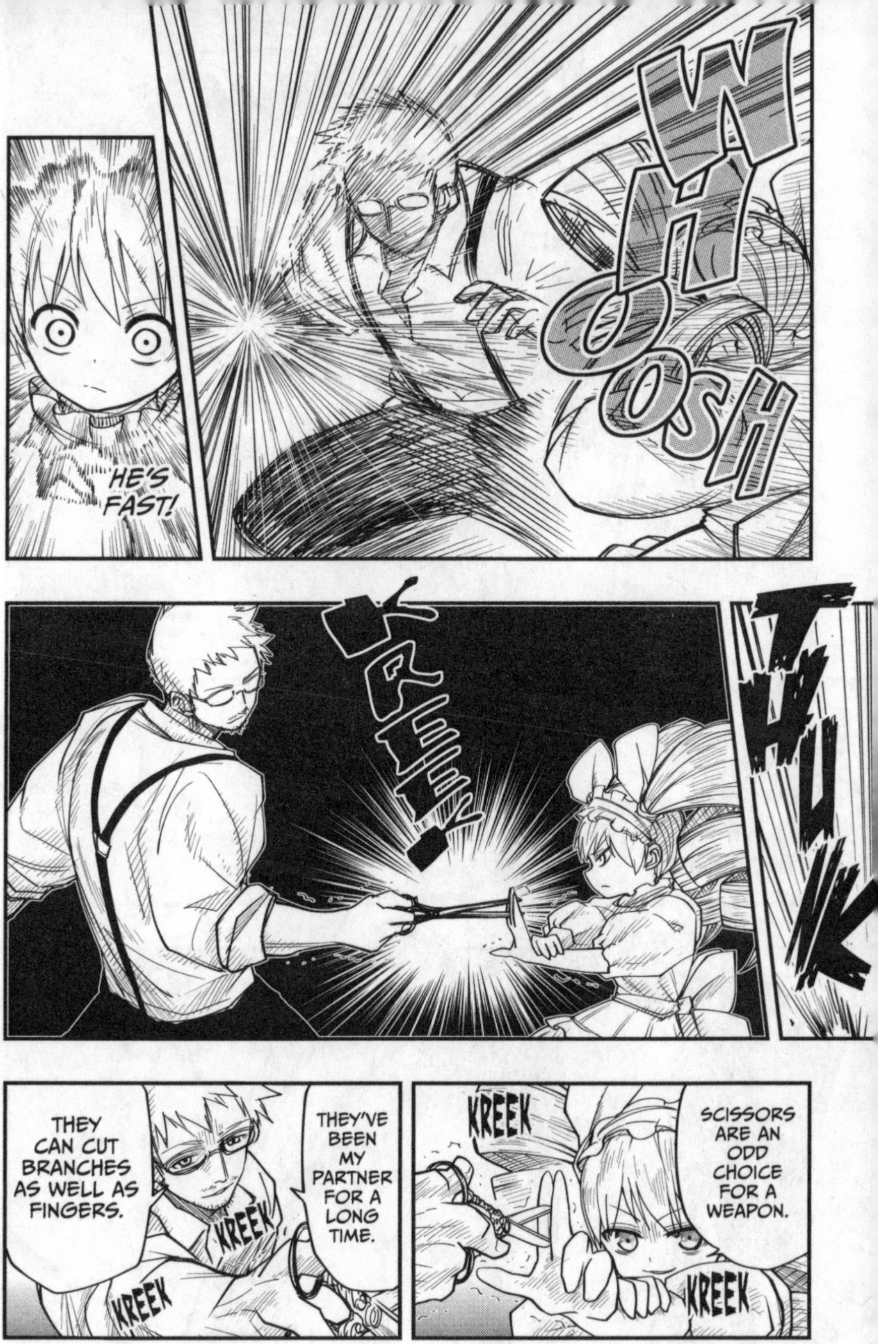
WHOOSH
HE'S FAST!
THUK
KREE
KREEK
SCISSORS ARE AN ODD CHOICE FOR A WEAPON.
KREEK
THEY'VE BEEN MY PARTNER FOR A LONG TIME.
THEY CAN CUT BRANCHES AS WELL AS FINGERS.
KREEK
KREEK

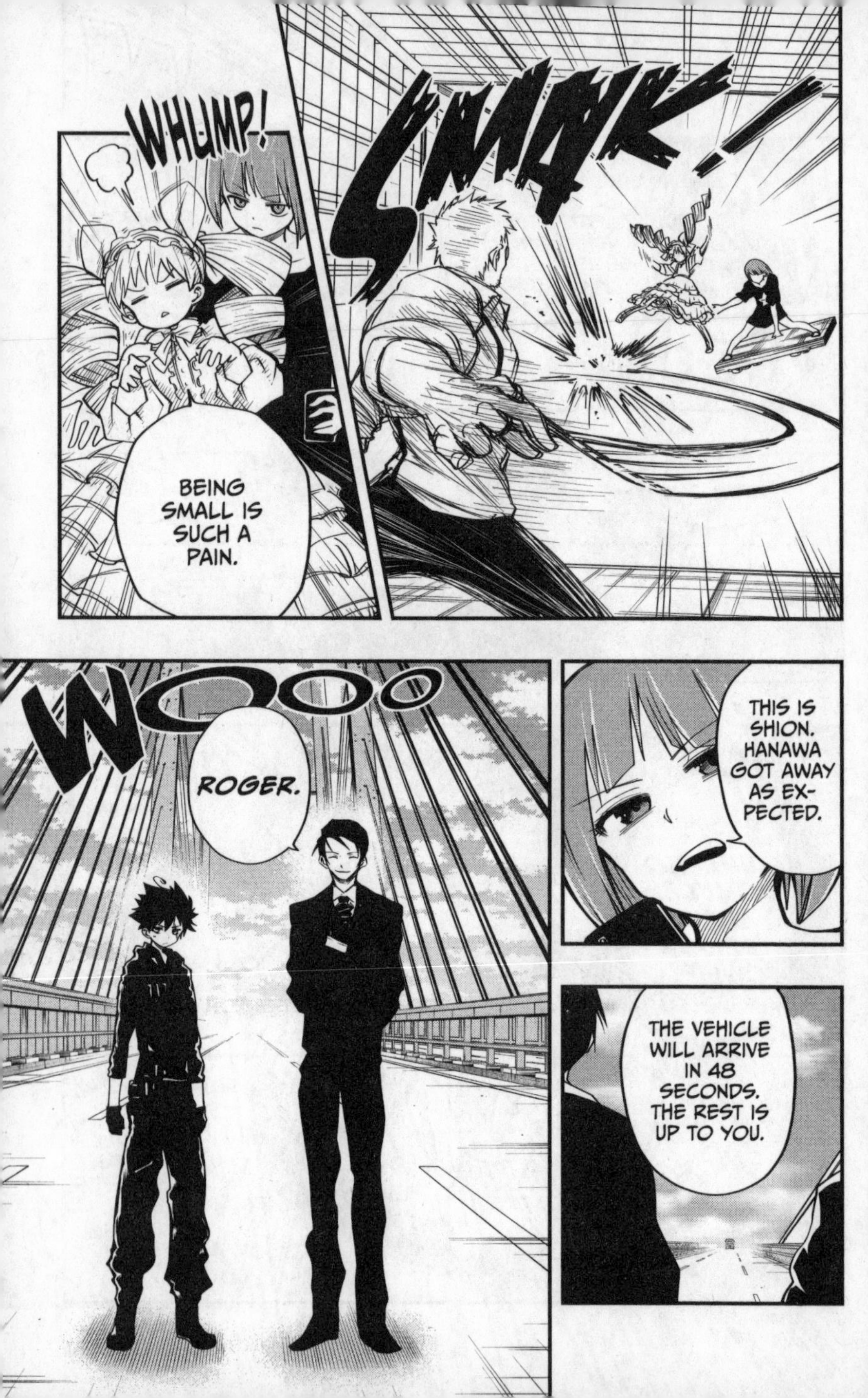
SMAK!!
WHUMP!
BEING SMALL IS SUCH A PAIN.
THIS IS SHION. HANAWA GOT AWAY AS EX-PECTED.
THE VEHICLE WILL ARRIVE IN 48 SECONDS. THE REST IS UP TO YOU.
WOOO
ROGER.

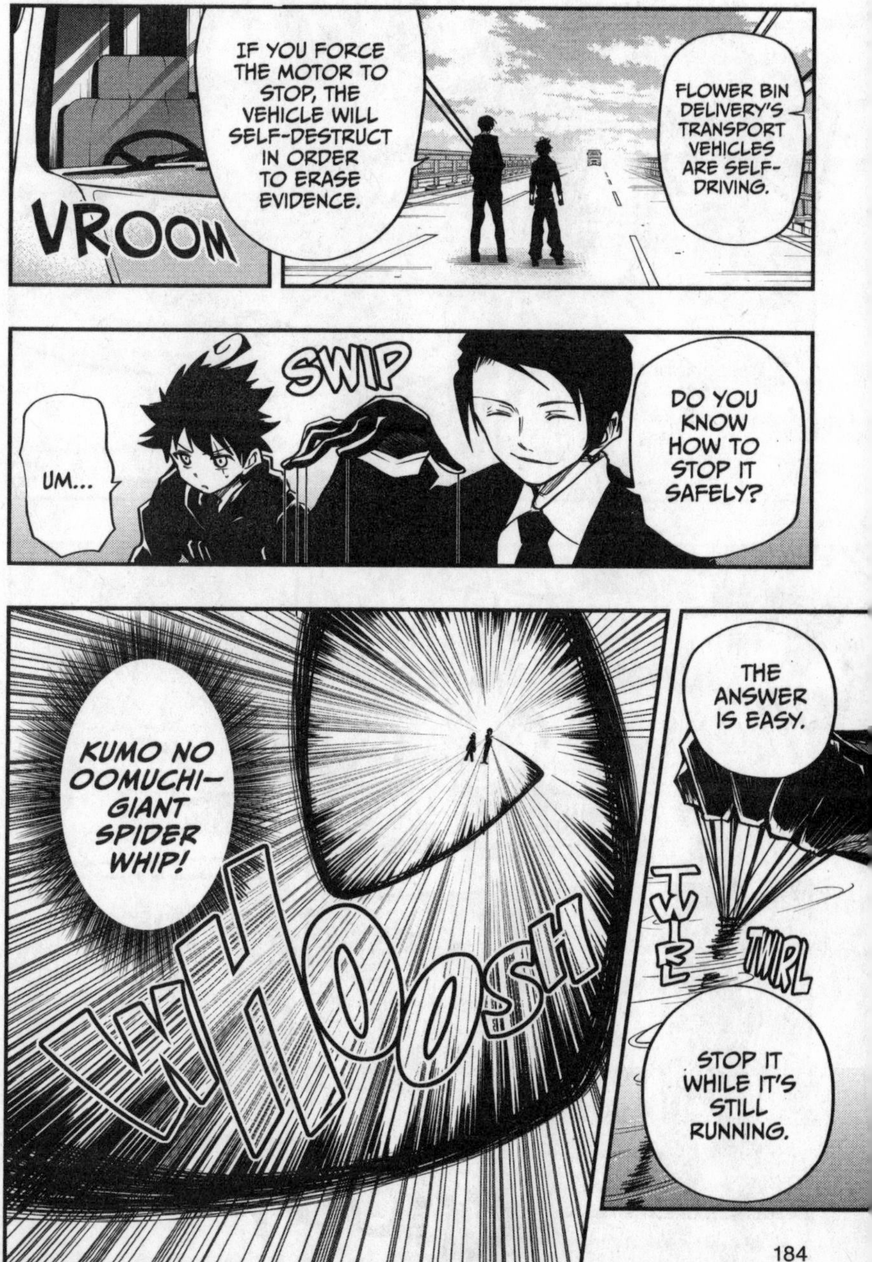
FLOWER BIN DELIVERY'S TRANSPORT VEHICLES ARE SELF-DRIVING.
IF YOU FORCE THE MOTOR TO STOP, THE VEHICLE WILL SELF-DESTRUCT IN ORDER TO ERASE EVIDENCE.
VROOM
DO YOU KNOW HOW TO STOP IT SAFELY?
SWIP
?
UM...
THE ANSWER IS EASY.
TWIRL
TWIRL
STOP IT WHILE IT'S STILL RUNNING.
KUMO NO OOMUCHI-GIANT SPIDER WHIP!
WHOOSH

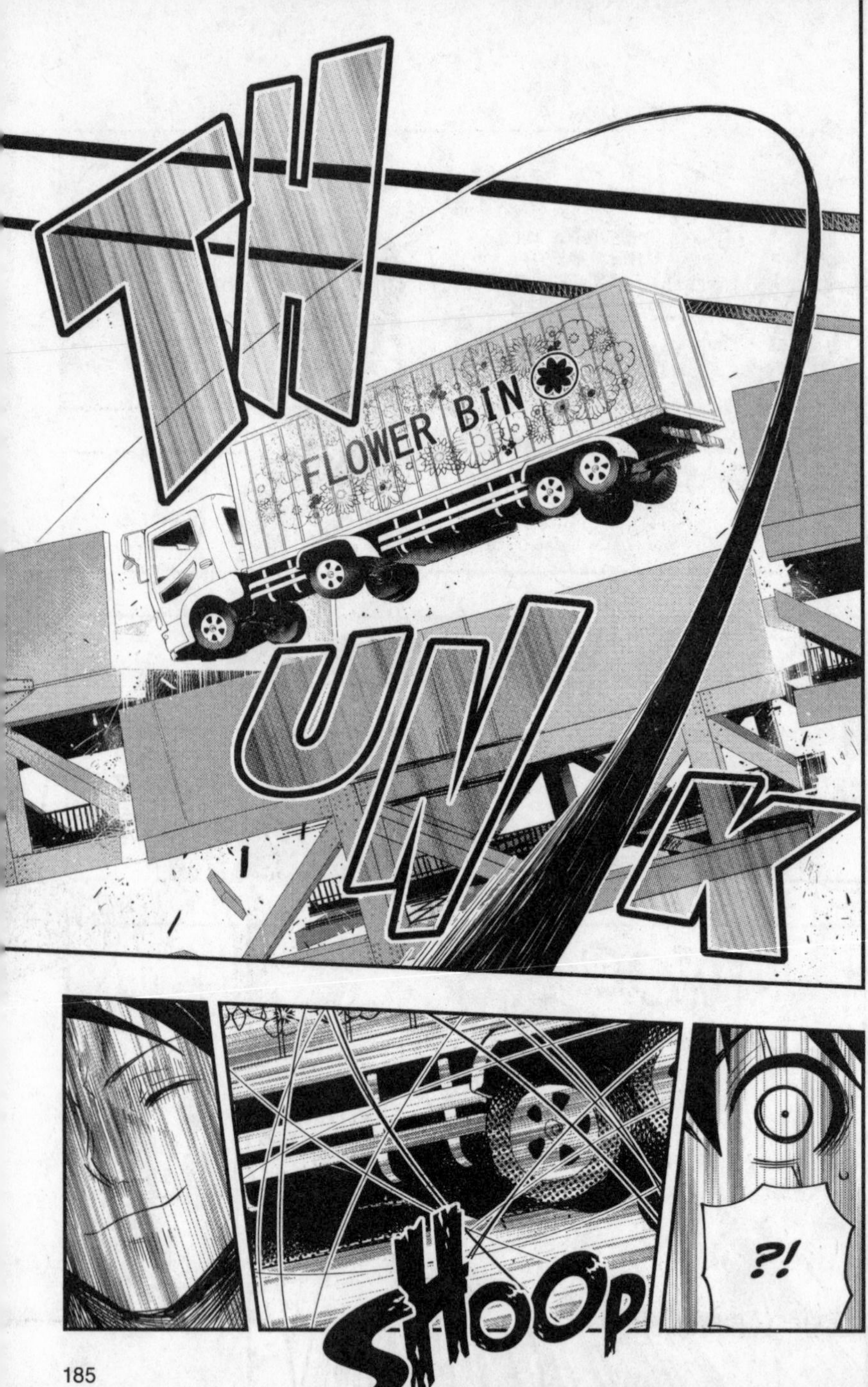
THUNK
FLOWER BIN
?!
SHOOP

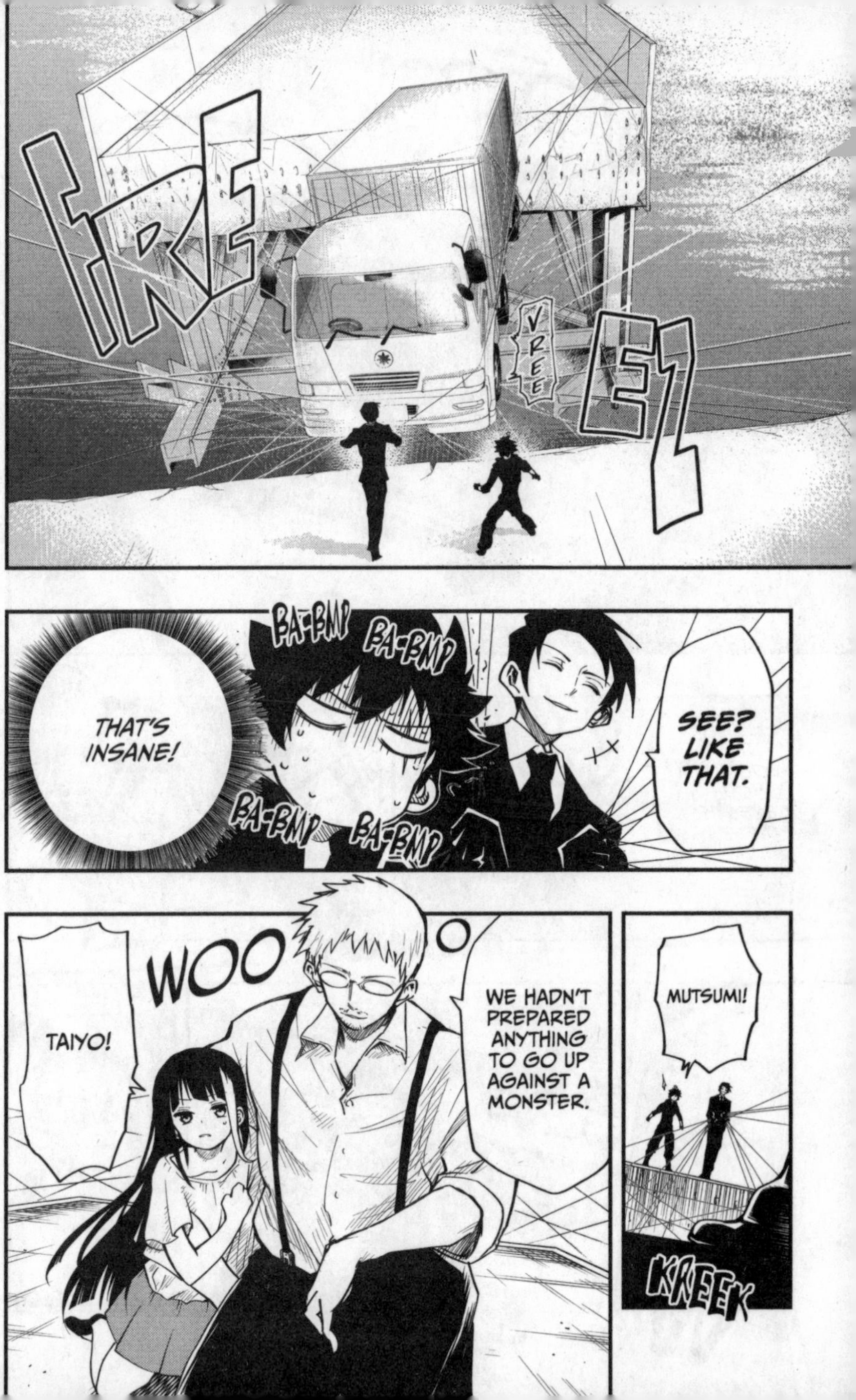
VREE
SEE? LIKE THAT.
BA-BMP
BA-BMP
BA-BMP
BA-BMP
THAT'S INSANE!
MUTSUMI!
KREEK
WE HADN'T PREPARED ANYTHING TO GO UP AGAINST A MONSTER.
WOOO
TAIYO!

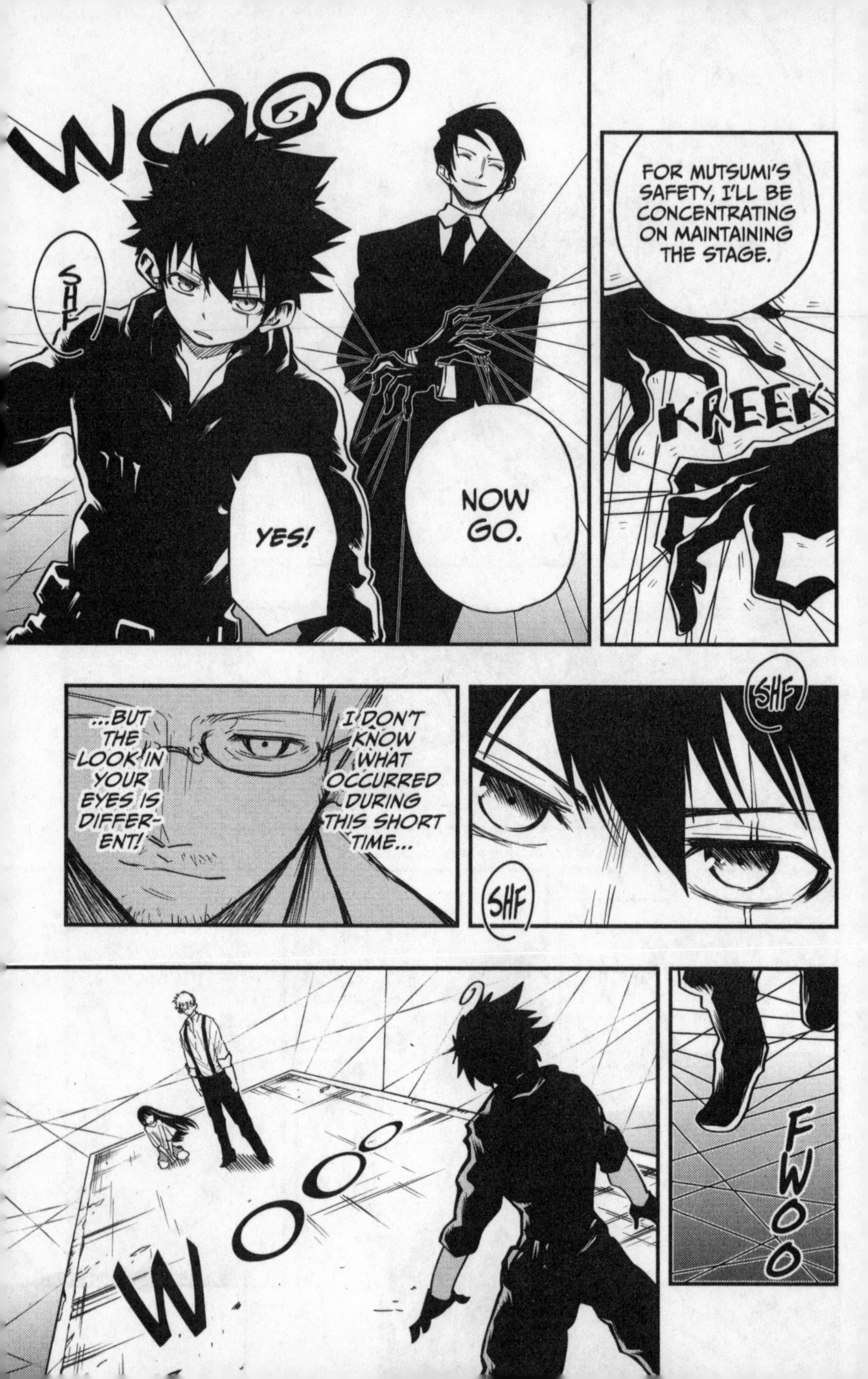
FOR MUTSUMI'S SAFETY, I'LL BE CONCENTRATING ON MAINTAINING THE STAGE.
KREEK
WOOOO
NOW GO.
YES!
SHF
SHF
SHF
I DON'T KNOW WHAT OCCURRED DURING THIS SHORT TIME...
...BUT THE LOOK IN YOUR EYES IS DIFFER-ENT!
FWOOO
WOOOO

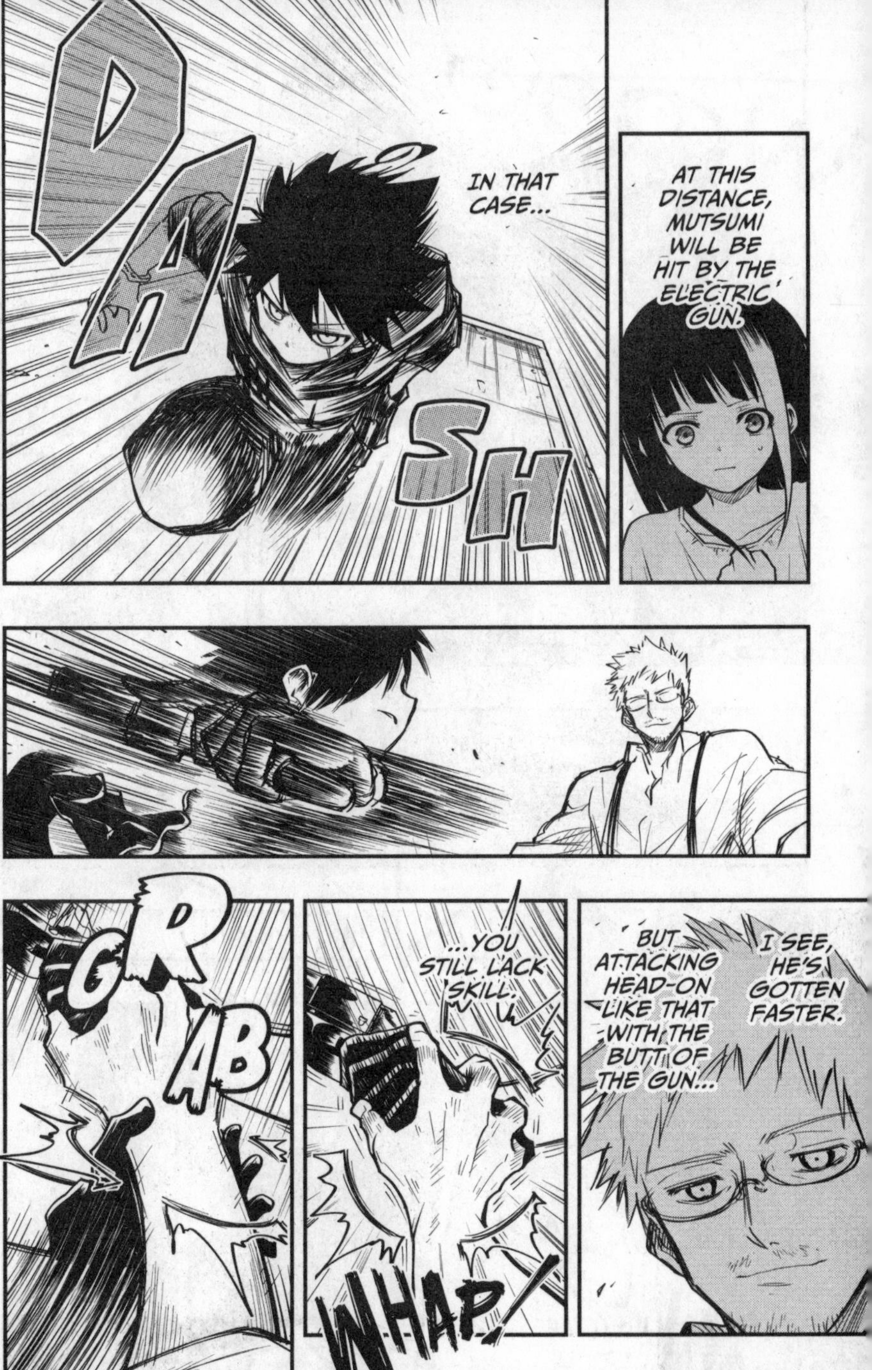
AT THIS DISTANCE, MUTSUMI WILL BE HIT BY THE ELECTRIC GUN.
IN THAT CASE...
DA
SH
I SEE, HE'S GOTTEN FASTER.
BUT ATTACKING HEAD-ON LIKE THAT WITH THE BUTT OF THE GUN...
...YOU STILL LACK SKILL.
WHAP!
GRAB

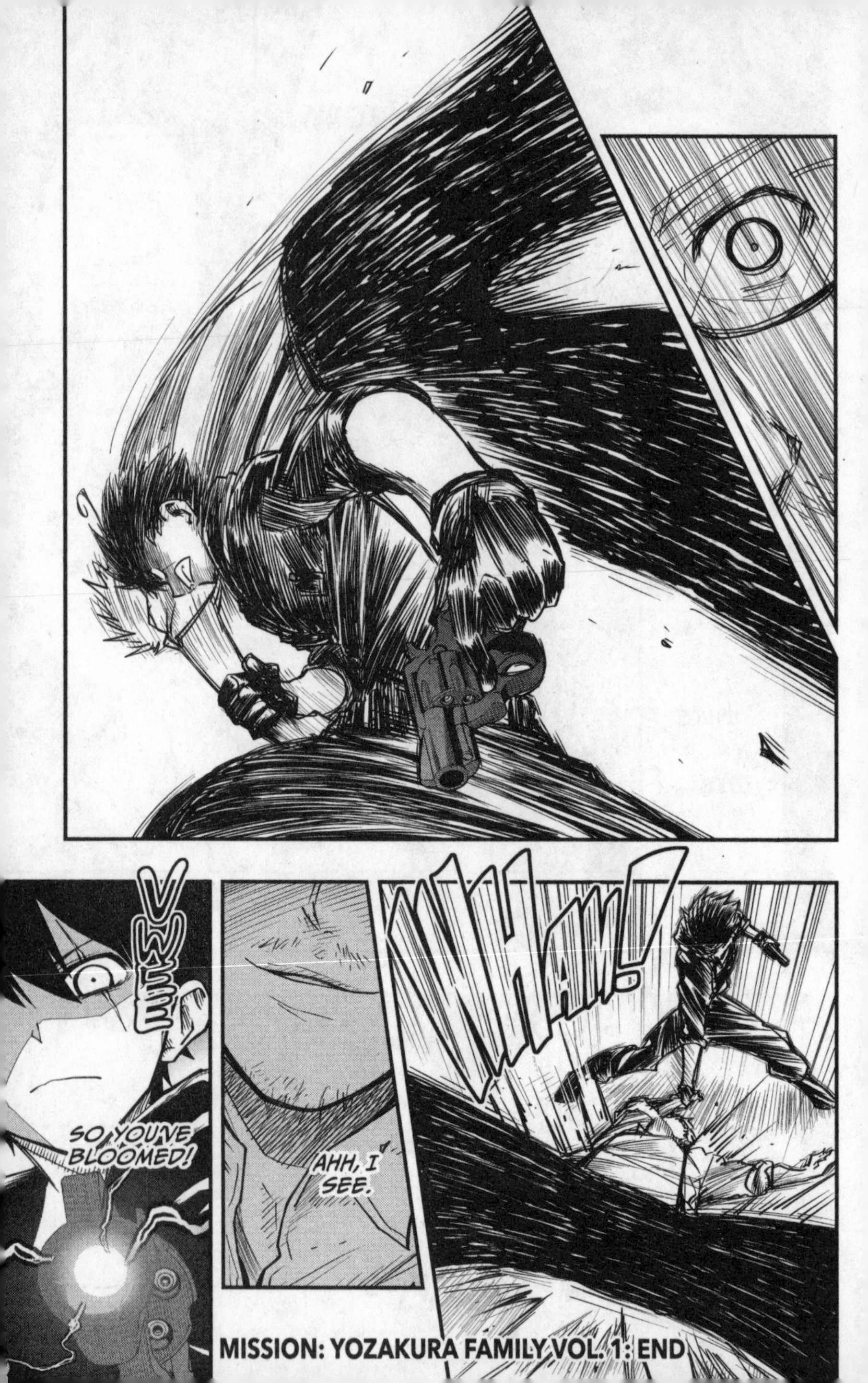
WHAM!
AHH, I SEE.
VWEE
SO YOU'VE BLOOMED!

MISSION: YOZAKURA FAMILY VOL. 1: END

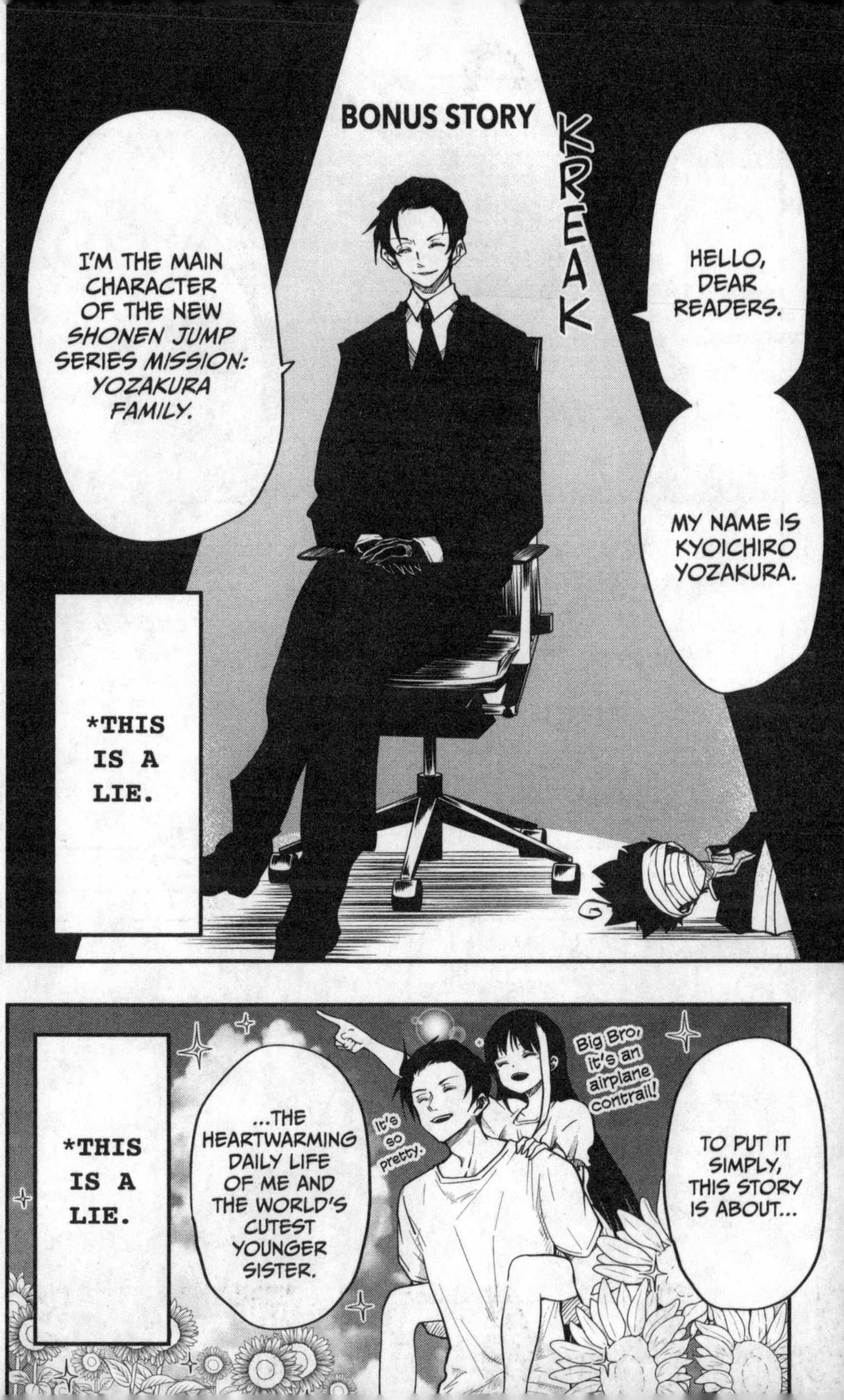
BONUS STORY
KREAK
HELLO, DEAR READERS.
MY NAME IS KYOICHIRO YOZAKURA.
I'M THE MAIN CHARACTER OF THE NEW *SHONEN JUMP* SERIES *MISSION: YOZAKURA FAMILY.*
*THIS IS A LIE.
TO PUT IT SIMPLY, THIS STORY IS ABOUT...
Big Bro, it's an airplane contrail!
It's so pretty.
...THE HEARTWARMING DAILY LIFE OF ME AND THE WORLD'S CUTEST YOUNGER SISTER.
*THIS IS A LIE.

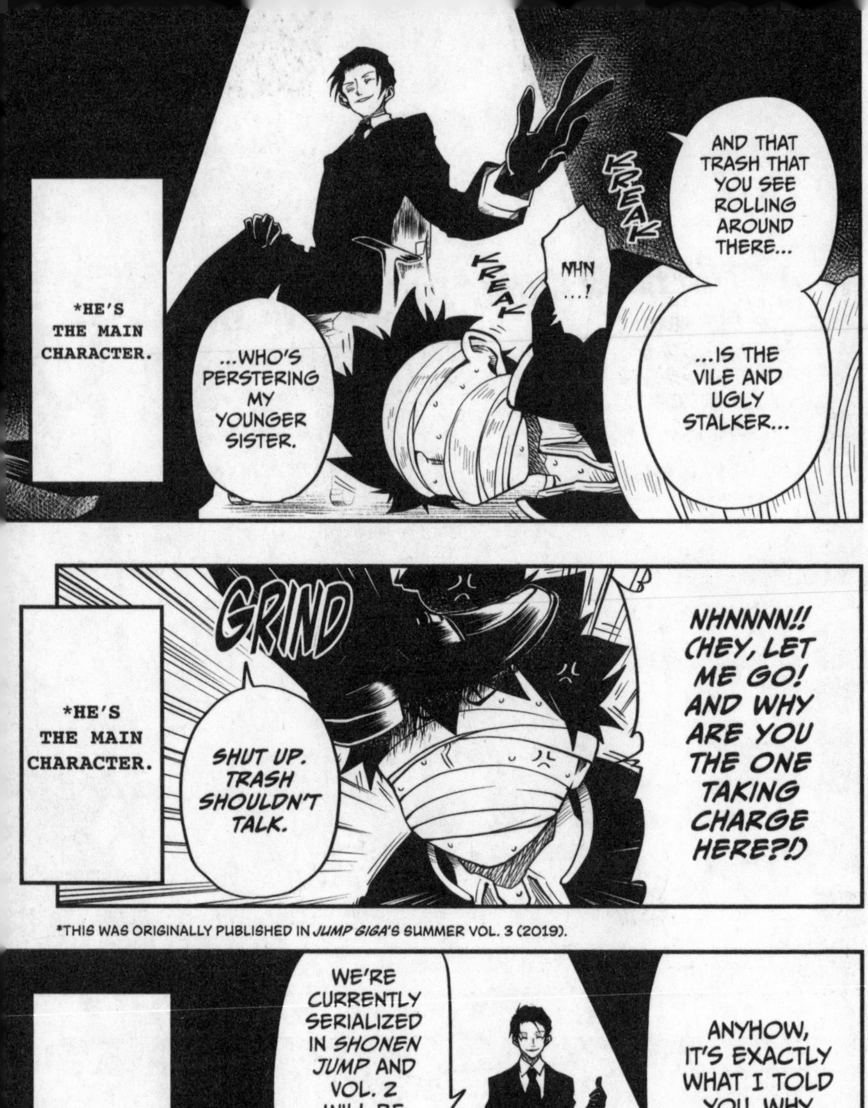
AND THAT TRASH THAT YOU SEE ROLLING AROUND THERE...
KREAK
NHN ...!
KREAK
...IS THE VILE AND UGLY STALKER...
...WHO'S PERSTERING MY YOUNGER SISTER.
*HE'S THE MAIN CHARACTER.
NHNNNN!! CHEY, LET ME GO! AND WHY ARE YOU THE ONE TAKING CHARGE HERE?!
GRIND
SHUT UP. TRASH SHOULDN'T TALK.
*HE'S THE MAIN CHARACTER.

*THIS WAS ORIGINALLY PUBLISHED IN *JUMP GIGA*'S SUMMER VOL. 3 (2019).

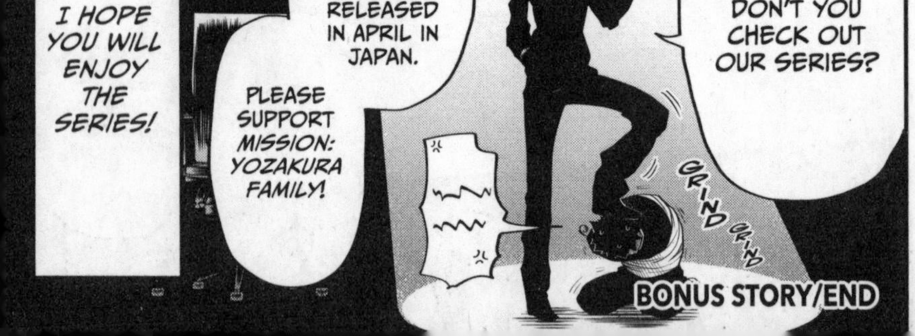
ANYHOW, IT'S EXACTLY WHAT I TOLD YOU. WHY DON'T YOU CHECK OUT OUR SERIES?
WE'RE CURRENTLY SERIALIZED IN *SHONEN JUMP* AND VOL. 2 WILL BE RELEASED IN APRIL IN JAPAN.
PLEASE SUPPORT *MISSION: YOZAKURA FAMILY!*
GRIND GRIND
I HOPE YOU WILL ENJOY THE SERIES!
BONUS STORY/END

YOU'RE READING THE WRONG WAY!

Mission: Yozakura Family reads from right to left, starting in the upper-right corner. Japanese is read from right to left, meaning that action, sound effects, and word-balloon order are completely reversed from English order.

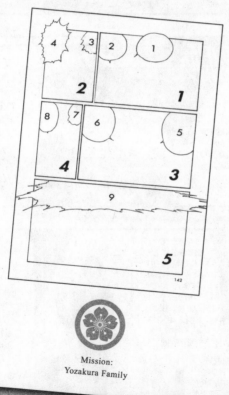

Mission:
Yozakura Family